D1545929

THE AESTHETICS AND AFFECTS OF CUTENESS

Cuteness is one of the most culturally pervasive aesthetics of the new millennium and its rapid social proliferation suggests that the affective responses it provokes find particular purchase in a contemporary era marked by intensive media saturation and spreading economic precarity. Rejecting superficial assessments that would deem the ever-expanding plethora of cute texts trivial, *The Aesthetics and Affects of Cuteness* directs serious scholarly attention from a variety of academic disciplines to this ubiquitous phenomenon. The sheer plasticity of this minor aesthetic is vividly on display in this collection which draws together analyses from around the world examining cuteness's fundamental role in cultural expressions stemming from such diverse sources as military cultures, high-end contemporary art worlds, and animal shelters. Pushing beyond prevailing understandings that associate cuteness solely with childhood or which posit an interpolated parental bond as its primary affective attachment, the essays in this collection variously draw connections between cuteness and the social, political, economic, and technological conditions of the early twenty-first century and in doing so generate fresh understandings of the central role cuteness plays in the recalibration of contemporary subjectivities.

Joshua Paul Dale has edited a special issue of *East Asian Journal of Popular Culture* on Cute Studies and created an online bibliography for this emerging field. Dale teaches cultural studies at Tokyo Gakugei University.

Joyce Goggin is a Senior Lecturer at the University of Amsterdam, where she teaches and conducts research in literature, film, television, and media studies. She is currently co-editing a collection of essays entitled *At the Intersection: Game Studies and Literary Theory* to be published in 2017.

Julia Leyda is an Associate Professor of Film Studies in the Department of Art and Media Studies at the Norwegian University of Science and Technology in Trondheim. She is co-editor of *Extreme Weather and Global Media* (Routledge, 2015) and *Post-Cinema: Theorizing 21st-Century Film* (REFRAME, 2016).

Anthony P. McIntyre is an Associate Lecturer in Film Studies at University College Dublin. He is finishing a monograph, *Millennial Tensions: Generational Affect and Contemporary Screen Cultures*.

Diane Negra is the author, editor, or co-editor of ten books. A member of the Royal Irish Academy, she serves as Professor of Film Studies and Screen Cultures and Head of Film Studies at University College Dublin. She is Co-Editor-in-Chief of *Television and New Media*.

THE AESTHETICS AND AFFECTS OF CUTENESS

Edited by
Joshua Paul Dale, Joyce Goggin,
Julia Leyda, Anthony P. McIntyre,
and Diane Negra

Routledge
Taylor & Francis Group
NEW YORK AND LONDON

First published 2017
by Routledge
711 Third Avenue, New York, NY 10017

and by Routledge
2 Park Square, Milton Park, Abingdon, Oxon OX14 4RN

Routledge is an imprint of the Taylor & Francis Group, an informa business

Library of Congress Cataloging in Publication Data
The aesthetics and affects of cuteness / edited by Joshua Paul Dale,
Joyce Goggin, Julia Leyda, Anthony P. McIntyre, and Diane Negra.
LCCN 2016032172| ISBN 9781138998759 (hardback) |
ISBN 9781138998766 (pbk.)
Subjects: LCSH: Charm. | Childishness. | Animals—Miscellanea. |
Human-animal relationships. | Aesthetics, Modern—21st century.
LCC BH301.C4 A37 2016 | DDC 155.2/5—dc23

ISBN: 978-1-138-99875-9 (hbk)
ISBN: 978-1-138-99876-6 (pbk)
ISBN: 978-1-315-65852-0 (ebk)

Typeset in Bembo and Stone Sans
by Florence Production Ltd, Stoodleigh, Devon, UK

CONTENTS

NOTES ON CONTRIBUTORS

César Albarrán-Torres is Lecturer in Media and Communication at Swinburne University of Technology in Melbourne, Australia. He has been widely published as a film and literary critic, author, and translator. His research focuses on what he calls "gamble-play media," hybrid platforms where gambling and digital interactive media intersect.

Megan Arkenberg is a graduate student in the English department at the University of California, Davis. Her research focuses on formal and discursive interchanges between scientific writing and Gothic, supernatural, and science fiction literature from the nineteenth century to the present, as well as Queer Theory and the history of sexuality.

Joshua Paul Dale has been a full-time faculty member in the Department of Foreign Languages and Foreign Literatures at Tokyo Gakugei University since 1995. He is the editor of "Cute Studies," a special issue of *The East Asian Journal of Popular Culture* (April 2016, Vol. 2.1), and is the author and curator of the *Cute Studies Bibliography*, an online resource for scholars working in this emerging area. Dale's work spans cuteness studies, gender studies, and performance studies. He is also a performance practitioner with over two decades of stage experience.

Michael DeAngelis is Associate Professor of Media and Cinema Studies at DePaul University. He is the author of *Gay Fandom and Crossover Stardom: James Dean, Mel Gibson, and Keanu Reeves* (Duke University Press 2001) and editor of *Reading the Bromance: Homosocial Relationships in Film and Television* (Wayne State University Press 2014). He is currently working on a book for SUNY Press on therapy in the cinema of the Sexual Revolution.

Nadia de Vries holds an MA in English literature from the University of Amsterdam. She is currently a PhD student at the Amsterdam School for Cultural Analysis, where she conducts research on the aestheticization of mourning in web-based cultures. She is also the author of two poetry collections: *First Communion* (2015) and *R.I.P. Nadia de Vries* (2016).

Joel Gn is Lecturer at SIM University (UniSIM), Singapore. He obtained a PhD in Communications and New Media at the National University of Singapore, with a dissertation on the phenomenological implications of cuteness in technological artefacts. His work centers on philosophical engagements with design aesthetics, new media, and East Asian popular culture.

Joyce Goggin teaches literature, film, and media studies at the University of Amsterdam. She has published on a variety of media (literature, painting, film, television, (video) games, comics, toys) and topics ranging from hermeneutics, deconstruction, and feminism, to playbour, addiction, and affect. She is currently co-editing a collection of essays entitled *At the Intersection: Game Studies and Literary Theory* to be published in 2017.

Elizabeth Legge, Associate Professor in the Department of History of Art at the University of Toronto, works on Dada, Surrealism, and contemporary Canadian and British art. She has written on psychoanalysis in early Surrealism (*Max Ernst: The Psychoanalytic Sources*, UMI 1989) and on Michael Snow's landmark film *Wavelength* (Afterall 2009). Her articles and reviews have been published in *Representations*, *Art Journal*, *Art History*, *History of Photography*, *Oxford Art Journal*, and *Journal of Canadian Art History*.

Julia Leyda is Associate Professor of Film Studies in the Department of Art and Media Studies at the Norwegian University of Science and Technology in Trondheim, as well as Senior Research Fellow at the Graduate School for North American Studies in the John F. Kennedy Institute at the Freie Universität Berlin. She has edited or co-edited several books, including *Extreme Weather and Global Media* (with Diane Negra, Routledge, 2015) and *Post-Cinema: Theorizing 21st-Century Film* (with Shane Denson, REFRAME 2016). Her current book projects center on the financialization of domestic space in twenty-first-century US screen culture and on climate change fiction and film.

Anthony P. McIntyre is Associate Lecturer in Film Studies at University College Dublin and Managing Editor of *Television and New Media*. He has published chapters and articles in numerous scholarly edited collections and journals and is finishing a monograph, *Millennial Tensions*, examining the cultural and affective interplay of generational cohorts, screen cultures, and politics. He has another book project in development, examining transnationalism in Irish media.

Diane Negra is Professor of Film Studies and Screen Culture and Head of Film Studies at University College Dublin. A member of the Royal Irish Academy, she is the author, editor, or co-editor of ten books. She is Co-Editor-in-Chief of *Television and New Media*.

Allison Page is Visiting Assistant Professor of new media studies in the School of Critical Social Inquiry at Hampshire College. Her work has been published in the *Journal of Consumer Culture, Television and New Media, Cultural Studies / Critical Methodologies*, and *Feminist Media Studies*. She is currently working on a book project preliminarily titled *Pedagogies of Slavery: Race, Media, and Citizenship*.

Katy Peplin received her PhD in the Screen Arts and Cultures program at the University of Michigan. Her dissertation traced the animal on screen from Topsy the elephant to Grumpy Cat, and her research interests include non-human media, documentary theory and ethics, media policy and law, and digital pedagogy.

Maria Pramaggiore is Professor and Head of Media Studies at Maynooth University in County Kildare, Ireland. She has published five books and more than thirty articles in film and media studies on gender and sexuality, Irish cinema, stardom and celebrity, and experimental film. Her most recent book is *Making Time in Stanley Kubrick's* Barry Lyndon: *Art, History & Empire* (Bloomsbury 2014).

ACKNOWLEDGMENTS

The editors would like to thank Laura Butler, Simon Jacobs, Naomi Hill, Stacy Grouden, Deb Pelton, Erica Wetter, Mia Moran, Maya Davis, Umar Massood, Parisa Haghshenas, Rebecca Gordon, Mark Tynan, Christopher Shore, the Amsterdam School for Cultural Analysis (ASCA), the Amsterdam Centre for Globalization Studies (ACGS), Maire Coyle and the University College Dublin Seed Funding Visiting Professorship Scheme, the Center for International Education at Northern Arizona University and its Director Harvey Charles, Gerardine Meaney, John Brannigan, and the Humanities Institute of Ireland.

1

THE AESTHETICS AND AFFECTS OF CUTENESS

Joshua Paul Dale, Joyce Goggin, Julia Leyda, Anthony P. McIntyre, and Diane Negra

Cuteness is a powerful affective register whose social proliferation since the turn of the millennium has been striking. When a Reddit user in 2014 asked Tim Berners-Lee, inventor of the World Wide Web, to name one use of the internet that he did not anticipate, he answered with just one word: "kittens" (Berners-Lee; Merriman). His widely quoted comment points to one of the incongruities that inspire this book: the avalanche of attention accorded to cuteness within popular culture juxtaposed with the notion that it is not a "serious" area of inquiry. Better understanding this paradox, in which the global phenomenon of cuteness is on the surface judged trivial based on the kinds of responses it often evokes, is increasingly urgent given the sheer range and rapid growth of "cute cultures." In acknowledging the worldwide reach of cute aesthetics and affects, the essays gathered here constitute one of the first attempts to direct serious scholarly investigation to this pervasive phenomenon. Noting that prior streams of scholarship invariably separate cute aesthetics from cute cultures of emotion, this book seeks to pinpoint the relationship between this aesthetic and the affective responses it evokes. A fundamental question this volume addresses is whether or not cuteness is a function of subjective judgment, or a quality inherent to the objects we experience as cute, or a complex interplay between these two.

A traditionally vernacular discourse, cuteness is undergoing a notable migration into institutions associated with the guardianship of high culture. In spaces like museums, galleries, and airports, historical knowledge is increasingly materialized through cute objects and rhetorics. We contend that cuteness is indeed more than a facile commodity aesthetic, and that in fact the cute aesthetic and its affects raise a number of deep-rooted political concerns. For example, in *The Aesthetics and Affects of Cuteness* we demonstrate that indulging in and communicating through cuteness provides an important coping strategy for subjects caught up in the precariousness inherent to neoliberal capitalism, and is thus central to the establishment of contemporary (inter)subjectivities. In addition, cuteness increasingly constitutes a performative aesthetic and form of communication for those who seek to enact, represent, or reference cuteness (whether positively or negatively) through and within self-presentation, affiliations with fandom, and other collective modes of expression. Furthermore, the power differential between a subject affected by cuteness and an ostensibly powerless cute object has serious implications when it is expressed through differences such as gender, race, class, age, nationality, and species, as a number of the authors in this collection argue.

Cute Origins

Numerous historical cultures of sentimentality that didn't overtly use the term "cuteness" may nevertheless have put the notion in play. Current usages of the word "cute" can be traced back at least as far as the 1850s in American and British English, where the term was aligned with children, women, the domestic sphere, and a particular form of "feminine spectacle" (Merish 192). Although these associations remain, the rapid rise of cute culture(s) in the twenty-first century has seen an explosion of cute commodities, characters, foods, fashions, and fandoms, leading to an inevitable expansion and dispersal of meanings and connotations. As a result of its seeming innocuousness and emotive appeal, the cute aesthetic has come to inform variously gendered subjectivities, as in, for example, the widespread popularity of cute animal characters among teen and adult women evidenced in the swarms of mostly female attendees at the sold-out Hello Kitty Con, a celebration of the character's fortieth birthday held in Los Angeles in October/November 2014 (Hinson). However, studies of cuteness today are not limited to femininity nor female-identified subjects, and a number of essays in this collection track the availability of cuteness as a masculine performative mode. We understand cuteness as a repertoire that is made use of by a variety of constituencies and for a variety of purposes.

Although cuteness is global, as the Japanese character Hello Kitty's worldwide reach would seem to attest, it also has much longer historical roots in Japan, home to early manifestations of cuteness during the Edo period (1603–1868), when images of cuteness often appeared in paintings and prints (Yano; Museum of Fuchu City). Much later, in the 1970s, Japan experienced a further boom in the dissemination of cute aesthetics in the form of *kawaii*, meaning literally "lovable," "cute," or "adorable," and its associated cultural practices. This boom rapidly spread throughout East Asia, and now has a growing global presence. Japanese *kawaii* culture, from Hello Kitty and other cute characters to manga, anime, cosplay, and fashion, has become an important indicator of globalization as well as a significant economic driver virtually everywhere (see Allison; Napier; Yano). As several contributions to this volume assert, the importance of Japanese *kawaii* in the genealogy of cute aesthetics gives the lie to the taken-for-granted dominance of "Western" cultures that betrays what is too often an unthinking replication of neo-Orientalist, center-margin geographies of knowledge within humanities scholarship today.

While eschewing Eurocentrism, our volume nevertheless attends to cultural distinctions within the realm of cuteness. One key difference between the English word "cute" and its equivalents in other languages, including Japanese, assists in delineating these cultural differences: in the eighteenth century, "cute" was a shortened form of "acute," and used to describe a sharp-witted or cunning person.[1] As Joshua Paul Dale points out in his chapter, by grafting the adorable or lovable onto this prior meaning, the normative English-language definition also retains a degree of suspicion towards the cute: a sense that the object's ability to provoke a cute affective response may be a pretense intended to manipulate the subject. "Don't be cute!" is a relatively common admonition in English, yet has no direct translation in major European or Asian languages. It is precisely this powerful ambiguity of "cute" and its capacity to simultaneously assuage and insult, to sugar-coat while critiquing, that several of the essays in *The Aesthetics and Affects of Cuteness* enlist as a critical tool to examine the acerbic sincerity of many contemporary manifestations of cuteness.

Defining Cuteness

Building on Charles Darwin's proposition that infants must have some quality arising from natural selection that prompts adults to care for them, Konrad Lorenz inaugurated the scholarship on cute affect in 1943 when he delineated his *Kindchenschema*, or "child schema": a set of physical and behavioral characteristics common to young children and baby animals alike. The aspects of cuteness that he identified and schematized, namely "a relatively large head, predominance of the brain capsule, large and low-lying eyes, bulging cheek region, short and thick extremities, a springy elastic consistency, and clumsy movements" would, Lorenz claimed, trigger an involuntary desire to nurture in adults (*Studies* 154–62). One pertinent example of Lorenz's rubric is outlined in Stephen Jay Gould's 1979 essay, "Mickey Mouse Meets Konrad Lorenz." In this essay, which is possibly the first published writing devoted entirely to the aesthetics of cuteness, Gould explains how Disney artists tailored the appearance of their famous mouse over the first fifty years of Mickey's "life," progressively aligning the cartoon character with Lorenz's child schema. A 1985 study on the evolution of the teddy bear found similar results (Hinde and Barden). Recent scholarship, however, is beginning to discern still more precise aesthetic qualities of cuteness that may precipitate an affective response, including not only body size and proportion as in Lorenz's schema, but also color, texture, motion, and sound (Cheok and Fernando 301–07). In this regard, it is interesting to note that Mickey Mouse was originally a trickster figure described as "a rambunctious, even slightly sadistic fellow," but, as Gould also argues, along with his softening appearance that went from black and white to color, Mickey's personality also softened and became "cuter" and friendlier as he achieved the status of a national—and global—icon (95).

Lorenz's belief that the childish cute features he identified would inevitably induce an instinctive need to care for vulnerable human young in adults has been challenged and largely overturned (see Lehrman). While subsequent studies conducted by behavioral psychologists from the 1970s onward confirmed the overall efficacy of the child schema, researchers gradually abandoned Lorenz's assumption that cuteness comes with an "innate releasing mechanism" that causes adults to involuntarily give themselves over to caring and nurturing behaviors. Hence, as the aesthetic drew increasing scholarly attention, definitions of cuteness became more nuanced, and discussions in the early 1990s in the *British Journal of Aesthetics* focused on critiquing and refining notions of empathic cuteness (see Moreall "Cuteness"; Sanders; Moreall "Response"). These debates interrogated the assertion that cuteness functions solely to make adults feel agreeably disposed toward their vulnerable and completely dependent offspring, and it has now become clear that reactions to cuteness are not merely Pavlovian responses over which we have no control.

As Dale suggests, whether our response to cuteness is innate or learned, cuteness may be best understood as an appeal—intentional or unconscious, made by an animal- or human-like entity—that seeks to trigger a particular affective response. Importantly in this regard, Daniel Harris and Lori Merish have both addressed cuteness and its liminal positioning with regard to freakishness and the grotesque, and identified a certain ambiguity in the appeal of cuteness. Their findings imply, furthermore, that cuteness is not always overdetermined, monolithic, or unproblematic, and this complexity makes it possible to construe cuteness as an aesthetic category in its own right. Moreover, seen in this light cuteness as an aesthetic takes on a significant degree of malleability, allowing for the attachment of antagonistic categories while still retaining the capacity to precipitate an affective response in some (though not all) observers.[2] The relationality of cuteness is highlighted in various ways in this volume; for instance, Elizabeth Legge underscores in her analysis of Jeff Koons that the cute can never exist in quarantine. In her account it is subject to various pressures from the expectations of art as well as from the theory that informs it. Tracking the incorporation of cuteness within contemporary military cultures, Maria Pramaggiore notes how a cycle of "mashup" videos disseminated on YouTube sees US soldiers recreate (primarily female-produced and often genderqueer) pop music videos, a striking instance of cute relationality. While such texts attest to cuteness's centrality in recalibrations of twenty-first-century masculinity, the cultural work these portrayals of active military service personnel indulging in gender play achieves must be viewed in light of their emergence at a time when sexual assault in the military was under intense public scrutiny.

In discussing the derivation of the English word "cute" from "acute," Sianne Ngai perceptively notes that "cute exemplifies a situation in which making a word smaller—or, if you like, cuter—results in an uncanny reversal, changing its meaning into its exact opposite" (*Our* 87). This transformative dialectic provocatively resonates with the fact that the cute often "cute-ifies" the spectator, as in, for instance, the tendency of adults to speak in "baby talk" to newborn infants, or the seemingly opposite compulsion to smother, molest, or even bite the cute object indicative in adjective choice (e.g. "huggable" and "squeezable") (Poltrack; Ferro). Ngai points to the aptness of this neat reversal considering the continual shifting of response that both she and Harris find central to the cute: what she terms an "oscillation between domination and passivity, or cruelty and tenderness" (*Our* 108).

The power differential at the heart of the relationship between subject and (cute) object that results in Ngai's "cute-ified" subject also involves a partial dismantling of the subject, in which the intimacy offered by the cute object serves to blur the boundaries between that object and the " cute-ified," baby-talking subject. This shift may be best understood through recent scholarship on cute affect in which cuteness is linked to "mentalizing," or the tendency to ascribe mental states to objects. In this way, cuteness encourages affiliative tendencies and social engagement as well as nurturing: "Cuteness is as much an elicitor of play as it is of care. It is as likely to trigger a childlike state as a parental one" (Sherman and Haidt 248). The desire to enter, if only for a moment, a state of being that renders the world unthreatening and playful comprises a compelling link between the aesthetics of cute and cute affect. As the remainder of this introduction demonstrates, beyond instigating caretaking behavior, cuteness also fosters several other key subject/object dynamics such as shared affect, empathic responsiveness, prosocial behaviors including communication and companionship, and the quelling of contemporary anxieties.

Cuteness, Coping, and Labor

Among other goals, this book seeks to investigate cuteness's relation to the value calculus of capitalism, noting new forms of cute production and consumption whose ideological character is typically (although not inevitably) conservative. In the current phase of neoliberal capitalism, uncertainty and contingency are keynotes of a range of subjectivities, particularly in relation to new technologies. A central concern of *The Aesthetics and Affects of Cuteness* will therefore be to situate cuteness in the complex of power relations that comes with a neoliberalizing economy and its accompanying cultures. We propose further research into the cultural functions of the cute aesthetic and its affects that in a variety of ways purport to "help" people cope with the impacts of neoliberalization. For example, a growing body of research attests to the deleterious impact that post-Fordist corporate and industrial practices have had on notions of community and stability in the workforce, a trend often conceptualized under the term "precarity" (Gill and Pratt; Neilson and Rossiter; Standing; Boltanski and Chapello). In this vein, for example, Richard Sennett, writing in the late 1990s, chronicled the feelings of impermanence and instability brought about by increased technological change within the workplace, a shift that displaced older forms of solidarity. With these observations in mind, another way of contextualizing cuteness is as a mode of temporality aligned to or disruptive of what Benjamin Noys calls the "malign velocities" of contemporary capitalism.

Updating research in this vein, Melissa Gregg has traced how rapid technological developments in the white-collar office have led not to the expected easing of workload but its opposite, due in part to new developments such as "presence bleed," that is, the increased inclination for staff to continue working outside office hours at home via digital technologies such as email and smart phones (2). This piling on of work during allegedly off hours has motivated Germany's Ministry of Labor to ban contact with employees by phone or email outside of office hours, in hopes that the business world will adopt similar measures to prevent burnout and allow workers real downtime ("Living"). In France, buried within a highly unpopular piece of labor legislation primarily benefiting employers, is a law asserting the right of workers to disconnect: it prohibits digital communication to workers from their employers except during regular working hours (Collins). But the more popular solution to this problem is the expedient implementation of "fun" office practices (paintball office parties, casual Fridays) and a cute aesthetic that informs various office décor elements (coffee mugs, posters) with supposedly stress-releasing messages such as "You wanted it when?" or "Keep calm and avoid junk food" (Fleming). In her chapter in this volume, Allison Page tracks the imbrication of cuteness within such neoliberal conflations of work and leisure. Her analysis of the reality TV program *LOLwork* (2012–), set in the offices of a company specializing in the development and distribution of cute media, finds that, perhaps unsurprisingly, the smart office is a complex site for the mingling of neoliberal mandates and the consumption of cuteness as a form of what Page deems "cruel relief." In Japan, where decades-long economic malaise has diminished the country's former "jobs for life" policies and rendered employment for many workers newly insecure, one reaction has been to buoy up the population through the promotion of a burgeoning cute culture informed by the desire to *iyasareru*, that is, to relax and escape from an alienating, exhausting work environment. This is perhaps best embodied by the cute character Rilakkuma, an office worker's bear friend whose name means relaxing bear and who loves to sleep and lounge around the house (Stevens). As the official website explains, "You will be dragged into Rilakkuma's world and become lazy and relaxed." In Nadia de Vries's chapter about cute consumables in Japan, she demonstrates that the popular character Gudetama represents the apotheosis of anti-workaholic cute culture: it is a lazy egg who doesn't want to wake up, covering itself with a slice of bacon and whining, "Five more minutes!" This is not to suggest that cultures of cuteness reside purely (or even chiefly) in Asia. Recent scholarship has begun to investigate the mediating role of the cute in multicultural environments such as that of the contemporary US, where, as Rebecca M. Gordon notes, "Latino/a identity bears an ambiguous relation to the racialized and classed aesthetics of cute" (Gordon; see also Julia Leyda's chapter in the volume). By addressing the affective potential of cute aesthetics around the globe, our collection seeks to bring to light the implicit connections between new neoliberal regimes of increasingly flexible, technology-dependent work cultures and the ubiquitous explosion of cuteness in the twenty-first century. One of the most important potentialities of cuteness may be its capacity to interrupt the high symbiosis between State and market.

The rise of cuteness at the current moment of economic instability is also attributable to the increased sense of isolation and loneliness engendered by jarring changes in daily life that many scholars take up in analyses of contemporary culture. In *The Connection Gap: Why Americans Feel So Alone*, for example, Laura Pappano suggests that contemporary lifestyle regimes have led to a proliferating population of what she deems "the new lonely," who are "overstimulated, hyperkinetic, overcommitted, striving, under-cared-for, therapy dependent, plugged in, logged on, [and] sleep-deprived" (8). Lauren Berlant has similarly conceptualized the effects of neoliberalism and particularly its capacity to induce feelings of insecurity as a result of job precarity. Hence, she has defined the twenty-first-century present as a time of "impasse," where "people find themselves developing skills for adjusting to newly proliferating pressures to scramble for modes of living on" (*Cruel* 8). Indeed, Berlant further characterizes the present as a time when the popular fantasies that serve to sustain life such as upward mobility, political and social equality, and durable intimacy are increasingly fraying (*Cruel* 3).

Cute images do not merely soothe and help to ease the kinds of anxieties over job security just outlined and the resulting financial insecurity of more and more workers. Sharing cute images online may also mark participation in a like-minded community, or constitute an aspirational declaration of the type of person one wishes to be perceived as by that community, which we explore further below (Baron). In addition, cuteness may be mobilized by new media entrepreneurs to monetize their personal brands. In Singapore, for example, popular social media "influencers" deploy cuteness in three distinct strategies, which Crystal Abidin terms "the Doll," "the Darling," and "the Dear," to win empathy from their many followers while convincing them to purchase products and services advertised on their blogs and other social media platforms (Abidin).

In considering specific iterations of technology and their affects, however, Jonathan Crary sees the smartphone in particular as emblematic of the social and economic reorganization that has occurred over the last three decades under neoliberal capitalism, and here once again, cute images are pivotal. The paradoxical tendency of modern technology to at once offer us greater connectivity yet deliver further atomization is encapsulated in this device which, according to Crary, leads to "the parcellization and fragmentation of shared zones of experience into fabricated microworlds of affects and symbols," such as cute emoticons (53). It seems that one of the prominent features of cuteness is its strength in delivering such easily shared "affective hits," a tendency increasingly exploited in new developments in communications technology. It is our view that such shareable cuteness encourages extended engagement with the computer, smartphone, or tablet, keeping attention focused on the screen, while shaping contemporary (inter)subjectivities and ostensibly offering coping strategies for dealing with numerous troubling aspects of the present.

So while the consumption of typically brief cute online images may be usefully understood in relation to various ways in which media users may seek relief from a bombastic, all-encompassing work environment, there is also a downside. In escaping the constant exhortations to productivity by venturing to more entertaining corners of the internet, we are ironically obliged to employ the same technologies we use for work, while producing minable data to be exploited in many, frequently undesirable, ways. Equally ironic is the result of recent research suggesting that viewing cute content at work, rather than being a distraction, may actually make contemporary office workers more productive (Nittono). Moreover, in that same provocative study, the author suggests that cute images provide a source of temporary consolation for contemporary workers, and in so doing they ironically strengthen the economic and existential viability of neoliberal regimes. In many respects, cute content as a whole complies with the description Luke Stark and Kate Crawford provide of emojis when they note that "these graphic forms are exemplary of the tensions between affect and a liberating human potential, and as a productive force that the market continually seeks to harness through the commoditization of emotional sociality" (2). In *The Happiness Industry*, William Davies issues a call to resist "smartness" in the techno-corporate sense the term has acquired. If we position cuteness as the fantasy of respite from imperatives of constant information-seeking, we might come to perceive it as an effort to rebuild the empathetic sociality a critic like Davies sees as incompatible with the corporatization of happiness and wellness.

Cute Consumption, Nostalgia, and Adulthood

A profusion of studies has also investigated how to systemize the design of cute products in order to produce an affective response in consumers, testifying to the heightened commercial value of cuteness in neoliberal regimes (see Cheok; Cho; Miesler et al.). Cat food producer Friskies, for example, has launched a wildly successful three-minute advertising spot entitled "Dear Kitten," now boasting more than twenty-seven million hits on YouTube, in which a sardonic cat dispenses advice to a kitten who has joined the household. Moreover, the very existence of studies that explain how to use cuteness in experience marketing, as well as the overwhelming number of cute animals and characters that front an endless variety of products on TV and other media, underscores the contemporary currency of cute as an affect-producing aesthetic that is simultaneously participatory and a target of profit-seeking companies (see Klingman).

One further link between contemporary subjectivities and the consumption of cute images is proposed by Radha O'Meara, who reads the prevalence of cute cat videos in the light of ubiquitous surveillance technologies that scrutinize contemporary citizen-subjects. She posits that the unself-consciousness of cats is fundamental to their online popularity, an aspect of their demeanor that offers viewers modes of enjoyment and in particular "[the ability] to imagine the possibility of freedom from surveillance, and to experience the power of administering surveillance as unproblematic" (O'Meara). This viewing position comprises a complex relationship due to the reversal of position in which the one who is watched becomes the watcher. This vacillation in power staged by cuteness, noted by Ngai and others, is key, we contend, to the pleasures of many forms of cute content, especially in an era when, as noted, numerous aspects of neoliberalization such as precarity in the labor market and the withdrawal of social safety nets engender widespread feelings of uncertainty and powerlessness.

Given these last observations, it is illuminating to situate the rise of cute aesthetics within the context of political depression, a concept that has recently been theorized by Berlant and others; this is particularly striking in recent mobilizations of pop culture nostalgia. Political depression refers to an affective context in which citizen subjects have reached a state of exhaustion due to the "brutal relationship of ownership, control, security and their fantasmatic justifications in liberal political economies" (*Cruel* 261). According to Berlant, political depression marks many recent lifestyle trends that signal a retreat from the brutalities of such a system. An article in the *Guardian* from November 2013, for instance, decried the trendy millennial penchant for "Cath Kidston and cupcakes, baking and beards" (Walker). The argument asserts that, unlike previous generations who met economic turmoil with countercultural rebellion, differentiating them from their parents, millennials are "so world-weary, jaded, and out of onwards oomph that they feel going backwards is the only option." Certainly the immense popularity of domestic-oriented television programs such as *The Great British Bake Off* (2010–) and designer-retailers such as Kidston, whose products are known for their twee aesthetic featuring patterns made up of tiny animals, attest to a contemporary aesthetic that relies on tropes of nostalgia, cuteness, and diminutiveness. Another commentator, in a piece provocatively critiquing what he terms "cupcake fascism," has even identified in that cutest and most nostalgic of all cakes, "the desire of an infantilized populace to hide from the world while imposing bourgeois values" (Whyman).

This confluence of cuteness and conservative nostalgia also drives a 2014 advertising campaign by British biscuit manufacturer McVities. Comprised of three different advertisements, each one pairs cute content with the theme tune of a television program popular in 1980s Britain: in one, a family opens a packet of McVities Digestives and a succession of puppies emerge from the packet, as the theme of the popular mystery series *Murder, She Wrote* (1984–96) plays in the background (see Figure 1.1). The affective impact of cuteness in combination with nostalgia is central to the campaign, with one of the marketing directors claiming, "We want to build that sense of the family of feeling you get from our biscuits" (Vela). At the same time, "the sense of family" that the producers of this advertisement want to disseminate complies with conservative, heteronormative, and culturally monolithic calls to British values that gained prominence at the time of broadcast, notably encapsulated in the surge in popularity of the anti-immigration and Eurosceptic UK Independence Party (UKIP) that precipitated a swing to the right among all the main UK political parties.

These ads are, moreover, explicitly designed with the potential for sharing via social media on video platforms such as YouTube. This self-conscious bid for virality is manifest in the ways in which these advertisements leverage nostalgia, technology, and cuteness, a powerful combination that simultaneously bolsters a consumerist imperative and provides affective comfort in the face of an uncertain present. Here it is helpful to recognize, with Svetlana Boym, how "technology and nostalgia have become co-dependent as new technology and advanced marketing stimulate ersatz nostalgia—for the things you never thought you had lost—and anticipatory nostalgia—for the present that flees with the speed of a click" (10).

Sociologist Jennifer M. Silva has similarly identified nostalgia as a common affective prop in her study of the travails of working-class young people in the US, citing the risk society such youth inhabit as a major contributing factor to this ambivalent yearning for the past. As she explains, "in a larger social climate of insecurity in which risks are increasingly redistributed from the state and onto the individual, the freedom from tradition more often leaves [people] longing for the connections—and constraints—of the past" (145). Cuteness, in tandem with nostalgia, is one of the primary aesthetics that can establish the intimate, mediated publics in which texts

FIGURE 1.1 A gaggle of puppies emerges from a biscuit packet to create "a family of feeling."

can circulate and form sites of connection that bolster a twenty-first-century retreatism through which to evade the vicissitudes of the present.

The expanding registers and repertoires of cuteness, furthermore, speak to important shifts in social definitions of adulthood. Literary scholar Robert Pogue Harrison devotes an entire book to juvenescence, which he describes as "a wholesale biocultural transformation that is turning large segments of the human species into a 'younger' species—younger in looks, behavior, mentality, and, above all, desires" (Harrison). Similarly, Christopher Noxon notes the contemporary emergence of "a new breed of adult, identified by a determination to remain playful, energetic and flexible in the face of adult responsibilities" (2). Recent controversies over the large and growing adult readership of Young Adult (YA) fiction and A.O. Scott's 2014 polemic about the death of "grown-ups" have appeared at a time when the affective re-positioning and cultural valuing of maturity are in evident transition (Thompson; Graham; Wolitzer). Commercial culture, recognizing this, increasingly makes appeals to children and adults as co-consumers. To account for this shift, Thomas Lamarre links the evolution of a more juvenile and cute Mickey Mouse discussed above to "the general fate of cartoon heroes drawn from folklore in the modern era" as they move across media platforms (123). He traces this not only to the expansion of marketing to children, but also to an increasing loyalty among adults towards the products they loved in childhood. These two factors combine to create more edgy fare for kids and more cute characters loved by adults. Lamarre concludes: "It is frequently difficult to say whether we are seeing a juvenilization of adults or a precocious maturation of children" (Lamarre 123). For Jesse Barron, "We're in the middle of a decade of post-dignity design, whose dogma is cuteness. One explanation would be geopolitical: when the perception of instability is elevated, we seek the safety of naptime aesthetics." The Pokémon Go phenomenon of 2016 notably depended on the game's ability to superimpose a layer of cuteness derived from the digital domain onto material reality. In Barron's assessment, "there is no better example of cuteness applied in the service of power concealment than Pokémon Go." The blurring of boundaries between childhood and adulthood, as well as the expansion of nostalgic consumerism described above, has enabled cuteness to come to the fore in forging new affective bonds, as Joyce Goggin's chapter on the 1960s line of toy dolls, Kiddles, exemplifies. She argues that the cute interpellations associated, with childhood consumption are increasingly actively recycled to incentivize adult re-consumption in the collectible marketplace, as César Albarrán-Torres analyzes in his chapter on the cuteness deployed by gambling machines.

Cute Communities and Shifting Gender Configurations

When we bond with others by sharing cute images, what forms of belonging are being constructed? Sara Ahmed's concept of "happy objects" offers a useful approach to this question. In an essay in which she interrogates the spreading of certain forms of affect, in particular happiness, she posits that such transmission can often be attributed to "certain objects that circulate as social goods" ("Happy Objects" 37). Similarly, as contributions to this volume by both Katy Peplin and Allison Page demonstrate, the sharing of cute objects and images establishes a commonality with others drawn to the pleasures of consuming such material. Such sharing, often via online message boards and chat rooms, establishes what has been variously termed an "affective community" (Ahmed *Promise*; "Happy") or "intimate public" (Berlant *Female*). Indeed, the ease of online sharing since the emergence of Web 2.0 is no doubt central to the formation of such communities brought together through proliferation of online cute content. The concept of "memetic cuteness" extends Limor Shifman's definition of memes as "pieces of cultural information that pass along from person to person, but gradually scale into a shared social phenomenon" to specifically explain the virality of cute online content (18).

The professional cuteness curators at the popular website BuzzFeed seem well aware of this when they propose that people might wish to share cute images of animals as a way of demonstrating to others their care and empathy (Baron). Harnessing the communicative power of the internet, new coping strategies centered around a shared love of cuteness have facilitated the establishment of fan communities, whether or not these fans are pursued by the (designers of the) cute objects themselves. Celebrities such as Zooey Deschanel, for example, actively cultivate a cute image to gather and inspire fans. Leveraging cuteness through a careful manipulation of her self-presentation, or "star text," enables Deschanel to "neutralize political fracture points of race and gender by evoking a paternal response or a sense of belonging to a juxtapolitical intimate public" (McIntyre, "Isn't" 15). In the case of Deschanel as with many others, the parent–child relation inherent in many theories of cute affect offers provocative approaches to understanding communities of cuteness.

In an interview with Daniel Harris almost a decade after the publication of his book *Cute, Quaint, Hungry, and Romantic* (2001), the author notes that, due to the advent of the Internet and social media, "there is a change in the availability of these [cute] images [. . .]. The medium has made us hungrier for this stuff" (Windolf). It is our contention, however, that the technological progress that contributes to a rampant sense of emotional precarity and increased workloads, as well as the constant pressure to keep up with such technological developments, has been central to the increased cultural predominance of cuteness and the online communities that form around it. That is, it is not merely the variety of means through which to disseminate cute content that social media provide that has led to the explosion of such content. Rather, it is a function of a number of the concomitant affective changes brought about by the shift to an "attention economy" as described by Crary. Given these observations, we seek to elucidate what exactly it is about this aesthetic that makes it so resonant with distressed contemporary subjectivities.

Other cuteness-oriented fan communities have arisen completely unexpectedly as outpourings of unsolicited fan adoration. For example, "Bronies," a rapidly growing participatory community of largely male fans of the animated US TV program *My Little Pony: Friendship is Magic* (2010–),[3] consciously redefine their own masculinity through their shared love of an animated television show aimed at young girls. An ongoing, though self-reported, sociological study of fandom has interviewed almost 60,000 fans, and cited the "life guidance" that fans report receiving from the show as the most surprising result of the survey. Almost two thirds of Bronies reported improvement in their prosocial behavior after becoming fans of the show, hinting at the power of cute animated ponies, or the power of social bonding over those ponies, to cause real-world effects.[4] As Venetia Laura Delano Robertson, in an analysis congruent with our own characterization of contemporary social atomization (above), summarizes, "the canny combination of [*My Little Pony: Friendship is Magic's*] sub-cultural qualities and the value of non-human but human-like role models or avatars speaks intimately to a group of individuals typically bound up in anonymous internet networks" (34; see also Pramaggiore).

Nevertheless, despite the input of cuteness in such emerging gender formations, this protean aesthetic can also be deployed in texts depicting forms of hegemonic masculinity that are increasingly perceived as being either outmoded or under duress (Carroll; Leonard). A common trope across a number of US sitcoms sees beleaguered alpha male characters rail against an increased feminization of the modern world exemplified by the popularity of cute dogs. Ron Swanson (Nick Offerman) in *Parks and Recreation* (2009–15) and Mike Baxter (Tim Allen) in *Last Man Standing* (2011–), for example, are political conservatives coded as inheritors of nineteenth-century frontier modes of masculinity through their association with activities such as hunting and fishing and are shown demonstrating antipathy toward cute dogs. In one episode of *Last Man Standing* ("Bring your Daughter to Work Day"), Mike delivers the weekly video podcast for Outdoor Man, the shop he runs, and praises the vicious hunting dogs cave men used before disparagingly referencing the cute dog he is holding which was "bred entirely to be adorable." The scene ends with Mike mock-threatening to shoot the dog with a gun currently on offer at the store, itself reminiscent of a scene in *Parks and Recreation* where Swanson instructs a co-worker to "take [a puppy] outside, and shoot it" after the animal licks his face. The repeated refrain voiced by Mike that "just because something is new doesn't mean that it's better" conflates changing animal–human relationalities (examined in more detail below) with the changing gender dynamic in both public and private spheres that constitutes the main premise of *Last Man Standing*.

The liminal space where cuteness merges with the grotesque is also a staging ground for narratives of masculinity under duress. Seth MacFarlane, the creator of *Family Guy* (1999–), subverts the cuteness inherent to teddy bears in the film *Ted* (2012) and its 2015 sequel, in which he voices the eponymous, hard-drinking, pot-smoking, lascivious toy bear brought to life by his owner's wish. The film represents a combination of cuteness and raunch culture (Levy) that capitalizes on the aesthetic's liminal relation to the grotesque. Similarly, the FX series *Wilfred* (2011–14) features a manic-depressive male with social anxiety who sees his neighbor's dog as a man in a fluffy dog suit, a creature which increasingly leads him into trouble. As Anthony P. McIntyre argues in his chapter in this volume, both *Ted* and *Wilfred* treat cuteness as something that can trick women yet which masks a more animalistic and transgressive nature, a representational strategy which revives long-standing carnivalesque and symbolic cultural tropes incorporating human-animal hybridization (Stallybrass and White 27–79) and which ties these to revivified notions of masculinity in a contemporary context where patriarchal authority is perceived as being in retreat.[5]

Cute Compassion and Communication

A striking example of the new culture of cuteness is to be found in a recent update of the famous 1987 "L'Enfant" Poster which showcased a buff young man cradling a seemingly delighted baby (see Figure 1.2). The widely circulated image worked to ratify an emergent social fantasy that the practice of "family values" would not diminish the social power or erotic capital of masculinity in an era in which lifelong personal fitness has become a neoliberal mandate. The re-focalization in the updated version looks to the cute animal as both needful of care and a companion who can illuminate the self. Similarly, in this volume, Michael DeAngelis identifies the prevalence of similar cute images in gay-oriented media, arguing that both cute animal and buff male are engaged in a "synergistic process . . . [that] authorizes approach and . . . facilitates fantasies of accessibility and closer engagement with the object of desire" (p. 203 of this volume). Cuteness's role in establishing a fantasy of accessibility is further developed in this author's analysis of the star Chris Pratt. Positing a diachronic "depth model" of stardom in which viewers attend to a celebrity over the course of their career, DeAngelis suggests that Pratt's current appeal lies in no small part in his former out-of-shape condition, notably evoked in his character, Andy Dwyer, in *Parks and Recreation*. The soft-to-hard transition evident in his current buff physique thus incorporates both his former cute and approachable character, as well as an identificatory and aspirational fantasy of body transformation that resonates with a contemporary culture that valorizes such physical self-work.

In an oft-quoted passage from his 2001 book, Harris argues that cuteness "aestheticizes unhappiness, helplessness, and deformity . . . [involving] an unconscious act of sadism on the part of its creator, who makes an unconscious attempt to maim, hobble, and embarrass the thing he [sic] seeks to idolize" (5). The first sentence of this paragraph, however, is seldom quoted: "Cuteness, in short, is not something we find in our children but something we do to them" (5). As we noted above, in order to characterize children as cute-ified by their

FIGURE 1.2 The iconic earlier image of man and baby has been more recently
updated in a way that speaks of the new affective centrality of cute
animals.

parents to the "squeezable" point of abuse, Harris ignores the physical
characteristics of children that supposedly invoke a Lorenzian cuteness response
in many (albeit not all) adults. Theories of cute affect, however, provide a logical
basis for understanding how cuteness may aestheticize such negative qualities: when
an object with cute characteristics seems in need of extra care, it has the potential
to prompt a stronger cuteness response allied with nurturing. Therefore, in order
to approach the topic of the affective bonds that comprise our response to cuteness,
an analysis of compassion is essential.

Berlant notes the complexity of this "human emotion" in phrasing which is
remarkably similar to much recent commentary on cuteness ("Introduction" 3).
As she explains, "there is nothing simple about compassion apart from the desire
for it to be taken as simple, as a true expression of human attachment and
recognition" ("Introduction" 5). If we take the example of "Animals with Casts,"
a Tumblr with archives dating from 2009 to early 2014 devoted to a huge
collection of images of injured animals wearing casts, we can clearly see the affective
link between compassion and cuteness, with its rich reservoir of implications about
power, posthumanism, and anthropomorphism. This collection of images also
yielded a photo book that explains, "Most people see the words 'animals with
casts' and think 'how cute' and 'how awful' at the same time" (Segal 1). Drawing
out emotions such as repulsion, compassion, and affection, images of animals
recovering from physical trauma act on viewers in complex ways that are
deliberately amplified when the images are shared with friends online.

One reason for the affective power of cuteness is its essentially atemporal nature
and its metaphoric ability to condense a number of thoughts and sentiments,

thereby lifting us briefly but compellingly out of linear syntax. Moreover, as Sheila Murphy has noted, cute images that are shared on the internet reemerge in cycles and it can be difficult to locate the exact provenance of a particular piece. The widely shared image of a panda (see Figure 1.3) that was purported to be hugging a policeman's leg after the March 2011 earthquake and tsunami in Japan is a prime example. With its evocation of vulnerability and appeal to human compassion, a common response seems to be the viewing subject's identification with the human in the picture, a feat made significantly easier by the fact that only a leg is visible in the most popular version of the viral image.

However the photograph was actually taken in 2006 when the panda had just arrived at a Taiwan zoo as a gift from China, rather than during the aftermath of the Japan disaster. Snopes.com, a popular website that traces the origins of such memes, uncovered the fake, yet veracity seems to be of little consequence to those who enjoy the image's cuteness, which attests to the power of cute online images to deliver the same affective hit regardless of the accuracy or extent of our knowledge of their context ("Pandamonium"). Likewise, the complete disregard for the temporal coincidence of image and event speaks to the atemporal nature of cuteness, and accounts for why cute images are repeatedly re-shared and may proliferate on the internet in intermittent waves.

FIGURE 1.3 This panda image, purporting to show a distressed panda after an earthquake, remains popular online despite being publicly debunked.

Free Messaging Whenever, Wherever

Send free one-on-one and group texts to your friends anytime, anywhere!
LINE is available for a variety of smartphone devices (iPhone, Android, Windows Phone, BlackBerry, and Nokia) and even your PC.

FIGURE 1.4 An ad for the messaging app LINE showcasing its capacity to replace words with stickers representing emotional responses.

In their capacity to elicit compassion and complicated affects through uncomplicated sincerity, emoticons, emoji, and cute images are currently undergoing an enormous surge as a communication style in another unanticipated effect of new technologies. These emoticons and attachments fill an affective gap in an era in which face-to-face communication is increasingly rare and the positioning and motivation of our digital correspondents is hard to grasp in the absence of traditional physical cues. One example of such a technology is the mobile app LINE that originated in South Korea and Japan, a hybrid of social media and text messaging. One of the most popular features of this hugely successful smartphone app is its ability to communicate emotional states through the inclusion of cute or amusing virtual cartoon "stickers" in one's messages, which are lucrative because some sets of stickers are free while others must be purchased. Frequently, these stickers comprise the entirety of the message, with no accompanying text. An invitation for drinks after work, for example, may be politely declined with an image of a cute bear busily flinging papers across a desk. In response, Facebook and other social media networks have added their own sticker capabilities to their messaging technologies.

Changes in the culture surrounding "companion species" likewise frame depictions of animal cuteness in important ways that are also inextricably linked not only to an increase in emotional precarity that comes as a result of neoliberal economic practices as outlined above, but also to the neoliberal logics of consumption (see LaForteza; Haraway *Companion*). For example, a reality TV series like *My Cat from Hell* (2011–), which disciplines feline and human subjects, suggests some of the ways that the achievement of domesticity is increasingly linked to interspecies harmony. At the same time, *My Cat from Hell* encourages the consumption of luxury cat foods, toys, and grooming accessories through product placement, while promoting a general trend to the consumption necessary in order to achieve the domesticity promoted in the show. Moreover, in addition to the proliferation of cute animals in the media, monetizing human/animal sociality in the form of cat cafes—a twenty-first-century form of commodifying cute animals in real life—exemplifies the complex intersection of the desire for cute animals and for public consumerism that goes beyond consuming cute images. The trend has spread from Taiwan and Japan, where cat cafes have existed for many years, to multiple countries in Asia, the Middle East, Australia, the US and Europe—these public spaces allow paying customers to relax and purchase food and drink along with physical proximity to and contact with cute cats and other humans similarly enchanted by them.

Cute Encounters: Anthropomorphism and Animals

Anthropomorphism is a subset of the skill of mentalizing, or the ability to imagine the mental states of others, including interpreting—or misinterpreting—the facial expressions of animals and even inanimate objects. In other words, feeling that something is cute creates a relationship to that object. This process may bring us closer to animals, or other humans, but this logic also functions if the cute object is a toy, a doll, or a fictional character. The photo book *Face to Face* by François and Jean Robert collects pictures of everyday objects that resemble human, animal, or machine faces—as in the example of a bag that appears to have a face due to the placement of snaps and zipper (see Figure 1.5). This book's fascinating exercise in the phenomenon of pareidolia begs the question of how intentionally industrial designers incorporate anthropomorphic motifs into their products. Furthermore, the disarming of the subject that occurs through assigning a mental state to a cute object may engender new forms of human subjectivity based on the expression and sharing of cute affect. For example, Julia Leyda's and Joel Gn's chapters in this volume address the complex, and often fraught, relationships between cute machines and their human companions.

Another subset of anthropomorphism is the fantasy of "zoomorphism": the expression of human qualities in animal form, which has given rise to the participatory subculture of "furries" who gather together wearing animal costumes and expressing animal identities. Attendees at "Anthrocon" in Pittsburgh, who numbered over 6,000 in 2015, were estimated to bring in $5.7 million to the local economy (Ruth). Though "furries" are a relatively small subculture at present, the phenomenon of interacting with people in animal suits is thoroughly mainstreamed elsewhere in theme parks such as the Disney parks around the world and the increasingly "theme-parked" Times Square in New York. In Japan, where there are hundreds of official and semi-official animal characters representing local communities who appear regularly at promotional events as well as brand mascots for every conceivable commercial product and service, interacting with people

FIGURE 1.5 One striking effect of reading *Face to Face*, a book of anthropomorphic images, can be a shift in ways of seeing, in which the viewer begins to search for (and find) human-like facial features in everyday objects.

Source: © Francois & Jean Robert photography, www.francoisrobertphotography.com. Image reproduced by kind permission of the artists

dressed as animals is a common experience (Occhi). As some of the chapters in this volume argue, anthropomorphism is key to new technologies of cute embodied not only by representations of cuteness such as emoji or online images, but also in new forms of subjectivity IRL, or "in real life." Significantly, these new subjectivities are dependent upon communicating through cuteness in the form of human/animal sociality, which then shapes "real life" cute encounters. Additionally, as McIntyre argues in his analysis of manifestations of "in-crisis masculinity" in this volume, while a longstanding trope in film and television, anthropomorphism is still a key component in indexing contemporary shifts in gendered subjectivity across these media.

As the LINE app's myriad anthropomorphized animal characters indicate, cuteness notably spans both the human and the non-human and it is this intersection that comprises a key site within its ideological terrain. Dogs and cats are privileged in the internet economy of cuteness, but have by no means cornered the market with viral videos and other cute images routinely featuring

FIGURE 1.6 "Furries" dressed in animal suits at the New Orleans Comic Con 2012 Wizard World at the Morial Convention Center.

Source: © Infrogmation of New Orleans, Wikimedia Commons/CC-BY-SA-3.0

pandas like the one from the Taiwan zoo and Brown and Cony in LINE, as well as otters, rabbits, horses, hamsters, deer, meerkats, and numerous other animal species. Even beyond the realm of online images and in addition to anthropomorphism, however, it is clear that major changes in human/animal relations frame the growing interest in animal cuteness in important ways.

We see cuteness as a crucial cultural driver in the complex negotiations that take place on the mediated terrain of human–animal subjectivities. While big-budget animated film franchises like *Kung Fu Panda* (2008; 2011; 2015) and Marvel's summer smash *Guardians of the Galaxy* (2014; forthcoming 2017) leverage animal cuteness[6] in bids to attract intergenerational audiences, with the effect of assuaging the political and social anxieties latent in their plots, we are cognizant of a broader shift in the meanings and uses of animality itself. In addition to CGI and animated animals, screen cultures of cuteness also appeal to audiences using "real" animal content: television's Animal Planet channel has made a specialty of broadcasting series such as *Too Cute* (2011–14), focusing on stories about puppies and kittens, with the tagline, "a world where cuddly knows no bounds and a place where fluffy reigns supreme." With internet sites such as YouTube initially being the primary outlet for cute content, such series represent attempts by television producers to regain lucrative ground lost to such emerging technologies by repackaging similar material in standardized schedule-friendly formats, just one example of the dynamic recalibration currently in progress as the older technology seeks to reassert its relevance to twenty-first-century viewers.

At a time when existing structures of sociality are coming under duress, animals are serving as facilitators for safe forms of socialization and enabling us to attribute to them a set of positive values perceived to be declining in everyday social life. Certainly the rise of cat cafes, dog parks, pet spas, and other spaces of human–animal interaction indicate the growing significance of domesticated animals as social proxies in middle-class culture. The use of animals to redress social deficits is striking especially in an era in which Western societies worry about citizens' "emotional intelligence," and pinpoint recurrent failings associated with moral callousness (Goleman; Grant). Such contexts help to make meaningful the rise of cute empathic animals. Given the concerns just outlined, one of the challenges of this book will be to critically engage with the intricate interplay between subjectivity, affect, and, ultimately, consumption that has resulted in the unprecedented popularity of cute comforting texts, as well as a broad spectrum of cute merchandise.

Spreadable Cuteness: Interspecies Affect

Domesticated animals have smaller bodies than their wild counterparts, along with curlier tails, floppier ears, spotted (piebald) coats, shorter extremities, and wider faces (Darwin). These are among the physical characteristics that tend to trigger a cuteness response in humans (Lorenz). Furthermore, tameness—that is, the willingness to approach and engage with humans—is also a key element of cuteness as it operates across species (Dale). Because social engagement with domesticated animals is commonly predicated upon a cute appearance linked to tame behavior, the place of pets in human society is a crucial concern of cuteness scholarship.

David Grimm has noted in *Citizen Canine* that pets occupy a position of enhanced affective value in contemporary US society, with pet ownership increasingly prized as a critical emotional bond tantamount to a familial tie.[7] As he goes on to suggest, the dog or cat that we share our bed with might be providing us with indispensable closeness and affection, thereby filling mounting emotional voids which Grimm attributes to the centrality of technology and disintegrating human relationships (12; 227). The transfer of human desires for comfort, sociality, and haptic intimacy to pets is evident in the rise of cat cafes as mentioned above, but also the ever-widening array of consumer goods and services targeting pet owners: gourmet dog foods, dog day spas, and rather notably the emergence of websites like PetDating.com, whose avowed purpose is "to serve as an online community for pet owners who want their pet to enjoy a long, healthy, and fulfilling life in the company of another pet." The vast expansion, and in some cases creation, of pet service industries featuring deluxe grooming and personalized carers who deliver precise reports on the experiences of the pet when walked and groomed also bespeaks the growing value placed on pets in today's society.

Recent scholarship on "companion species," notably by philosopher Donna Haraway has begun to explore the complexity of human animal interaction and its centrality to contemporary subjectivities (*Companion*; *When*).[8] While interspecies relationships have been a constant throughout human history, increasingly the uses to which animals are put are moving beyond the practical (farming, hunting, transportation) and toward the emotional. The centrality of animals in the coping strategies that people develop when facing the emotional vicissitudes of the present is becoming more and more apparent. For instance, a 2013 *New York Times* article examining the phenomenon of "emotional support animals" on US flights shows how such contemporary coping strategies are reshaping both legal and medical discourses (Witz). The article details a growing trend among travelers to obtain written documentation from doctors attesting to the necessity of having an animal on board the plane. The calculation with which media companies such as NBC-Universal have sought to capitalize on animal cuteness is apparent in the addition of therapy dogs to the personnel lineup on the popular morning program *The Today Show* and on The Weather Channel, which in 2014, announced a search for the dog with which network personnel would travel to storm-ravaged communities to comfort victims (Greenwood).

The exchange of interspecies affect mediated through tameness and cuteness working in concert is vital to the newly attributed importance of companion species to the emotional health of humans. Such shifts are visible, for instance, in emergent social practices encompassing not only publicly communing with cats in cafes as previously noted but also with dogs in university stress-relief rooms, and even airports such as San Francisco International ("For Stressed"). That airport's website includes a page entitled "Meet the Wag Brigade" where one can peruse profiles of the numerous certified therapy dogs who now roam the airport in "pet me" vests ("Meet").[9] Perhaps more scientifically, animal-assisted therapy, based on E.O. Wilson's biophilia hypothesis, also asserts the usefulness of animals in soothing human emotions, in helping patients to relax and open up to therapists more easily, as well as in caring for those hospitalized with physical ailments such as heart failure (American Humane Association; Cole et al.).

Representations of human-pet relationships have always found a place in film and television cultures, and today's mediascape is no exception. It is evident that cuteness accords well with the multi-platform sales strategies of the contemporary convergent media environment and animal celebrities are particularly adept figures in convergent promotional economies. When Ashleigh Butler danced with her dog Pudsey to win the sixth season of *Britain's Got Talent* in 2012, this proved only the opening salvo in a commercial onslaught that would come to include television and theater appearances and in 2014 the feature film *Pudsey: The Movie*. Cute animals likewise have the power to stage (or not) the otherwise not necessarily guaranteed humanity of humans. Such a phenomenon appears particularly evident in the improved fortunes of homeless London street performer James Bowen whose decision to write about his cat materialized in the bestselling book *A Street Cat Named Bob: And How He Saved My Life*, the vast success of which has spawned four follow-up books and a movie deal (Flood). In this case, a particularly sympathetic-seeming and personable cat rendered visible his previously abject owner. Thus alongside the rise of middle-class pet cultures, particularly in cosmopolitan urban locations noted above, pets are also made to serve as proxies and brokers for "safe" social encounters, or to provide companionship for alienated city dwellers. Cute pets, it would appear, have the ability to convey the human value of otherwise devalued and marginalized owners. A far more troubling instance of the relative ease with which people sympathize with pets arose in the immediate aftermath of Hurricane Katrina. As David Sedaris acerbically observed, many television viewers were moved to donate money when they saw a cocker spaniel marooned forlornly on a rooftop, finding it easier to feel empathy for sad-eyed animals than human victims. Such viewers, according to Sedaris:

> emptied their pockets when a cocker spaniel was shown standing on a rooftop . . . "What choice did I have?" they asked. "That poor thing looked into the camera and penetrated my very soul." . . .
> The eyes of the stranded grandmother, I noted, were not half as piercing. There she was, clinging to a chimney with her bra strap showing, and all anyone did was wonder if she had a dog.

The cases above attest to dramatic recalibrations of inter-species relationality resulting from a wide array of cultural-economic factors. The contemporary sense of precarity brought about by increasingly neoliberalized "risk" societies (Beck; Silva) serves as an affective keynote to our changing interactions and responses to pets and other animals. Cuteness, as we have demonstrated, plays a fundamental role in many instances of such change, with animals often enlisted for the empathic sustenance and consolation they can provide in a variety of contexts. One of the more pressing questions raised by such inter-species recalibrations is to what extent the readily available affective hits cute animals provide mark an individualistic rerouting of empathic economies, thereby increasingly rendering suffering that would otherwise have provoked our outrage, sympathy, or ameliorative actions invisible.

Political Cuteness

One main function of this collection is to interrogate connections between cuteness and the political. While on the surface the two may seem to have little connection, the complex interplay between economics, ideology, and affect attest to the fact that aesthetics are woven into the fabric of our lives and cuteness is increasingly central to negotiations between public and private spheres. Asserting that while the Web was initially developed as a tool for physics researchers to share their work, Ethan Zuckerman states that "Web 2.0 was invented so that we could share cute pictures of our cats." Yet, while decrying these "mundane" uses for such technologies, Zuckerman posits his "cute cat theory of digital activism," asserting that Web 2.0 "can be extremely powerful in the hands of digital activists, especially those in environments where free speech is limited" (quoted in Shifman 119). Moreover, while seemingly dismissive of cute content itself, Zuckerman's theory provoked designer and internet theorist An Xiao Mina to assert the necessity of cute images and humor in repressive regimes such as China, as a means of getting online political content past censors:

> [Zuckerman] creates a dichotomy between people who share pictures of their cats and people who engage in political activism. In other words, cute cats and activist messages leverage the same tools, but they're fundamentally different. But with Chinese political memes, the cute cats *are* the activist message.

As An Xiao Mina points out, cuteness needs to be considered within its cultural and political contexts: perhaps in the US and Europe, these are usually separate uses of social media, but where Chinese political memes are concerned, the cute object is the subversive message, and the following example is a case in point.

Created by Hong Kong designer Michael Miller Yu, a mashup image of a celebrated protest image and a contemporary cute artwork went viral in China in June 2013 on the anniversary of the 1989 Tiananmen Square massacre in which students and pro-democracy demonstrators challenged the Chinese government with a series of stand-offs and sit-ins in and around Beijing (Blussé). The original iconic photograph of the single protester, dubbed Tank Man, who halted a line of tanks, had quickly become the visual symbol of the resistance movement. In Yu's mashup, the army tanks are replaced by a long line of rubber ducks: images of Dutch artist Florentijn Hofman's 26-meter-high floating artwork, which had recently concluded a tour of East Asian harbors. The cute ducks in this composite photo work as a substitute for tanks in a way that points to the policy of censorship while simultaneously eliding it. Indeed, the mashup was also quickly censored by the authorities, who temporarily made "big yellow duck" an unsearchable term on Chinese microblogging service Weibo (Blussé). As a political statement, this image strategically deployed the helplessness of cute objects—a line of giant rubber ducks—to highlight the absence of the threatening tanks that were present in the widely circulated original image in a way that simultaneously recalls the peaceful nature of the students' protest.

In a similar vein, Christine Yano has noted the influence of the Hello Kitty brand empire in proliferating Japan's "soft power," which exercises authority through subtle, non-aggressive means (5). This concept can be deployed by official institutions as well as characterizing more generally a national pop culture phenomenon: McVeigh coined the term "authority cuteness" to describe efforts by authority figures or centers of power to soften hierarchical relations by displaying weakness through the strategic deployment of cute products or images (150–56). Examples of this process used by East Asian state institutions include the series of cute mascots used by the Japanese police, and the cute manga-like images that adorn posters for the Japanese military, or "Self Defense Force" (McVeigh 150–51). Similarly, the Taiwanese Democratic Progressive Party has produced a series of cute products as political commodities to promote both the party and its head, Chen Shui-Bian, including "A-Bian" dolls modeled on his image (Chuang 4). Japan's "authority cuteness" also includes the public safety sector's tendency to soften the exercise of authority by communicating warnings through cute images and cartoons on posters and supporting construction barricades with cute anthropomorphic animals (see Figure 1.7). In this volume, Pramaggiore interprets the YouTube mashup videos of soldiers performing in recreations of popular music videos as compelling examples of authority cuteness that while foregrounding a sense of gender play, ultimately "[shore] up the government and media discourses that seek to present gender relations in the US as enlightened so as to justify military intervention [as the rescue of women oppressed by Islam]"(p. 100 of this volume).

The terrain of political cuteness is broader than we have space to show here, but a further example speaks to how contentious political disputes can be materialized in such contexts. Originally an East German traffic signal icon, the "Ampelmann" figure was repositioned after reunification as a cute sign of the transcendence of partition. Vigorously marketed to tourists in Berlin, and embossed on every manner of commodity, the Ampelmann now illustrates the quieting effect over history that cute marketing can impose. "Endowed with humaneness and cuteness," as Svetlana Boym recognizes, the Ampelmann currently works to secure a precariously unified urban identity (196).

In a new age of political violence, in which the sharing of cuteness is dramatically accelerated through the use of social media, cute images and rhetorics can symbolically soothe the fears of terrorism. In November 2015, following the terrorist attacks in Paris but months before the attacks at the Brussels airport, amid the search for suspects, the Belgian police requested that Brussels residents refrain from using social media to post material that might contain sensitive or revealing information. Consequently, a number of residents took to Twitter using cat pictures featuring the cats as suspects, military personnel, or even suspicious packages, as Gilles Bordelais tweeted, alongside an image of a kitten wielding a machine gun at a window, "They haven't got a chance! We haz kittens!" (Rogers). Such social media practices at a time of great fear and concern underscore the ways in which cuteness has emerged as a ready repertoire for sense-making in various political contexts.

FIGURE 1.7 Japanese authority cuteness manifests frequently in the use of animal cartoon shapes in road construction barricades warning pedestrians and drivers to proceed with caution.

Source: Photo by Joshua Paul Dale

Cuteness and/as Manipulation

While the concept of soft power has been a mainstay of contemporary political strategy for some time, fresh anxieties concerning the use of affect to manipulate both consumers and voters are emerging, especially in relation to new technologies. For example, when it became known in summer 2014 that Facebook had been conducting secret studies on how to manipulate users' moods through content displayed in their personal feed, there was widespread condemnation in the popular press. A scientific study of the Facebook experiment published by employees of the company along with scholars from Cornell University concludes that "[e]motions expressed by friends, via online social networks, influence our own moods, constituting [. . .] the first experimental evidence for massive-scale emotional contagion via social networks" (Kramer et al.). The social network's capacity to invisibly control the spread of "emotional contagion" may have been the most alarming factor, as a UK House of Commons member of the media select committee exclaimed, "[t]hey are manipulating material from people's personal lives and I am worried about the ability of Facebook and others to manipulate people's thoughts in politics or other areas" (Booth). In this volume,

Megan Arkenberg's chapter illustrates how the vacillation of cute objects between categories such as dangerous/vulnerable and precious/disposable creates an ambiguity that renders them both amenable to manipulation by authoritarian structures and available as a tool to critique such institutions.

The role of cuteness in mass manipulation is a central feature of a 2013 episode of the UK television series *Black Mirror* (2011–) which indexes a growing unease with the potential for affective influence in the heavily mediated political arena. "The Waldo Moment" portrays a dystopian view of the impact of cuteness on the public sphere. The story follows a failed stand-up comedian, Jamie Salter (Daniel Rigby), who voices and performs (through motion capture) as a blue bear named Waldo on a late night comedy program. Waldo is a clear example of the cute/grotesque border that Harris identifies in *Cute, Quaint, Hungry, and Romantic*, with the exaggerated features common to anthropomorphized cute animals, yet with the ability to decapitate himself, for instance, and to indulge in graphic carnivalesque feats involving masturbation. Waldo runs for office and finishes second, based on his cuteness combined with his anti-establishment rhetoric that targets the perception of privilege and elitism at the heart of the polity. The episode ends as Waldo has become an international political brand and a now washed-up Jamie is beaten by police after throwing a bottle at Waldo's image projected on a screen.

In "The Waldo Moment" we see an inversion of the nostalgic political quietism that cuteness more commonly fosters, as well as an articulation of some of the fears that development studies scholar Guy Standing anticipates as a result

FIGURE 1.8 In a scene reminiscent of UK comedian Russell Brand's 2013 appearance on *Newsnight*, Waldo is interviewed on a current affairs news program.

of growing economic and social precarity. Standing argues that the resulting disenchantment leaves open the possibility that populist demagogues may marshal widespread discontent for right wing purposes (148–54), an assessment that finds corroboration in the US given business mogul Donald Trump's transition from reality television celebrity to "legitimate" political contender. That said, however, the marshaling of discontent that arises from feelings of vulnerability is not the sole preserve of any one political ideology. As the political interventions in recent years of left-leaning comedians such as Russell Brand in the UK and Beppe Grillo in Italy have shown, the affective power of unelected popular figures can have significant purchase in a time of political depression. Cuteness as a pop culture aesthetic already saturating social media offers a ready-made vehicle, as the *Black Mirror* episode and the Facebook experiment remind us, with which to undermine individual and collective affective agency in both public and private spheres.

The HBO satirical news program *Last Week Tonight with John Oliver* (2014–) provides another telling example of an interface between political depression and modes of cuteness. The program's host, known primarily in the US from his time as writer and performer on Comedy Central's *The Daily Show with Jon Stewart* (1999–2015), introduces a lengthy commentary on the fractious issue of capital punishment following a botched execution in Oklahoma by acknowledging the high seriousness of the topic and promising if the audience stays with him they will "watch tiny hamsters eating tiny burritos, together" (see also Allison Page's chapter in this volume). The entire piece attests to the increasing reluctance of many viewers to engage with traditional political platforms, a fact borne out by the proliferation of such comedic/political shows including not only the two mentioned above but also *The Colbert Report* (2005–15), *Newswipe* (2009–10), and *10 O'Clock Live* (2011–13) in the UK, as well as the popularity of satirical news websites such as *The Onion*. During the 12-minute segment Oliver presents the audience with staggering facts relating to the execution of innocent people, political apathy in the face of such false convictions and the exorbitant costs of execution in comparison with life imprisonment, as well as capital punishment's inefficacy as a deterrent before eventually making good on his promise, showing audiences the aforementioned cute hamster video which had gone viral on YouTube that week, concluding, "and that is how you end a comprehensive segment on the death penalty." This ability of cuteness to mollify in the face of disquieting truths is just one of the many instances of cuteness inflecting political discourse detailed above. Indeed, the sheer range of these examples indicate the affective plasticity of cuteness with regard to issues pertaining to the public sphere, a quality that *The Aesthetics and Affects of Cuteness* seeks to elucidate. While the popularity of cuteness might be attributed to its inoffensiveness in an era of heightened sensitivities, complex identity politics, and political factionalization, we believe and seek to show here, that the story is far more complex.

Conclusion

Taking analytical note of a representational phenomenon of such size and scope that journalist David Ehrlich has referred to it as the "cuteness-industrial complex," *The Aesthetics and Affects of Cuteness* aims to consolidate existing studies of cuteness and to extend the scope of scholarship on its complex positioning. At the same time, the essays published in this collection all, in some way, draw connections between cuteness and the social, political, economic, and technological conditions of the early twenty-first century. While the work of writers such as Daniel Harris and Sianne Ngai has helped to increase our understanding of the aesthetic impact of cuteness by highlighting the power imbalance between the spectator and the cute object, the forms and functions of cuteness still needs further explication, particularly as it proliferates as a shared affective response through an increasing variety of media platforms and real-world events and situations. Tracing how vectors of age, gender, ethnicity, sexuality, nationality, and species shape (and are shaped through) cuteness, this selection of essays also addresses a range of vehicles for the expression and consumption of cuteness, including local and globalizing developments in product design, military cultures, toys, comics, video games, social media, internet memes, television, movies, YouTube videos, and mobile apps, as a means of further understanding this ubiquitous aesthetic and the affects that inform it.

Notes

1   That sense of suspicion has not entirely disappeared in some national usages, and indeed in the Irish context the notion of the "cute hoor" to designate a crafty person (most often in political and business contexts) is still widespread. Similarly, in parts of the southern United States, referring to someone as "the cutest little old thing" is often a polite means of checking an irritating or intrusive interlocutor.

2   The grotesque yet also cute title character of *E.T.* (1982) is perhaps the best known example, maintaining some features of conventional cuteness (large eyes, diminutive stature, wobbly walk) along with characteristics usually perceived as unattractive (leathery skin) (Merish).

3   *My Little Pony* originated as a line of Hasbro toys aimed at young girls in 1983. The toys have been revamped several times in the intervening years. The 1980s and 1990s saw a number of animated specials and series furthering the franchise including *My Little Pony: The Movie* (1986), however the brony phenomenon has been primarily associated with *My Little Pony: Friendship is Magic*.

4   The researchers acknowledge various weaknesses of their study: for instance, their sample was drawn from Brony fan sites, and involved retrospective questions about subjective memories. Both therapists, they also note that subjective impressions of behavioral improvements, regardless of their accuracy, represent a favorable outcome from a therapeutic perspective. See Edwards et al.

5   For an arguably more progressive deployment of comedic cuteness that foregrounds the vulnerability at the heart of the aesthetic as well as its connections to the grotesque, see McIntyre's analysis of US comedian Sarah Silverman's work ("Sarah").

6   In addition to the amusingly aggressive genetically-engineered raccoon Rocket, *Guardians* also features a saturnine sentient tree named Groot who turns out to be the most popular character (Willmore).

7   We are of course aware that the positioning of animals in this way has crucial historical precedents. Nicholas Daly, in his study of the nineteenth-century city, for instance, generates an insightful analysis of pets in that era, summarizing their position as follows: "Status symbols, playthings, part-time controllers of vermin, objects of emotional cathexis, these animals had a complex position in the household" (158).

8   See also John Berger's highly-influential essay "Why Look at Animals?" for an early examination of the role capitalism plays in our evolving relationship with the animal world (Berger).

9   Airports are sites in which broad social shifts are often distilled. Many trends (in fields as varied as consumer practices and security) that become commonplace throughout wider society often emerge (or are significantly intensified) within airports. See, for instance, Marc Augé's *Non-Places*.

Works Cited

Abidin, Crystal. "Agentic Cute (^.^): Pastiching East Asian Cute in Influencer Commerce." Cute Studies, special issue of *East Asian Journal of Popular Culture* 2.1 (2016): 33–47.

Ahmed, Sara. *The Promise of Happiness*. Durham, NC: Duke University Press, 2010.

——. "Happy Objects." *The Affect Theory Reader*. Ed. Melissa Gregg and Gregory J. Seigworth. Durham, NC: Duke University Press, 2010. 29–51.

Allison, Anne. *Millennial Monsters: Japanese Toys and the Global Imagination*. Berkeley, CA: University of California Press, 2006.

American Humane Association. "Animal-Assisted Therapy." *American Humane Association*. 2013. Online. 30 Dec. 2014.

Augé, Marc. *Non-Places: Introduction to an Anthropology of Supermodernity*. London: Verso, 1995.

Baron, Zach. "Where the Wild Things Go Viral." *GQ*. Condé Nast, Mar. 2014. Online. 30 Dec. 2014.

Barron, Jesse. "The Babysitters Club." *Real Life*. Real Life Magazine, 27 July 2016. Online. 1 Aug. 2016.

Beck, Ulrich. *Risk Society: Towards a New Modernity*. London: Sage, 1986.

Berger, John. "Why Look at Animals?" *About Looking*. New York: Pantheon, 1980. 1–28.

Berlant, Lauren. "Introduction: Compassion (and Withholding)." *Compassion: The Culture and Politics of an Emotion*. New York: Routledge, 2004. 1–13.

——. *The Female Complaint: The Unfinished Business of Sentimentality in American Culture*. Durham, NC: Duke University Press, 2008.

——. *Cruel Optimism*. Durham, NC: Duke University Press, 2011.

Berners-Lee, Tim. Interview. AMA [Ask Me Anything]. *Reddit.com*. Reddit, 12 Mar. 2014. Online. 30 Dec. 2014.

Blussé, Julie. "Ducks Not Tanks, Says Yu, Creator of Weibo's Banned June 4th Meme." *Radio Netherlands Worldwide*. Radio Nederland Wereldomroep, 5 June 2013. Online. 30 Dec. 2014.

Boltanski, Luc, and Eve Chapello. *The New Spirit of Capitalism*. London: Verso, 2006.

Booth, Robert. "Facebook Reveals News Feed Experiment to Control Emotions." *Guardian*. Guardian News and Media, 30 June 2014. Online. 6 July 2014.

Boym, Svetlana. *The Future of Nostalgia*. New York: Basic, 2001.

Carroll, Hamilton. *Affirmative Reaction: New Formations of White Masculinity*. Durham, NC: Duke University Press, 2011.

Cheok, Adrian David. *Art and Technology of Entertainment Computing and Communication: Advances in Interactive New Media for Entertainment Computing*. London: Springer, 2010. 232–43.

Cheok, Adrian David, and Owen Noel Newton Fernando. "Kawaii/Cute Interactive Media." *Universal Access in the Information Society* 11 (2012): 295–309.

Cho, Sookyung. *Aesthetic and Value Judgment of Neotenous Objects: Cuteness as a Design Factor and its Effects on Product Evaluation*. Diss. University of Michigan, 2012.

Chuang, Yin C. "Kawaii in Taiwan Politics." *International Journal of Asia Pacific Studies* 7.3 (2011): 1–17.

Cole, Kathie, Anna Gawlinski, Neil Steers, and Jenny Kotlerman. "Animal-Assisted Therapy in Patients Hospitalized with Heart Failure." *American Journal of Critical Care* 16.6 (2007): 575–85. Online. 30 Dec. 2014.

Collins, Lauren. "The French Counter-Strike against Work E-Mail." *New Yorker*, 24 May 2016. Online. 26 May 2016.

Crary, Jonathan. *24/7: Late Capitalism and the Ends of Sleep*. London: Verso, 2013.

Daly, Nicholas. *The Demographic Imagination and the Nineteenth-Century City: Paris, London, New York*. Cambridge: Cambridge University Press, 2015.

Darwin, Charles. *The Expression of Emotion in Man and Animals*. London: John Murray, 1872. Reprint. *Darwin Online*. Online. 20 Dec. 2014.

Davies, William. *The Happiness Industry: How The Government and Big Business Sold Us Well-Being*. London: Verso, 2015.

Edwards, Patrick, et al. "How the Fandom Changed my Life Data." *Brony Study*, 2012. Online. 27 May 2016.

Ehrlich, David. "From Kewpies to Minions: A Brief History of Pop Culture Cuteness." *Rolling Stone*. Rolling Stone, 21 July 2015. Online. 10 June 2016.

Ferro, Shaunacy. "Why Do We Want To Squeeze Cute Things? Studying How Adorable Animals can Turn us Aggressive." *Popular Science*. Bonnier, 24 Jan. 2013. Online. 31 Dec. 2014.

Fleming, P. "Workers' Playtime? Boundaries and Cynicism in a Culture of Fun Program." *Journal of Applied Behavioral Science* 41 (2005): 285–303.

Flood, Alison. "Bob the Street Cat Books Sell 1m Copies in UK." *Guardian*. Guardian News and Media, 18 Mar. 2014. Online. 31 Dec. 2014.

"For Stressed College Students, A Doggone Good Way to Relax." *USA Today*. Gannett, 3 May 2012. Online. 30 Dec. 2014.

Gill, Rosalind, and Andy Pratt. "In the Social Factory? Immaterial Labor, Precariousness, and Cultural Work." *Theory, Culture, and Society* 25.7–8 (2008): 1–30.

Goleman, Daniel. *Emotional Intelligence: Why It Can Matter More Than I.Q.* New York: Bantam, 1995.

Gordon, Rebecca. "'So Cute It's Sick': The Chicano/Latino Disruption of Cute in *Ugly Betty* and *Juana la Virgen*." Modern Language Assoc. Conference, Austin, TX. 7–10 Jan. 2016. Address.

Gould, Stephen Jay. "Mickey Mouse Meets Konrad Lorenz." *Natural History* 88.5 (1979): 30–36. Rpt. as "A Biological Homage to Mickey Mouse" in *The Panda's Thumb: More Reflections in Natural History*. New York: Norton, 1980. 95–107.

Graham, Ruth. "Against YA." *Slate*. Slate Group, 5 June 2014. Online. 30 Dec. 2014.

Grant, Adam. "The Dark Side of Emotional Intelligence." *Atlantic*. Atlantic Monthly Group, 2 Jan. 2014. Online. 19 Sept. 2016.

Greenwood, Arin. "Butler the Therapy Dog Has an Important Message for Bo and Sunny Obama." *Huffington Post*. AOL-Verizon, 5 May 2014. Online. 20 June 2016.

Gregg, Melissa. *Work's Intimacy*. London: Polity, 2011.

Grimm, David. *Citizen Canine: Our Evolving Relationship with Cats and Dogs*. New York: Public Affairs, 2014.

Haraway, Donna J. *Companion Species Manifesto: Dogs, People, and Significant Otherness*. Chicago, IL: Prickly Paradigm, 2003.

——. *When Species Meet*. Minneapolis, MN: University of Minnesota, 2007.

Harris, Daniel. *Cute, Quaint, Hungry, and Romantic: The Aesthetics of Consumerism*. New York: Basic, 2000.

Harrison, Robert Pogue. *Juvenescence: A Cultural History of Our Age*. Chicago, IL: Chicago University Press, 2014.

Hinde, Robert A., and Les A. Barden. "The Evolution of the Teddy Bear." *Animal Behavior* 33 (1985): 1371–73.

Hinson, Tamara. "Inside the Cult World of Hello Kitty." *Guardian*. Guardian News and Media, 30 Nov. 2014. Online. 30 Dec. 2014.

Klingman, Anne. *Brandscapes*. Cambridge, MA: MIT Press, 2007.

Kramer, Adam D.I., Jamie E. Guillory, and Jeffrey T. Hancock. "Experimental Evidence of Massive-Scale Emotional Contagion through Social Networks." *Proceedings of the National Academy of Sciences of the United States of America*. 111.24 (2014): 8788–90. Online. 30 Dec. 2014.

LaForteza, Elaine. "Cute-ifying Disability: Lil Bub, the Celebrity Cat." *M/C Journal* 17.2 (2014). Online. 30 Dec. 2014.

Lamarre, Thomas. "Speciesism, Part III: Neoteny and the Politics of Life." *Mechademia* 6 (2011): 110–36.

Lehrman, Daniel S. "A Critique of Konrad Lorenz's Theory of Instinctive Behavior." *Quarterly Review of Biology* 28.4 (1953): 337–63.

Leonard, Suzanne. "Escaping the Recession? The New Vitality of the Woman Worker." *Gendering the Recession: Media and Culture in an Age of Austerity*. Eds. Diane Negra and Yvonne Tasker. Durham, NC: Duke University Press, 2014. 31–58.

Levy, Ariel. *Female Chauvinist Pigs: Women and the Rise of Raunch Culture*. New York: Free, 2005.

"Living Offline: Minister Halts After-Hours Contact for Staff." *Spiegel Online International*. Spiegel Online, 30 Aug. 2013. Online. 30 Dec. 2014.

Lorenz, Konrad. "Die angeborenen Formen möglicher Erfahrung. [The innate conditions of the possibility of experience.]" *Zeitschrift für Tierpsychologie* 5.2 (1943): 245–409.

——. *Studies in Animal and Human Behavior*. Vol. 2. 1950. Trans. R. Martin. Cambridge, MA: Harvard University Press, 1971.

McIntyre, Anthony P. "*Isn't She Adorkable!* Cuteness as Political Neutralization in the Star Text of Zooey Deschanel." *Television and New Media* 16.5 (2015): 422–38.

——. "Sarah Silverman: Cuteness as Subversion." *Hysterical! Women in American Comedy*. Eds. Linda Mizejewski and Victoria Sturtevant. Austin, TX: University of Texas Press, forthcoming 2017.

McVeigh, Brian. *Wearing Ideology: State, Schooling, and Self-Presentation in Japan*. Oxford: Berg, 2000.

"Meet the Wag Brigade." *Fly SFO*. San Francisco International Airport, n.d. Online. 30 Dec. 2014.

Merish, Lori. "Cuteness and Commodity Aesthetics: Tom Thumb and Shirley Temple." *Freakery: Cultural Spectacles of the Extraordinary Body*. Ed. Rosemarie Garland-Thomson. New York: New York University Press, 1996. 185–203.

Merriman, Chris. "Tim Berners-Lee Didn't Expect so Many Cats on the World Wide Web." *Inquirer.* Incisive Business Media, 13 Mar. 2014. Online. 7 July 2014.

Miesler, Linda, Helmut Leder, and Andreas Herrmann. "Isn't it Cute: An Evolutionary Perspective of Baby-Schema Effects in Visual Product Designs." *International Journal of Design* 5.3 (2011): 17–30.

Mina, An Xiao. "Social Media Street Art: Censorship, China's Political Memes, and the Cute Cat Theory." *An Xiao Studio.* An Xiao Mina, 28 Dec. 2011. Online. 10 July 2014.

Morreall, John. "Cuteness." *British Journal of Aesthetics* 31.1 (1991): 39–47.

——. "The Contingency of Cuteness: A Reply to Sanders." *British Journal of Aesthetics* 33.3 (1993): 283–85.

Murphy, Sheila. "I Can Has Cute: Why and How Online Cute Animal Videos Matter." Society for Cinema and Media Studies Conference, Seattle, WA. 19–23 March 2014. Address.

Museum of Fuchu City. *Kawaii Edo kaiga* [*Very Cute Pictures of Old Edo*]. Tokyo: KyuryuDo, 2013.

Neilson, Brett, and Ned Rossiter. "From Precarity to Precariousness and Back Again: Labor, Life, and Unstable Networks." *Fibreculture Journal* 5 (2005). Online. 25 Dec. 2014.

Napier, Susan J. *From Impressionism to Anime: Japan as Fantasy and Fan Cult in the Mind of the West.* New York: Palgrave-Macmillan, 2008.

Ngai, Sianne. "The Cuteness of the Avant-Garde." *Critical Inquiry* 31.4 (2005): 811–47.

——. *Our Aesthetic Categories: Zany, Cute, Interesting.* Cambridge, MA: Harvard University Press, 2012.

Nittono, Hiroshi, Michiko Fukushima, Akihiro Yano, and Hiroki Moriya. "The Power of *Kawaii*: Viewing Cute Images Promotes a Careful Behavior and Narrows Attentional Focus." *PLoS ONE* 7.9 (2012). Online. 30 Dec. 2014.

Noxon, Christopher. *Rejuvenile: Kickball, Cartoons, Cupcakes, and the Reinvention of the American Grown-Up.* New York: Basic, 2007.

Noys, Benjamin. *Malign Velocities: Accelerationism and Capitalism.* Winchester: Zero, 2014.

Occhi, Debra "Consuming Kyara 'Characters': Anthropomorphization and Marketing in Contemporary Japan." *Comparative Culture* 15 (2010): 77–86.

O'Meara, Radha. "Do Cats Know They Rule YouTube? Surveillance and the Pleasures of Cat Videos." *M/C Journal* 17.2 (2014). Online. 30 Dec. 2014.

"Pandamonium: Panda Hugs Japanese Policeman." *Snopes.com.* Snopes.com, 22 Mar. 2011. Online. 25 June 2014.

Pappano, Laura. *The Connection Gap: Why Americans Feel so Alone.* New Brunswick, NJ: Rutgers University Press, 2001.

Poltrack, Emma. "Why Do We Want to Bite Cute Things, Like Adorable Newborn Babies?" *Scientific American.* Scientific American, 16 Oct. 2014. Online. 30 Dec. 2014.

Pramaggiore, Maria. "The Taming of the Bronies: Animals, Autism, and Fandom as Therapeutic Performance." *Alphaville* 9 (2015): n.p. Online. 10 June 2016.

Richard, Frances. "Fifteen Theses on the Cute." *Cabinet* 1.4 (2001). Online. 3 July 2014.

Robert, François, and Jean Robert. *Face to Face.* Baden: Lars Müller, 1996.

Robertson, Venetia Laura Delano. "Of Ponies and Men: *My Little Pony: Friendship is Magic* and the Brony Fandom." *International Journal of Cultural Studies* 17.1 (2014): 21–37.

Rogers, Katie. "Twitter Cats to the Rescue in Brussels Lockdown." *New York Times.* New York Times, 23 Nov. 2015. Online. 24 Nov. 2015.

Ruth, Daisy. "The Business of the Furry Convention: Anthrocon Estimated to Bring in $5.7 Million to Pittsburgh." WTAE Pitttsburgh, 2015. Online. 27 May 2016.

Sanders, John T. "On 'Cuteness.' " *British Journal of Aesthetics* 32.2 (1992): 162–65.

Scott, A.O. "The Death of Adulthood in American Culture." *New York Times Magazine.* New York Times, 11 Sept. 2014. Online. 30 Dec. 2014.

Sedaris, David. "April and Paris." *New Yorker.* New Yorker, 24 Mar. 2008. Online. 15 Dec. 2014.

Segal, Julia. *Feel Better, Little Buddy: Animals with Casts.* San Francisco, CA: Chronicle, 2011.

Sennett, Richard. *The Corrosion of Character: The Personal Consequences of Work in the New Capitalism.* New York: Norton, 1998.

Sherman, Gary D., and Jonathan Haidt. "Cuteness and Disgust: The Humanizing and Dehumanizing Effects of Emotion." *Emotion Review* 3.3 (2011): 245–51.

Shifman, Limor. *Memes in Digital Culture.* Cambridge, MA: MIT Press, 2014.

Silva, Jennifer M. *Coming Up Short: Working-Class Adulthood in an Age of Uncertainty.* New York: Oxford University Press, 2013.

Stallybrass, Peter, and Allon White. *The Politics and Poetics of Transgression.* Ithaca, NY: Cornell University Press, 1986.

Standing, Guy. *The Precariat: The New Dangerous Class.* London: Bloomsbury, 2011.

Stark, Luke, and Kate Crawford. "The Conservatism of Emoji: Work, Affect and Communication." *Social Media and Society* (2015): 1–11.

Stevens, Carolyn. "Cute but Relaxed: Ten Years of Rilakkuma in Precarious Japan." *M/C Journal* 17.2 (2014). Online. 27 May 2016.

Thompson, Derek. "Adulthood, Delayed: What Has the Recession Done to Millennials?" *Atlantic.* Atlantic Monthly Group, 14 Feb. 2012. Online. 21 Oct. 2013.

Vela, Matt. "This British Biscuits Ad is the Cutest Thing Ever Put on Television." *Time.* Time-Warner, 12 Feb. 2014. Online. 10 July 2014.

Walker, Harriet. "Young People Are Dressing like Their Parents: It's Coziness Commodified." *Guardian.* Guardian News and Media, 2 Nov. 2013. Online. 25 June 2014.

Whyman, Tom. "Beware of Cupcake Fascism." *Guardian.* Guardian News and Media, 8 Apr. 2014. Online. 25 June 2014.

Willmore, Allison. "Ranking the *Guardians of the Galaxy* Characters." *BuzzFeed.* BuzzFeed, 14 Aug. 2014. Online. 31 Dec. 2014.

Windolf, Jim. "Addicted to Cute." *VanityFair.* Condé Nast, Dec. 2009. Online. 3 July 2014.

Witz, Billy. "Emotional Support, with Fur, Draws Complaints on Planes." *New York Times.* New York Times, 15 Nov. 2013. Online. 13 Dec. 2014.

Wolitzer, Meg. "Look Homeward, Reader: A Not-so-Young Audience for Young Adult Books." *New York Times.* New York Times, 17 Oct. 2014. Online. 30 Dec. 2014.

Yano, Christine R. *Pink Globalization: Hello Kitty's Trek Across the Pacific.* Durham, NC: Duke University Press, 2013.

Zuckerman, Ethan. "Cute Cats to the Rescue? Participatory Media and Political Expression." *Ethanzuckerman.com.* Online. 10 July 2014.

2

THE APPEAL OF THE CUTE OBJECT

Desire, Domestication, and Agency

Joshua Paul Dale

As the title of this volume indicates, cuteness occupies both the aesthetic and affective realms. As an affect, cuteness comprises a set of visual and/or behavioral characteristics capable of triggering a physical and emotional response in the body of the subject: what we may term the "Aww" factor. As an aesthetic category, this response is manipulated for a variety of purposes: commercial to be sure, but also artistic and self-expressive. The extant scholarship on cuteness tends to privilege one realm or the other. Quantitative analyses, which concentrate on affect, have isolated a specific set of stimuli that tends to cause a cuteness response in most people. However, this approach risks reducing cuteness to an autonomic, pre-subjective reaction that stands outside cognition, and thus apart from the production of meaning, the exercise of intention, and subjective agency in general. On the other hand, qualitative studies that privilege the aesthetic realm focus on cuteness as an aesthetic judgment, which emphasizes the agency of the subject encountering cuteness while defining cute objects as fundamentally passive.[1]

In this chapter, I aim to rectify this bifurcation of scholarly approaches by defining cuteness as a potential, rather than instinctive or reflexive, human response to a definable (albeit not completely defined) set of stimuli. The place taken by cognition lies at the heart of this distinction. As Marta Figlerowicz writes, the various branches of affect theory all circle around the central question of timing (3). Does experience run ahead of consciousness, or vice versa?

Brain Massumi defines affect as "irreducibly bodily and autonomic": an experience of intensity distinct from, and prior to, both cognition and emotion (28). Ruth Leys, on the other hand, argues in an extensive critique of this position that there is insufficient neurological evidence to support the claim that affects arise without intention and are separate from cognition (439). In taking this indeterminacy into account, I characterize the affective reaction to cuteness as potential rather than predetermined in order to account for the fact that difference is at work in the response to cute objects. The fact that humans in many different cultures have evolved a preference for cute things does not explain the values, intention, or meaning that various people or groups assign to this response. It does not even account for the simple happenstance that one person may find a particular object to be cute, while the same object may leave another unmoved. The realm of aesthetics brings this instability to the fore, highlighting the rich variation that results from individual and cultural differences in the apprehension of cute objects.

One particular cultural difference, however, has had a significant effect on this apprehension. As I show below, the derivation of "cute" from "acute" predisposes English speakers to view cute objects—living and non-living—as inherently manipulative and cunning. Scholarship on the aesthetics of cute has been strongly influenced by this linguistic bias. My definition of cuteness, on the other hand, proceeds from the affective reaction to a cute object, which I contend is fundamentally benign rather than adversarial. Thus I argue that antagonistic qualities such as violence, aggression and sadism are not intrinsic to the concept of cuteness. However, such qualities are frequently *attached* to cute objects in the aesthetic realm, a difference I make clear by briefly comparing the English cute to the Japanese *kawaii*.[2] Furthermore, while aggressive feelings do arise in a subject overwhelmed by cuteness, I maintain that this excess affect discharges towards the *subject* in order to preserve a vulnerable cute object from harm.

Scholars of cute affect, on the other hand, face their own difficulties when they take Konrad Lorenz's *Kindchenschema* or child schema as their primary model (155). The child schema lists the juvenile features—present in domesticated animals such as puppies, bunnies, and birds as well as children—that trigger a cuteness response (154). Decades of scientific research has verified that the *Kindchenschema* reliably produce a cuteness response in most people. However, the theory of instincts that Lorenz employs to ground his child schema is highly problematic in the way it universalizes this response. In demonstrating the efficacy of the child schema, researchers have tended to accept the theory that informs it due to a lack of alternatives. An important hypothesis, however, proposes social engagement as the primary motivation behind the cuteness response, and the work that explores this reconfiguration has important implications for the study of both the aesthetics and affects of cuteness (Sherman and Haidt, Nittono).

In my reading, the alternative hypothesis of social engagement allows for a new theory of agency on the part of the cute object, which I develop through the case study of a newly domesticated animal: Siberian silver foxes. By exploring the fox's transition from wild animal to tame pet, I identify the array of behavioral characteristics associated with the cuteness response that demonstrate its power to both initiate and enhance intra- and inter-species affiliative behavior. The new leitmotifs I propose include: prosocial behavior; emotional reactivity; cooperative action/play; and companionship/friendship. I conclude that expressions of cuteness, whether they emanate from animals, objects, or people, comprise a form of agency: namely, an appeal aimed at disarming aggression and promoting sociality.

The Dark Side of Cute

As noted in the introduction to this volume, the word "cute" first appeared in the eighteenth century as a shortened form of "acute," and was used to mean clever or sharp-witted. In the nineteenth century, cute became an American colloquialism and attained its modern meaning, but the definition still includes "cunning": an echo of the original aphaeresis that still reverberates three centuries later. Thanks to its inclusion of this disparate element, the English cute is capable of appearing in utterly un-cute contexts. Transcripts of the House of Un-American Activities Committee (HUAC) provide a telling example. When labor organizer David Brownstone was interrogated by the committee in 1957, he refused to answer their questions by pleading both the First and Fifth Amendments, suggesting that the committee itself was unconstitutional: a statement that chairman Edwin Willis twice dismissed as a "cute little speech" (Brownstone). Willis's remark was meant to demean Brownstone's defense as sly and self-serving. Attaching "little" to "cute" sarcastically references the latter's meaning as endearing in a further attempt to trivialize.[3]

When expressed in English, the concept of cute thus includes a fundamental ambivalence. In its definition of this word, the OED quotes two Aldous Huxley novels from the 1940s that include the phrase "indecently 'cute'": one referring to an affected French accent, the other to an overly dressed boy. Huxley's association of cuteness with an excess of feeling that runs beyond the bounds of decency is thus staged through pretense and artificiality.[4] This ambivalence is a double-edged sword. On the one hand, the fact that it reflects a quality of the English term that is absent from "cute" in major European and Asian languages may provide insight into the concept of cuteness as it operates cross-culturally. On the other hand, as I demonstrate below, the unique etymology of the English cute and the resulting ambivalence in its connotations is just as likely to lead arguments about the general nature of cuteness towards unfounded universalizing or generalizing.

The negative connotations attached to the English word cute due to its aphaeresis from acute inform much of the analysis of cuteness as an aesthetic category. Literary essayist Daniel Harris even finds a sadistic component lurking in the heart of cuteness:

> Cuteness, in short, is not something we find in our children, but something we *do* to them. Because it aestheticizes unhappiness, helplessness, and deformity, it almost always involves an act of sadism on the part of its creator, who makes an unconscious attempt to maim, hobble, and embarrass the thing he [sic] seeks to idolize. (5)

For Harris, cuteness is a simple commodity aesthetic that has no existence outside the subject. In his view, cuteness is always imposed upon a passive object, and the selfish drive to enjoy it that lurks behind any desire to nurture or engage a cute object blindly pursues its own ends, to the point of causing the object harm.[5] Though Harris's essay is more concerned with provocation than consistency, Sianne Ngai has attempted a detailed proof of his association of cuteness with sadism that is worth close examination.

In academic studies of this aesthetic, the association of cuteness with violence is most fully articulated in Ngai's book: *Our Aesthetic Categories: Zany, Cute, Interesting*, which offers a brilliant and sustained analysis of the importance of cuteness to contemporary culture. Ngai treats cuteness as the primary aesthetic of consumption and the domestic sphere. However, Ngai also follows Harris in asserting that cuteness has a sadistic side resulting from the selfish demand of the subject who encounters small, helpless cute objects (65). She maintains that the demand for care made by such objects results in "a desire to belittle or diminish them further" on the part of a subject that feels unfairly manipulated by cuteness (3). For Ngai, this desire leads to aggressive acts that only magnify the quality that occasions them. Maintaining that squeezing a plush toy creates a deformation that makes it cuter, she writes, "the more objectified the object, or the more visibly shaped by the affective demands and/or projections of the subject, the cuter" (65). This is a problematic generalization, for the claim that deformation always makes an object cuter fails to account for individual differences in the response to cute objects.[6]

Furthermore, Ngai finds a potential for violence flowing in the other direction as well; that is, stemming from the cute object. The helplessness that is part of its presentation, she maintains, leads to fantasies of the revenge this powerless object may take on the subject who interpolates it as cute (87–88). Thus Ngai declares, "violence is always implicit in our relation to the cute object" (85). Furthermore, the connection Ngai draws between helplessness and aggression leads her to argue that this "paradoxical doubleness is imbedded in the concept of the cute from the start" (85). In this fashion, Ngai casts the relationship between subject and cute object as fundamentally adversarial.

I contend that Ngai misreads the qualities intrinsic to cuteness as an affective response because her argument is too invested in the particular way this concept is expressed in the English language. Therefore, when Ngai asks:

> How are we to read the unusual readiness with which cute reverses into its opposite? Is it a sign of the aesthetic's internal instability, or how the experience of cuteness often seems to lead immediately to feelings of manipulation and betrayal? (85–86)

I argue for a separation of the former from the latter. The claim that the cute aesthetic is inherently unstable is very different from asserting that the experience of cuteness inevitably leads to feelings of manipulation and betrayal. These last qualities are clearly drawn from the English aphaeresis of acute to cute explained above. This is why Ngai, like Harris, sees cuteness as a judgment made by the subject—something that the subject imposes on the object—rather than a quality intrinsic to the object *qua* agent (87; 88).[7]

When cuteness is expressed as an aesthetic by incorporating it into a commodity, a work of art, or a form of entertainment, designers or artists may well attempt to bend the excess affect that often accrues in the subject encountering cuteness towards the object, or create a fantasy scenario in which the cute object seems to have power over the subject. In the aesthetic realm, the subject's fantasy shapes the object in the encounter with cuteness: subsequently, this fantasy rebounds to shape the subject as well. This is the "internal instability" of cuteness in operation. Moreover, this instability is expressed in astonishing variety by an aesthetic that is distinct from the English cute; namely, Japanese *kawaii*.

In making her case that violence is embedded in the aesthetic of cuteness, Ngai takes her main examples from Japanese artworks and characters, and states explicitly that cute and *kawaii* are the same aesthetic (78). This is not the case. The modern word *kawaii* comes from the word for pitiable (*kawaisou*), but unlike English, this meaning is no longer a part of *kawaii*: in fact, at present the word has no negative connotations (Nittono 81).[8] *Kawaii* has saturated Japanese culture to the extent that it has become a " 'standard' aesthetic of everyday life" (McVeigh 135). It is even employed by state agencies, politicians, and large companies to soften their exercise of power (McVeigh 150). Furthermore, the rapid expansion of *kawaii* since the 1970s has resulted in repeated iterations and cycles that I argue make *kawaii* more complex and varied than other aesthetics of cuteness (see de Vries in this volume). This decades-long expansion has seen many antagonistic elements attached to *kawaii*, resulting in substantial trends in Japan for ugly-cute, grotesque-cute, and disgusting-cute, to name just a few (Aoyagi and Yuen 101).[9]

Such complexity makes the aesthetic of *kawaii* a fertile ground for investigating the dark side of cuteness, particularly since the Japanese term cleaves so closely to the affective state of experiencing cuteness (Nittono 82). Furthermore, a focus on this affective state bridges the gap between the aesthetics of cute and *kawaii*, allowing for insights that may apply to both (Nittono 80). It also offers a way to more closely parse the propinquity of cuteness and its opposites, such as violence and aggression. I maintain that when these qualities are attached to cuteness for artistic purposes they serve to critically reflect upon, rather than embody, the subject's relation to cuteness. My argument hinges on the particular catharsis that occurs when high affect and approach motivation (the desire to engage with an object) appear in a subject overwhelmed by cuteness. It leads me to contest Harris and Ngai by arguing that the aggression that accompanies the feeling of being overwhelmed by cuteness is not sadistic, but masochistic.

Cute Aggression

D.W. Winnicott's well-known "transitional object" (1–34), often a stuffed toy that substitutes for the maternal presence as a child matures and serves as an outlet for both love and aggression, also appears as Ngai's "cute object par excellence" (89–90). This example works well when the cute objects in question are non-living commodities such as toys, since both affection and aggression are common during children's play (see Goggin in this volume). However, when the cute object is alive, the consequences of giving in to the aggressive impulses caused by an excess of cute affect(ion) and squeezing it hard are self-evident and potentially disastrous.

Human beings retain the capacity for violence, even during the encounter with an unthreatening and harmless cute object. However, I argue that the physical response triggered by cute affect effectively disarms the subject and imposes an imperative against harming the cute object. Free will notwithstanding, the world is not knee-deep in dead babies and puppies. The first thing children learn about cute animals is not to squeeze them too hard. Furthermore, if we take the affective response to cuteness, whether genetic or acquired, as fundamentally concerned with the need for adults to socially engage with children as outlined below, then a robust imperative against harming a cute object becomes important for species survival.

Yet, it is understandable that the encounter with cuteness seems fraught with the possibility of violence, because the profound effect of this encounter on the subject occupies the high end of the intensity scale. "It's too cute!"; "I just can't handle it!"; and, "It's so fluffy I want to die!" are all expressions common to this experience (Angier; Ferro). All testify to the tension building in the subject experiencing the high positive affect that characterizes a strong cuteness response. How is this excess energy discharged? Ngai argues that the encounter with a cute object contains no catharsis: that the cuteness response does not facilitate action (Ngai "Interview"). By shifting from aesthetics to the realm of affect, I argue that there *is* a catharsis built into the cute response, the purpose of which is to avoid the negative outcome (whether this is considered to be evolutionary or social in origin) that would accrue if this excess affect were discharged in a harmful fashion onto the body of a living being.

A study on responses to cute stimuli focusing on the "playful aggressions" that often accompany the feeling of being overwhelmed by cuteness found playful growling, squeezing, biting, and pinching were common reactions along with clenched fists and gritted teeth (Aragón et al. 2, 4). Importantly, the authors distinguish these behaviors from the intent to harm a cute object, hypothesizing instead that the feelings of aggression that accompany the positive experience of cute affect are involved in regulating strong emotions (2). In agreeing with this hypothesis, I also take note of the verbal responses common to the experience of being overwhelmed by cuteness, which include not only the above utterances, but also cooing, squealing, exclamations of "Aww," and so on. In these examples a subject alters itself through linguistic and behavioral self-limitation: language devolves, vocal cords tighten, fists clench, and teeth grit when in the thrall of a cute object in the service of preventing harm from coming to it. In this fashion, the aggression that accompanies the feeling of being overwhelmed by cuteness is directed away from the cute object and towards the subject.[10] Here we discover a subject who, faced with an excess of cuteness, discharges affective energy away from the cute object and towards *itself*, to the point of embracing infantile behavior and the reduction in higher cognitive functions seen in the examples above. In my view, this process serves to protect the cute object from potentially harmful aggression while simultaneously allowing further engagement with it.

To illustrate this point, I turn to graphic designer Mori Chack's cute character "Gloomy Bear" (Figure 2.1). Gloomy is a pink bear (though red in tooth and claw), a character that has appeared on various goods in the mode of Hello Kitty since the year 2000. However, Gloomy's backstory explains that this bear is two meters tall and has a tendency to violently attack the humans who love him,

FIGURE 2.1 After being attacked again by Gloomy Bear, a bloodied Pity hugs his friend.

Source: © Mori Chack

especially Pity, the boy who rescued him from abandonment as a cub (Chack). Gloomy is not out for revenge or motivated by hatred. Once a harmless cub, his play became violent as he grew to full size. Since it is his nature as a wild animal to attack, Gloomy is innocent in his violence. As his backstory explains, "he can never remember that he's not supposed to attack humans" (Chack). What accounts for the popularity of this character? Why do Gloomy's many fans enjoy the attacks of this violent bear?

Pity, the boy in the image, loves Gloomy even when blood streams from wounds inflicted by the bear. As I wrote above, though the Japanese *kawaii* derives from the word for pity, it no longer includes that meaning. Thus, though the boy is pitiable in Chack's scenario, it is the bear that is *kawaii*. Here, I note that the English cute may yield insight into the aesthetic of *kawaii*, for the attraction of Gloomy Bear to his fans hinges on the pleasure taken in being cut by cuteness that is suggested by the transformation of acute to cute. In other words, Chack's character reveals that the pleasure we take in not harming the cute object is essentially masochistic. By staging the pleasure we feel by being cut by cuteness, this violent bear and the boy who loves him anyway expose the psychic mechanism through which we are willing to harm ourselves in order to protect a cute object from our excessive love for it. This brings me to a key argument about the operation of desire in respect to cute objects that I formulate as follows: cute cuts the subject, not the other way round.

The subject apprehending cuteness directs the overwhelming affect produced by the encounter against itself, and takes pleasure in the intensity of this assault upon its sovereignty that manifests in a form of linguistic or behavioral self-limitation. The encounter with cuteness establishes an intimacy between subject and object, and the intensity of this experience blurs the boundaries between them. Though the pleasure that attends the cuteness response may well involve caring for a helpless object that must be protected, even from an excess of adoration, it is also the pleasure of play: of engaging with a cute object and of feeling one's sense of self altering under the pressure to preserve that object and one's bond to it. Thus, the encounter with cuteness is reciprocal rather than one-way. Before proceeding to explore this relationship in detail, I address the flaws in the argument that cuteness is based solely on the need to care for a fundamentally passive object: a misapprehension with a surprising persistence in the scientific literature on cute affect.

The Evolution of Cute Affect

Konrad Lorenz and his (Racist) Legacy

Charles Darwin first proposed that infants must possess innate qualities that prompt adults to care for them, thus increasing human reproductive success (Darwin "Expression"). However, the proper study of cuteness began with Konrad Lorenz.

A pioneer in the field of ethology, the scientific study of animal behavior as an evolutionary adaptive trait, Lorenz discovered the principle of imprinting in geese: the instinct that causes goslings to follow the first thing they see after hatching. In the 1940s, when Lorenz inaugurated the study of cuteness, he did so by extending his theory of animal instincts to human behavior. In the battle over nature versus nurture, or innate versus acquired behavior, Lorenz was emphatically on the side of the former, and this has important implications for the contemporary use of his ideas. The characteristics listed in Lorenz's *kindchenschema* that cause a cuteness response include: a large head relative to body size, large and low eyes, bulging cheeks, a plump body shape with short and thick extremities, a spongy elastic consistency, and wobbly movements (Lorenz 154).

Lorenz did not measure human babies to make the drawing in Figure 2.2. Instead, he based it on his close observations of animal behavior (Nittono 85).

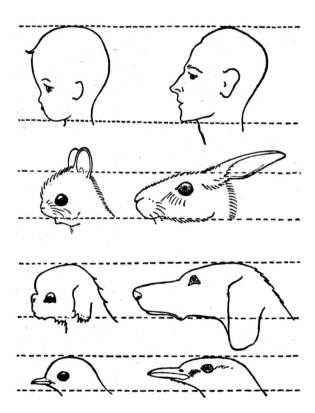

FIGURE 2.2 Konrad Lorenz's *Kindchenschema* (child schema) of cross-species juvenile cute characteristics continues to exert a strong influence on the study of cuteness.

Source: © Taylor and Francis

Nonetheless, Lorenz maintained that the same "Innate Releasing Mechanisms" (IRMs) that he believed governed animal instincts also applied to humans (154–162). Lorenz was unapologetically rigid in his approach, considering any variation of the cuteness response as "misplaced," an aberration or misfiring of an instinctual mechanism that solely expressed nurturing behavior (158). He assumed that his child schema operated like a key in a lock, releasing caregiving behaviors in humans without conscious intervention.[11] Thus, Lorenz presented his child schema as universal in the grandest sense: that is, as a genetically based and species-unspecific instinct specifically related to caregiving. Babies need care, runs his argument; and their cuteness compels us to provide it. However, there are significant problems with Lorenz's attempt to universalize the operation of the cuteness response in humans, which I address below.

In the 1960s and 1970s, scientists began to test Lorenz's theory by asking adults to judge the cuteness of either drawings or photos of children's faces. Though subsequent decades of scientific studies broadly confirmed the efficacy of the child schema, they did not prove Lorenz's hypothesis that this response is an instinct that automatically releases caregiving behavior (Alley 650). However, lacking an alternative theory, researchers still tended to accept Lorenz's hypothesis of an instinctual basis to the response to cuteness, which led them to privilege caregiving in their work (Little 775; Glocker et al.; Kringelbach et al.). Gradually, Lorenz's theory of IRMs fell out of favor in a variety of fields (Lehrman "Critique"; "Semantic"; Hinde *Animal*; *Ethology*), and from the 1980s onward researchers began to back away from Lorenz's ideas (Archer and Monton 217): for example, changing his terminology to consider cuteness as a "positive affective response" rather than an instinct (Alley 653). Studies that consider other cute stimuli have found that the child schema works not only for images of children, but also dogs, cats, teddy bears, and even utilitarian objects such as "baby faced" car fronts (Fullard; Little; Archer and Monton; Miesler et al.).

However, since Lorenz's theory was never definitively disproven, it is still cited even in recent studies (see Miesler et al.). When testing the speed of the cuteness response in the brain, a 2008 study found that activity in the medial orbitofrontal cortex—the area of the brain associated with reward behavior—occurred faster and more powerfully when subjects viewed cute infant faces as opposed to adult faces (Kringelbach et al.). The images were shown for only 300 milliseconds at a time, and the burst of brain activity occurred 130 milliseconds after viewing the cute image, which suggests a reaction to cute infant faces before consciousness has time to play a role (Kringelbach et al.). The authors of this study claim several times that this data provides evidence of Lorenz's instinctual IRMs, though in fact it only demonstrates that cute images draw attention quickly, not that any particular behaviors are thereby elicited.

The continuing appearance of IRMs in studies of cuteness is highly problematic considering that Konrad Lorenz, father of the science of ethology, was also a Nazi. He joined the National Socialist Party in 1938, and published two articles during the war that supported eugenics and justified Nazi efforts to prevent interbreeding by people of (so-called) different races (Klopfer 203). Furthermore, in private letters written during the war, Lorenz argued for racial standards of beauty that elevated Aryan ideals, and deemed inferior such groups as "urban Jews and gypsies" (Klopfer 205). Lorenz repudiated these ideas after the war, and reconciled with his colleagues Nikolas Tinbergen and Karl Von Frisch, opponents of the Nazi regime who shared the Nobel Prize with Lorenz in 1973 (Klopfer 204). However, throughout his career Lorenz continued to argue that human instincts operate universally and require the "correct" stimuli, writing in 1971 that he was still convinced that an IRM lies hidden "at the very root of every emotional judgment" (341). In fact, Lorenz believed that an instinctual response lies at the heart of every aesthetic and ethical judgment (161). Lorenz may have repudiated his wartime participation in "Aryan science," but he never changed his theory of human instinct that, as Peter Klopfer points out, is derived as much from Nazi ideology as it is from the study of animal behavior (206, 207).

Lorenz proposed two things: a concept and a theory. The concept, his child schema, has undergone over sixty years of experimental testing that has demonstrated its efficacy in evoking the cuteness response, if not universally, then at least in a broad range of people. In addition, the child schema is still evolving. Additional characteristics, such as certain colors, textures, sounds, and shapes have also been found to trigger a cuteness response in many people (Cheok 233–243). Lorenz's theory of IRMs, on the other hand, continues to easily slip into racism. In 2015, a tabloid news article in the *Mail Online* called "The Science of Cute" attempted to explain Lorenz's child schema with a graphic of a child's face that identified not only large eyes, chubby cheeks, and so on as cute characteristics, but also a new element: "a rosy complexion" (Tyler and Woollaston). With this simple addition, suddenly children with light skin that can show pink are pronounced "scientifically" cuter than children with dark skin. This example shows the danger lurking behind Lorenz's conflation of instinct, aesthetics, and ethics: namely, that unquestioned acceptance of the former is likely to lead to bias in the latter.

Post-Lorenzian Cuteness: The Social Engagement Hypothesis

Though it did not prove the existence of Lorenz's IRMs, Morten Kringelbach's brain scan study cited above does suggest that objects conforming to Lorenz's child schema attract our attention immediately, even before we have time to think. But what happens after that? Perhaps this attraction is merely a reflex: an involuntary, pre-cognitive reaction such as gagging from disgust. Or, our response to cute objects could be considered to be both an affective reaction and an emotion in its own right (Nittono 85–88). Though the precise nature of the cuteness response has not yet been determined, I argue that even if cute objects swiftly draw our attention as Kringelbach's study suggests, the disarming surge of tenderness thus prompted involves other, cognitive factors, such as recognizing the power differential at work between the self and a non-threatening cute object. Here, I maintain, is where aesthetics enter the picture.

A cute object is capable of triggering cute affect (the "Aww" factor). However, when different people look at the same object, some will find it cute while others won't. We turn to the realm of aesthetics to account for these differences. Yet much of the extant scholarship on cute aesthetics faces limitations due to its over-reliance on Lorenz's theory that parental, care-giving instincts are at the heart of the cuteness response. This is apparent in Lori Merish's foundational article on cuteness and commodity aesthetics when she writes: "the cute demands a maternal response, and interpolates its viewers/consumers as 'maternal'" (186). Of course, maternal—or paternal—feelings often do accompany our response to cute objects. However, I believe there are alternative points of origin for cute affiliations.

In fact, a new hypothesis has emerged that links the cuteness response to prosocial behavior in general, and considers the child schema merely an example, rather than the essence, of this response. Psychologists Gary D. Sherman and Jonathan Haidt find that cuteness encourages affiliative tendencies and elicits social engagement more consistently than nurturing, writing: "Cuteness is as much an elicitor of play as it is of care" (4). While they do not deny that cuteness may elicit care—which is also a form of social interaction—Sherman and Haidt suggest that the primary and immediate function of the cuteness response is to motivate sociality (4). They point out that cuteness is at its peak, not when children are newborn and require the most care, but rather at the age they tend to become more social, from approximately 10 months to 3 years (5). Moreover, they also cite research that finds children with happy or excited expressions that invite social interaction are judged to be cuter, notable because elicitors of compassion—likely to lead to caregiving—comprise negative expressions and other cues of distress. Thus, these scholars argue that: "Altogether, in the features that amplify cuteness and in the traits that are attributed to those possessing cuteness, social engagement is the recurring theme, more so than caretaking" (5).

Furthermore, Hiroshi Nittono's research extends Sherman and Haidt's findings by unpacking the culturally non-specific phenomenon of the affective response to cuteness as it manifests in *kawaii*. Citing international studies on cuteness as well as his own survey results on *kawaii*, Nittono finds that objects judged to be *kawaii*/cute, whether they conform to the child schema or not, tend to: draw attention and interest; induce positive feelings; increase carefulness and narrow the field of attention; and improve interpersonal relationships (89, 90).

Though these researchers greatly expand the field of cuteness studies, they focus on the subject of the encounter with cuteness. In the following section, I analyze the implications of the social engagement hypothesis in order to explore the other side of the equation: namely, the cause and nature of the agency that may be pursued by cute objects. Focusing on companion animals, I make the case for an additional basis for cuteness stemming from the suite of inherited characteristics—

morphological, physiological, and behavioral—common to domesticated animals, in order to reveal additional leitmotifs of this affective response that may expand the discourse of cuteness. These include emotional reactivity, shared affect, empathic responsiveness, and prosocial behavior such as play, communication, and companionship.

Cute Agency

The Siberian Silver Fox Experiment

In *The Variation of Animals and Plants Under Domestication*, Darwin documents the common set of characteristics exhibited by domesticated animals of various species: their bodies tend to be smaller, their tails more curly, their ears floppier, their coats piebald (spotted), their extremities shorter, and their faces wider (Darwin, cited in Ratliff). There are other shared characteristics that make up the domestication phenotype, but these are the morphological traits that trigger the cuteness response in humans. In addition to a domesticated animal's appearance, its behavior may also solicit this response. Tameness—that is, the willingness to approach and engage with humans—is a key element of domestication. As I established above, cute appearances and behaviors are not merely incentives to provide care; they also comprise a call for social engagement, which is reflected in the behavior of domesticated animals as opposed to their wild counterparts.

It has long been assumed that these traits were bred into domesticated animals by humans, rather than emerging under the pressures of natural selection. After all, in choosing which animals to breed for a new generation, wouldn't people include such aspects as affection and cuteness? Tameness also makes animals more responsive to human social cues: for example, dogs can locate hidden food in response to a social cue such as gaze direction or pointing (Hare 61). In addition to making animals more pleasing to the eye, the piebald coats characteristic of domesticated, but not wild, animals would make the former easier to see against the solid background of forest or field. However, this theory that tameness and the cute characteristics associated with it were selected by humans does not answer all the questions related to domestication. For example, why doesn't this potential exist in every species? Only around fifteen of the 148 species of large mammals have been domesticated. If this is a human-initiated and controlled process, then why have numerous attempts to tame, for example, zebras, always failed (Ratliff)?

The alternative to human selection of desired traits is "self-domestication": the theory that some animals were able to exploit new ecological niches by overcoming their natural fear and aggression towards humans. Both may have worked in concert over thousands of years. However, self-domestication suggests there may be an inherent potential for domestication present in the genomes of some species, but not others. The domestication of dogs from wolves, therefore, may have taken place in two stages. The first would have involved self-domestication, in which a few less aggressive or fearful wolves began to approach human settlements, gradually behaving in a more prosocial way towards humans as they acclimated to their presence (perhaps feeding from human refuse). Once they were slightly friendly, humans could start the second stage of intentional breeding (Hare, Wobber and Wrangham 573, 574). The evidence for self-domestication is strongly supported by a fascinating, ongoing experiment involving not dogs but foxes.

In 1959, the Institute of Cytology and Genetics in Novosibirsk, Siberia began an experiment to breed tameness into a population of silver foxes (*Vulpses vulpes*). Their guiding hypothesis was that domestic animals such as dogs could have resulted from selection for a single behavioral trait unrelated to physical appearance: namely, friendliness towards people (Trut 160, 161). Under heavy selective pressure by the research team, who chose only those kits who would approach a gloved hand inserted in their cages by a masked researcher, the breeding population of foxes soon began to demonstrate remarkable features: "In the sixth generation, there appeared pups that eagerly sought contacts with human, not only (tail) wagging, also whining, whimpering, and licking in a dog-like manner" (Trut, Oskina, and Kharlamova 351). In the early 1970s a worker at the Institute who took a fox home found that it would come when he called its name (Ratliff). Even more surprising was the fact that the appearance of the foxes also began to change, showing a high prevalence of floppy ears, curly tails, and piebald coats. Moreover, later in the program, the foxes' legs, tails, snouts, and upper jaws shortened, while their skulls widened (Trut, Oskina, and Kharlamova 353).

FIGURE 2.3 Exotic animal importer Mitchel Kalmanson chooses a tame fox for a client at the Novosibirsk Institute.

Source: ABC News

The cute characteristics and behavior presented by these foxes, which are now being sold as pets—evident in several YouTube videos—were a result of weakened aggressive and fear-avoidance responses (Trut, Oskina, and Kharlamova 351).[12] The socialization period in mammals, which starts in infancy and allows animals to explore their environment and form attachments, is limited in wild animals by an early onset of the fear response. The results of the fox experiment, however, "found that selection of the foxes for tameability slowed down the development of the fear response and shifted it to later dates" (Trut, Oskina, and Kharlamova 354).

The above factors resulted in foxes that share not only the morphology and physiology of pet dogs, but aspects of their behavior as well. I have already mentioned the tail-wagging, whining, and licking they display. In addition, subsequent studies conducted on these foxes show that they are adept at comprehending human gestures: for example, they follow a pointed finger to locate hidden food (Hare and Tomasello 439). Trut and her research team do not train the foxes: they limit human contact to measuring approach behavior in selecting which fox kits to breed.[13] Dogs, too, are able to read human communication cues even without extensive, individual exposure to humans (Hare and Tomasello 440, 441). Thus, the ability to comprehend human gestures in dogs and the tame Siberian foxes is an inborn trait, a direct result of domestication, that appears in concert with the other morphological and physiological changes described above that are also common to both. This suggests that traits for a cute appearance and behavior are integrated in the genome of both species: in other words, that loci may exist that co-regulate morphological-behavioral traits in both dogs and foxes (Trut, Oskina, and Kharlamova 357). Below, I outline the implications that the foxes' transition into lovable pets has for the study of cuteness.

The Appeal of Cuteness

What accounts for the tremendous profligacy of the cuteness response: the way it transfers easily to a wide range of objects? Perhaps it is more than just an adaptation that evolved as a means to encourage the socialization of children. It is possible that humans are a product of self-domestication as well. When applied to *homo sapiens*, the self-domestication hypothesis proposes that early humans self-selected for social abilities such as an enhanced ability to cooperate with each other, and emotional changes such as reduced fear and aggression in social encounters (Francis 287). It suggests that there was a gradual evolution of the limbic system in the human brain, the substrate of our emotional life, and an attenuation of the endocrine system, which regulates stress (Francis 289). The result was tameness, a trait shared by all domesticated animals. Evolutionary anthropologist Brian Hare takes this one step further by proposing that our neotenous appearance—that is, the tendency in humans for juvenile morphological and cognitive traits to persist into adulthood—is a byproduct of this self-domestication process (Hare, Wobber, and Wrangham 576). If this is true, then the linkage of tame behavior to a cute appearance common to domesticated animals such as dogs (and now Siberian foxes) is present in the human genome as well.

However, Hare may be taking this idea too far. Trut and her colleagues also bred a tame population of rats: but unlike the foxes, the rats did not develop a cute appearance (Francis 288). Even if humans have undergone self-domestication, the neotenous appearance of adults may not have resulted from this process. In either case, however, the self-domestication hypothesis still has an important relation to the power of cuteness. Science in general has overwhelmingly privileged intelligence—that is, the cognitive ability of our large brains—as the driving force behind the evolution of modern humans. The self-domestication hypothesis suggests that developing the qualities needed to work together cooperatively, which include the reduced aggressive behavior seen in *homo sapiens* and our companion species as compared to wild animals, was just as important. The profligacy of the cuteness response may have helped to conserve the qualities and behaviors associated with tameness, which may explain why people feel a desire to engage with a such a wide range of cute objects: that is, why an adaptation that most likely evolved as a means to socialize, protect and care for children so easily transfers to other objects.

Although this is a seductive idea, it is important to note the limits of any hypothesis that claims to explain species-wide behavior. In fact, the self-domestication hypothesis has a bad history. During the early twentieth century, it was enthusiastically embraced by the pseudo-science of eugenics. Viewing self-domestication as contributing to the weakness or "degeneration" of *homo sapiens*, many biologists of that time (Lorenz included) argued for both positive selective breeding and euthanasia of human populations deemed "inferior," which led directly to the Nazi program of racial extermination (Brüne 3). Therefore, I claim cuteness as a universal human *potential*, rather than behavior, in order to account for the fact that there are individual and social differences at work in the response to cute objects. In addition, though the self-domestication hypothesis stretches far back in time to account for the existence of the cuteness response, it says nothing about its development as a commodity aesthetic starting in the nineteenth century (Merish), and its radical expansion at the start of the twenty-first century (see Chapter 1 in this volume).

The Siberian silver fox experiment demonstrates several important points, namely: the potential for coexistence and cooperation with humans already exists in some wild animals; selecting for tameness reduces fear and aggression in future generations; and subsequently, morphological and behavioral markers of cuteness may appear. By connecting the domestication phenotype to cuteness, I am not only offering additional proof of the social engagement hypothesis: in addition, this alternative reading of cuteness allows for a stronger theory of agency on the part of the cute object. Instead of stemming solely from helplessness and dependence, cuteness is now intimately linked to companionship, cooperation, play, and emotional reactivity.

Since we share the qualities listed above with our companion species, this expanded discourse of cuteness helps to explain the power this affective response has to initiate and enhance both intra- and interspecies affiliative behavior. Behavioral scientists define the human cuteness response as high in "approach motivation." Now, we may extend that quality to the other side of the encounter: cute objects want to engage with us, too. Though this seems self-evident in the case of children and domesticated (or baby) animals, I believe that when faced with an inanimate object we find to be cute, our own desire to engage with it dictates the terms of the encounter. Therefore, I argue that *cuteness is an appeal to others.*

Conclusion

As I have shown in this chapter, some scholars incorrectly assign qualities such as violence, aggression, and even sadism to the core definition of cuteness. I attribute these misreadings to the fact that the English cute may still mean "clever" or "cunning," which creates the suspicion that a cute object may have ulterior motives: in other words, that its power over an "Aww-struck" subject may hide a desire to manipulate or control from a position of presumptive weakness. As I demonstrated above, this desire it is not intrinsic to the general concept of cuteness considered as an affective reaction to a definable set of stimuli. However, if we remove this presumed desire to manipulate from the heart of a cute object or character and transfer it onto its designers, then the suspicion engendered by the English term has a valuable role to play in cuteness studies. Megan Arkenberg's chapter, which follows this one, provides a substantial elaboration of the relationship between cuteness and manipulation in regulatory systems of control. Furthermore, because consumer products along with media and artistic produc-tions often seek to deploy cute affect for strategic ends, the aesthetics of both cute and *kawaii* provide many examples of cuteness strategically positioned alongside antagonistic qualities.

By questioning the dominance of Lorenz's theory of nurturing instinct and reformulating the underlying theory of cuteness under the rubrics of social engagement and domestication, this chapter argues that cuteness should be considered separately from the negative affects with which it often appears. In particular, I show that cute cuts the subject, not the other way round: i.e. that the playful aggression that often accompanies the feeling of being overwhelmed by cuteness rebounds upon the subject in an intense but pleasurable catharsis that serves to protect an unthreatening, vulnerable object from harm. My focus on prosocial, affiliative behavior allows qualities proper to a relationship of affinity to become integral to the cuteness response. The case of the newly tame Siberian silver foxes indicates that genes that result in an appearance humans find cute are expressed together with friendly, non-aggressive behavior in domesticated animals.[14] Incorporating these elements redefines the operation of both desire and agency in the relationship between subject and cute object. By focusing on affect, I have shown how cuteness is connected to domestication in its broadest sense: the taming of the wild and dangerous, and the concurrent valuing of cooperation and companionship, in our companion animals and in ourselves.

Bringing these insights to the realm of aesthetics, I argue that cuteness should be seen as a disarming surge of purely positive feelings such as affection and tenderness that also involves a cognitive reaction in which the power differential between subject and object comes into play. Discrete aesthetics of cuteness such as cute and *kawaii* come together at this level. When a cute/*kawaii* object successfully affects us, either due to its design or through its self-presentation, it serves to blur the boundaries between self and other (Merish 186, 188). Based on my analysis of the desire and agency that inform the concept of cuteness, I suggest that cuteness may be viewed as a performative act expressing affinity. That is, in its attempt to cause this particular affective response, cuteness is fundamentally an appeal to others: an invitation to sociality that we respond to as if it were an act of agency. Feeling that an object is cute or *kawaii* means responding to this appeal, a process in which one discovers oneself *already* drawn into the orbit of a lovable and intimate other. Reactions to this realization are multivalent and may be ambivalent: yet, the very instability that accrues in our responses to cuteness is part of the fascination of this emerging field of study.

Notes

1 In this chapter, "subject" refers to a person who experiences or is able to experience an affective reaction to cuteness. "Object" refers to the thing (person, animal, toy, character, etc.) that may cause this reaction by displaying a combination of the visual and behavioral characteristics described below.
2 Although the distinction between cute and *kawaii* aesthetics is elucidated at several points in this chapter, for the sake of brevity the former term is used as general nomenclature.
3 The association of the two words is longstanding, as one of the earliest examples of the modern use of cute in the OED is an 1857 reference that includes the same modifier: namely, "What cute little socks!" referring to a doll's costume. The earliest example of the modern "cute" in the OED, however, is from an 1834 novel that actually refers to a clever invention.
4 These qualities also appear in the common expression: "Don't be cute," which references the earlier meaning as an exhortation not to be cunning.
5 Harris recommends a complete boycott of cuteness, which he believes to operate like rose-colored glasses that prevent parents from enjoying children in their "natural, unindoctrinated state" (16).
6 When lecturing or speaking about cuteness, I frequently display the image of the two frog bath sponges, one being squeezed, one not, that Ngai employs to make this point. When I ask which one is cuter, only about half of the audience chooses the unsqueezed frog, indicating that deformation is not always seen as cute.
7 When, in a footnote, Ngai addresses the cute object as an actively desiring agent, she finds it to simultaneously embody delight, satiation, and rapacious desire. In other words,

she reduces cute agency to a temporarily satisfied, yet always recurring, infantile need (249n36).

8 Nittono establishes the contemporary usage of *kawaii* in several ways, most notably by analyzing the results of three surveys he distributed to 558 Japanese university students.

9 Respectively, *busukawa*, *gurokawa*, and *kimokawa*.

10 The burble of sounds emitted by the subject enraptured by cuteness is also found in "baby talk." This set of speech characteristics directed at young children has been discerned in a wide variety of languages, cultures and time periods (Zebrowitz, Brownlow and Olson 144). Thus, the characteristic verbal responses to a cute object are not only indicative of a catharsis directing aggression towards the subject, they are also a form of communication suitable for an object in an immature stage of development. Studies have shown not only that children judged to be cuter elicit more baby talk from adults, but also that these children perform better in subsequently administered cognitive tasks (Zebrowitz, Brownlow and Olson 156).

11 Megan Arkenberg's chapter in this volume investigates the persistence of this mechanistic viewpoint in present-day writings on cuteness.

12 As in other domesticated animals, the activity of the key hormonal regulator of stress and adaptation in the foxes, the hypothalamic-pituitary-adrenal (HPA) axis, became attenuated compared to foxes in the control group (Trut, Oskina, and Kharlamova 350).

13 The initial cohort for the experiment was taken from fur farms, in which generations of wild foxes raised in cages had become habituated to the presence of humans, yet were still wild (Trut 163).

14 Except for the aforementioned rats, whose appearance didn't change with domestication.

Works Cited

Alley, Thomas R. "Head Shape and the Perception of Cuteness." *Developmental Psychology* 17.5 (1981): 650–54.

Angier, Natalie. "The Cute Factor." *New York Times*. New York Times, 2 Jan. 2006. Online. 2 Mar. 2014.

Aoyagi, Hiroshi, and Yuen, Shu Min. "When Erotic Meets Cute: Erokawa and the Public Expression of Female Sexuality in Contemporary Japan." *East Asian Journal of Popular Culture* 2.1 (2016): 97–110.

Aragón, Oriana R. et al. "Dimorphous Expressions of Positive Emotion: Displays of Both Care and Aggression in Response to Cute Stimuli." *Psychological Science* 26.3 (2015): 1–15. *Sage Journals*. Online. 2 Feb. 2015.

Archer, John, and Soraya Monton. "Preferences for Infant Facial Features in Pet Dogs and Cats. *Ethology* 117 (2011): 217–26.

Brownstone, Sydney. "I Still Can't Believe There's a Jewish Democratic Socialist from Brooklyn Who's Already Won a Presidential Primary: Bernie Sanders Reminds Me of My Family." *Stranger*. Index Newspapers, 9 Feb. 2016. Online. 23 Mar. 2016.

Brüne, Martin. "On Human Self-Domestication, Psychiatry, and Eugenics." 21 *Philosophy, Ethics, and Humanities in Medicine* 2 (2007). *PMC*. Online. 20 Mar. 2016.

Chack, Mori. "Gloomy, the Naughty Grizzly." *CHAXGRAFFITO*, 2000. Online. 23 Mar. 2016.

Cheok, Adrian David. *Art and Technology of Entertainment Computing and Communication: Advances in Interactive New Media for Entertainment Computing*. London: Springer, 2010.

Darwin, Charles. *The Expression of Emotion in Man and Animals*. London: John Murray, 1872.

Ferro, Shaunacy. "Why Do We Want to Squeeze Cute Things?" *Popular Science*. Bonnier, 24 Jan. 2013. Online 28 Apr. 2014.

Figlerowicz, Marta. "Affect Theory Dossier: An Introduction." *Qui Parle: Critical Humanities and Social Sciences* 20.2 (2012): 3–18.

Francis, Richard C. *Domesticated: Evolution in a Man-Made World*. New York: Norton, 2015.

Fullard, William, and Anne M. Reiling. "An Investigation of Lorenz's 'Babyness.'" *Child Development* 47.4 (1976): 1191–93.

Glocker, Melanie L, et al. "Baby Schema in Infant Faces Induces Cuteness Perception and Motivation for Caretaking in Adults." *Ethology* 115.3 (2009): 257–63.

Hare, Brian. "From Nonhuman to Human Mind: What Changed and Why?" *Current Directions in Psychological Science* 16:60 (2007): 60–64.

Hare, Brian, and Michael Tomasello. "Human-like Social Skills in Dogs?" *Trends in Cognitive Sciences* 9 (2005): 439–44.

Hare, Brian, Victoria Wobber, and Richard Wrangham. "The Self-Domestication Hypothesis: Evolution of Bonobo Psychology is Due to Selection Against Aggression." *Animal Behavior* 83 (2012): 573–85.

Hare, Brian et al. "The Domestication of Social Cognition in Dogs." *Science* 298 (2002): 1634–36.

Hare, Brian et al. "Social Cognitive Evolution in Captive Foxes is a Correlated By-Product of Experimental Domestication." *Current Biology* 16 (2005): 226–30.

Harris, Daniel. *Cute, Quaint, Hungry, and Romantic: The Aesthetics of Consumerism*. Cambridge, MA: De Capo, 2001.

Hinde, Robert A. *Animal Behavior: A Synthesis of Ethology and Comparative Psychology*. London: McGraw-Hill, 1970.

——. *Ethology: its Nature and Relations to Other Sciences*. Oxford: Oxford University Press, 1982.

Klopfer, Peter. "Konrad Lorenz and the National Socialists: On the Politics of Ethology." *International Journal of Comparative Psychology* 7.4 (1994): 202–8.

Kringelbach, Morten L., et al. "A Specific and Rapid Neural Signature for Parental Instinct." *PLoS ONE* 3.2 (2008): e1664. Online. 18 Dec. 2015.

Lehrman, Daniel S. "A Critique of Konrad Lorenz's Theory of Instinctive Behavior." *Quarterly Review of Biology* 28.4 (1953): 337–63.

——. "Semantic and Conceptual Issues in the Nature-Nurture Problem." *Development and Evolution of Behavior*. Eds. Lester R. Aronson et al. San Francisco, CA: W.H. Freeman, 1970. 17–52.

Leys, Ruth. "The Turn to Affect: A Critique." *Critical Inquiry* 37:3 (2011): 434–72.

Little, Anthony C. "Manipulation of Infant-Like Traits Affects Perceived Cuteness of Infant, Adult and Cat Faces." *Ethology* 118 (2012): 775–82.

Lorenz, Konrad. "Part and Parcel in Human and Animal Societies." 1950. *Studies in Animal and Human Behavior, Vol. 2*. Trans. Robert Martin. Cambridge, MA: Harvard University Press, 1971.

Massumi, Brian. *Parables for the Virtual*. Durham, NC: Duke University Press, 2002.

McVeigh, Brian J. *Wearing Ideology: State, Schooling and Self-Presentation in Japan*. Oxford: Berg, 2000.

Merish, Lori. "Cuteness and Commodity Aesthetics: Tom Thumb and Shirley Temple." *Freakery: Cultural Spectacles of the Extraordinary Body*. Ed. Rosmarie Garland-Thomson. New York: New York University Press, 1996. 185–203.

Miesler, Linda, et al. "Isn't it Cute: An Evolutionary Perspective of Baby-Schema Effects in Visual Product Designs." *International Journal of Design* 5.3 (2011): 17–30.

Ngai, Sianne. "Our Aesthetic Categories: An Interview with Sianne Ngai." *Cabinet* 43 (2011): n. pag. Online. 20 Mar. 2016.

——. *Our Aesthetic Categories: Zany, Cute, Interesting.* Cambridge, MA: Harvard University Press, 2012.

Nittono, Hiroshi. "The Two-layer Model of 'Kawaii:' A Behavioral Science Framework for Understanding Kawaii and Cuteness." *East Asian Journal of Popular Culture* 2.1 (2016): 79–95.

Ratliff, Evan. "Taming the Wild." *National Geographic* (2011). Online. 20 Mar. 2016.

Sherman, Gary D., and Jonathan Haidt. "Cuteness and Disgust: The Humanizing and Dehumanizing Effects of Emotion." *Emotion Review* 3.3 (2011): 245–51. *SAGE Publications.* Online. 22 Feb. 2014.

Trut, Lyudmila N. "Early Canid Domestication: The Farm-Fox Experiment." *American Scientist* 87 (1999): 160–69.

Trut, Lyudmila N., Oskina, Irina, and Kharlamova, Anastasiya. "Animal Evolution During Domestication: The Domesticated Fox as a Model." *Bioessays* 31.3 (2009): 349–60.

Tyler, Jodie and Victoria Woollaston. "The Science of Cute." *Mail Online.* Associated Newspapers, 23 Sept. 2015. Online. 23 Mar. 2016.

Winnicott, Donald W. *Playing and Reality.* New York: Routledge, 1971.

Zebrowitz, Leslie A., Sheila Brownlow, and Karen Olson. "Baby Talk to the Babyfaced." *Journal of Nonverbal Behavior* 16.3 (1992): 143–58.

3

CUTENESS AND CONTROL IN *PORTAL*

Megan Arkenberg

Recent scholarship has depicted cuteness as an aesthetic category fraught with ambivalence. Sianne Ngai observes that cuteness provokes urges towards both "domination and passivity, or cruelty and tenderness" in its viewers (108), and other scholars note that cute objects can retain their cuteness even as they acquire additional, seemingly incongruous traits, such as "freakishness" (Merish 188), deadliness (Shiokawa 119), and monstrosity (Brzozowska-Brywczyńska 218–21). It is surprising, then, considering the range of its affective and aesthetic paradoxes, that cuteness is so frequently described as simple and unsophisticated—as an aesthetic that we "discern easily and react to automatically" (Morreall 46). If cuteness appears to act systematically, however, this capacity has important implications for the aesthetic's role in contemporary life. Indeed, the cute objects that populate our world move within a number of controlling systems, from economic systems of valuation and exchange to the systems of circulating emotion that Sara Ahmed has called "affective economies" (119). With its capacity to viscerally generate affects, the supposedly minor, ambivalent aesthetic of cuteness in fact plays a powerful role within the structures of modulation that—as Deleuze has argued—constitute power's primary channels in "societies of control" (4).

Thus, as cuteness gains increasing prominence in contemporary life, it becomes vital to address its role in contemporary arrangements of power. Scholars have not yet examined the interconnections of cuteness, its aesthetic incongruities, and its function within such systems. In this chapter, I argue that Valve Software's popular videogames *Portal* (2007) and *Portal 2* (2011) offer a valuable case study for understanding the role of this paradoxical, "mechanistic" aesthetic within systems of control. According to digital media scholar Alexander Galloway, videogames, by virtue of their algorithmic nature, are uniquely suited to a critique of contemporary "protocological" arrangements of power, and this characterization appears especially apt for the *Portal* series, which Michael Burden and Sean Gouglas have read as "an algorithmic exploration of human struggle against algorithmic processes" (Galloway 106; Burden and Gouglas).

Extending these scholars' insights, I argue that *Portal* makes cuteness central to its exploration of systematic power. As both a videogame and a cultural phenomenon, *Portal* demonstrates how cuteness's ambiguities enable its functions within various controlling systems described below. Additionally, by exacerbating these ambiguities over the course of gameplay, the games engineer players' affective responses to cute objects, directing players' attention to the controlling systems in which such objects function. Ultimately, *Portal* suggests to its players that cuteness is not only a tool of systematic control, but also a path to critique, and potentially a mode of resistance.

This analysis considers *Portal*'s linking of cuteness and systematic control in two different realms: first, on the level of narrative and gameplay, and second, within the games' wider cultural contexts of production, marketing, and fan reception.[1] In gameplay, *Portal* players take on the role of Chell, a human test subject trapped in the Aperture Science laboratory, who must navigate a series of obstacle-course-like "test chambers" under the manipulative supervision of an artificial intelligence named GLaDOS.[2] This game environment is inhabited by two classes of ambiguously adorable objects: the Sentry Turrets, robotic machine guns with cheerful voices and friendly personalities, and the Companion Cube, an inanimate box that Chell befriends and is later forced to "euthanize" in order to progress to the next test chamber.

Both objects—the Sentry Turrets and the Companion Cube—demonstrate the vacillation between power and powerlessness that defines cuteness as an aesthetic, and this vacillation determines the nature of both gameplay and fan reception. Within the game, these objects engage players in a series of violent encounters, which generate conflicting affective responses and compel players to examine the systems of valuation by which they judge cute objects as desirable or disposable. Thus, the games suggest that cuteness is systematic in its own right, rooted in biologically determined responses to weaker entities, while the very regularity of these responses allows cuteness to be harnessed by systems of economics. Outside of gameplay, enthusiastic fan responses to *Portal*'s cute objects trace additional connections between cuteness and systematic power in contemporary life. Indeed, because fan responses often imagine a continuity between the events of the game and "real life," they prove especially useful for addressing *Portal*'s questions about the viability of resistance: namely, can cute objects offer an escape from the very systems in which they function?

An example from *Portal* fan culture illustrates more concretely how *Portal*'s cute objects underscore the ambiguities of cuteness, and how these ambiguities shape the objects' functions within systems of control. Shortly after *Portal 2*'s release in April 2011, a fan named Jonathan Guberman posted a video demonstration

of a homemade Sentry Turret plush toy on his personal blog. Guberman's plush
Turret is equipped with motion sensors and a speaker that plays clips from the
game's audio, enabling the toy to respond exactly like its in-game counterparts
when it is approached, picked up, and knocked over. The project prompted
amusingly contradictory responses from fans such as Mike Nathan of *Hack-a-Day*,
who blogged about the toy under the headline "Portal Turret Plushie is Cute
and Harmless," and Nick Bungay of *NerdBastards.com*, who reported "It's Cute
and Deadly." By inviting readers to imagine both harmlessness and deadliness
adhering to the cute plush toy, Nathan's and Bungay's headlines establish
continuity between fan culture and gameplay, gesturing to the vacillating
dangerousness and vulnerability of the Sentry Turrets within the *Portal* games.
While potentially deadly to Chell, the in-game Turrets are easily deactivated by
the player, who can pick them up, drop them, or topple them over with a click
of the S key.

Guberman's video develops this contradiction at length, intercutting audio of
the Turret's threatening voice lines, such as "Target acquired," with clips of the
toy being manhandled by a largely off-screen presence. Interacting with the plush
Turret, the player restages the violence of player–Turret encounters within the
game while rendering all of the actual aggression one-sided. Moreover, the toy's

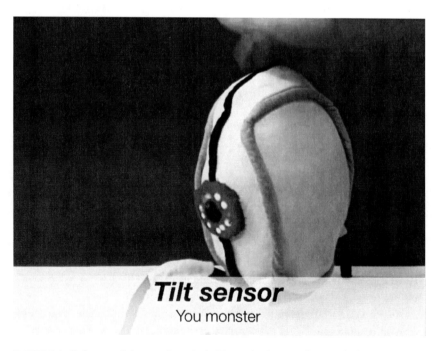

FIGURE 3.1 Guberman's interactive plush Turret is about to be toppled over in a
playful imitation of the violent encounters within the *Portal* games.

responsiveness to being dropped or tipped seems to encourage its handler to abuse it. It is the toy's powerlessness in the face of this abuse—as much as its round, soft, and disproportionate appearance—that establishes it as "cute." Cuteness thus bolsters the circulation of aggressive affect, since insofar as the toy's vulnerability encourages further interaction, it promotes further violence. In the community of emotion that the plush Turret generates, even desire for this cute object becomes expressed through aggressive rhetoric, as a commenter on Bungay's article demonstrates: "I would kill to have one of these. Or a dozen . . ." (shadowmaat).

If the Turrets' vacillation between power and vulnerability produces an economy of aggressive affect, the desire for a proliferation of these plush toys illustrates an ambivalence about cuteness that is more recognizably economic. Cute objects oscillate between singularity and plurality; between valuable uniqueness, as entities that solicit personal relationships with their viewers, and disposability, as mass-produced objects. This dynamic is central to cuteness's function in consumer capitalism, wherein, as Anne Allison argues, cute commodities offer consumers the "intimacy of friendship" even as they cultivate a drive for acquisition (13). Thus, *Portal*'s Turrets mimic cute objects in the twenty-first-century marketplace, at once soliciting engagement as singular entities and operating as a class of undifferentiated things. Within the games, each Turret speaks of itself in the first person singular, emphasizing its unique relation to the player—"I see you," "Put me down," "I don't hate you"—while at the same time, the mechanics of gameplay encourage players to see Turrets as interchangeable. Visually identical, the robots appear throughout the game environment in groups of two or three, and all the members of a group can often be deactivated through the same strategy—even through the same series of mouse clicks. The commenter's desire for "a dozen" of Guberman's plush toys, then, alludes to the abundance of Turrets within the game world, and also suggests that the Turrets instantiate a broader point about the nature of cute commodities, namely that the desire for a cute object expands into an acquisitive urge for many cute objects. Thus, cute things easily enter the economic realm of mass production. Bungay makes this point explicitly, if facetiously, concluding his article about the Turret plush by demanding that Guberman "shut up and take my money. Mass produce these now" (Bungay).

Valve Software, the corporation behind *Portal*, took notice of such fan commentary, and developed marketing materials and merchandise that tap into fan desires to own the games' cute objects. A 2011 promotional video for *Portal 2* parodies irresponsible corporate capitalism by advertising the Sentry Turrets—military-grade weapons—as an "investment opportunity" newly available to home consumers (Valve, "Investment"). Later that year, *Portal* fans really were able to "invest" in the Sentry Turrets when an officially licensed plush toy became available from the online store ThinkGeek (Mitchell).

Valve's production of licensed plush toys demonstrates with particular aptness how corporate systems can harness the desire for personal engagement with cute things. Just as the official plush Turret seems to have been prompted by

Guberman's homemade version, an official Companion Cube plush had become available once fans began sewing their own, shortly after the original game's 2007 debut (see Jetlogs). In these instances, the plush object's cuteness serves corporate interests uncannily well, allowing the toys to enter mass production while preserving the sense of enchantment usually reserved for handmade objects. Nevertheless, the tension between singularity and plurality remains distinctly visible in this context—even inspiring a light-hearted form of critique. Fans quickly noted an ironic contrast between the Cube's function in gameplay, where its singular status is a significant plot point, and its new role as a mass-produced consumer product, ready to enter an economic system of valuation. One videogame blog announced, tongue-in-cheek, "Portal's plush companion cube puts a price on friendship" (Kietzmann).

Such fan responses demonstrate how the *Portal* games use the aesthetics of cuteness to promote a critique of systematic control. Although the incongruous traits of cute objects like Guberman's plush toy perpetuate their function within systems of production, valuation, and circulating affect, the affects generated by cuteness also kindle tension between *Portal* players and controlling systems, as Valve's corporate policies stirred fans to comment on the co-optation of affective attachment by economic concerns. Player interactions with *Portal*'s cute objects are always embedded in systems, from the "testing" procedures and corporate protocols of the game narrative, to the algorithmic structure of gameplay, to the corporations and fan communities surrounding the games themselves. Throughout these interactions, cuteness offers a powerful means of engaging players' affects and attachments, which the game manipulates in order to bring attention to the controlling systems in which players are entangled. As they become attentive to these systems, players seek ways to resist their demands. Thus, *Portal* encourages us to see the ambiguous traits of cute objects as providing a rich site for both the deployment and the critique of systematic control.

The Mechanics of Cuteness

Before examining the strategies by which *Portal* effects this critique, it is useful to consider how cuteness's association with systematic control has developed. The dominant strain of cuteness scholarship beginning with Konrad Lorenz has operated under the assumption that cuteness acts systematically on those who interact with it, producing particular affective responses "with Pavlovian predictability" even before its integration into specific economic or emotional controlling systems (Harris 2). Moreover, the systematic nature of cuteness is central to its key ambiguity, namely its integration of power and powerlessness.

That is, when imagined as an automatic trigger for affective responses, cuteness unites physical weakness with the capacity to make overwhelming emotional demands. As Ngai notes, a cute object's demand for the subject's affection suggests that cuteness is "not just the site of a static power differential, but also the site of a surprisingly complex power struggle" (11). If "cute" generally describes objects that are vulnerable to violence and incapable of exerting much physical force, cute objects are nevertheless granted a power of their own. Psychologists Gary D. Sherman and Jonathan Haidt have found that cuteness tends to cause us to integrate objects into our "moral circle": the set of entities the harming of which is "morally proscribed" (245). Moreover, the intense appeal of cuteness can produce a sense that the *subject* is under the cute object's control. For those who fall under its spell, the cute thing's demands for attention and engagement may seem irresistible, to the point of eliciting violent desires such as squeezing or squishing (Ngai 64; see also Aragón et al.).

Importantly, cuteness's integration of physical weakness and emotional influence drives its function within systems of affective and economic exchange. According to Daniel Harris, the sense that we owe protection and love to cute objects is what makes cuteness "essential for the marketplace," as cute products demand to be adopted—that is, purchased—by the consumer (4). But if cuteness's paradoxical power is key to its role within systems, where does this paradox originate? How do we explain the ability of adorably powerless things to exert such compelling control over their viewers?

The portrayal of cuteness as a systematic trigger derives from its earliest context of academic study: the field of ethology. Linked to cybernetics, the science of control and communication, early ethology viewed the human organism as a kind of "mechanism" whose behaviors are dependably elicited by certain inputs (Wiener 15). In 1943, Lorenz identified cuteness as one of these inputs, or "innate releasing mechanisms," and observed that objects appear cute when their features and proportions approximate those of human infants, producing an air of vulnerability and need. Therefore, Lorenz argued, cuteness acts as a releasing mechanism for parental drives related to protection and caregiving (154–60).

Throughout early writing on cuteness, the cybernetic control model under-lying Lorenz's ethology surfaces in technological metaphors. For example, Lorenz depicts cute affect as part of a "highly differentiated system" of triggers and responses, which interlock "like the teeth of a delicately constructed clock-work mechanism" (146). The mechanical nature of these biological processes is what enables vulnerability to exert its irresistible control. For Lorenz, cuteness is characterized by a particularly intense "compulsiveness of the releasing mechanism," which renders the impulse to protect cute animals "virtually irrepressible" (160).

While subsequent research has complicated Lorenz's model of the cute response, the metaphor of cuteness as an automatic mechanism continues to appear in cute studies.[3] One popular article describes the aesthetic as "a device," a "self-fulfilling system," and a product of "engineer[ing]" by natural selection (Richard). Writing for the *New York Times*, science journalist Natalie Angier employs the conceit of "the human cuteness detector," calibrated at such a low threshold that it locates cuteness in everything from animals to emoticons (Angier). The privileged place of such mechanical metaphors in discussions of cuteness is striking, given that the cybernetic conceptualizations that inspired these metaphors have become less pervasive in the cultural imagination. This is to say that a sense of cuteness as mechanical has largely outlived the context that produced it, so that cuteness now appears indelibly linked to systematicity. In turn, this linkage reinforces connections between cuteness and specific systems of control.

Significantly, the idea that the human mind identifies cuteness automatically and promiscuously often slides into a fear that cuteness's operations will be exploited. If the cute response originates in biological systems outside of conscious control, it opens us to manipulation by any system or entity that can harness cuteness. Thus, aesthetic philosopher Dennis Dutton notes that the profligacy of the cute response can generate a "sense of cheapness . . . and the feeling of being manipulated or taken for a sucker" (qtd. in Angier). Dutton's use of the word "cheapness," with its economic implications, is telling given that cuteness's manipulative power is often linked to consumerism. For instance, Richard notes that "cute" has become synonymous with "the manipulative gesture, the pre-packaged, consumable demonstration" of vulnerability, and Harris similarly aligns this "manipulative aesthetic" with "fake[ness]" and consumption (Richard, Harris 4). Such conjunctions of the manipulative and manufactured natures of cuteness suggest an anxiety that the cute objects commanding our affections may also be complicit in our subjugation to economic systems.

Therefore, in addition to tracing cuteness's long-standing association with systematic control, this review of cuteness research suggests that the ambivalences that generate cute things' roles within economic systems are themselves produced through the "mechanics" of cuteness. The ethological view of cute responses as "compulsive" constructs cuteness as powerful precisely insofar as it aestheticizes weakness. Furthermore, the alacrity and promiscuity of such responses helps to explain the paradox in which objects deserving of care become perceived as "cheap" and disposable.

Portal's lab environment parodies cybernetic concepts, namely the view that human responses are mechanized processes, by featuring an A.I. program that "tests" a human subject's capacity to respond to her situation with standardized tools and procedures. Through this context, *Portal* primes its players to expect manipulation from the cute objects within the game. However, as players become aware of the ambiguous nature of these objects—at once threatening and vulnerable, disposable and precious—the game's narrative and mechanical systems put increasing pressure on players' responses to cute things, demanding that players examine the systems surrounding them.

Friendly Fire: The Aperture Science Sentry Turrets

The Sentry Turrets are a sinister variant of paradoxically powerful cute objects, in that they not only demand affection, but also threaten violence. They first appear in *Portal*'s Test Chamber 16, where GLaDOS warns Chell that the "usual" test has been replaced by "a live fire course designed for military androids" (Valve). If players initially underestimate the danger of the small, tripod-mounted oval at the chamber's entrance, they are quickly disabused of this faulty assessment when Chell passes the Turret's motion sensor, inciting a volley of machine-gun fire. As GLaDOS's warning suggests, the Turrets change the way players interact with the game environment. While previous levels required players to solve spatial puzzles in order to move Chell through the test chambers, the only goal of Chamber 16 is to get Chell from one door to the other without being killed by a Turret. Consequently, the game shifts from a series of puzzles to a series of violent encounters, as Chell uses the tools at hand to blast, crush, or topple each opposing Turret so that she can advance to the next portion of the test.

As objects whose sole purpose is to kill or be disabled, the Turrets challenge conventional understandings of "cute." Nevertheless, they have spawned a range of fan responses that specifically emphasize their cuteness, from plush toys like Guberman's to a Steam Community fan page unambiguously titled "*Portal Turrets are Cute*." Thus, if the Turrets are not as helpless and vulnerable as cute entities are traditionally thought to be, they still demand players' affection. Their cuteness primarily results from design elements that invoke friendliness, playfulness, and eagerness for interaction. One of the Turrets' most conspicuously "cute" features is their high-pitched, childish voice, which hails Chell with an unthreatening "There you are!" before the guns begin firing. They likewise offer a reassuring "I don't hate you" after Chell disables them.

In their appeals for engagement and interaction, the robotic Turrets echo the design logic of other cute technological products. Scholars of popular culture have noted that companies use cute designs to "impart positive feelings" towards new technologies, whose cuteness makes them appear familiar and unthreatening to customers (Cheok 230; see also Hjorth; Allison). With their minimalist and curvilinear form, the Turrets invoke the technological aesthetic of the "blobject," defined by science fiction author Bruce Sterling as "a physical object that has suffered a remake through computer graphics" (Sterling). Blobject aesthetics achieved popularity at the turn of the twenty-first century, when products like the Apple iMac and the Volkswagen New Beetle were redesigned in bright colors and clean, flowing outlines. In the same way that blobjects' uncomplicated forms make these electronic gadgets appear accessible and user-friendly, the Turrets' minimalist design projects friendliness and approachability.

Additionally, the Turrets share with other cute technologies an air of independent animacy, so that while Turrets and other blobjects are clearly the products of manufacturing, they nevertheless appear to be "living" entities in their own right. Depictions of these cute things therefore minimize the role of human labor in their manufacture. Sterling, employing the passive voice, writes that blobjects are "designed on a screen" and then "blasted into being in a burst of injection-molded goo" (Sterling). This account neatly parallels the *Portal 2* promotional video, which shows Turrets being customized, manufactured, and shipped to consumers without any human intervention. As part of a general absence of human figures in the games, this auto-generation of machines by machines gives Turrets a sense of independent agency: they are not only objects, but also entities with which players can have personal interactions. To apply a term from Sherman and Haidt's study of cute responses, the Turrets' apparent self-sufficiency encourages "mentalizing," or relating to an object "*as if* it has a thinking, intending mind" even when one knows that it does not (246, original emphasis). Sherman and Haidt find that viewers commonly mentalize cute consumer products, and this process elicits a range of social behaviors, including the desire "to touch, hold, pet, play with, talk to, or otherwise engage with the cute entity" (249). With their cute vocalizations, friendly futuristic design, and ostensible agency, the Turrets encourage such affectionate responses, even as their capacity for lethal aggression makes it necessary for players to topple them over, drop them through portals, or crush them with storage cubes.

As I have suggested, however, such merging of cuteness and aggression is not as contradictory as it may appear. Indeed, violence is part of the fabric of cuteness from the moment of its production. For Harris, cuteness aestheticizes "unhappiness, helplessness, and deformity," suggesting "an act of sadism on the part of its creator, who makes an unconscious attempt to maim, hobble, or embarrass" an object in order to make it adorable (5). Sterling depicts blobject production as another markedly violent event, in which products "suffer" through computer-aided design before being "blasted" into whatever shape their creators desire. Moreover, Ngai has suggested that the characteristic textures of cute things are ones that invite physical domination. Hence cute objects demonstrate their "responsiveness to the will of others" through softness and squishiness, which allow them to be aggressively deformed by their handlers (Ngai 64). Across these descriptions, verbs like "blast," "maim," and "squish" stand out for their physicality, demonstrating that there is a darker side to the common desire to "touch, hold, pet, [and] play with" cute things (Sherman and Haidt, 249).

A desire for violent physical contact may also factor into the affective economies that cuteness produces. By making its viewers feel overpowered and controlled, cuteness can provoke aggressive emotions such as frustration or the aforementioned feeling of being "taken for a sucker" (Angier). All of this suggests that, despite their overt violence, the Sentry Turrets are not simply an example of the "anti-cute," as one theorist has termed the "monstrous" or "empowered cute" (Brzozowska-Brywczyńska 219). Rather, their deadliness provides an alibi for an explicit working-out of the violence that cuteness always already implies. Thus, Sentry Turrets enable *Portal* players to justify their ostensible desire to aggress cute things by confronting them with cute objects that fight back.

The Turrets' violence alerts players to what Ngai calls the "complex power struggle" embedded in cuteness, and sanctions players' own aggressive responses. But *Portal* does not resolve the tension between power and vulnerability so neatly, given that in the aftermath of the player–Turret encounter, the defeated Turret changes from empowered to abject. Lying awkwardly on the test chamber floor, a disabled Turret elicits the player's pity, thereby reinforcing the object's cuteness and troubling the boundary between acceptable and unacceptable violence. On the one hand, violence against Turrets is required by both GLaDOS's sadistic "testing" procedures, in which Chell is an unwilling participant, and the protocological structure of the videogame that players themselves follow. On the other, a disabled Turret's pathetic reassurance that it bears Chell "no hard feelings" may make players probe their complicity in these systems, leading them to question what makes the game's violence against cute things so enjoyable or amusing. Put differently, can players disavow their enjoyment of the cute objects' distress if they continue to play the game?

This question gains urgency as the Turrets' affective demands become increasingly dramatic over the course of the games. In short, *Portal* escalates the violence that players must commit against Turrets to an unjustifiable level. While players only need to knock over the Turrets in Test Chamber 16, subsequent levels require shooting the cute robots with High Energy Pellets or toppling them into pits of corrosive liquid. In *Portal 2*, moreover, players must burn Turrets with laser beams, blast them with globs of experimental gels, and catapult them across chambers on special launch platforms. As the violence escalates from the first to the second game, the unfailingly polite Turrets become noticeably less sanguine about their eminent demise. While a deactivating Turret in the first game might announce "Nap time!" and wish Chell "Good night," a Turret being blasted with a Thermal Discouragement Beam emits a sequence of disturbing wails, such as "Ouch, it burns" and "Please stop." The increasingly excessive violence that players must commit as they advance through the games prompts them to interrogate the logic behind their responses to cute objects.

This logic entails not only affective structures of aggression, but also economic systems of evaluation. Indeed, violence against cute things demonstrates cuteness's ambivalent relation to disposability. Sentry Turrets are rendered disposable by both the game design, which deploys them in indistinguishable groups, and players' destructive actions in accordance with the game's dictates. Disposal is, of course, the frequent fate of mass-produced cute things, and Sterling writes of blobjects "littering" the earth, having become "common as dirt." Therefore, if cuteness is both common and instantaneously gratifying, viewers have little incentive to form long-term attachments to cute things. Emily Raine's enquiry into the "economy of cuteness" finds that "disposable affective moments are precisely what cute is all about," and in their frequency and brevity, players' interactions with Turrets over the course of the *Portal* games reflect this commodity logic, resulting in "a series of disposable connections with equally disposable cute things" (202).

In reflecting this logic, however, the games expose it to critique, so that in *Portal 2*, a line of in-game dialogue informs players that Aperture Science, like contemporary consumer capitalism, allows adorable objects to proliferate and therefore become devalued. GLaDOS mocks Chell's affection for the Companion Cube, another of the games' cute objects, by saying "We have warehouses full of the things. Absolutely worthless. I'm glad to get rid of them" (Valve). These lines, delivered by the game's villain and spoken on behalf of the sinister Aperture Science Corporation, are intended to make players question their own value-calculations. Thus, while players must treat the Turrets as disposable for as long as they participate in the game, they are also forced into awareness of the systems that produce this devaluation. And even as *Portal*'s systems require players to violently devalue cute things, other aspects of gameplay—such as a burning Turret's unnervingly childlike cries—prompt resistance to this devaluation and its effects. Indeed, fan responses such as Guberman's plush toy suggest that the Turrets' cuteness carries an affective appeal beyond what can be exhausted in gameplay. As the game trains them to resist controlling systems, *Portal* players build enduring connections with cute objects, even—or perhaps especially—when the systems around them devalue these connections.

Fratricide: The Weighted Companion Cube

The narrative of the Weighted Companion Cube similarly encompasses cuteness, violence, and disposability. Like the Sentry Turrets, the Companion Cube strains conventional understandings of cuteness. Despite its adorably alliterative name, it is essentially a gray storage crate, only distinguishable from similar crates throughout the game environment because of the pink Valentine hearts decorating its sides. Furthermore, *Portal* seems to encourage an ironic attitude towards the Cube's emotional appeals. While GLaDOS introduces it in Test Chamber 17 as an independent entity that "will accompany [Chell] through the test chamber," she also warns that "perceiving inanimate objects to be alive" is one of the psychological "symptoms" produced by Aperture Science testing (Valve, *Portal*). Nonetheless, *Portal* players consistently develop attachments to the Companion Cube, and the game relies on these attachments to generate the emo-tional pull of the test chamber's infamous conclusion, wherein GLaDOS informs Chell that the Cube "must be euthanized" in an Emergency Intelligence Incinerator before she can progress to the next level. Thus, the Cube's narrative is closely integrated with the game's critique of systematic control, demonstrating how cuteness can simultaneously function within systems and incite resistance to those systems.

The Cube's association with systematic control begins with its parodic appropriation of what I earlier called "the mechanics of cuteness," that is, the idea that cuteness automatically triggers particular behaviors and affects. If cute objects usually demand affection due to their weakness, the Cube's cuteness must first be manufactured, since it lacks softness and smallness, and is more likely to support Chell than to demand her protection. Indeed, throughout the puzzles in Chamber 17, the Cube functions as an extension or surrogate for Chell's more vulnerable body, serving as a step up to otherwise inaccessible surfaces and shielding her from deadly High Energy Pellets. Therefore, the game must use dialogue to generate a sense of cute dependency, and GLaDOS issues the Cube to Chell with the direct instruction to "take care of it."

This line of dialogue is vital to understanding the Companion Cube's role in *Portal*. As game designers Kim Swift and Eric Wolpaw explain in an interview, an early design for Test Chamber 17 ran into problems when players forgot to bring the storage crate, which was necessary for solving the level's puzzles, through the entirety of the test chamber sequence (Swift and Wolpaw). Since the game's other levels contain an abundance of crates, players were trained to see them as common and easily replaceable. Therefore, demonstrating an almost ethological conception of vulnerability as a "releasing mechanism" for care, the designers inserted GLaDOS's dialogue to make players feel responsible for the Cube's well-being, and it worked. As Wolpaw reports, "After that, no one ever forgets [sic] the box" (Swift and Wolpaw).

By employing an illusion of neediness to get players attached to the Cube, *Portal* imitates marketing techniques associated with cute consumer products. As Harris notes, "[a]dvertisers have learned that consumers will 'adopt' products" that project an aura of dependency (5). In its "advertisement" to players as a potential friend, or perhaps a pet (another read on "companion"), the Companion Cube mimics the cute commodity in consumer capitalism, "stand[ing] (in) for . . . the warmth and intimacy of friendship" (Allison 13). Yet the Cube enacts this role with an important difference, given that it never seeks to hide the means by which its "consumer" is manipulated. *Portal*'s "marketing" of the Cube proves so successful, in part, because its attempts to make us love it are transparently obvious, and the game's self-reflexive irony ensures that the player never feels "taken for a sucker."

Once the Cube's transparent manipulation succeeds in getting players emotionally invested in its well-being, *Portal* uses this investment to carry the game's most powerful thematization of systematic control, namely the infamous euthanization scene. At the close of Test Chamber 17, GLaDOS directs Chell to "escort" her Companion Cube to an Incinerator and informs her that she cannot progress to the next level until the Cube has been destroyed. After coming to view the Cube as a friend, players are suddenly forced to see it as a disposable tool that has served its purpose. Thus this scene brutally reminds players that their interactions with cute objects are structured by various systems of valuation. The game also links the Cube's disposal to scientific protocols: the euthanization of her "friend" may be another experiment that Chell, as a human test subject, must complete to serve GLaDOS's research program. Noting that the euthanization dramatizes "[o]bedience to authority, particularly scientific-institutional authority," Burden and Gouglas have compared this scene to the Milgram experiment, in which test subjects showed a willingness to electrocute other "volunteers" when commanded to by the experimenter, a scientific authority figure (Burden and Gouglas). I would add, however, that *Portal* presents scientific authority as just one of many societal values that exert control over subjects. When pressuring Chell to euthanize the Cube, GLaDOS invokes a number of systematic authorities, including "state and local statutory regulations," "eight out of ten Aperture Science engineers," and "an independent panel of ethicists." The euthanization scene may therefore be read not as an allegory of any particular system, but of systematic control more generally.

Considering, furthermore, that the euthanization scene is a scripted element in a videogame, it becomes clear that additional systems are implicated in the Cube's destruction. In another interview, Wolpaw suggested that the Cube's incineration was necessitated by videogame narrative conventions. Realizing that the game had not properly "trained" players to use the Emergency Intelligence Incinerators, which would play a key role in Chell's final confrontation with GLaDOS, the writers went back and inserted the Incinerator at the end of Chamber 17 (Laidlaw and Wolpaw). Perhaps most troubling for players, however, is their own complicity through the system of gameplay. As GLaDOS warns Chell, "Testing cannot continue until your Companion Cube has been incinerated." *Portal* thus demands that players weigh the cost of progressing to the next level against the value of refusing to destroy the Cube. Like the conflicting affects that the Turrets generate, conflicting valuations of the Companion Cube force players to acknowledge their own role within controlling systems.

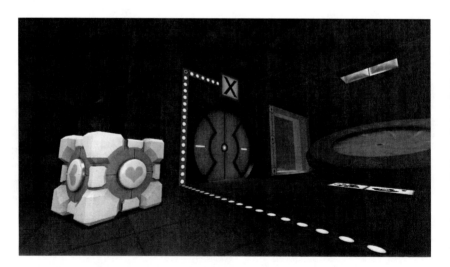

FIGURE 3.2 The Companion Cube awaits its fate at the end of Test Chamber 17. Players may only progress beyond this point if they use the Emergency Intelligence Incinerator at right to "euthanize" their Cube.

Fantasies of Resistance

For many players, this awareness of the game's controlling systems incites resistance. *Portal* uses players' increasing consciousness of their position within oppressive systems to inspire insurgency, culminating when Chell deposes these systems' representatives in the final battles. But players also practice forms of resistance that exceed the games' narratives. The Companion Cube's euthanization provokes particularly intense responses, as players search for ways to refuse the game's demand that they choose between playing the game and saving the Cube. A YouTube query for "How to save the Companion Cube" yields, at the time of writing, over five thousand results. One video explains not only how to save the Cube, but "how to keep it with you as a friend [sic]" when Chell leaves the test chamber, suggesting the centrality of cute affect to these displays of resistance (studioMAXIMO).

Other players accept that they must comply with controlling systems to progress beyond the euthanization scene, but find alternative forms of resistance outside of gameplay. In search of what Ngai calls "an ever more intimate, ever more sensuous" relation to the cute object, many fans sew or purchase Companion Cube plush toys (3). The rhetoric around these plush objects links out-of-game crafting with in-game control, so that one blog, offering a downloadable Companion Cube sewing pattern, promises that "you can finally hug your best friend" (JetLogs). Similarly, ThinkGeek's advertising for the official plush Cube engages players in the fantasy that buying a plush toy will enable them to resist GLaDOS's demands: "Finally, you can choose NOT to incinerate!" ("*Portal*"). ThinkGeek goes on to propose an alternative, utopian vision in which, rather than euthanizing the Cube, players can "squeeze it, feed it cake, and love it long time [sic]"—a fantasy vision of purely sensual enjoyment, beyond concerns of power or economics.

While ThinkGeek's fantasy appears more amusing than inspiring, it speaks to cuteness's potential as a vehicle for resistance. The desire to resist controlling systems by maintaining an intimate connection with cute objects reveals cuteness's utopian potential; for, as Ngai argues, cuteness:

> has a certain utopian edge, speaking to a desire to inhabit a concrete, qualitative world of use as opposed to one of abstract exchange. There is thus a sense in which the fetishism of cuteness is as much a way of *resisting the logic of commodification*—predicated on the idea of the "absolute commensurability of everything"—as it is a symptomatic reflection of it. (13, my emphasis)

Of course, this utopianism does not offer a strong proscriptive vision. Just as it is hard to imagine lingering in Test Chamber 17 with an un-euthanized Cube, as either a test subject or a *Portal* player, it is difficult to envision a "concrete, qualitative world of use" as more than an interval of hugging. The actual compelling fantasy that both *Portal* fans and Ngai offer is that interactions with a cute entity, and its singular set of phenomenal qualities, can constitute resistance to systems of control. If saving the Companion Cube lets players defy the system, wherein having "warehouses full" of certain things renders them "worthless," the popularity of Companion Cube plushes suggests that fans further challenge utility- or scarcity-based valuations by taking pleasure in the Cube's cute phenomenal qualities. Indeed, we might argue that the impulse to rescue the Cube from disposal mirrors "the fantasy of rescuing a commodity's phenomenological side" that cuteness enables (Ngai 66). The idea that cute objects can provide grounds for resistance as unique collections of sensuous phenomena offers one way to understand the Companion Cube graffiti, poetry, and collage art scattered throughout *Portal*'s final test chambers. This artwork, purportedly produced by one of GLaDOS's previous victims, presents the Cube as both a martyr around which resistance to GLaDOS can rally, and as a cute phenomenal image in which test subjects and players can take pleasure outside the concerns of controlling systems even as they remain locked in struggle against those systems.

The question remains: Does *Portal* sustain the fantasy that cuteness may offer an escape from systems of control? While the first *Portal* ends with Chell being dragged back into the laboratory that she has spent the entire game attempting to leave, the conclusion of *Portal 2* appears more hopeful. As Chell wanders into a field, finally released from the wreckage of the Aperture Science facility, GLaDOS sends a slightly charred Companion Cube bouncing after her. This final scene, free from systems or social structures of any kind, recalls Ngai's description of cuteness as "a kind of pastoral" that reflects "our desire for a simpler, more intimate relation to our commodities" (31). Chell and the Cube appear ready to realize the utopian promise of cuteness that Ngai identifies, though it is hard to imagine what would follow in this pastoral fantasy (13).

Significantly, however, fan responses reveal that the same tensions and ambivalences generated by the games continue to circulate outside of gameplay, and the culture around *Portal* proves uncannily capable of reincorporating displays of resistance. For example, if we see fans' attempts to "save" the Companion Cube as a way to escape the game system, a scene in *Portal 2* appears to counter such insurgency. In this segment, ironically titled "The Escape," the Turrets take over the Cube's role as cute victims facing incineration. Chell must sabotage the Turret Redemption Line—a recycling system that identifies defective Turrets for disposal—by switching the system's evaluative mechanism so that it destroys functioning Turrets instead of broken ones, ensuring that only harmlessly defective Turrets are deployed against her in the future. The Redemption Line scene teaches players to see Turrets as victims within a system that ruthlessly eliminates them if they fail to conform to a standard of utility.[4] As the player turns the incinerating laser on the Turrets, Chell makes the disturbing discovery that the robots "do feel pain, of a sort" (Valve Corporation, *Portal 2*). Nevertheless, their function in a violent system requires that they be eliminated to ensure Chell's own safety.

The Turrets' ambivalent function as both victims and enemies—sentient beings and disposable tools—renders compliance and escape equally unacceptable. Like the Companion Cube's euthanization, this scene generates abhorrence for the systems that destroy the Turrets, but also maintains that their destruction is necessary, since players can only progress in the game by replacing Aperture's system of valuation with an equally brutal one of their own. Thus the difficult Turret Redemption scene suggests that *Portal*'s meditation on systems of control is effective precisely because it refuses to offer a clear escape from these systems. Rather, the games promote fantasies of awareness and resistance.

If this reading seems pessimistic, it is worth interrogating the game's proposed alternative, which leaves Chell stranded in a field with her adorable Cube and nothing further to do. Interestingly, while the game's final image provides Chell and the beloved Cube with a happy ending, *Portal* fans have shown greater appreciation for the game's *pen*ultimate scene, in which a group of opera-singing Turrets serenade Chell with a celebratory aria. Cornering Chell in a freight elevator as she makes her way to the surface, the Turrets open their carapaces and emit the sound of accordions in place of the expected gunfire. The Turret Opera's potential to delight relies on careful arrangements in terms of both the scripting of player expectations and the musical performance itself. As each Turret plays its designated role to produce the full effect of the scene, the game suggests that play, like cuteness, requires a system.

Conclusion

The *Portal* games demonstrate how cuteness's distinctive features, including the assumed mechanical nature of cute responses and viewers' ambivalent valuations of cute objects, produce its role in various systems, from affective to economic. In turn, the association of cuteness with systematic control informs the ambivalence of cute affect. Popular notions of the cuteness response as unconscious and irresistible, combined with cute objects' ability to entrap their viewers in systems of exchange, reveal a strong sense of cuteness as disempowering. Indeed a recent study found that aggressive responses to cute things arise in order to counter the "overwhelming" positive emotions that cuteness inspires in some subjects (Aragón et al.). These subjects experience their own emotions as "unmanageable," suggesting that interactions with cute objects can be discomfiting even when the objects themselves receive "positive appraisals" (Aragón et al. 2).

Portal, then, asks us to consider the role of aggression in reinstating the subject's power during these disempowering encounters. In reality, aggressiveness or animosity towards a cute object is rarely acted upon. In requiring players to act out aggression towards the Turrets and the Companion Cube, *Portal* gives subjects a way to reassert power vis-à-vis cute things, and indeed, the fact that such violence is part of the game's entertainment value demands that players acknowledge the pleasure attached to harming cute objects. At the same time, it is important that the game presents the directive to harm cute objects as coming from a system external to the player. As cuteness remains capable of generating affection even in subjects who feel manipulated by it, the suffering of cute objects incites players to resist the systems that threaten cute things. If cuteness begins by disempowering subjects, *Portal* suggests, it can also prompt them to "take the power back" from systems of control.

Ultimately, even in its association with control, cuteness remains linked to play. Propounding neither simplistic escapism nor pessimistic compliance, *Portal* suggests that the systems surrounding cuteness may afford pleasure, insofar as they encourage strategizing and playful competition. Even though such systems can appear exploitative, ruthless, and worthy of resistance, the fact that players take pleasure in the struggle against them—as in the struggle between player and game, or even the complicated power struggle that cuteness elicits—suggests that these are systems we are not so eager to escape.

Notes

1   For more on the role of fan communities and fan production in making meaning from popular media, see Jenkins et al.
2   GLaDOS, pronounced similarly to Gladys, is an acronym for Genetic Lifeform and Disk Operating System, which suggests GLaDOS's role as the game's most obvious representative of systematic power.
3   For a recent study of the instantaneous nature of cute recognition, see Kringelbach et al.
4   Ian Bogost has argued that videogames derive their persuasive and instructive power from their capacity to engage players in procedures, which in turn "make claims *about how things work*" (29, original emphasis). Thus, in having players complete a series of actions to sabotage the Turret Redemption Line and then requiring them to witness the Turrets' destruction, the game makes a procedural argument about the Turrets' vulnerability and the player's implication in violent systematic power. See Bogost, especially 28–35.

Works Cited

Ahmed, Sara. "Affective Economies." *Social Text* 22.2 (2004): 117–39. *Project MUSE*. Online. 14 Sep. 2015.
Allison, Anne. *Millennial Monsters: Japanese Toys and the Global Imagination*. Berkeley, CA: University of California Press, 2006.
Angier, Natalie. "The Cute Factor." *New York Times*. New York Times, 2 Jan. 2006. Online. 2 Mar. 2014.
Aragón, Oriana R. et al. "Dimorphous Expressions of Positive Emotion: Displays of Both Care and Aggression in Response to Cute Stimuli." *Psychological Science* 26.3 (2015): 1–15. *Sage*. Online. 2 Feb. 2015.
Bogost, Ian. *Persuasive Games: The Expressive Power of Videogames*. Cambridge, MA: MIT Press, 2007.
Brzozowska-Brywczyńska, Maja. "Monstrous/Cute: Notes on the Ambivalent Nature of Cuteness." *Monsters and the Monstrous: Myths and Metaphors of Enduring Evil*. Ed. Niall Scott. Amsterdam: Rodopi, 2007. 213–28.

Bungay, Nick. "It's Cute and Deadly: An Interactive *Portal* Turret Plush." *NerdBastards.com*. Nerd Bastards, 25 Apr. 2011. Online. 22 Feb. 2014.

Burden, Michael, and Sean Gouglas. "The Algorithmic Experience: *Portal* as Art." *Game Studies* 12.2 (2012): n. pag. Online. 14 Feb. 2014.

Cheok, Adrian David, and Owen Noel Newton Fernando. "Kawaii/Cute Interactive Media." *Art and Technology of Entertainment Computing and Communication*. Ed. A.D. Cheok. London: Springer, 2010. 223–54.

Galloway, Alexander R. "Allegories of Control." *Gaming: Essays on Algorithmic Culture*. Minneapolis, MN: University of Minnesota Press, 2006. 85–106.

Guberman, Jonathan M. "*Portal* Turret Plushie." *Up, Not North*, n.d. Online. 22 Feb. 2014.

Harris, Daniel. *Cute, Quaint, Hungry and Romantic: The Aesthetics of Consumerism*. Cambridge, MA: De Capo, 2001.

Hjorth, Larissa. "Cute@keitai.com." *Japanese Cybercultures*. Eds. Nanette Gottlieb and Mark McLelland. London: Routledge, 2003. 50–59.

Jenkins, Henry, Joshua Green, and Sam Ford. *Spreadable Media: Creating Value and Meaning in a Networked Culture*. New York: New York University Press, 2013.

Jetlogs. "Companion Cube Plushie Sewing Pattern." *JetLogs.org: Web Design, Video Games and Papercraft*. Jetlogs.org, 29 Oct. 2007. Online. 10 Mar. 2014.

Kietzmann, Ludwig. "*Portal*'s Plush Companion Cube Puts a Price on Friendship." *Joystiq*. AOL, 14 Dec. 2007. Online. 13 Mar. 2014.

Kringelbach, Morten L., Annukka Lehtonen, Sarah Squire, Allison G. Harvey, Michelle G. Craske, Ian E. Holliday, Alexander L. Green, Tipo Z. Aziz, Peter C. Hansen, Piers L. Cornelissen and Alan Stein. "A Specific and Rapid Neural Signature for Parental Instinct." *PLoS ONE* 3.2 (2008): e1664. Online. 18 Dec. 2015.

Laidlaw, Marc, and Eric Wolpaw. "Valve's Writers and the Creative Process." Interview by Kris Graft. *Gamasutra*. UBM Tech, 2 Nov. 2009. Online. 16 Mar. 2014.

Lorenz, Konrad. "Part and Parcel in Human and Animal Societies." 1950. *Studies in Animal and Human Behavior*. Vol. 2. Trans. Robert Martin. Cambridge, MA: Harvard University Press, 1971. 115–95.

Merish, Lori. "Cuteness and Commodity Aesthetics: Tom Thumb and Shirley Temple." *Freakery: Cultural Spectacles of the Extraordinary Body*. Ed. Rosemarie Garland-Thomson. New York: New York University Press, 1996. 185–203.

Mitchell, Richard. "Official Plush *Portal* Turrets Deploying This December." *Joystiq*. AOL, 18 Oct. 2011. Online. 13 Mar. 2014.

Morreall, John. "Cuteness." *British Journal of Aesthetics* 31.1 (1991): 39–47. *Project MUSE*. Online. 10 Sep. 2015.

Nathan, Mike. "*Portal* Turret Plushie is Cute and Harmless." *Hack-a-Day*. Hackaday, 25 Apr. 2011. Online. 22 Feb. 2014.

Ngai, Sianne. *Our Aesthetic Categories: Zany, Cute, Interesting*. Cambridge, MA: Harvard University Press, 2012.

"*Portal* Turrets are Cute." *Steam Community*. Valve, 12 July 2011. Online. 15 Mar. 2014.

"*Portal* Weighted Companion Cube Plush." *ThinkGeek: Stuff for the Smart Masses*. ThinkGeek, n.d. Online. 10 Mar. 2014.

Raine, Emily. "The Sacrificial Economy of Cuteness in *Tamala 2010: A Punk Cat in Space*." *Mechademia 6: User Enhanced*. Ed. Frenchy Lunning. Minneapolis, MN: University of Minnesota Press, 2011. 193–210.

Richard, Frances. "Fifteen Theses on Cute." *Cabinet* 4 (2001): n. pag. Online. 17 Feb. 2014.

shadowmaat. Weblog comment. *NerdBastards.com*. Nerd Bastards, 25 Apr. 2011. Online. 22 Feb. 2014.

Sherman, Gary D,. and Jonathan Haidt. "Cuteness and Disgust: The Humanizing and Dehumanizing Effects of Emotion." *Emotion Review* 3.3 (2011): 245–51. *Sage*. Online. 22 Feb. 2014.

Shiokawa, Kanako. "Cute but Deadly: Women and Violence in Japanese Comics." *Themes and Issues in Asian Cartooning: Cute, Cheap, Mad, and Sexy*. Ed. John A. Lend. Madison, WI: Popular, 1999. 93–107.

Sterling, Bruce. "When Blobjects Rule the Earth." SIGGRAPH 2004. Los Angeles Convention Center, Los Angeles. Aug. 2004. Address. Rpt. in *Viridian Note*. Online. 28 Feb. 2014.

studioMAXIMO. "How to Save and Keep Companion Cube!!!" *YouTube*. YouTube, 9 Mar. 2011. Online. 10 Mar. 2014.

Swift, Kim, and Eric Wolpaw. "GDC: A *Portal* Postmortem." Interview. *Edge Online*. Future, 23 Feb. 2008. Online. 16 Mar. 2014.

Valve Corporation. *Portal*. Valve, 2007. Computer software.

——. *Portal 2*. Valve, 2011. Computer software.

——. "Investment Opportunity #3: Turrets." Video. *Official Portal 2 Website*. Valve, 2011. Online. 8 Mar. 2014.

Wiener, Norbert. *The Human Use of Human Beings*. Boston, MA: Houghton Mifflin, 1950.

4

"THIS BABY SLOTH WILL INSPIRE YOU TO KEEP GOING"

Capital, Labor, and the Affective Power of Cute Animal Videos

Allison Page

Introduction

In the second episode of the Bravo reality series *LOLwork*, viewers are given a glimpse of the contradictions that characterize a twenty-first-century "creative economy" office space. A show that epitomizes Bravo's broader uptake of content featuring new forms of labor and branding imperatives, *LOLwork* follows the staff of Cheezburger, the company that makes "lolcats" and other cute animal media, securing more than 700,000 daily global viewers and more than 2 million page views per day.[1] Based in Seattle, Cheezburger is a hip workplace: the office space is colorful and laidback, with a couch, a foosball table, a boss who uses a standing desk, and no cubicles of any kind. Indeed, the space itself is emblematic of a post-Fordist blurring of work and leisure, similar to the cool "new economy" environments described in a *New York Times* article about millennial workplaces with an "aggressively playful vibe" (Widdicombe). As Andrew Ross demonstrates in *No-Collar*, such "permissive" workplaces, "designed both physically and philosophically to chase off the blues," emerged during the 1990s tech boom (10). Cheezburger's staff is comprised primarily of young creatives who dress casually, love animals, and grew up steeped in Internet culture. In this particular episode, "Career Day," the staff are working on Saturday ("caturday") in order to host junior high students, "the future customers of icanhazcheezburger," interested in learning about how the business runs. When one of the students asks Content Director Paul, who is depicted throughout the show as a cynical curmudgeon, "Don't you have a lot of fun?" Paul replies, "Sort of, but here's what happens: when you work, doing things that you like, the thing that you like suddenly becomes the thing that you hate, and so you have to learn to love and hate something at the same time." In a manner suggestive of the ways in which neoliberal capitalism captures and instrumentalizes passion and desire, Paul underscores how work has destroyed his previous relationship to creativity. Throughout the series, Paul is the voice of anti-work critique, struggling with what Kathi Weeks describes as "work as a requirement, work as a system, work as a way of life" (3). Later in the same episode, he tells the camera, "I gave the kids a leg up today. They're going to know that work is hell and they're going to be ready for it." In response, the show cuts to student McKenzie, who concludes, "I think working at a place like this would be a lot of fun, actually" ("Career Day"). McKenzie's comment functions as a way to render Paul's anti-work perspective baseless.

Throughout the season, *LOLwork* strives to make Cheezburger seem fun and enlightened, supportive of creativity and innovation. Yet "creative" work is central to a late capitalist economy that exploits precarity and requires continuous productivity (McRobbie *Creative*). The show represents the Cheezburger office ethos as existing outside a neoliberal regime of precarious labor, as interesting and exciting rather than dull and crushing: the staff have parties, play games, and occasionally someone dresses up in a giant cat costume. But ultimately, the Cheezburger staff demonstrate that creating cute animal media *is* work—boring and commodified—even as the show tries to portray it as otherwise through discursive emphasis on creativity and fun. In this way, *LOLwork* represents a paradox: the Cheezburger staff make cute animal videos that uplift and distract bored workers while they themselves are in a work environment reliant on continuous productivity, affective labor, and instrumentalized creativity.

In this article, I situate the rise of cute animal videos within late capitalist affective circuits, focusing in particular on shifts in labor and the workplace. Drawing on Lauren Berlant's theorization of "cruel optimism," which describes the attachment we have to things that are detrimental to us, I suggest that cute animal videos operate as a form of what I term "cruel relief." I contend that the affective pull of cuteness—and cute animals in particular—offers a disruptive affective excess that provides a tool for coping with not just the drudgery of work and office life, but also the devastations of neoliberalism and its attendant social and political effects. One such effect includes the proliferation of a productivist ethos that bleeds into every arena of life such that any semblance of separation between work and "life" is eroded (Graeber 20–22). This overvaluation of work is part of capital's quest to capture the "rest of life beyond work"—its "times, spaces, rhythms, purposes, and values" (Weeks 29). In this way, readily available reservoirs of mediated cuteness function as a consolation, not only making work more bearable but also ameliorating work's role as a disciplinary apparatus. As Weeks argues, "postindustrial production employs workers' minds and hearts as well as their hands . . . post-Taylorist labor processes increasingly require the self-management of subjectivity so that attitudes and affective orientations to work will themselves produce value" (31). Similarly, Melissa Gregg contends that there are a "limited range of affective states and subjectivities permissible in workplaces," especially those requiring a certain professional "cool" ("On Friday" 250). Cuteness, I argue, is central to this form of self-managing capitalist subjectivity.

In order to theorize this relationship between cuteness and neoliberalism's grip on work and subjectivity, I examine the rhetoric used to frame cute animal media. Photographs of baby animals, animal cams following puppies, and websites devoted to "procrastination at insanely cute levels" are frequently captioned in ways that underscore cuteness's ascribed motivational functions even if on paradoxical terms as in "This Baby Sloth Will Inspire You to Keep Going" (Hall). Cute animals thus offer respite from what Berlant has termed "crisis ordinariness," where crisis is not exceptional but quotidian (7). I suggest that their wide availability as a tool of procrastination softens (and thus strengthens) capitalism and the imperative for 24/7 productivity (Crary 3). I draw from *LOLwork* to demonstrate how this paradigmatic post-Fordist workplace highlights the necessity of cuteness to neoliberal labor.

Cuteness and Capitalism

Cute animal media are routinely dismissed as frivolous and irrelevant at best, and the portent of the "downfall of modern society" at worst (Zimmerman),[2] ushering in a world of apathetic complacency. In March 2014, a *New Yorker* cartoon featured a man and a woman in a living room staring at a television with shocked expressions, captioned with, "It's finally happened. They've replaced the nightly news with cat videos" (Smaller). In 2010, Neil Genzlinger wrote a hyperbolic and tongue-in-cheek review for the *New York Times* about the animal "takeover" of television, film, and new media, suggesting that the "vacant-eyed armies of people who are watching idiotic cat and dog videos on the Internet" could be doing more significant and productive things with their time:

> "Surprised Kitty" is 17 seconds long. That means humans have wasted roughly 484,500,000 seconds watching this thing. That's more than 15 years. It took just over a year to build the Empire State Building; about four years to construct the Golden Gate Bridge; eight to land a man on the moon. In the time that we collectively were watching "Surprised Kitty," we collectively could instead have done all those things and still had a year to sit back and admire our work.

Genzlinger describes a scenario in which individual consumption of cute animal videos precludes collective action on what he considers more meaningful pursuits. Similarly, within a subset of the academic left, the viewing and sharing of cute animals has come to stand in for passivity, apathy, and stupidity (Morozov 81).

The "cute cat" image has a longer genealogy than the now commonplace lolcats. During the 1870s, photographer Harry Pointer took around 200 photographs of his cats, first posing them in "realistic" postures and then shifting to scenes of cats drinking tea, sitting at the table, or riding a bike, often with humorous captions (Figure 4.1).

In 1894, Thomas Edison produced a silent short of two cats boxing complete with miniature boxing gloves.[3] Decades later, Harry Frees dressed up his animal subjects in cute clothing and photographed them, publishing a photography book in 1929 titled *Animal Land on the Air* (Lamar). In "Why Look at Animals," John Berger details how representation of animals began long before the advent of film, television, and photography, yet as these technologies developed, they produced new forms of knowledge about animals, and as Berger notes, animals were "always the observed" (14). The erasure of animals from everyday life accompanied capital's advance, as industrialization and urbanization required new forms of labor and a shift from agrarian lifestyles to urban ones. Ordinary contact with animals receded during the late eighteenth through the nineteenth century due to a reconfigured daily life; as such, animals were marginalized and brought back as a new type of commodity to be engaged during leisure time via "public zoos, realistic animal toys, pet-keeping" (Chris x). Developing Berger's argument, Cynthia Chris describes how this new commodification of animals underscores the relationship between capital and colonialism. The logics of containment, display, and observation underwriting zoos were the same used to represent and display a "supposedly primitive Other . . . observed as entertainment" (Chris x–xi).

FIGURE 4.1   Harry Pointer's "Rinking at Brighton" features cats on roller skates in his photography studio in Brighton.

Further, the technologies used to produce images of animals were those used to constitute visual representations of colonial subjects.

In our own era, the proliferation of cuteness and cute animals has occurred alongside downward pressure on wages, increased job precarity, dramatic wealth concentration, austerity regimes, the militarization of the police, endless war, further environmental degradation, and increased surveillance, all of which are bound up with neoliberal ideals of risk management and the ever increasing corporatization and commodification of daily life.[4] In order to account for this broader social, political, and economic context, scholarship on cuteness has begun to consider the relationship between cuteness and capital. For example, Daniel Harris argues that cuteness is a humanist (and narcissistic) category central to consumer culture, and affords humans an opportunity to extend power over the cute object (11). In their work on consumption, gender, and cuteness, marketing scholars Elad Granot et al. extend Harris's work to suggest that "cute" as a concept has "considerable power" that they link to a "rapidly expanding desire for cute, cuddly, reassuring consumption experiences" (75). The consumption of cute products, they argue, offers an emotional connection or experience that could "disguise and compensate for the very isolation of individuals in contemporary society" (82). Such isolation can be attributed in part to imperatives to work ever more hours and in spaces and times once reserved (for some) as those of leisure and rest. For Jonathan Crary, the "separation, isolation, and neutralization of individuals" is perpetuated by the compulsory nature of contemporary media culture that shapes how, where, and when we consume: "Visual and auditory 'content' is most often ephemeral, interchangeable material that, in addition to its commodity status, circulates to habituate and validate one's immersion in the exigencies of twenty-first-century capitalism" (52). Along these lines, in their analysis of emoji as "prophylactic" features of neoliberalism, Luke Stark and Kate Crawford suggest that emoji "help people in digital environments cope emotionally with the experience of building and maintaining social ties within hierarchical technological platforms and unjust economic systems that operate far outside of their control" (8). Similar to what I am suggesting about cute animal media, Stark and Crawford point to the possibility that affective excess might escape the logics of capital even as capital seeks to capture, contain, and use it. The discourse around cute animal media often implies that we are collectively suffering (to varying degrees) from the affective impacts of neoliberalism, including loneliness and isolation, yet the cuteness provided is our salve or reward. In addition to offering emotional connection or experience, cuteness and cute animal media assuage neoliberalism's effects—in this way, cute animal videos are not simply distraction but rather, acknowledged reprieve.

Cute animal videos thus go hand in hand with an acknowledgment of the deleterious effects of neoliberal capital. As a form of cruel relief, cute animal videos provide a reprieve from the onslaught of daily life under neoliberalism. For Berlant, "cruel optimism" describes a relation that exists "when something you desire is actually an obstacle to your flourishing" (1). The optimism becomes cruel when "the object/scene that ignites a sense of possibility actually makes it impossible to attain the expansive transformation for which a person or a people risks striving" (Berlant 2). Simultaneously, the optimism is cruel because one is confirmed by (and perhaps derives pleasure from) a relation that is actually damaging. In other words, the very thing one imagines will bring about change or possibility is that which makes it impossible. Along these lines, I conceive of cruel relief as a form of relief that is cruel in its evanescence. Cute animal videos help us to exist by providing a momentary form of connection, a tug, a charge, a moment of respite. The relief is cruel because it is so fleeting and because it normalizes neoliberal capital and work, thus intensifying the subjection of the relieved subject. Cuteness and cute animal media thus soften capitalism and help us to endure and become "adjusted to injustice."[5]

A parody of this dynamic was presented in a May 2014 episode of *Last Week Tonight with John Oliver* where host John Oliver promised viewers a cute animal video as a reward for enduring a 12-minute segment on botched executions and the US death penalty: "Let's do this then, let's talk about the death penalty," proposes Oliver.

> And before you turn this show off, there was a YouTube video this week of tiny hamsters eating tiny burritos, and it's as magical and as uncomplicated as you think. And if you make it to the end of this story, I promise we will watch it together, OK? But you have to stay with us to get it." (*Last Week*)[6]

Here, the fleeting break provided by cute animals operates as an incentive for viewers to momentarily engage a form of state violence that seems intractable before the reprieve. This break becomes even more important for viewers and users who inadvertently encounter a depressing news story. In a blog entry acknowledging the comforting power of cute animals, Justine Keogh notes:

> When we're surfing the internet, which many of us have to do on a daily basis, it's inevitable that we're going to come across some kind of depressing headline or upsetting news story. The abundance of cute animals on the internet means we've always got somewhere to go to cheer ourselves up when all the negativity gets too much for us. Stop thinking about the dark stuff for a while and let an animal make you smile.

Cute animals provide cruel relief, a much-needed break from new norms of work and productivity that further bolster capitalism and erode anti-work resistance. As the Oliver example suggests, cruel relief extends beyond work to provide an affective disruption to the negative emotions produced by a variety of events, including the racism of the death penalty.

Embattled Workspaces

During the 1970s, an economic, political, and cultural transformation took place that redefined the meanings of white-collar work and office workspaces in the United States. With the imposition of late capitalism and the ensuing shift from Fordism to post-Fordism—aided by new communication technologies and a feminizing workforce—work began to reach ever further into what was once, for some, considered leisure time. As the service economy grew, so did the demand for affective and immaterial labor (Hochschild; Lazzarato). The overvaluation of work operates in tandem with neoliberal forms of responsibilization, where one must effectively self-manage and self-optimize in order to navigate a society without a safety net (Rose 146). As David Graeber notes, jobs under neoliberalism are no longer lifelong. Rather, the average worker changes careers at least five times, and one must continually strive to stay current and relevant by under-going continuous training and education in order to be mobile. This demand for constant productivity is one of the hallmarks of post-Fordist capitalism, where clear distinctions between work and "play" have eroded, and leisure activity is (or should be) productive.

In turn, this extends the workspace into daily life: "labor is performed via phone in the car, on email walking down the street, or at home after putting the children to bed" (Galloway 120). Crucially, such work outside the parameters of the office goes unrecognized, and the "purported convenience of the technologies obscures the amount of additional work they demand" (Gregg, *Work's* 2). Even the supposed leisure and pleasure of a converged media landscape actually heightens the work imperative for women, as Laurie Ouellette and Julie Wilson have detailed in their research on the female audiences of lifestyle and self-help advice guru Dr. Phil (549). Such a blurred boundary between work and life constitutes a change for those workers who were once able to leave work at the office. Life itself is a site of valorization, where anything can be monetized. According to Tara McPherson, "[o]ur email and our Twitter feeds always beckon. . . . We write reviews on Yelp or Amazon, and our labor is harvested" (Jenkins). Social media and digital devices contribute to a presentist, "always-on, perpetually connected" temporality that aligns with late capital's demands for continuous productivity. Melissa Gregg highlights how this "always-present potential for engaging with work" constitutes a new form of affective labor (3).

It is important to note that what Gregg terms "presence bleed," the erasure of "firm boundaries between personal and professional identities," refers to certain types of middle-class work and workers (2). Arlie Hochschild, Angela Davis, Angela McRobbie, and others have pointed to the ways that for workers minoritized by race, gender, class, and sexuality, there has always been a blurred work/life boundary and never a hard and fast distinction between leisure and work. Further, as Tavia Nyong'o argues, the "vocabulary of precarity" is often universalizing and although it may capture "one aspect of neoliberal governmentality," it "fails to adequately represent the full violence of global capitalism in all its dimensions," thereby limiting possibilities for resistance (158). Nyong'o points to the significance of attending more precisely to capital's entanglement with race and heteropatriarchy.

This erasure of a line between work and leisure is evident throughout the season of *LOLwork*. Employees are shown working in situations that mask their labor through discursive emphasis on creativity and cuteness. For example, episode 4, "Coffee is for Closers," begins with shots of the staff hanging around in their open-plan workspace, joking with one another, looking at their phones, and apparently not working. Sarah, the site's Art Director, tells the camera, "Working here for a people watcher is kind of an ideal situation . . . You can do your work and still be entertained by people not doing work." Paul defends what appears to be goofing off, noting, "Lots of times, good ideas pop into your head when you're doing something else. So what's most important is being able to do something else." On the one hand, the staff's leisureliness is implicitly condemned by the show, which frames it as laziness and lassitude; at the same time, it is also considered part of what constitutes creative work in a supposedly creative economy. Yet immediately following these scenes, Cheezburger CEO Ben reprimands his staff during their daily morning meeting, holding up a Cheezburger-produced image of a cat napping in front of a computer at an office, captioned with "Work: Where All Your Best Naps Take Place." Ben tells them,

> I know that our job kind of looks like this and I love it. It's fun and games and we're creative and all that, and I totally get it. And I encourage some of this. But, there are things that need to be accomplished, things that we need to be able to deliver because people rely on us to do so, and it's a business. ("Coffee")

The expansion of work into everyday sites that (for some) were formerly not considered spaces of labor has coincided with the "internal collapse of the workspace itself, as the 'bored at work' classes invent new ways to slack off on the job, surfing the web, and otherwise circumventing the necessities of workplace always-on performance" (Galloway 120). Yet in the case of *LOLwork*, I suggest that this ongoing ambiguity between work and play perpetuates an understanding of digital labor as leisure rather than work. When the staff of Cheezburger "surf the web," they are not slacking off. In an economy reliant on creative and immaterial labor, goofing off online is not outside of capitalism; in other words, even their supposed slacking is labor rather than mere distraction.[7]

In her research on self-branding, reality television, and immaterial labor, Alison Hearn argues that television series like *The Hills* model the "ostensibly labor-free world of the attention economy" by showcasing and promoting the commodification of the self, where one's "performance of personality and job-appropriate selfhood" becomes profitable (67–68). Along with programs like

The Real Housewives franchise, forms of reality television "provide templates for the communicative and image skills required for profit-generating self-performance in all sectors of the economy" (64). Similarly, *LOLwork* narrates new forms of affective labor and offers a glimpse into the types of workspaces that require cuteness. These shows represent one side of reality television's enmeshment with neoliberalism and late capitalist subjectification processes. The flip side to shows like *LOLwork* includes the spate of reality programming that constitutes what Ouellette terms "dispossession TV," comprised of shows centered on pawn shops, auto and home repossession, and storage units that "take the logic of self-enterprise to its final conclusion" (71). Such programming, which demonstrates a total disregard for people suffering under neoliberalism, flourished after the 2008 recession when "recessionary profiteering" boomed (72). Reality television thus highlights the ravages of late capitalism while also espousing its benefits as portrayed on *LOLwork*.

To teach his creative team the meaning of hard work and discipline them into better appreciating the business aspect of the site, Cheezburger CEO Ben explains that they will work in advertising for the day. Ever the voice of anti-work critique, Paul tells the camera, "Our assignment is to discover what it feels like to be salespeople. Which means I'll finally figure out one of the factors that killed my grandfather." Similarly, Sarah is resistant to Ben's assignment, remarking, "This is ridiculous. I didn't come here to sell things to people." The rest of the episode focuses on the team's inability to channel their creativity into advertising, with Paul and co-worker Monda spending the day at a pet spa under the guise of researching ad possibilities and building relationships with potential businesses. Paul and Sarah both draw a line between their type of work (as creative, non-exploitative, non-life-threatening) and the material work of selling ads, which is implied by the show to be "real" work. At the end of the episode, team members Ali and Emily go to a farm to film some puppies as content for the site. Delighted by the dogs, Ali is reminded by Emily that they need to focus on getting cute videos rather than get distracted by the puppies. Over shots of Emily and Ali arranging the puppies for photos, Ali exuberantly narrates the puppies' experience, clearly overjoyed to be with the dogs. The fact of capturing cuteness as labor is erased by the pleasure it affords.

For Weeks, one of the defining features of neoliberal and "post-neoliberal regimes" is the inescapable demand "that almost everyone work for wages" despite the fact that a race to the bottom, overwork, and new technologies do not leave sufficient work to go around. Further, "postindustrial production employs workers' minds and hearts as well as their hands, and . . . post-Taylorist labor processes increasingly require the self-management of subjectivity so that attitudes and affective orientations to work will themselves produce value" (31). Cuteness plays a key role here: by making work more bearable, be it via cute animal media (created by Cheezburger) or actual cute animals themselves, as is the case for Ali, cuteness is central to capitalist subjectivity and post-Fordist workspaces.

Daily Dose of Cute

Weeks wants us to think of the workspace as a public site—one where political power might be mobilized and exercised—rather than a private one. She writes, "[T]he willingness to live for and through work renders subjects supremely functional for capitalist purposes" (12). I contend that cuteness is one way to obfuscate work's role as a disciplinary apparatus. Although they provide a means for rebelling from work in small ways, cute animals are also productive for capital, thereby intensifying cute animal media's role as cruel relief. A recent Japanese study found that looking at cute animals not only improved the viewer's mood, but also their work productivity, particularly in tasks requiring careful attention: "Cute features not only make objects more user friendly and approachable, but also induce careful behavioral tendencies in the users, which is beneficial in specific situations, such as driving and office work" (Nittono et al. 7). Cuteness and cute animals are thus the object of scientific inquiry regarding their usefulness to capital. Further, cuteness helps to create affective orientations toward work where one might critique workspaces but never fully launch a critique of the ethos of work itself. In fact, cute animal media routinely feature images or videos of animals themselves "working," often at computers. This anthropomorphic maneuver, while ludic and ostensibly light-hearted, suggests that even animals are subject to

FIGURE 4.2 In the neoliberal labor regime, work extends to everyone, including dogs.

the exigencies of work, and like humans, grumble about it. For example, the #SusieTheBoston image is captioned, "Trying to get her TPS Reports done. Someone has a case of the Mondays."[8]

As Berger contends, the "pettiness of current social practices is *universalized* by being projected onto the animal kingdom" (13). Capitalism and work are naturalized even as many cute animal media captions contain an implicit critique. Similarly, during the first episode of *LOLwork*, the staff are divided into teams and tasked with creating a new webseries for the site. Paired with Paul, Sarah narrates a video of chipmunks eating peanuts with a critique of capitalism: "I'm a man. I'm a *homo sapiens*. I think I'm better than everyone else. And you know what makes me happy? Capitalism. I control all the wealth," at which point she is cut off by Paul, who says, "I'm following you on this, but do you think it's maybe too dark?" Later in the season, Cheezburger's Chief Revenue Officer Todd, notes, "Revolutionary usually isn't good for our business" ("The Show"). The show's page on the Bravo website even features a "re-cat" written from the perspective of Cheezburger employee Will's cat, Winston. The re-cat features stills from the episode with captions questioning the staff's labor. One features an image of Sarah laughing with the caption, "Does not look like work." In another, "We start off this week's episode . . . in the closet? I guess LOLwork isn't always fun work" (BravoTV.com).

Value is thus being extracted from cuteness on at least two levels. First, Cheezburger generates revenue through advertising on its sites as well as from the users who freely provide their own images to the company. By "extracting value from pure information," what we do online is extremely productive for capital. Second, value is also extracted in the affective orientation to work that

FIGURE 4.3 On *LOLwork*, creative work is naturalized through fun.

cuteness helps to provide. For Crary, "Most images are now produced and circulated in the service of maximizing the amount of time spent in habitual forms of individual self-management and self-regulation" (47). Cute animal media offer a means to self-administrate: they assist with productivity and contribute to increased happiness.

The rise of cuteness alongside neoliberal capital works in tandem with the expectation of happiness. Scholars like Sara Ahmed, Barbara Ehrenreich, and William Davies highlight the proliferation of technologies of happiness and the rendering of well-being into a science. As part of the path to such happiness and personal fulfillment, corporations promulgate self-care practices like yoga, meditation, and mindfulness in order to further extract employee labor. The expectation of 24/7 productivity renders mindfulness and meditation necessary for "senior managers" as an antidote to the increasing stress of "always-on digital devices." The expansion of capital is in part responsible for this "explosion of political and business interest in happiness" (Davies 8). This scientific approach to happiness includes cuteness and cute animal media. Urging readers to not feel "guilty for indulging in a daily dose of cuteness," Shana Lebowitz writes that we can "instead think of it as a quick mood- and productivity-booster." Long-running though now defunct website Cute Overload referred to its blog posts as daily "happy pills," underscoring the pathology of unhappiness in a world requiring positivity, particularly vis-à-vis work. Describing ICanHazCheezburger, Ben emphasizes the centrality of happiness to the site: "People come here to escape reality . . . they want to see happy, smiling cats." The introduction to each *LOLwork* episode highlights Cheezburger's motto, "Make people laugh 5 minutes a day." Cuteness provides happiness and functions as a way to inculcate new affective imperatives in contemporary "information workplaces"; namely, that we must love work and that it must make us happy. Indeed, workers are "encouraged to feel a deep emotional attachment to their work" (Moran qtd. in Gregg, "On Friday" 39).

Cute Animal Videos as Cinema of Attractions

In August 2015, "How Cats Took Over the Internet" opened at the Museum of the Moving Image in Queens, New York. In conversation with the Walker Art Center's Internet Cat Video Festival, the exhibition offered a genealogy of the internet's love affair with cats and featured a reel of cat videos from the Walker's festival (Kingson). As briefly discussed in this book's introduction, the Walker's first festival in 2012 drew more than 10,000 viewers and garnered a frenzy of media attention, which fixated in part on the meeting of a degraded and feminized genre—the cat video—with the high art cachet of the Walker Art Center. Notably, the Walker has not claimed cat videos as "high art," but rather, emphasizes the experimental social nature of the festival. Notes festival producer Scott Stulen, "This social aspect is key: the festival isn't just about watching cat videos, because you can do that at home. It was about what's it like to watch cat videos with others" (Schmelzer and Stulen). In this way, the festival points to the relationality of affect, where "emotions are not simply 'within' or 'without'" but rather, "create the very effect of the surfaces of bodies and worlds" (Ahmed, "Affective" 117). Affect circulates, it sticks, it creates, it "sustains or preserves the connection between ideas, values, and objects" (Ahmed, "Happy" 29). At the same time, the festival's relationship to a highbrow institution such as the Walker certainly legitimated (for some) cat videos as cinematic; Tom Gunning's notion of "cinema of attractions" is instructive here.

As Gunning observes, early cinema emphasized exhibition over narration, where filmic techniques themselves were the attraction "and the point of the film" (66). Such "cinema of attractions" is "a cinema that bases itself on . . . its ability to *show* something," and is linked to new experiences of space and time. It is self-conscious, displaying its visibility in order to attract the spectator's attention rather than maintain a fictional world; in this way, spectators are directly addressed by the attraction (Gunning 64). Drawing on Sergei Eisenstein, Gunning notes that attraction "aggressively subjected the spectator to 'sensual or psychological impact,'" which in turn created a relationship to the spectator that emphasized "exhibitionist confrontation rather than diegetic absorption." This exhibitionist quality of early popular art was attractive to the avant-garde (including Eisenstein) because of its "freedom from the creation of a diegesis, its accent on direct stimulation" (Gunning 66). Further, for Eisenstein, such cinema offered the possibility of producing popular energy that could then be directed toward radical ends (Gunning 67). What interests me most about Gunning's theorization is the production of energy or affective excess spurred by exhibitionism. I suggest that a similar type of "stimulus" occurs with cute animal videos, which can be read as a contemporary "cinema of attractions." Although some develop narration (either human or ascribed animal), most cute animal videos emphasize affective connections—a sudden affective pull—between image and viewer.[9] Knowing this, the Walker's festival sought to create affective connections among *humans* via cat videos. In an era of increasing social isolation, the festival implicitly responded to capitalism's capture of affect and emotion by bringing people together, creating community and connection.[10]

Cruel Relief

For Jodi Dean, capitalism's seizure of affect and emotion occurs primarily through communication technologies. This results in what she terms "communicative capitalism," referring to "the materialization of ideals of inclusion and participation in information, entertainment, and communication technologies in ways that capture resistance and intensify global capitalism" (*Democracy* 2). Dean, thus, is highly skeptical of the touted political possibilities of the Internet, particularly the idea that online participation is inherently "good" or useful, or even excessive (and thus potentially a site of rupture) vis-à-vis capital. Whereas scholars like Henry Jenkins view the rise of mediated interactivity and participation as empowering and ripe with democratic possibility, Dean highlights the ways that this participation is easily aligned with neoliberalism and neoconservatism (*Blog* 104). In her work on blogs in particular, Dean draws on psychoanalytic theory to argue that the affective networks of the Internet ensnare us in a continuously moving flow of information and affect.

Cute animal videos are certainly implicated in these affective networks by their contribution to the flow of affects and intensities. A quick glance at the comments on the popular YouTube video of otters "holding hands"—just one iteration of the same video has more than 20 million views—demonstrates the affective pull of the video:

> "Awwww! :) Animals always, always find a way to keep me questioning my own species"

> "I just died from cuteness overload and am currently watching this in the afterlife"

> "this made me cry of [sic] happiness"

> "faith in humanity restored 100%"

> "I was having a bad day when i saw this now im feeling a whole lot better"

> "Almost 20 million views . . . oh the power of cuteness!"

Cute animal videos are imagined as powerful vehicles through which humanity is revived, consoled, and/or healed from the suffering of the day. The affective intensity of the videos is evident in hyperbolic viewer references to dying and crying, both typical rhetorical registers on cute animal video comment sections. Gregg cites Berlant's theorization of precarity as marking a space of "animated suspension" wherein people struggle to "gain a footing" ("On Friday" 252). As cruel relief, cute animal videos momentarily stabilize the suspended-ness of precarity.

Otters "holding hands" provides a moment's reprieve that can be continued by moving on to the next video, conveniently available in YouTube's sidebar. This endless movement locks "mediated subjects" into feedback loops, which for Dean are best understood as the "circuits of drive." Central to this process is the imperative to enjoy, and the anxiety that results when we are reminded, as Dean writes, "that we aren't enjoying enough, as much, or as well as others are." This attendant anxiety is also entangled with enjoyment, as affect is bound up with the flow in a process that "is intense; it draws us in" (*Blog* 92; see also Joshua

Paul Dale's chapter in this volume). Networks such as blogs and social networking sites are key contributors to the circulation of affect, which operates in this context as a binding technique. In the never-ending flow of communication (comments, likes, Tweets), a surplus of affect is produced for each moment—"a smidgen of attention that attaches to it"—which enables it to stand out before it becomes once again swept up in the wave. The resulting "affective networks" are not productive of actual community but rather *feelings* of community that circulate intensities we might trace (Dean, *Blog* 95–96).[11]

The common responses to cute animal media reveal such affective intensities. For example, 1) a mock-angry tone chastising the animal for "being so cute" and thus eliciting such an affective response. This is also evident in comments about visceral responses to the cuteness, e.g., vomiting, as exemplified by a comment on Internet celebrity Hamlet the tiny pig: "I am basically dying right now because of Hamlet. I am so in love with him and with his name I think I might throw up" (Conaboy); 2) declarations of happiness, joy, pleasure, e.g., BuzzFeed Animals's "25 Animal GIFs That Will Warm Your Cold, Dead Heart: It's time to let yourself feel joy again. Let these animals help you" (Shepherd); and 3) expressions of new-found faith in humanity, a response that points to what Chris has identified as a "zoomorphic" framework for understanding animals, wherein we look to animals to learn about ourselves. This has broadly shifted from an anthropomorphic view, although both are evident in the responses to cute animal media. The underlying presumption of each of these responses is that cute animal imagery softens and relieves hardened or emotionally numb humans. The supposed irresistibility of "adorable animals" is a guaranteed emotional salve (Adam Davis).

Although materials certainly travel through the web because they are meaningful to those who spread them, this circulation is outside neither capital nor Dean's affective circuits of drive. As she makes clear, networked communications and the attendant expansion of communicative capitalism thrive on interactivity and participation—indeed, "communicative capitalism fetishizes speech, opinion, and participation" (17). Any consideration of longevity, corporate influence, access, and "the narrowing of political struggle to the standards of do-it-yourself entertainment culture" is dismissed as outmoded and irrelevant (Dean, *Democracy* 17). The affective dimensions of the Internet work to keep us trapped in an ever-expanding flow of information *that we create* and that dangles enjoyment in front of us even as we are, in part, enjoying the process. Even as the flow makes us anxious, we get caught up in it and simultaneously derive pleasure from it.

Such enjoyment, I suggest, is connected to the productivist ethos of late capitalism, where the Internet's affective flow helps to maintain the regime of work. Dean herself fleetingly considers the affective pull of cute animal media, asking why people engage with and circulate "cute" and "funny" animal photos and videos. For her, this circulation happens not just "because cats are cute" but because of the affective ties to the imagery:

It's that the feeling that the cuteness accesses, the feeling that moves it, opens to something more, to a kind of beyond or potential. The dimension of affect is this "more than a feeling" that imparts movement. The potential here may be for connection (though one should be careful not to reduce affect to the intentions of the subject sending cute cat photos) but not necessarily—anyone who uses email knows how annoying forwarded cuteness can actually be . . . They all provide momentary, even fleeting, charges and intensities, interruptions and divergences. (*Blog* 115–16)

These momentary divergences are then folded back into the flow of information, thereby eradicating any possibility for rising above the rush of continuous circulation. In such fashion, Dean is pointing to the ways that joy and other pleasurable emotions are always already a part of capital.

But what of these charges and intensities? There is something more at work here than Dean argues—namely, the cruel relief of these affective charges offers ephemeral respite. The *Huffington Post*'s cute animals page provides an example of how cute animal media operate in affective capitalist networks.[12] The videos include titles like "Puppies Versus Stairs: Facing Off for the First Time" and "13 Adorable Cats 'Boxing'" and are updated daily. An "about" box explains the page thus:

There's nothing that can brighten a day quite like seeing a cute animal. Heartwarming stories about cute animals have ranged from a pit bull in love with a bunny, to a penguin being tickled . . . If you can spare to squeeze a few minutes of procrastination into your day, take a moment to enjoy one of the simpler pleasures in this world . . . cute animals. ("Cute Animals")

Here, the *Huffington Post* points to the ways cute animals are deployed for cheer and for uplifting procrastination, making plain the relationship between cute animal videos and work. Cute animals offer respite from the drudgery of 9–5 both in the procrastination the videos offer and in the momentary pleasure derived from seeing a cute animal. Thus, they become a significant tool of maintaining labor precarity. Moreover, as an article titled "Dog Taking a Shower Will Wash Away Your Stressful Work Week" suggests, cute animal videos can erase the stressors of labor, thus enhancing the function of capital (Jamieson). Workers will work more if they feel better.

On the "cute animal videos" page, the headlines reveal an implicit acknowledgment of how cute animals offer (cruel) relief. Described in terms of the comfort they provide, the videos include: "Lamb Hops Down the Hallway, Makes Everything Better in 6 Seconds"; "When this Baby White Rhino Gallops, Everything Feels Right in the World"; "Goose Does a Happy Dance, Probably Because it's Friday." Once again, work rhetoric captions the video. Cute animal videos are heavily promoted through witty, wry headlines and captions that point to an awareness of the ongoing present of "systemic crisis" (Berlant 10); they thus go hand in hand with an acknowledgment of neoliberalism's devastations.

Conclusion

At a moment when labor is precarious, policing is expansive, and mass extinction is occurring, seeking momentary relief via the tools most readily available to many of us—digital ones—makes sense as a way to cope with the conflation of work and leisure and the alienation and hyper-individualization of late capitalist life. Even media consumption has become more and more isolated, as viewing has moved from the public space of the movie theater to the family home to the "singular person strolling down the street wearing tiny headphones" (Dean, *Democracy* 4). I have argued here that the mechanism of cruel relief associated with the consumption of cute animal media symbolically ameliorates the exigencies of neoliberal work. Nevertheless other, perhaps more socially optimistic, prospects hover within reach. For instance, the Internet Cat Video Festival plays with the form of the cute animal video by making it a "social experiment" to encourage physical togetherness, going beyond cruel relief and possibly opening space to imagine alternatives to neoliberalism. The joys of cuteness and the relationality of affect may yet offer us a glimpse at another way to organize the world.

Notes

1 Jacquelyn Arcy has traced how these forms of feminized labor take place on the Bravo reality television series, *The Real Housewives of New York*.
2 In addition, Michael Moore opens *Capitalism: A Love Story* (2009) by attributing the imminent demise of the United States to a video of cats flushing toilets.
3 Several comments on the short refer to it as the "first cat video." See www.youtube.com/watch?v=k52pLvVmmkU.
4 See Klein; Harvey; Duggan; Alexander; Hong; Roy.
5 Cornel West, Lecture, Smith College, February 11, 2016.
6 John Oliver has used this maneuver on more than one occasion. As a reward for sticking with a February 2016 segment on abortion rights, Oliver showed viewers a video of baby sloths in a bucket. See Locker.
7 For critiques of digital labor's productivity for capital, see Terranova.
8 See also: www.thatcutesite.com/15-pictures-of-animals-working-on-computers/; http://omgcutethings.com/2013/11/06/animals-getting-sweat/.
9 Radha O'Meara has detailed how dog videos in particular rely on exhibitionism and similar modes of spectatorship to Gunning's "cinema of attractions." For O'Meara, cat videos "employ a unique mode of observation" because cats are indifferent to the camera's gaze. This, in turn, produces an "aesthetic of surveillance without inhibition," a rarity in an era where humans are aware of pervasive surveillance.
10 On the broader issue of technology and social isolation, see Turkle.
11 Workplaces are increasingly articulated as sites of community comprised of teams (e.g., Lululemon, Netflix) or even families. Thanks to Diane Negra for alerting me to this point.

12 I chose to focus on this site because the *Huffington Post* is considered a news source
rather than exclusively a site devoted to cute animals. A user can click from an article
about police violence to an image of a raccoon eating cat food.

Works Cited

Ahmed, Sara. "Affective Economies." *Social Text* 79 (2004): 117–39.
——. "Happy Objects." *The Affect Theory Reader.* Eds. Melissa Gregg and Gregory J.
Seigworth. Durham, NC: Duke University Press, 2010. 29–51.
Alexander, Michelle. *The New Jim Crow: Mass Incarceration in the Age of Colorblindness.* New
York: New Press, 2010.
Arcy, Jacquelyn. "Affective Enterprising: Branding the Self through Emotional Excess."
The Fantasy of Reality: Critical Essays on The Real Housewives. Ed. Rachel Silverman. New
York: Peter Lang, 2015.
Berger, John. "Why Look at Animals?" *About Looking.* New York: Pantheon, 1980. 3–28.
Berlant, Lauren. *Cruel Optimism.* Durham, NC: Duke University Press, 2011.
BravoTV.com. "Winston's Episode 6 Re-Cat." Online. 19 Nov. 2015.
Capitalism: A Love Story. 2009. Writ., Dir., Perf. Michael Moore. Dog Eat Dog-Weinstein,
2010. DVD.
"Career Day." *LOLwork.* Bravo. 14 Nov. 2012. Television.
Chris, Cynthia. *Watching Wildlife.* Minneapolis, MN: University of Minnesota Press,
2006.
"Coffee is for Closers." *LOLwork.* Bravo. 28 Nov. 2012. Television.
Conaboy, Kelly. "The Petting Zoo: The Week's Top 10 Animal Videos." *Videogum.com.*
1 Feb. 2012. Online. 25 Sept. 2015.
Crary, Jonathan. *24/7: Late Capitalism and the Ends of Sleep.* New York: Verso, 2013.
"Cute Animals." *Huffington Post.* Huffington Post, 13 Jan. 2016. Online.
Davies, William. *The Happiness Industry: How the Government and Big Business Sold Us Well-
Being.* New York: Verso, 2015.
Davis, Adam. "The BuzzFeed Animals Newsletter Will Turn Your Frown Upside Down."
BuzzFeed.com, 27 March 2016. Online. April 1, 2016.
Davis, Angela. *Women, Race, and Class.* New York: Random House, 1981.
Dean, Jodi. *Democracy and Other Neoliberal Fantasies: Communicative Capitalism and Left Politics.*
Durham, NC: Duke University Press, 2009.
——. *Blog Theory: Feedback and Capture in the Circuits of Drive.* Cambridge: Polity, 2010.
Duggan, Lisa. *The Twilight of Equality? Neoliberalism, Cultural Politics, and the Attack on
Democracy.* Boston, MA: Beacon, 2003.
Ehrenreich, Barbara. *Bright-Sided: How Positive Thinking is Undermining America.* New York:
Metropolitan, 2009.
Galloway, Alexander. "Does the Whatever Speak?" *Race After the Internet.* Eds. Lisa
Nakamura and Peter A. Chow-White. New York: Routledge, 2012. 111–27.
Genzlinger, Neil. "On Films and TV, Cats and Dogs Playing Cute." *New York Times,* 23
July 2010. Online. 13 Sept. 2014.
Graeber, David. *The Utopia of Rules: On Technology, Stupidity, and the Secret Joys of
Bureaucracy.* Brooklyn, NY: Melville House, 2015.
Granot, Elad, Thomas Brashear Alejandro, and La Toya Russell. "A Socio-Marketing
Analysis of the Concept of *Cute* and its Consumer Culture Implications." *Journal of
Consumer Culture* 14.1 (2014): 66–87.

Gregg, Melissa. "On Friday Night Drinks: Workplace Affects in the Age of the Cubicle." *The Affect Theory Reader*. Eds. Melissa Gregg and Gregory Seigworth. Durham, NC: Duke University Press, 2010. 250–68.

——. *Work's Intimacy*. Cambridge: Polity, 2011.

Gunning, Tom. "The Cinema of Attraction[s]: Early Film, Its Spectator, and the Avant-Garde." *Wide Angle* 8 (1986): 63–70.

Hall, Ellie. "This Baby Sloth Will Remind You to Never Give Up." *Buzzfeed.com*. 9 Sept. 2015. Online. 21 Sept. 2015.

Harris, Daniel. *Cute, Quaint, Hungry, and Romantic: The Aesthetics of Consumerism*. New York: Basic, 2000.

Harvey, David. *A Brief History of Neoliberalism*. New York: Oxford University Press, 2005.

Hearn, Alison. "Reality Television, *The Hills*, and the Limits of the Immaterial Labor Thesis." *tripleC* 8.1 (2010): 60–76.

Hochschild, Arlie. *The Second Shift: Working Families and the Revolution at Home*. New York: Penguin, 1989.

Hong, Grace Kyungwon. *The Ruptures of American Capital: Women of Color Feminism and the Culture of Immigrant Labor*. Minneapolis, MN: University of Minnesota Press, 2006.

Jamieson, Amy. "Funny Video: Dog Taking a Shower Will Wash Away Your Stressful Work Week." *People*. Time Inc., 3 Oct. 2014. Online. 15 Aug. 2015.

Jenkins, Henry. Interview with Tara McPherson. "Bringing Critical Perspectives to the Digital Humanities, Part One." *Confession of an Aca-Fan*. Weblog. 16 Mar. 2015. Online. 31 Oct. 2015.

Jenkins, Henry, Xiaochang Li, and Ana Domb Krauskopf. *If It Doesn't Spread, It's Dead: Creating Value in a Spreadable Marketplace*. MIT: Convergence Culture Consortium, 2011.

Keogh, Justine. "5 Reasons Why Animals Make the Internet a Better Place." *Broadband Mart*. Weblog. 14 June 2013. Online. 15 Nov. 2015.

Klein, Naomi. *This Changes Everything: Capitalism vs. the Climate*. New York: Simon and Schuster, 2014.

Kingson, Jennifer. " 'How Cats Took Over the Internet' at the Museum of the Moving Image." *New York Times*. 6 Aug. 2015. Online. 15 Feb. 2016.

Lamar, Cyriaque. "Even in the 1870s, Humans were Obsessed with Ridiculous Photos of Cats." *io9.com*. 9 Apr. 2012. Online. 13 July 2014.

Last Week Tonight with John Oliver. HBO. Season 1, episode 2. 4 May 2014. Television.

Lazzarato, Maurizio. "Immaterial Labor." Trans. Paul Colilli and Ed Emery. *Radical Thought in Italy: A Potential Politics*. Eds. Michael Hardt and Paolo Virno. Minneapolis, MN: University of Minnesota Press, 1996. 133–47.

Lebowitz, Shana. "Why Buzzfeed's Cute Animals Turn Us Into Click-Happy Zombies." *Greatist.com*. 16 Aug. 2013. Online. 5 Nov. 2015.

Locker, Melissa. "John Oliver Tackles Abortion on *Last Week Tonight* (With the Help of Some Sloths)." *Time.com*. 22 Feb. 2016. Online. 26 Mar. 2016.

McRobbie, Angela. "Reflections on Feminism, Immaterial Labor and the Post-Fordist Regime." *New Formations* 70 (2011): 60–76.

——. *Be Creative: Making a Living in the New Culture Industries*. Malden, MA: Polity, 2016.

Morozov, Evegyny. *The Net Delusion: The Dark Side of Internet Freedom*. New York: Public Affairs, 2011.

Ngai, Sianne. "The Cuteness of the Avant-Garde." *Critical Inquiry* 31.4 (2005): 811–47.

Nittono, Hiroshi, et al. "The Power of *Kawaii*: Viewing Cute Images Promotes a Careful Behavior and Narrows Attentional Focus." *Plos One* 7.9 (2012). Online. 1 Feb. 2016.

Nyong'o, Tavia. "Situating Precarity Between the Body and the Commons." *Women and Performance: A Journal of Feminist Theory* 23.2 (2013): 157–61.

O'Meara, Radha. "Do Cats Know They Rule YouTube? Surveillance and the Pleasures of Cat Videos." *M/C Journal* 17.2 (2014). Online. 9 Feb. 2016.

omgcutethings.com. http://omgcutethings.com/2013/11/06/animals-getting-sweat/.

Ouellette, Laurie. *Lifestyle TV.* New York: Routledge, 2016.

Ouellette, Laurie and Julie Wilson. "Women's Work: Affective Labor and Convergence Culture." *Cultural Studies* 25 (2011): 548–65.

Rose, Nikolas. "Governing the Enterprising Self." *The Values of the Enterprise Culture: The Moral Debate.* Eds. Paul Heelas and Paul Morris. New York: Routledge, 1992. 141–64.

Ross, Andrew. *No-Collar: The Humane Workplace and Its Hidden Costs.* New York: Basic, 2003.

Roy, Arundhati. *Capitalism: A Ghost Story.* Chicago, IL: Haymarket, 2014.

Schmelzer, Paul, and Scott Stulen. "The Nine Lives of the Internet Cat Video Festival." *Walker Art Center Magazine*, 28 Aug. 2013. Online. 10 Sept. 2015.

Shepherd, Jack. "25 Animal GIFs That Will Warm Your Cold Dead Heart." *BuzzFeed.com.* 4 Sept. 2014. Online. 30 Sept. 2015.

Smaller, Barbara. "Daily Cartoon: It's Finally Happened. They've Replaced the Nightly News with Cat Videos." *New Yorker.* 21 Mar. 2014. Online. 28 Nov. 2015.

Stark, Luke, and Kate Crawford. "The Conservatism of Emoji: Work, Affect, and Communication." *Social Media and Society* (2015): 1–11.

Terranova, Tiziana. "Free Labor: Producing Culture for the Digital Economy." *Social Text* 18.2 63 (2000): 33–58.

thatcutesite.com. www.thatcutesite.com/15-pictures-of-animals-working-on-computers/.

"The Show Must Go On!" *LOLwork.* Bravo. 7 Nov. 2012. Television.

Turkle, Sherry. *Alone Together: Why We Expect More from Technology and Less from Each Other.* New York: Basic, 2012.

Weeks, Kathi. *The Problem with Work: Feminism, Marxism, Antiwork Politics, and Postwork Imaginaries.* Durham, NC: Duke University Press, 2011.

West, Cornel. Lecture on Black History Month. Smith College. February 11, 2016.

Widdicombe, Ben. "What Happens When Millennials Run the Workplace?" *The New York Times*, 19 Mar. 2016. Online. 26 Mar. 2016.

Zimmerman Neetzan. "And So It Begins: Internet Cat Video Film Festival to Take Place Next Month in Minneapolis." Gawker.com, 10 July 2012. Online. 15 Oct. 2015.

5

"I'LL BE DANCIN'"

American Soldiers, Cute YouTube Performances, and the Deployment of Soft Power in the War on Terror

Maria Pramaggiore

A popular YouTube genre has emerged in which US military personnel restage music videos by Lady Gaga and Beyoncé ("Telephone"), Carly Rae Jepsen ("Call Me Maybe"), Ke$ha ("Blah Blah Blah"), Taylor Swift ("Shake it Off"), and others. These remix parodies, which originate in the combat theaters of Iraq and Afghanistan, are disseminated to millions of online viewers around the world, and the representational mode of cuteness they employ speaks to a number of social and political concerns. This chapter examines the global dynamics of US masculinity as exemplified by these videos: while these remixes seem to amplify anxieties associated with the precarity of twenty-first-century soldiering, they may also serve a potentially strategic purpose. Their often comic gender and sexual provocations resonate with official propaganda that justifies the US War on Terror through a starkly drawn dualism pitting a secular, enlightened, and egalitarian West against a patriarchal Islam whose oppressed women are in desperate need of rescue. The videos display a distinctive historical, geographical, and aesthetic trajectory. There are two generations of work: the earliest videos emerged around 2005 and tend to be located in Iraq rather than Afghanistan, which coincides with the logistics of the two wars in those countries, as the withdrawal of US troops from Iraq began at the end of 2007.

The early cohort of Iraq videos (2005–10) tends to cover male rap, rock, and reggae artists such as Eddy Grant and Vanilla Ice. First-generation videos include performances of "Eye of the Tiger" (Caholo, 2006); "Dance Party in Iraq" (MasterFX 2000, 2007), which includes both "Electric Avenue" (Eddy Grant) and "What a Feeling" (Irene Cara); and "Ice Ice Baby" (Iam918, 2007), songs possibly chosen because of lyrical references pertaining to the lives of soldiers. These videos are not invested in recreating the original music video in terms of choreography, sets, or costuming, as the more ambitious second-generation videos tend to do. They often betray a self-consciousness about the ambiguous sexuality that their remixing might imply.

The remake of Ke$ha's "Blah Blah Blah" (Doughty) signals a transition from the earlier cycle. Made in 2010, when the "Don't Ask, Don't Tell" policy was rescinded, the video is entitled "If the Army Goes Gay" and its performers overtly cite "gays in the military" in its opening moments. This introduction establishes the pretext for a series of shots of gyrating male soldiers who overtly court sexual objectification, enacting and embracing straight fears regarding the repositioning of men on the gender hierarchy. The comments uploaded on the video's YouTube page by its makers, "Codey Wilson and his elite step team of volunteers," include a pre-emptive appeal to critics and an apparently unwitting citation of the Tom Cruise vehicle *A Few Good Men* (1992), a citation that calls forth further associations with Cruise's earlier military-themed film *Top Gun* (1986), important for both its music video aesthetic and homoerotic subtext. Wilson's comments express a strategic ambivalence regarding gender and sexual politics as well as a defensive recourse to "political correctness":

> Don't give us a hard time for this, please? We're just a few good men trying to enjoy ourselves and get this deployment over with. No one is gay that we know of. Not that there is anything wrong with that! (political correctness). (Doughty)

A second wave of remix videos (2010–) relocates the action from Iraq to Afghanistan, recirculates female and genderqueer pop stars rather than rap or rock artists, and shifts from broad, laddish comedy to painstaking parody with intentional choreography and precise racial correspondences. Examples include "Telephone: The Afghanistan Remake" (malibumelcher), from 2010, a video that has garnered more than seven million views, a 2013 reenactment of the Miami Dolphins Cheerleaders' cover version of the Carly Rae Jepsen hit "Call Me Maybe" (YouTube Multiplier) with more than three million, and a 2014 video of a group of Marines singing along with the ubiquitous anthem "Let It Go" (itsMRich) from Disney's *Frozen* (2013).[1] The latter is not technically a remix: in it, Marines sing along over the original version, matching word for word, and inflection for inflection, enthusiastically projecting the affect of an audience of young girls. Although sung in the film by Elsa, a young adult character, "Let it Go" quickly became the province of online cuteness culture after parents began posting videos of their children's precocious versions of it. Capitalizing on that wave, the *Sun* in Britain and the *Huffington Post* in the US hosted online singalong competitions, generating endless cute compilation videos for all to enjoy.

A number of scholars have convincingly demonstrated that the American soldier embodies, informs, and reproduces cultural norms of hegemonic masculinity (Hooper; Connell; Barrett; Ehrenreich), which makes the apparent playfulness around gender in these videos, with male soldiers adopting the personas of women pop stars and fans, particularly compelling. Are these cute performances evidence that the humble male foot soldier—the grunt—has internalized Judith Butler's iconic notion of gender performativity and now enthusiastically participates in exposing the social construction of gender and sexual binaries? Or should we tread carefully, paying heed to the observations of gender and media studies scholar Yvonne Tasker, who argues against the facile interpretation of the action hero of 1980s cinema as a "*simplistic* embodiment of a reactionary masculine identity" (109, emphasis in original). She continues,

> Though masculinities are bisected and experienced through a range of differences, feminist film criticism often seems to map onto the cinema a peculiarly heightened narrative of male power and female powerlessness. It is in this sense that the eroticized male body comes to be critically spoken of as "feminized." (116)

In keeping with Tasker's injunction, it is important to examine the historical, generic, and textual contexts in which these male bodies appear. These are music videos, not narrative films, and they complexly eroticize the dancing male soldier body as they remix original works that exploit unconventional genders and sexualities. "Telephone," named best video of the decade by Billboard, is a paean to Quentin Tarantino's femme-fueled aesthetic of violence and pairs powerhouse performers Lady Gaga and Beyoncé; in it, overt reference is made to rumors of Lady Gaga's status as intersex. In Carly Rae Jepsen's "Call Me Maybe," a smash hit whose immense popularity was synonymous with numerous fan-made remixes (including one made by Justin Bieber and Selena Gomez), Jepsen's aggressive pursuit of an attractive man concludes with him indicating his preference for her male bandmate.

Gender and sexuality are central to the military remixes. The vast majority of the videos feature men and thus reassert the masculine character of militarized space despite—or because of—the 2012 rollback of the combat exclusion policy that barred women from the front lines. The performers are individuated, and yet they bear the marks of soldier conformity, communicated through their uniforms, tattoos, and hairstyles. These are not the cinematic bodies of movie stars but rather demotic digital bodies with ordinary, everyday features. The videos have less to do with shoring up celebrity personas and more to do with a critique of life in the military, as they offer a glimpse of its peculiar dialectic of boredom and danger. In what may be the ultimate act of defiance of soldierly expectations, the remix videos depict fit and disciplined male bodies that are at the same time unruly, as they persist in dancing on YouTube rather than taking seriously their duty of fighting, or supporting the fighting, in Afghanistan.

These remixes obey the logic of the viral music video. Maura Edmond notes that, in the YouTube era, music videos have become a dialogic, conversational hub around which a wide variety of mashups and remakes take place, which address a growing audience extremely literate not only in music video aesthetics but also in the rhetoric of parody, remixes, and fan cultural productions (314).

They rise to Jean Burgess's standard of spreadable content because they act as a "hub for further creative activity by a wide range of participants in the social network" (102) using "textual hooks and key signifiers" (105). Dozens of videos from the US military and that of other nations, such as Israel, participate in this network of creative remixing. Several videos have been produced at the Air Force and Naval Academies, moving the locus of activity away from the field of combat. After the "Call Me Maybe" military remix circulated, a Harvard fraternity produced a close parody as a sorority recruitment video. Within the military videos, key signifiers associated with the suburban teenager's YouTube vlog are replaced with the mise-en-scène of the combat film and video game: makeshift particle-board living structures, desert camouflage clothing, and a nonchalant familiarity with sophisticated weapons.

These macho military men display cuteness in action. Perhaps more than their appearance or abilities, the soldiers' committed homage to the work of women pop performers contributes to the potential charm of these videos. Comments left on YouTube pages suggest that viewers do find them charming: in 2016, Robert Byars wrote "the cheerleaders have the looks but the military has the moves . . . I call it even" (YouTube Multiplier). The performances transmit the soldiers' admiration as much as appropriation, while indicating their physical fitness as well as their resourcefulness in designing choreography, decorating sets, and conjuring up costumes.

The work of philosopher Graham Harman offers one way of understanding how such performances evoke the aesthetics of cuteness. Harman proposes a notion of cute incompetence, which helpfully moves beyond Konrad Lorenz's emphasis on the visual proportions of infancy (large eyes, large head) delineated elsewhere in this volume. Harman writes:

> certain actions are performed by certain worldly agents with a regularity and ease devoid of any hesitation. Horses gallop, donkeys eat, humans write letters, and native speakers of a language use it fluently. The labors of such agents become "cute" when they are slightly underequipped for their task: a newborn horse trying to prance on its skinny, awkward legs; a sweet little donkey trying to eat a big pile of hay with its sweet little mouth and tongue; a child handing us a thank-you note with imperfect grammar. (142)

Harman's binary of competence and incompetence is ultimately difficult to sustain, however. In the military remix videos, soldiers are cute when they approximate yet fail to fully perform the finer points of femininity, which is the case in "Telephone: The Afghanistan Remake" video. Uniformed soldiers with bulky muscles and enthusiastic, yet plodding dance moves trudge through the song with a ham-fisted dedication until a break halfway through that cuts to a large hangar where the soldier stand-in for Beyoncé and a number of campily dressed dancers gyrate wildly against a background of tacky, surreal wall decorations. Although modeled on the two-part original, the form of this 2010 video in some ways anticipates the "Harlem Shake" viral craze of 2013 (Keating).

In other videos, cuteness emerges when the soldiers match or exceed the codes of femininity: this is apparent in "Call Me Maybe." (See Figure 5.1.) The split-screen version of this video enables viewers to compare the Miami Dolphin cheerleaders' version of the Jepsen song to the meticulously observed parody produced by the soldiers in Afghanistan: background foliage in the former becomes green smoke in the latter; underwater shots are remade in outdoor showers. Competence is demonstrated through dance moves and camera moves: camera operators duplicate exact shot angles, while performers recreate the most minute gestures. There's a world of difference between these two videos, made in 2010 and 2014, respectively, in terms of costumes, sets, choreography, and production values. The short gestures and brief cuts of the "Call Me Maybe" video embody the GIF aesthetic more than the music video form.[2] Over the course of a few years, US soldier-fans have improved their technical competence and their physical skills at female pop star mimicry in equal measure. This may reflect the fact that, on a twenty-first-century battlefield populated by drones, autonomous weapons, and/or robot soldiers, mastering modes of technology such as videography is at least as important as, and threatens to become indistinguishable from, disciplining the human body through choreography.[3]

FIGURE 5.1 Shot-for-shot matching in "Call Me Maybe" highlights the soldiers' meticulously-observed parody.

These soldiers' cute performances turn on two axes, both of which are associated with hierarchical power dynamics. The first hierarchy involves gender: in the remixes, adult men across a spectrum of sexualities engage in mocking or parodying femininity in modes that are clearly meant to be playful, non-threatening, and non-violent, a move that invokes psychologists' Gary D. Sherman and Jonathan Haidt's conception of cuteness as "a mechanism that releases sociality" (4). The second axis is defined by the hierarchical organization of the military, which situates this gender play among the foot soldiers and support personnel prosecuting the US War on Terror. All volunteers, some of the men may have joined up after 9/11 as part of a modest uptick in patriotic enlistment (Dao), but the larger surge came during the recession in 2008. They occupy the lowest rungs on the military ladder and their fates rest in the hands of the policy-makers in Washington and the tacticians whose orders they are obliged to follow.

The complex cultural work of these remix videos takes place at the inter-section of two instances of hierarchy—gender and rank—and offers a compelling example of authority cuteness, as theorized by Brian McVeigh. Authority cute-ness articulates a dynamic of vulnerability and power that "effectively combines weakness, submissiveness, and humility with influence, domination, and control" (McVeigh 292). Drawing upon the work of McVeigh and that of feminist philosophers Bonnie Mann and Robin James, I consider the cute performances in these remix videos within the history of military drag and within the post-9/11 context, arguing that, while their dance-fueled play with gender and sexuality may challenge military hierarchies and raise concerns about the human costs of soldiering, it also shores up the government and media discourses that seek to present gender relations in the US as enlightened so as to justify military intervention as allegedly motivated by the ethical obligation to rescue women oppressed by Islam. Finally, I explore the linkages between these embodied expressions and US foreign policy, contending that the videos contribute to the deployment of "soft power" in the War on Terror.

Soldier Drag

Male soldiers performing as women is nothing new. Although a good deal of mid-twentieth-century Americana was spun from the heteronormatively whole-some United Service Organizations (USO) and its staging of patriotic militarism featuring acts like Bob Hope and Ann-Margret, the US military is no stranger to gender trouble. The military's gender nonconformity has begun to emerge in the wake of the 2010 rescission of the "Don't Ask Don't Tell" policy; however, ignorance of and open hostility toward soldier drag lingers in media commentary. When gay and lesbian soldiers put on a drag king and queen charity performance at Kadena AFB on Okinawa in March 2014, *Stars and Stripes*, the official newspaper of the US military, mistakenly reported that this was the first drag show held on an American military base (Tritten), and the conservative website

Freedom Outpost decried the soldiers as "hapless queens," characteristically linking soldier sexuality to geopolitical brinksmanship: "is there any wonder why Putin thumbs his nose at Obama?" (Brock).

In fact, American soldiers stationed in Okinawa during WWII took to the stage in 1941 for a drag burlesque revue featuring Tony Starr that was later written up in *Pacific Stars and Stripes*. At Fort Slocum on Long Island, a cross-dressing performance of "Swing Fever" was filmed and featured in a 1942 Universal Newsreel. Decades before these performances, drag was common among soldiers. "World War I was marked by an unprecedented efflorescence of cross-dressing in institutionalized military performance," according to David Boxwell (5). In *Soldiers of Song*, Jason Wilson documents concert parties among Canadian, British, American, and Australian soldiers, and Alon Rachamimov identifies forty-six German-language theaters in Russian POW camps that staged productions in which male soldiers played women characters.

One critical transmedial signifier of the importance of these drag perform-ances—one that we will encounter again in relation to the Iraq and Afghanistan videos—is their migration into media. The movement from the stage of POW camps to the screens of modern mass culture reinforces the centrality of these wartime experiences, converting them into cultural memory through popular entertainment. The traces of drag practices haunt Jean Renoir's classic film *La Grande Illusion* (1938) most prominently in the figure of Maisonneuve, but also in the recourse that the protagonist Maréchal makes to cross-dressing as a means of escaping the POW camp.

Marjorie Garber has argued that the history of military cross-dressing "attests to a complicated interplay of forces, including male bonding, acknowledged and unacknowledged homosexual identity, carnivalized power relations, the erotics of same-sex communities, and the apparent safety afforded by theatrical represen-tation" (55–56). Garber's "complicated interplay" and "carnivalized power relations" suggest the ways in which cute military performances in YouTube videos might be both unsettling to the American military—as threats to hierarchies based on gender—and at the same time tolerated as a "healthy" way for men to bond with one another and manage stress in a pressurized environment. When "Telephone: The Afghanistan Remake" went viral in 2010, Sgt. Aaron Melcher, the mechanic stationed in western Farah province with the 4th Brigade Combat Team of the 82nd Airborne who had created the video, reported that his superior officers saw it as a "morale booster" ("No Security Concerns"). Major Michelle Baldanza, the official spokesperson for the 4th Brigade, conveyed the same message in an email to McClatchy Newspapers. "The soldiers have a challenging mission there, and they were just having a good time and blowing off some steam in their downtime," she wrote (Fisher). Baldanza quashed speculation about breaches of security: "They did nothing illegal, immoral or unethical and the video did not violate our operational security at all" ("No Security Concerns"). One can only speculate as to whether the "top brass" in the military truly consider these videos to be good for morale, to be a useful tool in the War on Terror—potentially capturing hearts and minds abroad as well as garnering support for the troops at home—or merely find it impossible to control their circulation.

Authority Cuteness: Sex and Gender, Power and Danger

Within contexts of military and geopolitical power dynamics, the videos enact a brand of authority cuteness designed to mask the use of power within hierarchical organizations: "those in positions of power convince those below them they are in fact not intimidating" (McVeigh 299). Soldiers deployed in Iraq and Afghanistan, particularly those in support functions such as the mechanic shop that produced the "Telephone" remake, are subject to a rigid chain of command. As "boots on the ground," in the synecdochic parlance of the Department of Defense, they aren't even complete bodies, much less human beings in charge of their own fate. On the other hand, they are the foot soldiers enacting and enforcing American military dominance. McVeigh's analysis is applicable: "on the one hand [cuteness] reinforces vertical relations [. . .] but on the other it strengthens the notions that those in inferior positions require and need care and empathy from those in authority" (308). He aptly points out that "[c]uteness . . . effectively combines weakness, submissiveness, and humility with influence, domination, and control" (McVeigh 292).

The US soldier's low status within the chain of command in no way obviates his or her ability to enact deadly force against those "below"—particularly against civilians and combatants in occupied territories. Documented civilian deaths in Iraq after the 2003 invasion number 150,000 (Iraq Body Count); in Afghanistan the figure is 92,000 ("Costs of War"). These remix videos may seek to temper the violent threat of soldiering, soliciting viewers in the US as the audience for caretaking activities because the US population remains the ultimate (if largely symbolic) authority over the military, as manifested in the Defense Department's civilian leadership. US viewers of these soldier videos, watching their sons, brothers, fathers, and boyfriends enjoying gender-bending viral ventriloquism may experience the deployment of cuteness quite differently than people living in countries in which the world's dominant military power is actively engaged in combat operations.

The videos strategically allude to and mask the work of the soldier, sometimes employing gendered visual puns. Early in "Telephone: The Afghanistan Remake," an automatic rifle can be seen resting on the ground, as if the high-tech weapon has been tossed aside temporarily and forgotten amidst the rigorous body-focused acrobatics of the choreography. In "Call Me Maybe," the split-screen aesthetic juxtaposes the sexual allure invoked by close-ups of a Miami Dolphin cheerleader's hips with the matched shot of an artillery belt on a soldier's hips (see Figure 5.2). In subsequent shots, "Call Me Maybe" draws a comparison between the cheerleader's harmless weapons—pom-poms—and those of the soldiers—exploding mortars.

FIGURE 5.2 Aesthetic juxtaposition playfully conflates sexuality with destructive capability in "Call Me Maybe."

The videos may succeed in creating a sense of intimacy for American viewers because they are (among other things) a digital age's version of letters home. They follow in the tradition of Victory Mail during WWII and the Voices from Home audio recording program during the Vietnam War. To Americans, repeatedly enjoined to "support the troops" regardless of their position on the wars in Iraq and Afghanistan, the cute videos assert that these soldiers are in need of care (witness their makeshift living arrangements), yet are secure enough in their masculinity to toy with gender, to mock and mimic pop celebrities buoyed by girl power (for the videos that tend to be remixed depict assertive and violent women). These videos certainly distance the soldiers from the "baby killer" epithet, popularized by the *Rambo* movies and supposedly used to denigrate soldiers returning from Vietnam (although evidence for its usage remains scant).

The viral reach of these videos beyond an inner sanctum of male officers and combat buddies differentiates remix culture from earlier instances of soldier drag. If Vietnam is remembered as the first televised war and the Gulf War as the first cable TV war, then the War on Terror must be considered the YouTube war. Importantly, these remix productions emerge and circulate within a global media landscape populated by the shocking training and beheading videos distributed by Al Qaeda and ISIS. One important function for these cute performances is thus to serve as a rejoinder to the radically patriarchal masculinity attributed to "the terrorists" and "Islamic fundamentalists." These "kinder and gentler" American soldier performances—bringing George H.W. Bush's words into a new context—can thus function as double-edged swords, ideological and otherwise. The soldiers are potential killers but they are also cute-sexy-cuddly cheerleaders, and cheerleader-lovers. It's not coincidental that the "Call me Maybe" video, which offers the strongest evidence that male soldiers can become highly proficient in feminine mimicry, makes it clear in the closing credits that the soldiers are fans of the cheerleaders. Ironically, this suggests that their presumptive hetero-sexuality explains their lovingly precise parody.

Evoking the affects of cuteness in this manner modulates and softens male warrior iconography, an important factor for the US audience during a period in which the problem of sexual assault in the military came under public scrutiny. In 2012, a Pentagon-commissioned study revealed that unreported incidents of sexual assault had grown by 36 percent over the previous two years. Estimates placed the number of women and men in the US military who had been sexually assaulted at 26,000, a number that Defense Secretary Leon Panetta called "unacceptable" (Muirine). That same year, Kirby Dick and Amy Ziering's documentary examining this issue, *The Invisible War*, won the Audience Award at Sundance, was nominated for an Oscar, and was broadcast on PBS. In 2013, journalist Jesse Ellison of the *Daily Beast* reported that "rape is so endemic within the armed forces that a female soldier is more likely to be raped by a fellow soldier than killed in combat" (Ellison).

The problem of masculinity gone amok within the US military resonates with broader discourses of gender and power circulating after 9/11. In *Sovereign Masculinity: Gender Lessons from the War On Terror*, Bonnie Mann builds on the pioneering work of Cynthia Enloe, Susan Faludi, and Susan Jeffords to historicize post-9/11 masculinity and to question the assumption that masculine power binds itself to notions of rationality. She argues,

> the longstanding feminist analysis of the association of reason with masculinity, and emotion/unreason with femininity, doesn't tell a complex enough story for the US American context. In fact, in the United States sovereign masculinity is hybrid. In it animality, primitivity, instinct, and raw power mix with technical acumen (what is left of reason here) to form a powerfully seductive, heroic figure. (Mann 49)

For Mann, the quintessential projection of that heroic figure is William James, the protagonist of *The Hurt Locker* (2008), a film lauded for its seemingly apolitical depiction of the war in Iraq and simultaneously held up as proof of film industry progressiveness because its director, Kathryn Bigelow, was the first woman to win the Academy Award for Best Director. For Mann, James epitomizes "a kind of masculinity that is ferociously focused on triumph and survival" (52). This new American masculinity, she posits, "imagines itself to be, more often than not, the superior counterpart to rational, European-style manhood rather than a dislocated repetition of its expression" (45). The military remix videos certainly assert a ferocious focus on triumph and survival. Their lip-sync appropriation of pop divas like Gaga and Beyoncé allows the soldiers to enact what Robin James terms a resilience discourse. Organized by "Look, I Overcame!" narratives, resilience is complicit in neoliberal biopolitics, James argues, because it converts social, economic, and physical damage into social capital. Thus, the "cross-racial feminist alliance" that animates the Gaga–Beyoncé "Telephone" video incites patriarchal damage in the form of the black man who is Beyoncé's partner and victim in the video "so that Gaga can overcome it" (135, loc 2197). James considers resilient women key to neoliberal America, and connects them to global military conflicts: "the resilience of 'our' women is what distinguishes us from backward nations in need of white saviorism, drone strikes, and worse" (135, loc 2192).

The remixed US masculinity on display in these videos thus underscores a version of gender politics that affirms Samuel Huntington's "Clash of Civilizations" rhetoric and contributes to a version of Mann's sovereign masculinity. Here, superiority inheres in the irrational, playful, irreverent male body whose technical acumen can be demonstrated within the videos not only through the management of tanks, Humvees, and weapons, but also through the increasingly sophisticated performances of femininity and practices of filmmaking.

As was the case with the migration of stage drag from the POW camps of WWII to the silver screen in Renoir's film, the confirmation that making these videos represents something quintessential about the soldier's experience of the War on Terror is implied by the appearance of soldier videos made by two fictional television veterans: Gary in *Gary, Tank Commander* (2009) and John Bennett in *Orange is the New Black* (2014). Within the series diegesis, video extracts from both programs are available on YouTube, cementing this rite of passage as definitive of the post 9/11 male soldier's tour of duty and creating something of a *mise en abyme*. The example from *Orange is the New Black*, a program with aspirations to progressive gender and sexual politics, speaks explicitly to the way that the videos contribute to the ideological project linking enlightened gender politics to US global hegemony. The Afghan soldier filming the video of Bennett and his platoon-mates strutting around to No Doubt's "Hollaback Girl" is shown to have missed the point entirely when he trains the camera on the breasts of a woman soldier dancing in the background. The video's American soldier-director admonishes him, explaining that the video is only funny when the camera captures men performing as women. Unable to participate in the cute-inflected spirit of gender play as the US soldiers do, the soldier may be problematically fixated upon the voyeuristic exploitation of a western woman but proves to be less "backward" than his fellow Afghanis: he translates for Bennett, telling him that his Afghan compatriots (who subsequently throw a grenade into Bennett's tent) believe the soldiers to be gay.

I'll be Dancin': Hard Bodies, Soft Power

These remix performances can be differentiated from conventional drag shows, where professionally applied makeup and theatrical costuming are critical to establishing the illusion of femininity, because feminine mimicry is accomplished through gesture, movement, and dance. The soldiers perform body drag: evoking femininity primarily through choreography, dance, and gesture. The remix videos reassert masculine prerogatives through the appropriation of the movements and affect of the female celebrity and fan. Do they represent a new form of remasculinization for a US audience still recovering from 9/11?

Susan Jeffords's influential work on the remasculinization of America after the Vietnam War (*Hard Bodies, Remasculinization of America*) links the reclamation of white male privilege in the face of feminism and military defeat to revisionist narratives of the war, such as *Rambo: First Blood Part II* (1985), that reassert masculine dominance through the hard bodies of action–adventure film stars. Although the Gulf War (1990–91) was also characterized as a period in which American masculinity was reborn (Feinman), that conflict ultimately generated a dominant narrative of masculine vulnerability, one that brought the damaged male body into focus through the specter of Gulf War Syndrome and PTSD, calling into question rhetorics of physical dominance and psychological invulnerability (Kilshaw 184–86). Indeed, the rise in the diagnosis of PTSD for soldiers reflects a heightened awareness of the perilous nature of US soldiering, both for men historically (going back to the "shell shock" of WWI) and for those in contemporary theaters of war (Whitworth 110–11).

Bonnie Mann reminds us that politicians, journalists, and soldiers characterized the 9/11 attacks in highly masculinist terms involving castration and anal penetration. Mann observes:

> We come to understand that this [US cultural] imaginary reads the attack on the twin towers as a closely sequenced double act of penetration/rape (the planes fly into the buildings again and again) and castration (the scene climaxes and ends with the two towers collapsing) when we attend to the subsequent fantasies of revenge: cartoon drawings of missiles poised to anally penetrate Saddam Hussein, the slogan "USA: Up Saddam's Ass," a photo of soldiers spray painting a missile with the words "High Jack This Fags." A symbolic effort to redeem national sovereignty is articulated as a restoration of the power of the American phallus. (4–5)

At the same time, the American belief in its cultural, not merely its military, superiority is apparent in the desire to assert US gender relations as preferable to those of the societies from which the terrorist threats are thought to emerge. This double-edged ambition for military and cultural dominance requires an oscillation between the restoration of phallicism on one hand, and the deployment of the forms of cuteness placed on display in the military videos on the other.

Following in the footsteps of post-Vietnam remasculinization and Gulf War and 9/11 revictimization, these military remix videos, not surprisingly, both flaunt and flout the hardbody conventions that Jeffords associates with post-Vietnam American popular culture. They promulgate masculine military cuteness as they recode the male soldier's body: trained for combat, the men display their fitness by performing moves recognized as the province of the postfeminist body earning its keep through posing, modeling, cheerleading, and dancing. Incongruous uniforms and settings, synchronized choreography, childlike gestures, and campy settings create a comic dissonance that evokes the spectacle of children playing dress-up. These fit, potentially dangerous bodies have been redeployed for unproductive, unheroic pursuits such as dance.

According to Jane Desmond, dancing is "one of the most important arenas of public physical enactment," and is inevitably linked to "sex, sexiness, and sexuality" (7). Dancing wasn't always seen as incongruous for the warrior's body. During the reign of Louis XIV, dancing was touted as keeping a man in shape for battle, as the turned-out stance and controlled postures of ballet were seen as proper preparation for fencing and fighting (Desmond 9). By the nineteenth century, however, commentators such as Parisian ballet critic Jules Janin complained that men should not "[caper] aimlessly" when they were so obviously "made expressly to bear a rifle, saber, and uniform" (qtd. in Chapman 204).

The remix videos emanate from an American cultural context in which the dancing male body has transcended derogatory associations with gay disco and migrated into the territory of ironic metrosexual hypermasculinity. If disco overtly queered the proficient male dancer, the straight male dancing body could be celebrated in the continuing appeal of Kevin Bacon in *Footloose* (1984, remade in 2011) and Patrick Swayze in *Dirty Dancing* (1987). This figure was recently revivified when Channing Tatum's boyishly cute persona juxtaposed virtuoso feats of physicality in *Magic Mike* (2012) and *Magic Mike XXL* (2015), films that take as given the mainstreaming of stripper culture.

By focusing on the moving body, the videos also foreground anxieties regarding masculine vulnerability in an era that has witnessed significant social, economic, and technological changes in the culture of warfare. These changes include the entry of women into combat roles in light of the changing dispensation of the US military since 9/11, as well as the loosened adherence to the Army's Combat Exclusion Policy preventing women from serving in ground combat (which culminated in a lifting of the ban in 2012), the rescission of the Department of Defense's "Don't Ask Don't Tell" policy in 2010, the increasing privatization and outsourcing of military functions, and the development of drones and autonomous weapons, which threaten to render human fighting bodies redundant. According to recent reports, the Pentagon now has some 7,000 aerial drones, compared with fewer than 50 a decade ago (Bumiller and Shanker). The US government's fiscal year 2017 budget included $4.5 billion for drone research, development, and procurement ("Drone Spending"). In their attempt to humanize the US soldier, these remix videos negotiate the reality that the hardest bodies of the twenty-first century are not human bodies at all, but the robots that augur human obsolescence. The War on Terror is not only the first YouTube war; it is also the first drone war. The dancing men of these videos speak to the looming superfluity of the soldier body, perhaps as a blessing and a curse. And there are some tasks that drones and autonomous weapons/robot soldiers cannot undertake. US soldiers are expected to embody the use of force and to win "hearts and minds" across unstable regions (Lennon).

The videos thus position the male body within another important gendered narrative of the War on Terror: the policy debate regarding hard versus soft power, or the distinction between military force and the "cultural attraction" and "political values" (Nye) that win hearts and minds. Christine Yano argues that the Hello Kitty brand empire has proliferated Japan's "soft power," exercising a form of authority that operates through subtle, non-aggressive means (5). The remix videos may do the same thing: not only proposing an implicitly superior Western version of free expression, in contrast with the prohibition of dance and music in Taliban-controlled Afghanistan, for example, but also promulgating a notion of gender equality defined by equal opportunity objectification.

By deploying images of an American masculinity "secure enough" to adopt the position and gestures of female pop icons, these YouTube performances of cute soldiering, while ostensibly aimed at challenging the phallic masculinity embodied in military hierarchy, ultimately endorse claims of Western cultural and military superiority. The videos support the ideological dynamics in which claims of Western enlightenment are predicated on a (misrepresented) gender equality that is posed as anathema to Islamic fundamentalism. The Western press insistently places enlightened gender relations front and center, from Lisa Beyer's *Time* magazine piece "The Women of Islam," published just after 9/11 to British documentaries such as BBC Arabic's examination of one activist's attempts to free abducted women and children, *Yazidi Women: Slaves of the Caliphate* (2015), which circulates on YouTube.

Cute performances by US soldiers should be understood within the rubric of authority cuteness and sovereign masculinity, and recognized as being recuperated as part of the deployment "soft power" in the War on Terror, for US and international audiences. The deployment of the male soldiers' fit, dancing bodies through cute remix performances is inseparable from the US deployment of both soft and hard power. At the same time, the videos employ resilient celebrity divas to ventriloquize contemporary perceptions of male vulnerability in light of cultural and economic shifts over the last four decades.

Notes

1   These viewing figures are correct as of May 2016.
2   I thank Lenore Bell and Lucy Fife Donaldson for bringing this to my attention.
3   Thanks to Tony Tracy for convincing me of the importance of this point.

Works Cited

Barrett, Frank J. "The Organizational Construction of Hegemonic Masculinity: The Case of the US Navy." *Gender, Work, and Organization* 3.3 (1996): 129–42.

Beyer, Lisa. "The Women of Islam." *Time.* Time Warner, 25 Nov. 2001. Online. 16 Apr. 2016.

Boxwell, David A. "The Follies of War: Cross-Dressing and Popular Theatre on the British Front Lines, 1914–18." *Modernism/Modernity* 9 (2002). 1–20.

Brock, Janna. "US Homosexual Soldiers Caught Dancing in Drag at Okinawa for 'Fundraiser.'" *Freedom Outpost.* Freedom Outpost, 3 Mar. 2014. Online. 10 June 2016.

Bumiller, Elisabeth, and Thom Shanker. "War Evolves with Drones, Some Tiny as Bugs." *New York Times.* New York Times, 19 June 2011. Online. 16 Apr. 2016.

Burgess, Jean. "'All Your Chocolate Rain are Belong to Us'?: Viral Video, YouTube, and the Dynamics of Participatory Culture." *Video Vortex Reader: Responses to YouTube.* Eds. Geert Lovink and Sabine Niederer. Amsterdam: Institute of Network Cultures, 2008. 101–19.

Butler, Judith. *Gender Trouble: Feminism and the Subversion of Identity.* New York: Routledge, 1990.

Caholo, Orlando. "Iraq (Eye of the Tiger)." *YouTube.* YouTube, 7 Nov. 2006. Online. 28 May 2016.

Chapman, John. "Jules Janin: Romantic Critic." *Rethinking the Sylph: New Perspectives on the Romantic Ballet.* Ed. Lynn Garafola. Hanover, NH: University Press of New England, 1997. 197–241.

Connell, Raewyn W. "Hegemonic Masculinity: Rethinking the Concept." *Gender and Society* 19.6 (2005): 829–59.

"Costs of War." Watson Institute for International and Public Affairs. Brown University, 14 Dec. 2015. Online.

Dao, Kind. "They Signed Up to Fight." *New York Times.* New York Times, 6 Sept. 2011. Online. 10 June 2016.

Desmond, Jane. *Dancing Desires: Choreographing Sexualities on and off the Stage.* Madison, WI: University of Wisconsin Press, 2001.

Doughty, Rob. "Kesha Ke$ha Military Music Video for Blah Blah Blah (Gays in the Military?)." *YouTube.* YouTube, 14 May 2010. Online. 26 Apr. 2016.

"Drone Spending in the FY17 Defense Budget." Center for the Study of the Drone. Bard College, 15 Feb. 2016. Online. 18 Apr. 2016.

Edmond, Maura. "Here We Go Again: Music Videos after YouTube." *Television and New Media* 15.4 (2014): 305–20.

Ehrenreich, Barbara. *Blood Rites: Origins and History of the Passions of War.* New York: Metropolitan, 1997.

Ellison, Jesse. "Sexual Assaults Still Pervasive in Military Despite Official Outrage." *Daily Beast.* IAC, 13 May 2013. Online. 10 June 2016.

Enloe, Cynthia. *Bananas, Beaches and Bases: Making Feminist Sense of International Politics.* Rev. ed. Berkeley, CA: University of California Press, 2014.

Faludi, Susan. *Stiffed: The Betrayal of the Modern Man.* New York: Random House, 2011.

Feinman, Ilene Rose. *Citizenship Rites: Feminist Soldiers and Feminist Antimilitarists.* New York: New York University Press, 2000.

Fisher, Max. "Military Brass Likes Lady Gaga Parody." *Wire: News from the Atlantic.* 4 May 2010. Online. 10 June 2016.

Garber, Marjorie B. *Vested Interests: Cross-Dressing and Cultural Anxiety*. New York: Routledge, 1992.

Harman, Graham. *Guerilla Metaphysics: Phenomenology and the Carpentry of Things*. Chicago, IL: Open Court, 2005.

Hooper, Charlotte. *Manly States: Masculinities, International Relations, and Gender Politics*. New York: Columbia University Press, 2012.

Huntington, Samuel P. "The Clash of Civilizations?" *Foreign Affairs* 72.3 (1993): 22–49.

Iam918. "Vanilla Ice Remix (gotta see)." *YouTube*. YouTube, 7 May 2007. Online. 14 Dec. 2015.

Iraq Body Count. www.Iraqbodycount.org. Online. 10 June 2016.

itsMRich. "US Marines Watch *Frozen* and Sing Let it Go." *YouTube*. YouTube, 1 May 2014. Online. 26 Apr. 2016.

James, Robin. *Resilience and Melancholy: Pop Music, Feminism, Neoliberalism*. London: Zero, 2015. E-book.

Jeffords, Susan. *The Remasculinization of America: Gender and the Vietnam War*. Indianapolis, IN: Indiana University Press, 1989.

———. *Hard Bodies: Hollywood Masculinity in the Reagan Era*. New Brunswick, NJ: Rutgers University Press, 1994.

Keating, Abigail. "Video Making, Harlem Shaking: Theorizing the Interactive Amateur." *New Cinemas: Journal of Contemporary Film* 11.2–3 (2013). Online. 10 June 2016.

Kilshaw, Susie. *Impotent Warriors: Gulf War Syndrome, Vulnerability, and Masculinity*. New York: Berghahn, 2009.

Lennon, Alexander, ed. *The Battle for Hearts and Minds: Using Soft Power to Undermine Terrorist Networks*. Cambridge, MA: MIT Press, 2003.

Malibumelcher. "Telephone: The Afghanistan Remake." *YouTube*. YouTube, 23 Apr. 2010. Online. 26 Apr. 2016.

Mann, Bonnie. *Sovereign Masculinity: Gender Lessons from the War on Terror*. Oxford: Oxford University Press, 2014. E-book.

MasterFX200. "Dance Party in Iraq." *YouTube*. YouTube, 16 May 2007. Online. 28 May 2016.

McVeigh, Brian. "Commodifying Affection: Authority and Gender in the Everyday Objects of Japan." *Journal of Material Culture* 1 (1996): 291–312.

Muirine, Anna. "Pentagon Report: Sexual Assault in the Military Up Dramatically." *Christian Science Monitor*. 19 Jan. 2012. Online. 26 Apr. 2016.

"No Security Concerns." *News.com.au*. News Limited, 7 May 2010. Online. 10 June 2016.

Nye, Joseph. "Think Again: Soft Power." *Foreign Policy*. 23 Feb. 2006. Online. 10 June 2016.

Rachamimov, Alon. "The Disruptive Comforts of Drag: (Trans)Gender Performances among Prisoners of War in Russia, 1914–1920." *American Historical Review* 111.2 (2006): 362–82.

Sherman, Gary D., and Jonathan Haidt. "Cuteness and Disgust: The Humanizing and Dehumanizing Effects of Emotion." *Emotion Review* 3.3 (2011): 1–7.

Tasker, Yvonne. *Spectacular Bodies: Gender, Genre, and the Action Cinema*. New York: Routledge, 2012.

Tritten, Travis. "Gay, Lesbian Troops Perform in Drag at Kadena Air Base Fundraiser." *Stars and Stripes*. Defense Media Activity, 2 Mar. 2014. Online. 10 June 2016.

Whitworth, Susan. "Militarized Masculinity and Post Traumatic Stress Disorder." *Rethinking the Man Question: Sex, Gender, and Violence in International Relations*. Eds. Jane L. Parpart and Marysia Zalewski. London: Zed, 2008. 109–26.

Wilson, Jason. *Soldiers of Song: The Dumbells and Other Canadian Concert Parties of the First World War*. Waterloo, ON: Wilfrid Laurier University Press, 2012.

Yano, Christine. *Pink Globalization: Hello Kitty's Trek across the Pacific*. Durham, NC: Duke University Press, 2013.

YouTube Multiplier. "Miami Dolphin Cheerleaders versus US Military." *YouTube*. YouTube, 18 Jan 2013. Online. 14 Dec. 2015.

6

LIVE CUTENESS 24/7

Performing Boredom on Animal Live Streams

Katy Peplin

In the second season of the hit HBO television series *Silicon Valley* (2014–), the technology startup Pied Piper is looking for content to stream live (Berg). The team has built a powerful video compression engine, which will allow the company to broadcast video live in heretofore-unseen levels of quality. After a sequence of missteps, Pied Piper is forced to take the suggestion of Jared, their belabored business manager, and train the camera on the egg of a condor that is about to hatch. The image never changes (an incubating egg is static content indeed) and after the mother condor stops visiting the nest, Jared eventually alerts the habitat's caretaker to go and check on the status of the condor eggs. What was a routine event quickly turns dramatic as the human caretaker slips into the remote ravine where the condor nest is located. In front of the camera's watchful eye, the man is trapped, injured, and waiting for rescue in increasingly dire conditions. Hundreds of thousands tune in as the images go viral—the feed functioning perfectly to broadcast what it was never meant to see. As more tune in, the servers need to handle more and more traffic, and the technology becomes the center of the spectacle. The team scrambles to add servers to handle capacity and allow the technological infrastructure to handle the traffic, and the normally invisible mechanism that keeps the content available to viewers around the world is made visible. *Silicon Valley* is parodying the viewer that would sign on to look at video of an unhatched egg, but also pointing to the live nature of the camera, as what was deadly boring turns into a life and death situation. A rescuer turns the camera off, and viewers leave the feed as it goes black. The human subject was rescued, the technology handled the traffic, and the team moves on to their next challenge, but viewers are never updated on the state of the eggs. The animal live feed returns to the boring entity it was before, and leaves us to wonder: who is watching animals live and why? While *Silicon Valley* treats the Condor cam as a darkly absurdist gag, the scenario highlights much of what fascinates about the technology: 24/7 liveness, technological capacity and incapacity, the mundane and the unpredictable, and the complexity of early twenty-first-century viewing practices.

Animal "live cams" generate a noteworthy form of content available to the average consumer in the twenty-first century, with their lenses trained on a range of material from adoptable kittens growing up on screen to heavily curated views of sea animals in amusement parks whose ethics are under fire. These live streams, made possible by the cheap consumer cameras flooding the market and proliferating high-speed internet connections in the developed world, are viewed by thousands of people at a time, all around the world, despite their often static, if not downright soporific, content. From Shamu at SeaWorld to kittens in shelters, these cams are set up to promise uninterrupted access to animal lives and deliver the "liveness" that memes, videos, and other animal media often lack. I argue that this framing, and the very condition of liveness, exaggerates the intermittent qualities of cuteness present in the subjects being broadcast. Liveness, even and especially as it is presented in a mediatized commodity form, allows for a conflation of the embodied lives of animals pictured and the technical qualities of the video streams that present those lives to us. The stream presents the illusion of an uninterrupted view of animal lives that reframes the experience away from the contained cute moment and towards a temporality of boredom. Although it is not my purpose here, other scholars are beginning to explore how "the affective pulse of boredom is captured, broadcast, circulated, managed, and put to work in digital network culture" (van Doorn).[1]

No matter what the use of the cam or how it portrays the animals, this article argues that the sense of liveness, and the tenuous link to an embodied animal allows for effective and efficient commodification of cuteness. Live cams give a sense of personality, experience, and cuteness in real time that differentiates the animals depicted from those that appear in memes or short amateur videos. Thus the exchange of money, time, or affection is justified because of the existence of a "real" animal, and that the promise of cuteness can be accessed at any time. By capitalizing on the streaming, ever-refreshing nature of this technology, these cams perpetuate the idea that animals perform their cuteness organically, willingly, and for us, and all we need to do is train a camera on them to see it.

Here I examine three cases of the animal cam in order to demonstrate how the quality of boredom is used to authenticate an animal experience to various political, cultural, or commercial ends. First is the Shamu Cam, a feed from the embattled SeaWorld San Diego amusement park, which is set up to ostensibly display a "killer whale" when it is not actively performing as a way of validating the standard of care and treatment that whales receive in the park.[2] The camera, however, is configured in such a way, both structurally and rhetorically, as to limit access, demonstrating that live streaming need not necessarily equate to a true or realistic sense of a profilmic space, or the animal lives it contains. I then move to the most popular live stream in the world, that featuring the Decorah Eagles in Decorah, Iowa. The feed tracks a pair of nesting bald eagles during the incubation period, but broadcasts continuously. In contrast to the Shamu Cam, this feed is explicitly framed as scientific endeavor, and resists attempts to make the content "cute." I conclude with the live streaming kitten shelter cams which broadcast litters of kittens from birth to adoption, focusing on the Tiny Kittens feed from British Columbia, which is one of the most popular of its kind and operates under the banner of its own non-profit charitable status. The feed is structured to transform kitten behavior into consumable cuteness culture in its communal spaces and structured to create attachment to the kittens and fellow viewers. All three use the moments between explicitly cute or interesting animal behavior as a signal of the authenticity of the feed; the live nature of the feed may make for tedious viewing, but the moments of cuteness that punctuate the boredom reassure viewers that animal lives are as cute as we imagine.

Cuteness and Liveness

Animal live streams alternate between cuteness and boredom, constructing a narrative of access that allows viewers to appreciate real animal lives rather than manufactured or packaged animal performances. But this does not mean that cuteness is not at work to incentivize and capture viewers. I draw here from accounts by Lori Merish and Sianne Ngai, scholars who have worked to historicize cuteness as an element of public affective culture. Both establish how the affect of cuteness is constructed as a capitalist object, a literary focus, and a consumerist currency. I follow them in arguing that cuteness is much more than a feminized, easily dismissed affect; rather it is one that works in a network of relations that expose power imbalances between subject and object. As Ngai writes, "There is no judgment or experience of an object as cute that does not call up one's sense of power over it as something less powerful" (11). The "asymmetry of power" that Ngai describes speaks to the inherent imbalance between the object that is cute, weak, small, childlike, young, or worthy of protection, and the subject making the judgment, basing those assessments on his or her status as larger than, older than, and/or stronger than the object. In order to be cute, the subject must be diminished, though Ngai goes on to suggest that the judgment of "less than" upon which cuteness relies is not a static judgment, but a continuously negotiated struggle:

> But the fact that the cute object seems capable of making demands on us regardless, as Merish underscores—a demand for care that women in particular often feel addressed or interpolated by—suggests that "cute" designates not just the site of a static power differential but also the site of a surprisingly complex power struggle. (11)

It is the ongoing relationship of care that truly marks the cute as an object different from the pitied, the weak, or the small; a cute object must be swooned over, cared for, worried about; it becomes a subject of imaginative, if not actual, care that is coded as feminine. To be cute is to be weak, small, and powerless, yes, but in a way that demands a relationship between the subject and the object. If a kitten is alone in a forest, it may be small, hungry, or in need of care; it only becomes cute when observed, when it activates that affect in another being and creates a relationship of real or imagined dependence.

However, this affect in the body of the subject is transactional, dependent, and transient, and in the case of the live cam, continuously in need of refreshing. Natalie Angier writes that even though the pleasure of observing a cute object is as strong as other, more traditional pleasurable activities like "sex, a good meal, or psychoactive drugs like cocaine," we are taught to be suspicious of it. She describes the pleasure of cuteness being "routinely overridden by secondary feelings of suspicion," making the original pleasure "weak" (qtd. in Ngai 12). Especially for those not meant to notice or appreciate cuteness, this feeling of protection and pleasure is regularly sublimated by dismissing the pleasure as immature, feminine, or unsophisticated. Cuteness is reserved for juvenile objects, and those who appreciate it are similarly cast as juvenile, or overly invested in maternal feelings. Unlike a meme, which remains as a static image even as it is circulated and modified by individual users, the live cam allows access to a cuteness that is also evolving from moment to moment. Cuteness can shift, grow, and evolve over time and that weak affect can be constantly re-experienced as a remedy for its unsustainable nature.

The animal in a meme is separate from the animal in a live feed, and that difference is rooted in the liveness of the video feed, not the animal itself. Mary Ann Doane describes televisual time as "an insistent 'present-ness'—a '*this-is-going-on*' rather than a '*that-has*-been,'" in order to separate it from the "embalmed" time of film, and this condition of "this-is-going-on" persists into digital media spheres as liveness (222). Liveness is a condition less of presence and more of structural construction. I use the term here to indicate the sense of temporality, or lack thereof, that the media object conveys. I use it as such to distinguish from the sense of embodiment, or the feeling that the object being displayed is connected to a real, living body in proximate or distant space. Liveness relates to the sense that a viewer has, increasingly so in digital media culture, that the representation is unfolding in real time, or is captured without intervention. Philip Auslander argues that it is not the medium of recording or transmission that determines liveness; it is not an ontological quality. He writes that "the best way of thinking about that relationship is to understand liveness as a historically contingent concept continually in a state of redefinition and to look at the meanings and uses of live performance in specific cultural contexts" (Auslander 184). Liveness in this articulation becomes something that is framed, rhetorically or visually, for the viewer rather than being a quality that can be pinpointed in any specific ontological configuration. Liveness then becomes a quality ascribed to a live stream, rather than something inherent in the technology of its recording or broadcast, and thus it becomes important that the relationship between agentic viewer and observed animal be framed not only in terms of affective connection, but technological proximity.

This pair of concepts—cuteness and liveness—is essential in reframing the live stream as more than simple distraction, cultural curiosity, or form of crass capitalist consumption. The live stream works differently from other cute media objects—the moments that would otherwise be edited into a video or taken and used as a meme are buried within hours of animals sleeping, eating, or otherwise being uninteresting. Cute moments, and the affect that accompanies them, become the reward for consistent and patient viewing; a viewer earns a moment of cuteness after watching many boring moments, and with both categories of experience, can feel empowered to know the animal beyond its performance and as it "actually is." However, this sense of the cam showing the animal's actual existence is employed to varying ends. Not all boredom is created equal.

See for Yourself: Shamu Cam

Orca whales have built a dual reputation, beloved as companions based on representations (notably in the film *Free Willy* and its many sequels), but also are colloquially referred to as "killer whales" (Wincer). *Free Willy* creates a cute animal out of a narrative connection with children, with a plot that emphasizes just how dependent whales are on humans, and that template is effectively deployed by SeaWorld to fortify the species' cuteness. Logos for the park rely on a cartoon whale, teeth hidden behind an anthropomorphized smile, to suggest that despite the case made by the film, the whales are happy to be performing, happy to be contained, and happy to be made cute in shows for guests multiple times a day. While not typically cute in the small or vulnerable sense of the word, the animals have consistently been a top draw for the SeaWorld parks, and marketing for the park consistently emphasizes them (SeaWorld[r] Parks). The narrative that whales are safe is bound up both with nostalgia for the film's happy ending, and the perceived safety in captivity associated with the animals at SeaWorld. However, concerns have been mounting about the ethics of keeping orcas in captivity, spearheaded by the 2013 film *Blackfish*, a documentary that focused on the mistreatment, confinement, and training of orca whales, practices that ultimately resulted in the deaths of three human trainers employed by the park (Cowperthwaite). In the second quarter of 2015, SeaWorld Entertainment reported profits down 84 percent as compared to the same quarter of 2014, citing "increased brand challenges" as a reason for that catastrophic loss of profit ("SeaWorld Entertainment"). It seems that the risks of keeping marine animals in captivity are no longer adequately justified by park visitors' appetite to see dolphins, orcas, and other sea creatures up close, performing, or otherwise.[3]

With the brand in trouble and park attendance having been in decline for nearly a decade, SeaWorld took several steps that summer to bring guests into the park and assure them that the animals are well treated in their captivity. A centerpiece of the efforts was to install a "Shamu Cam" in orca tanks at various parks owned by SeaWorld across the country. Shamu is a stage name used for all orca whales in SeaWorld parks, and therefore the name is helpfully opaque— the cam could picture any of the twenty plus whales held across the three parks, signifying more a cute anthropomorphized character than wild animal. The most popular, or at least, best maintained camera feed featured whales in the San Diego park, which is bigger than those in Florida and Texas, and broadcast images from 9:00 to 5:30 pm, PST. When the camera was not live at night, when presumably the lighting conditions made it impossible to capture usable images, the feed displayed highlights from the previous day. The camera was intended presumably to assure viewers that even when not performing, the whales were safe and healthy in their tanks, swimming peacefully until their next show. The camera's low-quality feed (it streamed JPEGS, rather than full video, a choice that most likely reduced maintenance of the feed) made it moderately unpleasant to watch, and the feed never reached the level of popularity where it would have been featured on news outlets or heavily promoted in marketing materials for the park.

Some viewers quickly paid attention to the feed for an alternate purpose: to document signs of aggression and injury to the whales in the tanks. Videos were captured from the feeds, recut, and circulated in other venues, like YouTube, to demonstrate that the whales are aggressive towards one another, that they've sustained injuries from that aggression or from self-injurious behavior, like repeatedly chewing on gates or other tank features, or by repeatedly beating their bodies against the walls of their tanks.[4] What was presented as a view into these animals' lives when they are "off stage" became just that—confirmation that the lives of the whales in captivity were monotonous, cruelly confined, and unsafe. The feed was removed without fanfare at some point in 2013 just as criticism of the park and its whale captivity program was beginning to reach the mainstream media, after several high-profile accidents at the park, including one trainer's death, and the premiere of *Blackfish*. The camera was initially trained on the holding tanks so that anyone interested could verify that the whales were being well taken care of, but it seems instead that the low quality of the feed, the limited hours, and the sudden disappearance of the camera suggested that it was disrupting the happy and safe narrative the park was pushing in other outlets.

Other cameras, trained on turtles, stingrays, and penguins, remain viewable on the SeaWorld website, but are carefully framed so as only to include the public spaces of exhibits ("Shamu's"). Unlike the Shamu Cam, which was constructed to confirm that even the "off-stage view" of the whales could be broadcast, these new cams simply replicate what a patron would see at the park. Boring, easily replicated content of animals in an aquarium now constitutes the only views available live. Until the park is sure that the feed is being used for entertainment and promotion and not surveillance, liveness is simply not a quality that SeaWorld can offer to the public. A feed of whales swimming back and forth should be boring and repetitive, but instead, the restraints placed on the condition of liveness alerted viewers to the artificial nature of the view. What was meant to assure viewers that the park had nothing to hide was actually a liability, and viewers who came to see cute orcas instead saw mistreatment. As SeaWorld works to eliminate live orca performances in the coming years, it has become clear that the whale in live performance, either in person or on a video feed, can no longer be trusted to be cute.

You and Millions of Others: The Decorah Eagle Cam

While the writer's room might have found the idea that a camera trained on an incubating egg would make for captivating viewing absurd enough to drive an entire story line for *Silicon Valley*, the truth is that the most popular live feeds, animal or otherwise, drew rapt attention from viewers. The Decorah Bald Eagles, a nesting, bonded pair of eagles, have been tracked and filmed since 2007, with footage of the pair featured in a 2008 PBS documentary ("American Eagle"). However, the feed was transferred to the live streaming platform UStream in 2011, and with the exception of the 2013 season, where the pair built and hatched eggs in a new nest, every hatching season has been broadcast live around the world. It has been estimated that upwards of 300 million unique viewers have tuned into the feed at some point, making it far and away the most popular live stream broadcast ever ("World's"). The camera was first installed as a way to observe the nest without disturbing the pair and monitored by conservationists and other interested parties, but when its widespread appeal was discovered, it became important that the purpose of the feed be framed in contradistinction to the potentially trivial cuteness of baby animals.

In switching from a limited, monitoring stream to a public entertainment stream, the rhetorical framing and technological architecture surrounding the stream inevitably changed. The switch to UStream was made in part to allow for a more robust architecture and effective commodification of the stream, which in turn raises money to support the non-profit Raptor Resource Project (*Decorah Eagles*). UStream, and the money generated by its ad revenue, allowed for a bevy of upgrades—improved cameras and playback capabilities, and a social chat feature to run alongside the stream during the breeding season. Consequently, the feed exploded in popularity, as it was linked to by multiple online news sources and shared globally. In order to appeal to the widest range of viewers (and more importantly, investors), the cuteness of the baby eagles had to be minimized in order to preserve the scientific value of the tool (Figure 6.1). A large public educational push was built around the stream, and the Raptor Resource Project now maintains an extensive website with information about eagles and their habitats, and makes those resources available (with an ad-free stream) to schools around the world.

FIGURE 6.1   The Decorah Eagles cam offers live streamed animal images without overtly soliciting the enjoyment of cuteness on the part of the spectator.

After several years of broadcasting, a community of non-expert users have mobilized around the Decorah Eagles feed. Users capture significant moments from the feed and post them to video sharing sites like YouTube, often with their own commentary or visual enhancements like editing or title cards. Fundraising efforts are directly linked to the stream, with ads playing at regular intervals, interrupting the screen, donation links embedded in the webpage, and copious links directing back towards the RPP overall project site. These solicitations for contributions are always framed as work to "keep the feed going," and are directed rhetorically to a scientific or conservationist agenda rather than an anthropomorphized sense of supporting the eagles directly. The feed seemingly encourages engagement with the cuteness of the vulnerable animal bodies that need protection and (financial) support in order to drive viewership, while rhetorically keeping that affective relationship at bay by insisting on the scientific mission of the project.

The scientific, conservationist angle is heightened because of the insistence on keeping the feed and surrounding social spaces from lapsing into anthropomorphized cuteness. The mating pair of eagles is referred to as Mom and Dad, but all other eagles, including the juveniles, are referred to by alphanumeric names, like D1. Maintaining scientific protocols, individual viewers might lapse into cute anthropomorphized descriptions in Facebook comments or chat messages, ascribing bird behaviors to romantic love or other human emotions, however the RPP staff and official messaging never does so ("About Us"). The feed is a scientific tool shared with the public in order to build support for a conservationist agenda, but not as a therapeutic object or vehicle for community interaction. Cute moments, like a mother feeding a newly hatched chick, or a chick stretching its wings for the first time, are possible, but they are more often characterized as "amazing" or "majestic" or "never before seen," tying the experience into the much less trivial sense of the sublime. If, as Ngai argues, cuteness is indexed by its availability, this camera upon a mountain seems to emphasize not just the remote nature of the camera, but the inaccessibility of the eagle subjects (18).

The eagles dictate the terms of the eagle cam, moving closer to the model of the "critter-cam" that Donna Haraway explores where the animal's body becomes the vehicle for the camera, literally becoming the eagle's eye view. "Actual crittercam footage . . . is usually pretty boring, and hard to interpret," she writes, framing the pleasure as bound up with "scientific knowledge" that was inaccessible before the camera technology was introduced (Haraway 258–59). Viewers are not completely immersed in the world of the eagles because the camera does not replicate their embodied view through boundless flight, but the feed does seem to promise a view that is inaccessible to humans, except through technology. The vulnerable fledglings are in need of protection, and could easily be considered cute, and thus worthy of a viewer's investment, both affective and financial. The Decorah Eagle cam must work to emphasize the much "higher" scientific purpose of the cam, connecting it to the technological feat of this distance monitoring and the sublime character of the eagle as American symbol in order to keep this cuteness from verging into the trivial. Referencing a "male" scientific discipline to manage and control cuteness, the Decorah Eagles Cam thus stands in gendered opposition to the Tiny Kittens feed I will discuss shortly.

Watch Them Grow: Tiny Kittens and Shelter Cams

Perhaps the height of cute triviality is to watch kittens grow up on a live stream, when there are unwanted kittens born in shelters, barns, and alleys all around the world. David Giles, in his taxonomy of animal celebrity types, names the "promotional celebrity" animal, which after being publicized through a human interest piece or otherwise gaining a fan following, continues to "generate publicity for the zoo or other institution where they are kept" (119). Shelter live streams turn one or a few kittens into temporary internet celebrities, drawing attention to the long-standing mission of the shelter while capitalizing on the fleeting cuteness of these baby animals before they mature into the more complex character of full-grown cat.

The 24/7 live kitten stream is the innovation of Shelly Roche, a graphic designer and former Facebook employee who relocated to British Columbia and began to volunteer at a shelter. The webcam initially allowed her to monitor the litters of kittens she began to foster while she was out of the house, but eventually, interest in the stream reached beyond just her immediate fostering needs (*Tiny Kittens*). The Tiny Kittens project now broadcasts live litters of kittens from birth to adoption, often focusing on cats with pressing medical needs or that had been abandoned or discarded in some way. More than just a way to watch kittens online, the Tiny Kittens program has been highly successful in raising money for the umbrella shelter, Langley Animal Protection Society, or LAPS, with which it is associated, a classic function of the promotional celebrity animal. Donations can be made directly to the shelter, but Roche also appears often on camera asking for donations from an Amazon.com wish list of shelter supplies, food, and litter, forming a direct visual and spatial link between the kittens and the personal spending that viewers can engage in to support them. Viewers also have donated new technology, toys for the cats, and even tiny suitcases for them to pack up toys to take to their "furever" homes.

The Tiny Kittens chatters are inclined to use cutesy lolspeak constructions in their commentary and to some extent this is paralleled in the language used by Tiny Kittens itself which also notably plays up the idea that the kittens are rescued from cruel fates, unwanted and discarded, only to become cute, adoptable, and valued by this community and those that will eventually go on to adopt them. Flourishes of rhetorical cuteness such as "furever" homes and "furry tail endings" play up the romantic quality of Tiny Kittens, and encourage viewers to cast themselves as the "heroes" of the story as it unfolds. By watching the feed, using the vocabulary, and perhaps most importantly, supporting the efforts of Tiny Kittens, viewers become active parts of this idealized familial narrative, instead of passive consumers of its cuteness. Watching kittens can't be trivial if viewers are heroes, and while there might be more kittens every time you visit a local shelter, these kittens (thanks to your donations) are out of that system and into permanent homes. This relationship between animal subject and human viewer is much more intimate here than in the case of the Shamu or eagle cams, and this sense of maternal and material care for the vulnerable creatures makes this cuteness both more pronounced and more "feminine." While a picture of a kitten might induce a temporary affective burst, the live stream creates an embodied connection to these kittens, and the liveness heightens the sense of availability and proximity of the kittens to their network of caretakers. If scientific rhetoric demands that viewers maintain a "masculine" distance from the observed subjects, "feminine" viewing dissolves that boundary, encouraging emotional investment.

The kittens are, at the core, highly effective (and affectively charged) "celebrity" fundraisers, for the Tiny Kittens non-profit foundation supports not just the "on-screen" cats, but a wider, unseen population of needy felines. For a recurring monthly donation, or a one-time donation of $100, kitten lovers can become VIPs and have access to an HD webcam which is placed to facilitate "prime viewing" and also take part in raffles in order to win naming rights for kittens in future litters. Tax-deductible VIP status is regularly detailed and promoted on the publicity pages for Tiny Kittens and members regularly identify themselves as VIPs in various social spaces associated with the kittens. More than just passive consumers of these kittens as they grow up in front of the camera, viewers are frequently donors who give money to support both the technical needs of hosting such a large and popular video feed, and to support the actual kittens' physical needs. As Heidi Nast writes in her call for a new field of critical pet studies, this increasingly visible love of pets has "paralleled the growth of post-industrial service and consumption sectors under largely neo-liberal regimes of accumulation, [with] pets figuring as both commodities themselves and sites of intensely commodified investment tied to global inequalities" (Nast 897). What once was limited to in-person volunteering or local shelter support has turned, thanks to the live feed, into a global cause to which anyone around the world can contribute. Chatters perform this support by declaring what they have contributed, or asserting their VIP status, but they also perform their inability to fully participate in a fiscal sense, often announcing that while "money is tight," they have shared posts on Facebook to raise publicity and encourage others to donate. Financial support is best, but publicity to facilitate others to find the feed and support it is also appreciated.

The live nature of the Tiny Kittens live stream allows the animals to be treated differently from cats encountered in still image memes or in short video clips. The kittens are broadcast continuously excepting only technical interruptions, from pre-labor contractions to adoption into their new homes. The stream, started in order to monitor kittens in a foster situation, now exploits human interest in the cute, the fragile, and the adorable and provides constant incentive to tune in. Not unlike long-form experimental cinema, these feeds are both compelling and boring, progressing in real time and challenging the attention of the viewer.[5] Kittens, like their full-grown cat counterparts, sleep the majority of the day, and especially in the first few weeks of life, are contained in a small area and move very little. A viewer must tune in repeatedly, over the course of several months, in order to observe appreciable changes in the kittens, and many express their joy in watching the kittens grow and develop. This joy could be achieved in brief checks of the cam, or even from still pictures, which leads one to ask: why do some viewers watch live, or for hours at a time?

Alongside the video feed itself, there are several social spaces that are built in and around it. These social spaces consist of the chat function on the various live stream channels, as well as the Facebook and Instagram pages maintained by both Roche and fans of the kittens. The most consistent activity is in the chat spaces, especially on the free version of the feed (Figure 6.2). People from all around the world, at all hours of the day and night, comment on the activity of the kittens, using lingo picked up from Roche, derived from lolcats, and perpetuated by the chatters, calling food "fudz," referring to nursing as going to the "milker," or the "milkbar" being opened or closed, and any activity involving kittens running or scampering as "the zoomies." Regular chatters are recognized by screen name or avatar, and new chatters are directed to a long list of rules, vocabulary, and topics to avoid before they are welcomed into the social space. Even though very few chatters go on to adopt on-screen kittens, the entire community is framed

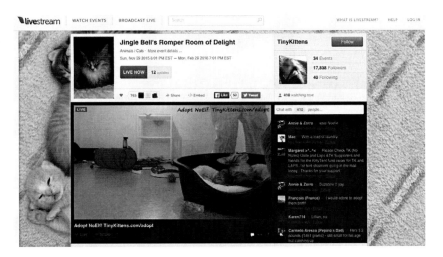

FIGURE 6.2 The Tiny Kittens live stream generates an active chat room in which viewers post detailed observations, often using a "cute-ified" vocabulary.

as directly contributing to their well-being simply by watching, chatting, and spreading the word about adoptions and donations.

The draw of liveness at least partially explains the fascination of this mode of cat media. Still images captured by Roche and posted onto social media sites show the kittens developing, highlighting the small changes in coat, size, bone structure, and physiognomy, but watching the kittens move on the feed allows for movement to be conveyed, interactions between the kittens to be observed, and a heightened sense of embodiment to be felt. The live nature of the feed ensures that even if Roche is not updating the social media feeds, viewers can feel empowered to "check in on" the cats and monitor their development personally. Rather than a recorded clip of the kittens uploaded to a video sharing site like YouTube, the live stream can be both more mundane and more immediate and vibrant, as the images are appearing constantly, in an ever-refreshing manner. When and if the cats experience a crisis or difficulty of some kind (an infection, lower than expected weight gain, physical impairment, etc.), viewers are empowered to observe the kittens and assess their progress themselves, and chatters pride themselves on length of time spent observing the kittens and the ability to pass valuable information to Roche or other chatters about when significant events happened. One chatter calmed others when one kitten appeared to be struggling to gain access to his mother to nurse, by saying, "Otto was just hooked on [to the nipple] about an hour ago, no need to worry," directing other viewers to the time stamp in the saved footage to verify the observation. In this way, viewers feel themselves not just to be passively consuming images of the kittens, but providing a seemingly valuable service through their viewing, directly impacting real kittens.

Chat activity is particularly heated during major events, like births or adoptions, and the role, imagined or real, of the chatters is most clearly enacted. Any time that a birth is imminent, disclaimers are posted on the main hub of communication, the Tiny Kitten's Facebook page, emphasizing that much could go wrong during a birth: kittens could be stillborn, the mother could prove unable to properly clean and prepare them after birth, or they could refuse to breathe, as well as the general warnings about blood and other fluids being present. "This is live, uncensored rescue kitten reality TV," the "PSA" urges; "labor and delivery is hard work, it can be messy and there may be times where we may have our hearts broken." Like trigger warnings in a classroom, these announcements are both meant to warn the viewer that upsetting (i.e. not cute) events may occur while highlighting the live nature of the feed and the unique access viewers are given to the birthing process. During births, chat can become contentious, as both the birth and the technology are open to discussion. During one birth, many criticized the picture or sound quality of the feed ("I keep getting error messages!!" and "is the feed frozen?") consistently asking for Roche to move the camera so that a better view would be possible ("can you move the cam?" and "I can't see anything ☹.") Others remarked that Roche's use of a flashlight to examine the mother during birth was cruel or unsuitable for the kittens as they adjusted to their new surroundings ("and those poor kitties don't need to see that light when they come out! Stop flashing that light!!!! I know their eyes are closed but the light can go through their eyelids kittens [sic]"). Chatters are quality control for the technology, and safeguard for the well-being of the kittens, and thus are imagined as much more active than other internet video watchers.

However, those who regularly observe the chat room and follow the kittens keenly feel the limits of this mode of observation. While the camera may capture events like eating, nursing, playing, or sleeping, it is not an infallible observational eye. The stream often struggles to broadcast in the highest definition, as the bandwidth required is much beyond that of a standard residential internet connection. The lower quality feed can have trouble broadcasting accurate or synced audio, or be so low-resolution that it becomes difficult to tell similar looking kittens apart. The angle of view is also limited, so if the kittens move to a new area, fall asleep behind a toy or piece of furniture, or otherwise escape the boundaries of the viewable area, they can disappear from view for hours at a time. Kittens are also notorious for "cam take-downs," where curiosity about the light and lens-focusing noise draws their attention and often results in the camera being knocked off a tripod and left to focus on the empty carpeted floor or ceiling for hours. Unlike with an edited clip, these moments are tolerated as the cost of live access, and astounding amounts of traffic and chat will occur even when the camera has been focused on carpet for more than a few hours. Liveness, whatever its limitations, has appeal beyond the still image, or short video.

While the chat may seem ancillary to the actual medium of kitten cams, in reality it serves a multitude of functions essential to framing and meaning making of the visual and audio material. The chat provides incentive and function for viewers to stay engaged and interested in the feed even when the stream itself is not captivating. It provides an outlet for viewers to communicate with each other, and build a community around the kittens. Chatting also allows viewers to communicate back to Roche, who often will sit with a computer monitoring the chat talking to the live stream, in a delayed question and answer session. By communicating intermittently with the humans appearing on screen, the chat can feel like a participatory space, with chatters able to actively comment upon and change the course of the stream. However, that power is largely illusory; it would be unreasonable to assume that the livestream's eight hundred average viewers can have personal or even indirect access to the events on screen. Of course Roche doesn't take into account each suggestion or recommendation about where furniture should be positioned, what toys should be purchased, or what kittens should be adopted together because they appear to get along well. However, the chat provides the illusion that this is possible, and thus perpetuates the idea that this is not only a live feed, but also an interactive one where viewers' engagement with the live stream, through watching and chatting, is valuable to the kittens and Tiny Kittens' mission writ large.

The chat serves a circuitous but essential function by furnishing character narratives for the cats themselves. Each kitten is given a name, and as the kittens develop, the chatters insist on noting features of the personality and behaviors of each kitten and creating narratives based around them. Kittens that aggressively feed or climb over each other to nurse are characterized as "determined," kittens that sleep are dubbed "calm" and "reserved." Just as with human infants, it is nearly impossible to observe personality traits in extremely young kittens as their lives are dominated by the need to feed and sleep. Anthropomorphism is certainly at work here, as the assigning of personality traits allows viewers to build more satisfying narratives about the (often dull) content they are consuming, but it also serves other, more economic functions. In order to make the cats attractive to viewers, potential adopters and perhaps most significantly, potential donors, characterizations play into narratives of cuteness, helplessness, and vulnerability that ensure continuing interest. Kittens born with difficulties (low birth weight, infections, congenital defects) quickly rise to prominence in the litter as viewers can more easily narrate their lives and extract meaning from otherwise unremarkable events. A kitten nursing is simply an animal following its biological imperative, but if that kitten was the runt of the litter, his or her nursing becomes a sign of resilience, determination, and survival in a character-based narrative. Adopting the fractious kitten, or the loving, attentive kitten, or the calm and relaxed kitten is much more satisfying than adopting one of six undifferentiated kittens in a litter, but the characterization comes at a cost. Animals are returned to shelters every day for not living up to their expected behaviors, and the risk of anthropomorphism is that it encourages adopting the neat narrative of the cat, rather than the complex, embodied reality of the cat. Chat reinforces and solidifies these narratives, which often continue into the lives of the kittens in their adoptive homes, where their new owners are encouraged to create and maintain public Facebook pages with visual and narrative updates on how the cats are adjusting to their new lives as feline micro-celebrities.

The Tiny Kittens live stream, and the chat that accompanies it, must work against the burdens of liveness and interactivity to add complexity and nuance into the character narratives created. The live stream is wildly popular because of the nature of the medium. The ever-updating content and illusion of interactivity has built a virtual community that busies itself by creating narratives to both inject meaning into the visually dull stream and create opportunities to leverage narrative for economic or personal gain, with online businesses making cat toys promoted on the stream, and Roche appearing to work with Tiny Kittens as a full-time profession. The cuteness of the cats is a draw, but only intermittently: the live nature of the stream, and the fiscal health of Tiny Kittens, depends on the repeat viewing and intense engagement with the cats being filmed. Narratives around the cats flatten the embodied experience of the cats into a trite anthropomorphized soap opera, but it provides easy monetization. Tiny Kittens raises awareness about unwanted cat populations everywhere, encouraging that viewers spay and neuter animals while simultaneously relying on unaltered animals for the raw material keeping the feed active.

All litters eventually grow up and leave the Tiny Kittens nest. Kittens only stay small for a few months, and are eventually adopted, forgoing minor celebrity life online for life in carefully vetted adoptive homes. But viewership numbers remain surprisingly consistent, suggesting a core community that remains committed not to the individual cats, but the social spaces produced around the live cam. Lauren Berlant argues that "an intimate public operates when a market opens up to a bloc of consumers, claiming to circulate texts and things that express those people's particular core interests and desires" (5). The intimate public of the Tiny Kittens space is on the surface bound together by the kittens themselves, a core interest of many of the self-proclaimed animal lovers who show up day after day to watch low-quality feeds of kittens sleeping and nursing. These chatters, who hail from all corners of the world (a fact that is often emphasized when one member initiates a "roll call" to have others announce where they are located), are strangers to one another just as they are strangers to the cats they consume, but share an intimacy all the same. While users attempt to bring chat topics back to the kittens, conversations often drift to the medical conditions (PTSD, anxiety, depression) that users claim are soothed by the kittens, or the shared feeling that these "unwanted and abused" kittens that the organization so proudly claims to rescue share an affinity with those watching who must defend their time spent watching kittens to those in their lives. As one chatter says: "even the smallest of toes and the tiniest of ears matter in this weary world," reflecting back the cultural unease that so many feel in our increasingly atomized culture. The reward for tuning in is not the sense of justice and protection found in monitoring the

Shamu Cam, nor the contribution to scientific knowledge promised in the Decorah Eagles cam, but a burst of affect and maternal instinct ritualized in the excited language of the kitten cam chatters, and is not without ideological import, as Chapter 1 in this volume so deftly argues. As viewers watch, care for, and donate to support these marginalized cats from sometimes thousands of miles away, the intimate public built around these cute kittens serves as a safe, welcoming space to exercise the weak, fleeting, "feminine" juvenile, but ultimately addictive affect of cuteness in real time, for as long as the internet connection holds out.

I Can't Believe You Watch That: Live Stream Appeal

Jonathan Crary has argued that the trope of 24/7 has come to stand for a "time that no longer passes, beyond clock time," marker and symptom of "neoliberal globalization . . . and Western modernization" (8). While it might be easier to relate this timeless quality back to the on-demand, binge-watching models of media that are facilitated by high-speed internet connections, and built into marketing and distribution plans as whole seasons of shows are released at once to be consumed outside of the fixed schedules of network television, that timeless quality is also present in the live streams examined here. Animal live streams, although consistently dismissed as trivial, model this phenomenon as sites where hours can pass where kittens are only sleeping, and the eagle cam broadcasts all year, despite the fact that the eagles only nest there for two or three months maximum. Unlike still photographs, edited films, or even live television, live feeds encourage the viewer to visit the animals rather than consume them, to incorporate them into the disordered rhythms of late capitalist lives. Just as work and play are no longer confined to set schedules, so too has cuteness been liberated: one only needs to log on for the next live affective hit, and the longer one watches, the more cuteness is available. The long form duration of the feed rewards careful attention in all of the cases detailed here. Viewers can feel a connection to animals as they grow and change, and because the live nature of the feed suggests that all aspects of the animal lives are being broadcast, it becomes easier to connect with the embodied animal being displayed.

Liveness stands in for embodiment, and by showing viewers all behaviors and not only the cute ones, these cams frame their visualizations as more true, more realistic, and more authentic than other media representations. Cuteness becomes an affective relationship that is earned by sifting through hours of non-cute material, a ratio that is much closer to that found "in the wild," and therefore more authentic. While of the examples discussed here, only Tiny Kittens traffics directly in the commodification of cuteness in order to engage its public, all three streams rely on the emotional connection to the animal to keep viewers engaged minute after minute, day after day. Live streams undermine the sense that animals are cute all the time by showing us the boring moments in between, but the constant performance is still oriented towards the viewer. Connections to the animals pictured allows for advocacy that can remove whales from captivity, facilitate financial contributions to shelters that allow more kittens to be adopted, or launch preservation initiatives for the habitats of endangered species. Animals on live stream cameras might not be cute all the time, but when they are, viewers experience it as an authentic cuteness, and therefore worthy of any number of types of investment.

Notes

1   Literary scholars taking up the subject of the banal and mundane include Saikat Majumdar, while the study of boredom in the field of psychology has seen several new works produced in the past ten years (Koerth-Baker).
2   SeaWorld, a brand of amusement parks around the United States, has come under fire from multiple sources because of its practice of keeping large sea mammals (orca whales, dolphins, sea lions) in captivity and using them as trained performers. The chain is experiencing financial distress, with profits down 84 percent in 2014 according to one report in the *Guardian* (Neate).
3   SeaWorld has recently announced that it will no longer be featuring orcas in performances at the park, although as of the time of this writing, the shows had not yet been phased out (Izadi).
4   A simple search of YouTube reveals several of these videos, and there are also numerous Facebook groups dedicated to documenting the cam's images.
5   Although films like Snow's *Wavelength* and Warhol's *Empire* engage directly with duration, perhaps the most direct comparison is with Gordon's *24 Hour Psycho* and its gallery installation, which allows patrons to enter in and watch portions of the film while remaining aware of the larger narrative that plays out over the entire 24-hour duration of the piece (Snow; Warhol; "Douglas Gordon").

Works Cited

"About Us." *Raptor Resource Project*. n.d. Online. 18 Dec. 2015.
"American Eagle." *Nature*. PBS, 15 Nov. 2008. Online. 18 Dec. 2015.
Auslander, Philip. *Liveness: Performance in a Mediatized Culture*. London: Routledge, 2008.
Berg, Alec (dir.) "Two Days of the Condor." *Silicon Valley*. HBO. 14 June 2015. Television. www.imdb.com/title/tt4185460/.
Berlant, Lauren. *The Female Complaint: The Unfinished Business of Sentimentality in American Culture*. Durham, NC: Duke University Press, 2008.
Cowperthwaite, Gabriela, dir. *Blackfish*. Magnolia Home Entertainment, 2013. Film.
Crary, Jonathan. *24/7: Late Capitalism and the Ends of Sleep*. London: Verso, 2014.
Decorah Eagles. Ustream. IBM, n.d. Online. 12 Feb. 2016.
Doane, Mary Ann. "Information, Crisis, Catastrophe." *Logics of Television: Essays in Cultural Criticism*. Ed. Patricia Mellencamp. Bloomington, IN: Indiana University Press, 1990. 222–39.
"Douglas Gordon: Timeline | MoMA." *The Museum of Modern Art*. MoMA, n.d. Online. 15 Feb. 2016.
Giles, David C. "Animal Celebrities." *Celebrity Studies* 4.2 (2013): 115-28. Online.

Haraway, Donna J. *When Species Meet*. Minneapolis, MN: University of Minnesota Press, 2008.

Izadi, Elahe. "SeaWorld Is Ending Its Killer Whale Shows in San Diego." *Washington Post* 9 Nov. 2015. Online. 15 Feb. 2016.

Koerth-Baker, Maggie. "Why Boredom is Anything but Boring." *Nature*. Macmillan, 12 Jan. 2016. Online. 10 June 2016.

Majumdar, Saikat. *Prose of the World: Modernism and the Banality of Empire*. New York: Columbia University Press, 2013.

Nast, Heidi J. "Critical Pet Studies?" *Antipode* 38.5 (2006): 894–906. Online. 18 Mar. 2016.

Neate, Rupert. "SeaWorld Sees Profits Plunge 84% as Customers Desert Controversial Park." *Guardian*. Guardian Media Group, 6 Aug. 2015. Online. 15 Feb. 2016.

Ngai, Sianne. *Our Aesthetic Categories: Zany, Cute, Interesting*. Cambridge, MA: Harvard University Press, 2012.

SeaWorld(r) Parks & Entertainment. *Behind The Scenes: Orca Care | SeaWorld(r)*. Film.

"SeaWorld Entertainment, Inc. Reports Second Quarter 2015 Results." Online. 5 Oct. 2015.

"Shamu's Underwater Viewing." *Seaworld Parks: San Diego*. SeaWorld Parks and Entertainment, n.d. Online. 18 Dec. 2015.

Snow, Michael, dir. *Wavelength*, 1967. Film.

Tiny Kittens. Tiny Kittens Society, n.d. Online. 15 Feb. 2016. http://livestream.com/tinykittens

van Doorn, Niels. "Broadcasting Boredom and the Attention Economy of Media Culture." 2016. Unpublished manuscript.

Warhol, Andy, dir. *Empire*. 1964. Film.

Wincer, Simon, dir. *Free Willy*. Warner Bros., 1993. Film.

"The World's Most Popular Live Streaming Video: 200 Million Eagles Fans Can't be Wrong." *Forbes*. Online. 17 Dec. 2015.

7

WHEN AWE TURNS TO AWWW . . .

Jeff Koons's *Balloon Dog* and the Cute Sublime

Elizabeth Legge

The recognition that category-defying, postmodern artist Jeff Koons's work thematically engages with cuteness is not unprecedented. Sheri Klein, for example, notes that "contemporary artists rely on the aesthetic of cuteness to lure viewers, in particular in the works by William Wegman and Jeff Koons" (112). Seeking to deepen these accounts, this article investigates a number of Koons's most recognizable works, in particular his metal sculpture *Balloon Dog* (1994–2000) in a series of five brilliantly colored stainless steel versions (*Blue, Magenta, Yellow, Orange,* and *Red*), through the lens of cuteness (see Figure 7.1).

Balloon Dog is a test case for the ways the cute marks its territory in the domain of high art. While not all of Koons's work fits the classic Lorenzian schema of cuteness or indeed subsequent theoretical work on the topic, Koons significantly adapts features of the cute to powerful and persistent effect. Indeed, *Balloon Dog* may be productively viewed as a prime example of a popular aesthetic of the cute and the kitsch, allied to product design of its time, introduced into an art world ordinarily impenetrable and impervious to those aesthetic registers. In that capacity *Balloon Dog* is something of a Trojan Horse, and as such it is particularly usefully analyzed through an aesthetics of cuteness. Its cuteness becomes further legible when it is situated in terms of the theory and criticism in the postmodern time period of its making, inviting questions surrounding what writing enables it and what writing it engenders. Ultimately then, the goal of this article is to elucidate key features of Koons's sensational and yet somehow enigmatic work that might otherwise be embarrassedly bypassed or hidden in plain sight.

Certainly, *Balloon Dog* has been hard to categorize. While it set a sales record for work by a living artist in a Christie's auction in 2013 (Vogel), it has often been dismissed as a glittery consumerist lure without much redeeming intellectual or critical purchase; or, at best, as the *New York Times* reviewer Jed Perl said in response to Koons's huge 2014 retrospective at the Whitney Museum in New York, as "catnip for intellectuals" (Perl). Koons's work raises questions of how far the cute, without the redeeming irony that might signal some critique of art as consumer goods, can be pushed toward conveying a generalized importance or portentousness while remaining cute, and of how much the cute can be compromised by being situated in the context of art and its critical reception— again, while remaining cute.

Balloon Dog's cute features are complicated by its size and its symbolic baggage. Physically, its cuteness begins with its little nose, made of the terminal knot of a balloon, the quintessence of a pert, popular cultural ideal of a child's nose, yearning to be tweaked; and, given the umbilical aspect of the balloon knot, there is something newborn to it—again, cute. That cuteness however is complicated by its keen stance, lean body, and show dog pose. While its legs might convey the pudgy cuteness of a toddler, and, in the film *Night at the Museum 2: Battle of the Smithsonian* (2009), the cuteness of *Balloon Dog* is emphasized through buoyantly

FIGURE 7.1 Arguably combining the cute with the kitsch, Jeff Koons's *Balloon Dog* challenges definitions of cuteness, just as the sculpture series unsettles notions pertaining to artistic seriousness and worth. *Balloon Dog*. 1994–2000. Mirror-polished stainless steel with transparent color. 121 × 143 × 45 inches/307.3 × 363.2 × 114.3 cm. 5 unique versions (Blue, Magenta, Yellow, Orange, Red).

animated locomotion, as it springily bounces and flails like a shambolic puppy; yet, when taken with the erect uninflated tip of its tail, we see a show clip and not a puppy (see also Ahmed). And then, a further complication is its imposing size: 10 feet tall and 12 feet long. Where *Balloon Dog*'s cuteness might be thought to be diminished by that size, it arguably amplifies its cuteness, inducing an anthropomorphizing sense of valiant overreaching on the part of the plucky little fellow. Given that cuteness has consistently been aligned with smallness by authors such as Konrad Lorenz and Sianne Ngai, the enormity of *Balloon Dog* is both surprising and perplexing.[1] Therefore, the pressure of its aspirational size is usefully thought of not so much in terms of the relations implied by "scale" as in terms of a more naïve, less architecturally or art-historically inflected "bigness," returning us to a childhood perception of our position in the relative scale of things. Seen in this light, the dog is like a giant toy aspiring to be a monument. Further, given its show dog aspect, *Balloon Dog* might claim to be the quintessence of its balloon breed, as if a monumental sculpture of itself: the equestrian statue of balloon animals. As such, it is also situated in the tradition of anthropomor-phized animals as instrumental symbols and mirrors of human subjectivity, serving human uses as social, political, and moral models (Baker 125).

In 2006, *Balloon Dog (Magenta)* was installed on the Grand Canal in Venice in front of the Palazzo Grassi, which housed French businessman François Pinault's art collection, and served as a trophy and emblem of the status of the major collector. At the Chateau de Versailles in 2008, in an exhibition largely funded by Pinault, it resonated with the equestrian statue of Louis XIV in the palace forecourt; and, installed under the baroque ceiling painting of the apotheosis of Hercules in the Sun King's grand chambers, it was as if another hero were waiting to be sucked up into the skies with the gods, fitting right in with the regal inflationary claims and ostentation of kings and collectors. In other words, Koons's political gesture of inflating what we would expect to be diminutive undercuts viewer expectations while destabilizing prevailing art hierarchies.

Another key feature of the dog's hybrid putative cuteness is its surface, both in its balloon origins as rubber stretched to tautness, and in its realization in glossy metal with a jewel-colored coat. Given the impulse to squeeze or poke or fondle a vulnerable creature, the *Balloon Dog*, insofar as it represents a swollen balloon, induces touch, in the way the giggling "Poppin' Fresh" Pillsbury Doughboy is always poked in his swelling tummy ("abdomen" won't answer to the cute effect) by a giant finger, and coyly pops right back. A corporate mascot invented in 1965, Poppin' Fresh is one epitome of the cute as marketed to the baby boom generation of which Koons is a member. Some of Poppin' Fresh's cuteness relies partly on the fact that he is made of pure white dough through and through, a perfected form of unfleshly embodiment, as if an immortal child: a modern equivalent of the cherubs and *putti* of art tradition.[2] Moreover, as with dough, prodding a balloon may be gratifying, but poking a balloon past its point of resilience until it pops is a darker gratification. *Balloon Dog* acknowledges the cuteness of poke-able, squeezable rubber objects (Ngai, *Our* 64–66); but insofar as it is made of steel, it resists any such indignity. That armored effect is in turn undermined by the hyper-reflective metal finish, which, paradoxically, creates another impression of vulnerability: the brightly colored steel looks as breakable as a Christmas ornament. Indeed, Koons played up precisely that illusion of fragility in the giant Easter eggs of his *Celebration* series, which anticipate our knowledge that most chocolate eggs, like cast metal sculptures, are hollow, and that real eggs break. The glittering emptied fragments of very thin steel eggshell in *Cracked Egg* (1994) make the illusion of frangibility explicit. *Balloon Dog*, too, goes back and forth between provoking us to pet it or pop it; that is, whether to pop it—insofar as it is a balloon—or to smash it—insofar as it is not a balloon.

To briefly contextualize Koons's *Balloon Dog*, it notably emerged in 1994 in a company of balloon dogs, including the artist Bruce Nauman's video installation *Coffee Spilled and Balloon Dog* (1993), and the poet Thomas Sayers Ellis's response to Nauman in the poem *Balloon Dog* (1993) (Sayers Ellis 22–25). In Nauman's installation, one video shows the artist repeatedly dropping and spilling a cup of coffee; and in the other, a man trying and failing to make a balloon dog. Both are in slow motion, which enhances the excruciating futility of the enterprise, and deepens and distorts the sound of the man breathing and balloon squeaking, as if plaintively. In a related work, *Falls, Pratfalls, and Sleights of Hand* (1993), exhibited in New York in February 1994, Nauman projected slow-motion videos of both dexterous and slapstick activities, including magic tricks, sliding on a banana peel, and two hands making a balloon dog (Hagen). Sayers Ellis's poem, written in response to Nauman's videos, is more poignant. It opens with terse implosive words—"Snap. Blow. Twist. Squeak" (Sayers Ellis 22)—that capture the feeling of the balloon's anthropomorphic vulnerability, as heard in Nauman's soundtrack, "Squeak" is the pleading of the small creature it is turning into, as if in being created it were having its neck wrung. Poignantly, the balloon dog, because it is not a real dog, cannot be "anybody's best friend" (Sayers Ellis 23).[3] The clown bringing it to life is "the only one capable" of "seriously loving old air and rubber" (Sayers Ellis 22). In its proneness to being squeezed, its smallness, anthropomorphic appeal, and childlike or pet-like dependence on the poet/clown's parental care and affection, the balloon dog in the poem manifests cuteness.

Where Nauman's videos are an endurance test for the audience, Sayers Ellis's balloon dog elicits the impulse to care for its "little balloon heart" (Sayers Ellis 22). That vulnerable and diminutive appeal resonates in a tragicomic way through cuteness. In responding to Nauman, the poem understands the making of the balloon dog as the bathetic or overly sentimental making of art. As a meta-phor for the creation of the poem that describes it, Sayers Ellis's balloon dog acquires a tenuous status: its leaking air is a kind of off-gassing of the poet's ego that enables the making of the poem (Sayers Ellis 23). At the poem's end, the balloon dog occupies a strangely dignified ambivalent position, caught between inconsequence and importance, between "what goes Pop" and "Art" (Sayers Ellis

25). Koons, like the poet, was likely in dialogue with Nauman, having been in an exhibition with him in 1993,[4] and his *Balloon Dog* too negotiates "what goes Pop" and "Art," conferring a compensatory status on the lowly created object as if inflating a balloon were a metaphor for expanded meaning. The relationship of Koons's *Balloon Dog* to art—his own and others', to what he says about art, and to the institutional and theoretical hierarchies and exigencies he faces down, inflect what is arguably a strange and anomalous cute.

Postmodern Koons and the Cute

To further frame the critical environment in which Koons's work evolved into his cute balloon animals—Koons's route to the cute—it is important to note that he emerged as an artist in New York in the mid-1980s, a cultural and temporal context informed by postmodern questions about the nature of the aesthetic. In his influential 1985 book *Postmodern Culture*, art critic and theorist Hal Foster expressed doubt that inherited categories of the "aesthetic" could remain valid, given "mass mediation," and he proposed an "anti-aesthetic" rooted in everyday vernacular culture as a mode of resistance to hierarchical orders of representation in art (xiii). In that context Koons was credible in a field of artists revisiting and ostensibly critiquing the grand American modernisms—Abstract Expressionism, Pop, Conceptual Art, and Minimalism—and the intellectual and critical claims made for them. Parody, pastiche, and the deadpan ironies of appropriation, taking existing images from commercial media and canonical art and redeploying them in skeptical a-historical collision, were the principal moves. As an index of the relative weight of these theoretical concerns, it was significant that the cover of the catalogue for the 1986 exhibition at the Boston Institute of Contemporary Art, *Endgame: Reference and Simulation in Recent Painting* (Joselit), listed the names of the A-list art historians (including Hal Foster), who wrote for it, rather than those of the artists (including Koons) exhibited in it. In the catalogue the artists' moves were theorized as engaging with the artwork's collapse into commodity fetish understood to be a critique of artistic mastery (Foster, "Future" 95).

In *Endgame*, Koons exhibited floating basketballs and the then brand new "wet/dry" vacuum cleaners in vitrines in his series *The Pre-New* and *The New* (1979). The work profited from the historical credibility attached to the Duchampian "readymade," especially as it was described by the philosopher Jean-François Lyotard in *Artforum*, as a technologically produced thing that no longer answers to any existing aesthetic or consensus of established taste (Lyotard, "Presenting" 64–69).[5] Koons evoked both the conventions of taxonomic museum display (ironically, since contemporary art had long escaped the glass case), and of department store display, allowing consumerist fantasy about brand new things to run interference with aesthetic contemplation.[6] In the *Endgame* catalogue, Foster saw in Koons a recognition of the way the commodity fetish replaces the use value of things within the economy of simulacra and signs, so that basketballs, vacuum cleaners, and works of art are fungible or exchangeable. Yet while giving the work this intellectual credit, Foster prophetically wondered whether Koons's "mediated" sculpture was in fact "more camp than critique?" ("Future" 98–99). Given Susan Sontag's foundational account of Camp as a "sensibility that converts the serious into the frivolous," Foster's question about Koons's tone and intentions was pointed (Sontag 275–92).

Koons seems to have taken Foster's critical concern about Camp as an action plan, since his next exhibition, *Banality* (1988), was mediated by Susan Sontag's point about, precisely, Camp-as-banality. Sontag argued that since an historical work of art is liable to lose its original moral or aesthetic relevance over time, its present-day audience is happily disengaged from any demanding intellectual or aesthetic response:

> Time liberates the work of art from moral relevance, delivering it over to the Camp sensibility . . . (Banality is, strictly speaking, always a category of the contemporary.) What was banal can, with the passage of time, become fantastic. [. . .] Thus, things are campy, not when they become old—but when we become less involved in them, and can enjoy, instead of be frustrated by, the failure of the attempt. (285)

Koons devised his own contemporaneity as banality, fast-tracking the passage of time that allows a work of art to become banal and "fantastic" within the mechanisms of Camp, going straight for already kitsch objects—things that are gratifying in excessive or sentimental ways—as stand-ins for art. In *Banality* iconographies and symbolic meaning are stripped of time-laden accumulated art historical weight and reconfigured as Camp. For example, that staple of Western cultural history, Ovid's account of the metamorphoses of gods and mortals turned to animals for purposes of sexual congress, seems to be reenacted with an eye to its cute anthropomorphizing potential. The cheerfully humanlike bear couple of *Winter Bears* (she with a valentine heart on her handbag), and the baby doll *Amore* (which, because it is also a teddy bear, might be the result of interspecies coupling) announce an Ovidian erotics reduced to a reductively sentimental "I heart" sticker. In *Bear and Policeman*, the bear, with an alarming grin, towers over the English bobby and toys with his whistle in a bit of unnervingly sexual Freudian stage business. The startled cartoon panther in *Pink Panther* embraces a stereotypically blonde bombshell while mugging at the viewer over her shoulder as if he doesn't know what to do next. In these works, Koons puts pressure on the indeterminate aesthetic of the cute, as if testing its capacity to absorb the dirty joke or impending violence. Here then, Ovidian rape and metamorphosis collide with childhood story books and cartoons in a squeamish limbo.

Koons's Camp is consistent with Pierre Bourdieu's sociological account of the ways that aestheticizing operations may be directed at things that are not art (xxviii; 169). Bourdieu addressed the class coding of taste: where Kantian beauty requires disinterestedness, working-class or popular taste of the "common people" looks to gratification as the legitimating ethos for art, conferring aesthetic status on "banal" or "common" objects (Bourdieu xxix; 470). For his *Statuary* (1986) series Koons produced stainless steel casts of corny ornaments—Koons refers to the medium as "poor people's platinum" (Schjeldahl, "Selling Points")—a "naughty" needle-wielding doctor about to inject a nurse's backside, a statuette of the comedian Bob Hope, a bust of Louis XIV (evoking the 1950s "Miami Beach French" decor of Morris Lapidus), and a "mermaid troll." These remind us that Koons's first forays into art were made for his father's interior decorating business (Deitch 216–17). In *Banality* he presents the tastes not only of Bourdieu's common people, but also of another generation, given the temporal distance of Camp, hence Sontag's complementary observation that Camp is to be found in the outmoded and in "all the elements of visual décor" applies here as well (Sontag 278). In other words, Koons worked his way into cute through Camp and kitsch; hence his route to the cuteness of *Balloon Dog* was through the modes of triviality legitimized and ironized by theoretical Camp. His work evolved within the context of cheap, glittery, and jokey objects that could be ironically deployed in terms of kitsch and Camp; and at the same time, it rejects the knowing ironies that that theorization demands and, through cuteness, goes for instant affect. His engagement with dominant critical and theoretical apparatuses over the course of his career, as I suggest below, takes the form of modifying them and stripping them of any features, especially irony, that might endanger the deployment of cuteness as if on its own terms for its own sake.

Koons's own artist statements, derived from popular self-help rhetoric, provide a safe lexical haven for the cute and amount to fridge magnet self-empowerment nostrums of "acceptance," meant to introduce his audience into the world of instant affect that enables the cute. As Foster intimated, Koons's work might once have been construed as critique of Conceptual Art's critique of the art work as consumerist object. But Koons rejects any such positioning. His project *Baptism*, published in *Artforum* in 1987, adopted a Conceptual Art look, pairing photographs and text to renounce the very "criticality" that fueled Conceptual Art. "Criticality gone," he announced, "liberating" himself into the "romance," "power," and "spirituality" of the "mainstream" (Koons). Nearly thirty years after his provisional praise in *Endgame*, Hal Foster now observes that Koons's slogans serve the manipulative "therapy culture" of neoliberal ideology that "seeks to promote our 'self-confidence' and 'self-worth' as human capital" ("At the Whitney" 23). Indeed, Koons echoes the vocabulary of Abraham Maslow's *Motivation and Personality* (1954), which became a commonplace of management studies (Libert). Maslow's famous "hierarchy of needs" proceeds from the lower registers of physical needs, up through creative expression, self-esteem, and social status, to the peak of "self-actualization." While an employer may get more out of an employee by addressing these needs, Maslow's rhetoric has a quasi-spiritual aspiration to ultimate "ego transcendence," since the gratification of basic needs alone can lead to boredom (xiv–xv). Similarly, Koons says: "I really believe that to have transcendence into the highest realms you have to have acceptance of others. You have to leave the self. You get so bored with the self" (qtd. in Perl; Maslow 104, 194). Where Maslow wrote that "even the normal member of our culture feels unnecessarily guilty or ashamed about too many things and has anxiety in too many unnecessary situations" (155), Koons urges an end to middleclass "guilt and shame." In his rejection of "judgments" in favor of "acceptance" (qtd. in Swanson; Lee 220), Koons seems to inhabit Maslow's highest peaks of fully self-actualized "motivational development," where creation is "spontaneous, guileless, open, self-disclosing, and unedited and therefore expressive . . ." (Maslow 66). This combination of the rhetorics of instrumental corporate psychology and consoling pop spirituality may be just the thing to frame a cute aesthetic if we are to understand its operations more fully.

To his blandly inclusive sayings, Koons adds an absolutely unrevealing interview technique borrowed from political spin. Given the increasing conflation of the artwork with the theoretical discourse that informs and justifies it in the "artist's statement," so that, with Minimalism and Conceptual Art in the 1960s, the work of art became its own theorized response (Morris), Koons's statements, or "talking points," are essential to his work, almost as a way of evacuating those expectations of the artist's statement. For example, when an interviewer proposed that the intensely mirroring surfaces of Koons's stainless steel balloon works might be designed to give a "certain Lacanian pleasure," alluding to the psychoanalyst Jacques Lacan's ubiquitous theoretical account of an infant's "mirror stage" identification with his reflection as a more powerful and competent self, Koons skirts the theory, firmly bringing matters back to his talking points: "I believe in love and life—in the past, the moment, and the future. Art invites you into human history" (Diehl). Here, all the implicit terms—love, life, time, art, history—might be liable to various theorized qualifications—sexuality, mortality, temporality, teleology, eschatology—but the only possible intellectual yield Koons offers could be summarized as a smiley "whatever," a word that constitutes an all-embracing and all-dismissing environment for cuteness.

Further Along the Path to the Cute

In what follows, I want to move on to a discussion of how Koons has policed or deployed language and critical terminology to give safe haven to the cute, in ways which are fundamental to questions that coalesce around the aesthetic consideration of cuteness. The critical response to *Banality* questioned what formulation of the aesthetic might serve the cute or allow it to communicate itself. Would it involve a kind of "critical slumming"? This dilemma is hyperbolized in the art critic Peter Schjeldahl's response to *Banality*: Koons's work is "staggeringly vulgar" and "as self-explanatory as a kick in the stomach," and yet, he concludes with a kind of aesthetic bulimia brought on by the all-too-accessible and gratifying: "I love it, and pardon me while I throw up" (*Hydrogen* 307).[7] This ambivalence points to a core aspect of the cute, which is that its directly pleasurable affect may be complicated by negative affect. For example, the subjects of one psychology study, when presented with increasingly infantile stimuli—baby pictures—experienced increasingly stronger positive feelings; but these feelings were expressed as simultaneous impulses to caress the baby and to pinch the baby, or to devour the baby, as in the commonplace, "I could eat you up" (Aragón et al.) (Which returns my argument to the Pillsbury Dough Boy.) Researchers hypothesize that such dimorphous or dual responses are adaptive as a way of regulating and tamping down overly positive emotions that threaten to be overwhelming (Aragón et al. 260). These mixed features are part and parcel of Jeff Koons's effects, and go some distance to explaining critics' frequent incapacity to deal with the work using extant critical vocabulary.

The powerful ambiguity of Koons's cute was fully fledged in the breakout figure in the *Statuary* series, *Rabbit* (1986), a dollar store plastic inflatable bunny embodying a familiar corny cartoon anthropomorphism transmuted to glossy stainless steel (Figure 7.2).

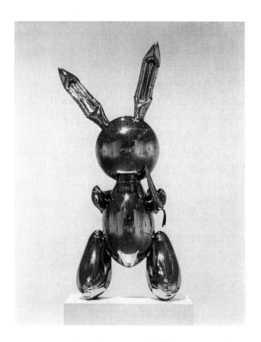

FIGURE 7.2 Constituting a challenge to machine aesthetic modernism, *Rabbit* at once invokes the childlike and the sexual in a piece where cuteness is hybridized with high aesthetic seriousness. Jeff Koons. *Rabbit*. 1986. Stainless steel. 41 × 19 × 12 inches/104.1 × 48.3 × 30.5 cm. Edition of three plus Artist's Proof.

Once stripped of the lurid colors and the goofy facial features of its original plastic prototype, *Rabbit* emerged as a brilliant challenge to the machine aesthetic modernism of Constantin Brancusi's sleek bronze *Bird in Space* (1928), and could be imagined, again, as ironic postmodern critique of the claims made for MoMA-sanctioned modernist "masterwork." *Rabbit* has a baby-like round stomach that invites patting or tickling, and its splayed little legs and vestigial arms suggest a toddler's characteristic side-to-side gait and inept grasp. Only forty-one inches tall, it is child size: we imagine we could pick it up. And yet there is an edge to the rabbit. Its strangely sharp pointed ears project like missile launchers, and at the same time are unnervingly fleshy and vulval, deeply grooved within their swelling edges. They set up a visual conversation with the rabbit's carrot as if a goofy phallic lingam and vaginal yoni. The witty coexistence of the cartoonish toy and the gravely abstract artwork; the immature and the sexualized; and the malleable and the armored submit cultural constructs of the childlike as cuteness to a certain stress. *Rabbit*'s cuteness is hybridized with high modernist seriousness.

If the *Statuary* and *Banality* works might have seemed jocular postmodern interventions, the *Made in Heaven* series (1989–91), Koons's sexual collaboration with the porn star Ilona Staller in many permutations pressed the cute into a more demanding service. The cutely childlike was Staller's principal sexual selling point—she recorded obscene lyrics to the tunes of children's songs and carried around a teddy bear. Her nickname, "La Cicciolina," was itself cute, a diminutive term for her pudenda, signifying the pudgily or pinchably cute in Italian. *Made in Heaven* provoked muted to hostile critical response (Russell). Koons's white heterosexual condomless narrative seemed tasteless at the height of the AIDS epidemic, and offensive to an art world distraught about the censorship of Robert Mapplethorpe's work and the consequent funding cuts to the National Endowment for the Arts. Using Staller's own sets and costumes, *Made in Heaven* staged a prelapsarian cuteness with giant butterflies, pastel-colored teddy bears, and wreaths of flowers, along with Koons's chubby putti, shaggy puppies, fluffy cat, and swelling bouquets of flowers in porcelain and polychrome wood. This might be taken as a pretty mockery of Mapplethorpe's somber cryogenic black-and-white photographs of sexualized flowers and homoerotic fetish practices; a prettiness interrupted by Koons's and Staller's unairbrushed and unwreathed genitals that punctuate the *Made in Heaven* series like a penetration of the Lacanian real into the cute sets of an orgasmic cartoon princess surrounded by adorable attributes.

Balloons and the Shiny

Made in Heaven led Koons not to a continuing exploration of sex as such, but, recalling erection metaphors, to the cute made large. As aesthetic judgments are always part of situations of intellectual and social positioning, the cute, tainted by sentimentality, has to look out for itself. It can ward off judgment either by being evermore disarmingly cute—the cat is cute, the kitten cuter—or by capitalizing on some not-so-cute element that might allow us to imagine that it has a concealed edge. An example of the latter tactic would be Takashi Murakami's creature *Mr. DOB*, a kind of manic Mickey Mouse who alternates between a rictus synchronized swimmer smile and fanged grin. Koons shares with Murakami the inflation of something small into something large, but avoids the openly monstrous. An example of the former tactic, of cutening the cute, is the way the little *White Terrier* from *Made in Heaven* was scaled up to the 40-foot-tall flower-covered *Puppy* (1992). That move submits the conventionally cute features of things that are small, pliable, powerless, and childlike to the pressures of scale, so that cuteness has to negotiate its role within the adult monumental, as if some agency had been thrust upon it. Installed outside the Bilbao Guggenheim, *Puppy* was meant to instill "confidence and security" ("Puppy"), as if for all its plushy puppyish nature it aspired to be a guard dog. This cuteness made large informed Koons's turn to big sculptures based on balloons, the first of which was *Balloon Dog* (1994).

Bearing in mind Koons's attention to artwork as consumer product, *Balloon Dog* resonates with the "cutifaction" of manufacturing in the early 1990s and the sophisticated product design of its time. As Marilyn Ivy has noted, Koons's monstrous balloon sculptures have the "shine and gloss of the commodity form and [the] sheen of glossy technical achievement" characteristic of 1990s product design (17). In this regard, Koonsian cuteness is related to the Italian manu-facturer Alessi's "Family Follows Fiction" houseware line (1993) that claimed to explore the creative processes of children and "primitive cultures" [sic] ("Gino Zucchino Sugar Castor"); that is, it tapped into the psychology of "reptilian" emotions and basic drives that inform product design ("Interview: Clotaire Rapaille"). Alessi's anthropomorphic designs, such as Gino Venturini's sugar dispenser, capitalized on the Lorenzian cuteness of large-eyed, entirely rounded, almost fetal shapes; as tools, they were toys that invited the simul-taneously affectionate and aggressive gesture of squeezing triggered by the cute. Similarly, the rounded contours of Jonathan Ives translucent Apple iMac G3 computers (1998–99) made the manufactured business tool neotenous, childlike, and pet-like. "Family" was explicitly part of the product concept for Alessi's series ("Stefano Giovannoni"), as well as for 1999 iMac ads promising "Family Vehicles for the Information Superhighway." Alessi and iMac designers capitalized on the "visual saliency bias" toward rounded surfaces that invite stroking and bright colors; and both the Alessi product line and iMacs, like Koons's *Balloon Dog* series, came in a range of five jelly-like colors.[8] The G3 was, as if consumable, advertised as "iCandy": "Yum" proclaimed one advertisement. This returns my argument to the ambivalent cuteness effect: "I could eat you up." Here, the baby boom generation's nostalgia for the toys, candies, artificial food coloring, enameled appliances, chromed cars, and psychedelic colors, and mythologized golden age of the traditional family of their postwar childhoods, was tapped for powerful emotional associations.

Balloon Dog was created for the *Celebration* series of paintings and sculptures inspired by the birthday party of Koons's infant son Ludwig. Since shortly after that party Ludwig's mother, La Cicciolina, abducted Ludwig to Italy, the *Celebration* works could seem a form of mourning for the lost son, a custody battle realized in the compensatory deployment of substitute objects—toys, gifts, party hats, cake, ribbons, foil wrap, Play-Doh, balloon animals. Like the highly reflective surfaces of the balloon sculptures, the paintings of the *Celebration* series are in dialogue with 1970s hyperrealist art, as if that unfashionably gratifying representational genre was another form of readymade. Especially the paintings of the hyperrealist Audrey Flack, featuring excessive heaps of glittering desirable things—jewelry, mirrors, glazed pastries, ornaments, flowers, butterflies, glistening fruit, water drops, and high-sheen satin—echo in *Celebration*. Flack's still lifes are in the *memento mori* tradition that warns of the transience of physical pleasures; but the *Celebration* works, given Koons's insistence on freedom from guilt, must override any such despondent message. Koons converts Flack's repertoire, redolent of stereotypically feminine adult gratifications, to a child's preferences.

In its painted version, *Balloon Dog* (1995–1998), seen in profile with the splayed show dog stance, glints with sharply delineated, high-contrast reflections, far more defined than the hazy sheen on its rubber prototype (Hochdörfer 237). The dog's body and the heavy foil gift wrap are mutually reflecting, and it is as if the balloon dog had emerged from the hole-like shadow in the foil behind it. Or, the dog and the foil are bringing one another into existence in the blaze of light, as the dog's tail seems to squiggle onto the foil above it as if extruding itself or transmuting into the same substance. Given the incongruity of bringing together Koons's cheery platitudes and Jacques Lacan's involute psychoanalytic theory, the celebration might have been organized by a Lacanian party planner intent on mustering all available *objets a* (objects of desire that are never fully attained, that may take the form of anxiously offered gifts), as a substitute for the absent son (Lacan, "Introduction" 84–87). Or, it is as if the famous passage in which Lacan describes the blinding glint of light from a sardine tin on the wave as a revelation of being uncomfortably looked at by something from elsewhere had been transferred to gift wrap (Lacan, *Four* 95). Of course, that road won't bear the traffic; and yet, there is a sense that the cute is put to the service of something less accessible that we cannot put our finger on.

The almost impossibly flawless, glassy reflective surfaces of the balloon sculptures of *Celebration* induce their own peculiar tactile appeal. Light seems to slide and flow over them, as if stroking. In theoretical terms, these shining surfaces could be situated in a constellation of postmodern considerations. Within the postmodern currency of Baudrillard's "simulacral" circulation of copies without original objects, glossiness offers a screen onto which compensatory fantasies can be projected (Bora 95). In Fredric Jameson's account of postmodernism as a "mesmerizing new aesthetic mode," "reality" and "present history" are reconfigured as "the spell and distance of a glossy mirage" (21). As the house style, or "sociohistorical expression" (Ngai, *Our* 32) of putatively ahistorical postmodern moves, representing an incapacity to depict the present or to engage history (Jameson 21), glossiness is to postmodernity as theorized flatness was to modernist art. There are "connotations of taste, wit, and socioeconomic power" in the terms we use to describe surfaces (Bora 99). The shiny can represent a value of the pristine and new, quite the opposite of the auratic value of "patina" that marks the passage of time over, say, an ancient bronze (Benjamin 3); and that gleam of the new may also be coded as cheaply gratifying. All of these possibilities inflect *Balloon Dog* as almost irresistible consumer lure. In the context of intellectual expectations that might be attached to art, any attention to Koons's dazzling surfaces is an uneasy compromise between knowing better than to fall for them, and falling for them. Here again, then, Koons mobilizes cuteness to confound categorization while subverting the expectations of viewers and critics alike.

A Dumb Aesthetic

Balloon Dog as show dog generates a syllogistic analogy of an art work and a dog: both are shown. A paradoxical effect of the show dog pose is that of all of Koons's balloon sculptures *Balloon Dog* is most clearly readable as what it represents—a dog—and in that clarity of form it is paradoxically amenable to modernist formalist assessment, while at the same time provoking associative narratives of the toy-like or pet-like. However hypothetically cheaply alluring, features of *Balloon Dog* cannot escape a pedigree in art. Looking at it, we feel the twisted pinches separating its component body parts, and that feature can be situated with respect to formalist arguments about the relations of part to whole in 1960s sculpture. Where the influential critic Michael Fried famously approved of the ways that, in Anthony Caro's abstract sculpture, each element inflected the others, rather than insisting on its own identity (161), the sculptor Charles Ray converted these abstract formalist principles to figural representation. Ray's *Oh! Charley, Charley, Charley* (1992) arrays eight highly realistic self-portrait sculptures engaged in auto-erotic play, in a chain of body parts touching body parts. Ray claimed a precedent for that configuration in Caro's work as described by Fried (Fried and Ray). *Oh! Charley, Charley, Charley* is at once formally elegant and, because it is so representational and because it is autoerotic, also seems to parody modernist claims for an art of purely formal relations. Given that Koons most certainly knew Ray's sculpture, which was shown at the same *Documenta 9* exhibition as Koons's *Puppy*, it is possible to understand the nodal points of contact that mark the expressive relations of parts to whole in the welded and bolted joins of a Caro, or in the fingertips to penis in the Ray, as being rearticulated in the pressure points of Koons's *Balloon Dog*. The balloon is compressed and twisted to start a new limb, as if submitting the august Caro principles to the squeezing and pinching operations triggered by the cute.

With respect to his contemporaries, Koons's qualifications of cuteness are in a countermanding dialogue with much darker work, such as the scatological, morbid, sexual, and caustic treatments of childhood and toys and animals in the work of other postmodern artists including Paul McCarthy, Mike Kelley, Jake and Dinos Chapman, Damien Hirst, Takashi Murakami (whose *Mr. DOB*, with its alternately fanged maw and fixed rictus-like smile, sometimes takes the form of giant balloons), and even in the grand mythopoetics of gonads in Matthew Barney. McCarthy, for example, has long directly parodied Koons. As Koons's *Puppy* stands guard outside the Guggenheim Bilbao, or as *Balloon Dog* was posted for several years outside the Palazzo Grassi on the Venice Grand Canal, McCarthy installed his own 80-foot-tall rubber version of a balloon dog outside the 2013 Frieze art fair, presumably to draw attention to the commerce of art and to Koons's spectacular success within it. McCarthy's version had chubbier, baby-like proportions, including a shortened body, as if beating Koons at his own game of cuteness; and then complicating matters by the inevitable association with McCarthy's other giant inflatables, the equally rounded and implicitly squeezable shapes of turds (which might yet be childishly cute in a poo-poo joke way) and butt plugs.

Balloon Dog's relative simplicity with respect to the contortionist composition of the other balloon works accentuates its pet-like appeal. Koons's subsequent balloon sculptures jettison the cute: the monkey and rabbit are almost impossible to identify without a label, and the swan looks like a striking cobra. Any residual cuteness is vanquished in Koons's most recent balloon work, *Balloon Venus* (2008–12), his version of the carved Paleolithic figure (ca. 25,000 BCE), the famous Venus of Willendorf. Realized in balloons, she is like a mutant Pillsbury Doughboy, all inducement to prod and poke her belly, but at the same time monstrous, as her proliferating balloon swellings of breasts and hair look something like a mushroom infestation. Naming this ancient figure "Venus" has its own cute incongruity, pitching her against the lofty European normative beauty. Koons says that he tried hundreds of balloons to choose the "perfect buttocks, breast, and head" (Lalinde), associating his process with the ancient artist Zeuxis's choosing among the ideal parts of many individual women to assemble his Helen of Troy. Wittily, a balloon knot, which had made the tweakable nose of *Balloon Dog*, represents *Balloon Venus*'s pudenda. Situating Koons's work in the context of his artist interlocutors shows the way he cute-ifies any august critical and formal issues, and, in doing so, tweaks the gravity of historical monumentality and abstraction, while arrogating these properties to cuteness.

A Sublime

Ngai has commented at length on the relationship of cuteness to the sublime as a sort of anti-sublime that declines to overwhelm us with its enormity and vertiginous vastness. Rather, cute objects, which are most often small, "present themselves as entirely available, as their commercial and erotic connotations make explicit" (*Our* 18). While Koons's work undercuts and reverses eighteenth-century notions of the sublime in terms of scale, *Balloon Dog*'s cuteness is hybridized with other aesthetic claims. Koons's work exerts a powerful sensory appeal and associative charm, in ways that contravene the Kantian disinterested aesthetic; Koons's statements effectively refute any beauty that might rely on educated—that is, informed about Kant—taste. If there could be an opposite of Kant's example of the wild tulip as an instance of the disinterested "beautiful," it would be Koons's balloon tulips, rendered in three tons of furled tumescent forms simultaneously seeming to flop and rise from a mirrored floor in casino magnate Steve Wynn's theater rotunda in Las Vegas (Kant 80; 140). With respect to the other principal Kantian aesthetic, the sublime, however, there is a curious analogy to the cute. The sublime is an aesthetic response brought on by phenomena of an immensity beyond our perceptual grasp, and is experienced as a "pleasure which is possible only by means of a displeasure" (Kant 260). Bathetically, this takes us back to the dimorphous nature of response to the cute as both intensely pleasurable and aversive, and to the research that proposes that, because the experience of the cute is overwhelming, it triggers a concurrent negative emotion to tamp it down. Ngai has distinguished the ambivalence of the Kantian sublime, which ultimately leads to a powerful resolution, from the cute, which provokes a weaker vacillating effect ("Cuteness" 811). That inability to resolve or achieve catharsis leads to another version of the sublime that is perhaps more pertinent to Koons.

The sublime had a currency when Koons was first emerging as an artist in New York, as re-envisioned in Jean-François Lyotard's influential essays in *Artforum*, "Presenting the Unpresentable: The Sublime" (April 1982) and "The Sublime and the Avant-Garde" (April 1984). Lyotard's definition of the "readymade" as a technologically produced thing that no longer answers to any existing aesthetic or consensus of established taste certainly applies to Koons's work of the mid-1980s ("Presenting" 64–69). Lyotard, who had imported the term postmodernism into philosophy, deplored postmodern art as opportunistic. For success, an artist had only to appropriate or pastiche an extant model and then destabilize it by folding in incompatible formulae and ornamentation to the point of "kitsch" or "the grotesque." A disinterested Kantian aesthetic of beauty and "pure" judgment of taste could not answer to such work that only flattered the "taste of a public that can have no taste" (Lyotard, "Sublime" 106). Lyotard consequently proposed that the ethical task of the avant-garde artist was to grapple with a new category of an "unpresentable" sublime ("Presenting" 64–69; see also Crowther 74). In much of Koons's work, that unpresentable assumes a mask of cuteness.

Given cycles of novelty within capitalist economies, Lyotard argued that where the dominant question in capitalism is "what is happening?" (colloquially, "what's new?"), the question posed by the avant-garde artist is the destabilizing "is it happening?" supposing or proposing that nothing at all might be happening *now* ("Sublime" 91; 106). For Lyotard, the ambiguous eruption of a contemporary sublime was in that "nothingness now" ("Sublime" 92). Arguably, Koons realized the re-theorized sublime in reverse, capitalizing on precisely what Lyotard saw as a crass reliance on the commercial appeal of the borrowed, juxtaposed, ornamental, and kitschy. And yet at the same time Koons's work aligned with a feature of Lyotard's sublime, which was to raise the possibility that nothing whatsoever is happening, but not at all in the indeterminate way that Lyotard had intended. Koons does not so much grapple with the problem of directing us to the unpresentable, but of overwhelming us with the unironically accessible, which in turn becomes uncomfortably ungraspable in its art context, neither one thing nor another. This can be directed forward to the indeterminate features of Ngai's "stuplime," the hybrid aesthetic provoked by postmodern artefacts, in which initial astonishment is "paradoxically united with boredom," inducing a kind of "desensitization, exhaustion or fatigue" (*Ugly* 271). Yet, arguably, *Balloon Dog* doesn't generate or admix that boredom or fatigue; rather, it is an excitation that doesn't quit, endlessly interfering with expectations of what it, as art, ought to be appealing to. Koons's work directs us to our inability to find a critical vocabulary for communicating Koons, far from the ethical register Lyotard imagined. In other words, the peculiar hybridity of cuteness in Koon's *Balloon Dog* illustrates the ways Koons fits into and evacuates the critical theories circulating through his career, in his evolution of a cute-sublime.

Scapegoat and Trojan Horse

With respect to this undecidability, the critic Blake Gopnik, an unqualified Koons admirer, has picked up Koons's remark that *Balloon Dog* is a "Trojan Horse" because it serves the infiltration of the echelons of high art with a complex cuteness (Sylvester 339). As Gopnik argues, Koons's "simplest, dumbest aesthetic" conceals an "ambush of almost every conventional aesthetic mode" (Gopnik). But if *Balloon Dog* is a Trojan Horse, how is it one, beyond the way that the emptiness of the balloon stands for the emptiness of cast sculpture? A Trojan Horse is a fairly open-ended metaphor: it might simply mean the consumerist commodity infiltrated into the art museum, analogous to money laundering. Koons, however, blandly says that what the Trojan Horse conceals is sexuality, referring to a brand name of condoms (Swann). With respect to that incongruous sexuality, Renu Bora has proposed two modes of perceiving texture. The first is "the surface resonance or quality of an object or material" that lets us know what it would feel like to stroke or touch just by looking at it (Bora 98). That is one thing that *Balloon Dog* impels us to do. At a deeper level of sensation, Bora proposes "Texxture," intensely operating on the sense of touch and physical pressure (as two Xs in a word generate a grating effect), inducing associations with eating and sex. The vocabulary of textural properties includes "brittleness," "elasticity," "bounciness," "hardness," and "stiffness" (Bora 99–100). (With Koons we could imagine a gleefully "teXXXtural" sexual domain, where multiplying Xs is a cute textual move.)

Or, again with respect to its Trojan sexuality, we might see *Balloon Dog*'s sausage-like properties in the light of psychoanalytic theory. The genderless *Balloon Dog* fulfills the criteria of Lacan's *objet a* both imagined as being separable from the rest of the body, and as a container or wrapping: the blown-up balloon as both the prophylactic for the absent Lacanian *objet a*-as-phallus and the unrepresentable phallus. That is, *Balloon Dog* as *objet a* embodies the cute as a trivial or marginal entity with respect to the intellectual substrata of high art, while at the same time claiming the enormous theoretical stature of *objet a* in critical discourse: as object of desire, *objet a* is derived from "*agalma*," the desirable thing hidden in an undesirable body, or treasure concealed in a box, discussed in Plato's *Symposium* (Lacan "Subversion"). That theorized hiddenness takes us back to the Trojan Horse as empty vessel of meaning, and to *Balloon Dog* as hollow.

Of course Koons's cute effects may be cheap thrills. Through Lacan's account of the sardine can, Robin Kelsey has proposed that Koons's mirroring surfaces create the impression that the works look back at us, showing us the embarrassingly "brutal indifference of our surrender to crass appeal" (72). That is, even as we lose ourselves in them, we become complicit in an exhibitionist artwork that is the equivalent of an Instagram "selfie." At the same time, *Balloon Dog*'s mirroring may be the contemporary all-American cultural equivalent of Wallace Stevens's glass jar that reorders the world around it, in *Anecdote of the Jar*:

> The wilderness rose up to it,
> And sprawled around, no longer wild.
> The jar was round upon the ground
> And tall and of a port in air. (60–61)

The convex reflective surfaces of Koons's balloon sculptures have the effect of taking whatever surrounds them into themselves, reconfiguring any environment into the lusciously rounded curves, in which art deco streamlining meets the petting zoo. It holds its own against mirroring: it takes the world in, rather than having the reflections of the world corrode its sleek wholeness. In spite of knowing better, we could say that the *Balloon Dog*, like Stevens's jar, "took dominion everywhere" (60–61).

That "dominion" might return us to a further complexity of the Koonsian cute sublime just elaborated, as part of a postmodern sublime. In *The Postmodern Condition*, Lyotard remarks on the way experimental art, in the form of the formless or abstract, had been abandoned in favor of art that offered familiar subject matter, that was well-crafted using familiar techniques. Such work offered the public a comfortable reassurance that they can understand and judge it without too much difficulty (Lyotard, *Postmodern* 76). It offered safe "good form" and signified a nostalgia for wholeness. Lyotard proposes an alternative to this, a postmodern sublime, "*novatio*," that might present the unrepresentable in a pleasurably recognizable form. That is, the sublime does not have to take an allusively abstract form. *Novatio* arouses a jubilant increase and intensification of "being" in the viewer by the sheer force of breaking old rules and generating new ones (*Postmodern* 81). Koons's dog, for all its pandering shiny, ingratiating, tacky cuteness may be the Trojan Horse in Lyotard's "war on totality," by offering the viewer a sort of reassuring, understandable form rendered glossy, shiny, gigantic, and cute. While it might appear to be a mascot of the general cultural "slackening" and "appease-ment" Lyotard deplores, it in fact parades *novatio* by taking the form of the unacceptably cute, breaking the terms and rules for art. Where modern art had tended to dread the pet-like domesticated, anthropomorphized animal with its sentimental baggage, Koons breaks that rule of decorum. Where in *Mother and Child Divided* (1991) Damien Hirst assaulted the sentimentality attached to motherhood by floating a bisected cow and calf in vitrines of formaldehyde, Koons comes at the rule-breaking problem from the opposite direction, by hypostatizing the sentimental.

Perhaps, then, there is a heroic ending for *Balloon Dog*. In Adorno's analysis, kitsch and art both objectify the feelings and desires we project onto them, sharing the predicament of being an object or limited "thingness" in the here and now, without any real efficacy (Ngai, *Our* 41). In spite of its claims to seriousness, art bears the *guilt* of being politically powerless, even ridiculous (Adorno 209). *Balloon Dog* may be the scapegoat of art's guilt, dramatizing the elisions of kitsch and art in the guise of the cute. Adorno wrote that "*[k]itsch* parodies *catharsis*" (312). In *Balloon Dog*, through the mechanisms of the cute, that would be turning awe to awww.

Notes

1   Smallness is consistently aligned with cuteness in most of the literature on the topic. To cite just one example, see Ngai's discussion in *Our Aesthetic Categories* of Stein (70), Adorno (102), or, more generally, her assertion that cuteness is an aesthetic organized around smallness and helplessness (78). See also the introduction to this book on Darwinian cuteness and its relationship to diminutive size (27), as well as to design and representation (12; 36). See also Chapter 1 in this volume.

2   Similarly, Ngai writes that "the epitome of cute would be an undifferentiated blob of soft doughy matter," and that "soft contours suggest pliancy or responsiveness to the will of others," in other words, cute objects invite poking, prodding, and pinching (*Our* 64). She further cites Daniel Harris who goes so far as to claim that "the cute object's exaggerated passivity seems likely to excite the consumer's sadism" (*Our* 65).

3   This recalls Ngai's notion that "'twittering' is how we imagine the language of cute beings" and that, as she quotes Merish, "[c]uteness generates ever more cuteness by drawing out 'small-sized adjectives and diminutive ejaculations' from those who perceive it in others" (*Our* 60).

4   The exhibition *Pour la vie: Gilbert and George, Jeff Koons, Bruce Nauman* ran at the CAPC: Musée d'Art Contemporain in Bordeaux, France, from 25 June–20 September 1993.

5   "Duchampian" here refers to artist Marcel Duchamp's practice in the early twentieth century of taking objects, most famously a urinal, and exhibiting them in museums as an ironic commentary on what he called "retinal" art, or art which is only visual.

6   See Taylor on the "aestheticization of commodities," and the elision of art and commodity, museums and department stores (15–54).
7   Similarly, Alexander Nagel: "The work made me a little sick, even as I felt an almost irresistible invitation to submit to it" (245).
8   Venturini's Alessi line is in yellow, green, red, blue, orange, and black; iMacs came in purple, blue, orange, green, and red.

Works Cited

Adorno, Theodor W. *Aesthetic Theory*. London: Continuum, 2004.
Ahmed, Tameer. "Balloon Dog." *YouTube*. 17 Dec. 2013. Online. 1 May 2016.
Aragón, Oriana R., Margaret S. Clark, Rebecca L. Dyer, and John A. Bargh. "Dimorphous Expressions of Positive Emotion: Displays of Both Care and Aggression in Response to Cute Stimuli." *Psychological Science* 26.3 (2015): 259–73.
Baker, Steve. *Picturing the Beast: Animals, Identity, and Representation*. Manchester: Manchester University Press, 1993.
Benjamin, Walter. "The Work of Art in the Age of Mechanical Reproduction." *Illuminations*. Trans. Harry Zohn. New York: Schocken, 1969. 1–58.
Bora, Renu. "Outing Texture." *Novel Gazing: Queer Readings in Fiction*. Ed. Eve Kosofsky Sedgwick. Durham, NC: Duke University Press, 1997. 94–127.
Bourdieu, Pierre. *Distinction: A Social Critique on the Judgement of Taste*. Trans. Richard Nice. Cambridge, MA: Harvard University Press, 1984.
Crowther, Paul. "The Kantian Sublime: The Avant-Garde and the Postmodern: A Critique of Lyotard." *Jean François Lyotard: Aesthetics*. Vol. 1. Eds. Victor E. Taylor and Gregg Lambert. London: Routledge, 2004.
Deitch, Jeffrey. "York to New York." Rothkopf 215–18.
Diehl, Travis. "After Jeff Koons: A Retrospective." *Los Angeles Review of Books*. LARB, 2 Sep. 2014. Online. 5 July 2015.
Foster, Hal. *Postmodern Culture*. London: Pluto, 1985.
——. "The Future of an Illusion, or the Contemporary Artist as Cargo Cultist." *Endgame*. Ed. David Joselit. Boston, MA: Institute of Contemporary Art, 1986. 91–105.
——. "At the Whitney: Jeff Koons." *London Review of Books*. LRB, 31 July 2014. 22–23.
Fried, Michael. "Art and Objecthood." *Art and Objecthood*. Chicago, IL: University of Chicago Press, 1998.
Fried, Michael, and Charles Ray. "Early One Morning." *Tate Etc.* 3 (2005). Online. 23 Nov. 2015.
"Gino Zucchino Sugar Castor." *Alessi*. Alessi, n.d. Online. 22 Jan. 2016.
Gopnik, Blake. "Jeff Koons: A Genius from Day One." *Artnet*. 18 Aug. 2014. Online. 23 Nov. 2015.
Hagen, Charles "Art in Review." *New York Times*. New York Times, 11 Feb. 1994. Online. 9 Feb. 2016.
Hochdörfer, Achim. "The Gift of Art." Rothkopf 235–38.
"Interview: Clotaire Rapaille." *The Persuaders*. PBS. 9 Nov. 2004. Online. 22 Jan. 2016. Transcript.
Ivy, Marilyn. "The Art of Cute Little Things: Nara Yoshitomo's Parapolitics." *Mechademia* 5 (2010): 3–29.
Jameson, Fredric. "The Cultural Logic of Late Capitalism." *Postmodernism, or, The Cultural Logic of Late Capitalism*. Durham, NC: Duke University Press, 1991. 1–54.

Joselit, David, ed. *Endgame*. Boston, MA: Institute of Contemporary Art, 1986.

Kant, Immanuel. *Critique of Judgment*. Trans. James C. Meredith. Oxford: Clarendon, 1953.

Kelsey, Robin. "Photography, Lacan, and the Genius of Jeff Koons." *Texte zur Kunst* 99 (2015): 62–73.

Klein, Sheri. *Art and Laughter*. London: I.B. Tauris, 2006.

Koons, Jeff. "Baptism: A Project for *Artforum*." *Artforum*. Artforum International, Nov. 1987. 101–7.

Lacan, Jacques. *The Four Fundamental Concepts of Psychoanalysis*. Trans. Alan Sheridan. London: Penguin, 1977.

——. "The Subversion of the Subject and the Dialectic of Desire in the Freudian Unconscious." *Écrits: A Selection*. Trans. Alan Sheridan. New York: Norton, 1977. 292–23.

——. "Introduction to the Names-of-the-Father Seminar." *Television*. Trans. Denis Hollier, Rosalind Krauss, and Annette Michelson. New York: Norton, 1990. 84–87.

Lalinde, Jaime. "How to Make a Koons." *Vanity Fair*. Condé Nast, 16 June 2014. Online. 12 Dec. 2015.

Lee, Pamela. "Love and Basketball." Rothkopf 219–24.

Libert, Barry, et al. "Why Businesses Should Serve Consumers' 'Higher Needs.'" *Knowledge @ Wharton*. 29 Aug. 2014. Online. 22 Jan. 2016.

Lyotard, Jean-François. *The Postmodern Condition: A Report on Knowledge*. 1979. Trans. Geoffrey Bennington and Brian Massumi. Minneapolis, MN: University of Minnesota Press, 1984.

——. "*Presenting the Unpresentable: The Sublime*." Trans. Lisa Liebmann. *Artforum*. Artforum International, Apr. 1982. 64–69.

——. "The Sublime and the Avant-Garde." Trans. Lisa Liebmann, Geoffrey Bennington, and Marian Hobson. *The Inhuman*. Cambridge: Polity, 1991. 89–107.

Maslow, Abraham H. 1954. *Motivation and Personality*. New York: Harper, 1970.

Morris, Robert. "Some Splashes in the Ebb Tide." *Artforum*. Artforum International, Feb. 1973. 42–49.

Nagel, Alexander. "Objects that are Only Boundaries." Rothkopf 243–46.

Ngai, Sianne. "The Cuteness of the Avant-Garde." *Critical Inquiry* 31.4 (2005): 811–47.

——. *Ugly Feelings*. Cambridge, MA: Harvard University Press, 2005.

——. *Our Aesthetic Categories: Zany, Cute, Interesting*. Cambridge, MA: Harvard University Press, 2012.

Perl, Jed. "The Cult of Jeff Koons." *New York Times*. New York Times, 25 Sept. 2014. Online. 6 Feb. 2016.

"Puppy." *Guggenheim Bilbao*. Guggenheim Bilbao Museoa, 2016. Online. 15 May 2016.

Rothkopf, Scott. "No Limits." Rothkopf 15–36.

Rothkopf, Scott, ed. *Jeff Koons: A Retrospective*. Ed. New York: Whitney Museum-Yale University Press, 2014.

Russell, Andrew. "Jeff Koons's 'Made in Heaven' Series: A Critical Compendium." *16 Miles of String*. 18 Oct. 2010. Online. 3 Mar. 2016.

Sayers Ellis, Thomas. *The Genuine Negro Hero*. Kent, OH: Kent State University Press, 2001.

Schjeldahl, Peter. *The Hydrogen Jukebox: Selected Writings of Peter Schjeldahl, 1978–1990*. Berkeley, CA: University of California Press, 1991.

——. "Selling Points." *New Yorker*. New Yorker, 7 July 2014. Online. 22 Jan. 2016.

Sontag, Susan. "Notes on Camp." *Against Interpretation and Other Essays*. London: Penguin, 1966. 275–92.

"Stefano Giovannoni." *Alessi*. Alessi n.d. Online. 27 April 2016.

Stevens, Wallace. "Anecdote of the Jar." *Collected Poetry and Prose*. New York: Library of America, 1997. 60–61.

Swann, Jennifer. "Jeff Koons's Balloon Dogs are Sex Machines, and More Surprises from the Artist." *LA Weekly*. LA Weekly, 25 Feb. 2014. Online. 25 Jan. 2016.

Swanson, Carl. "Jeff Koons is the Most Successful American Artist Since Warhol. So What's the Art World Got Against Him?" *Vulture*. 5 May 2013. Online. 27 Jan. 2016.

Sylvester, David. *Interviews with American Artists*. New Haven, CT: Yale University Press, 2001.

Taylor, Mark C. "Paper Trails." *Confidence Games: Money and Markets in a World Without Redemption*. Chicago, IL: University of Chicago Press, 2004. 15–54.

Vogel, Carol. "At $142.4 Million, Triptych is the Most Expensive Artwork Ever Sold at an Auction." *New York Times*. New York Times, 12 Nov. 2013. Online. 6 Feb. 2016.

8

CUTE TWENTY-FIRST-CENTURY POST-FEMBOTS

Julia Leyda

My interest in this chapter is to bring into conversation three currently productive fields of inquiry—cuteness studies, cultural studies of technology, and scholarship on postfeminist sensibilities—over the figure of the female android, taking up the question of how machine cuteness connects to axes of gendered and racial inequalities peculiar to twenty-first-century postfeminisms. Important work on gender can now be found within the burgeoning field of cuteness studies, focusing, for example, on the "manic pixie dreamgirl" figure, the cute female star texts of Parker Posey or Zooey Deschanel, and cute masculinities in contemporary raunch cultures, gay aesthetics, and the military (as showcased in this book), to name only a few.[1] Additionally, millennial culture's fascination with robotics and AI has inspired an array of provocative studies across the rich intersection of science and technology studies with film and media studies, including recent books by Despina Kakoudaki and Jay Telotte, among others. Moreover, as Rosalind Gill maintains, today's media culture creaks under the weight of recurring tropes of neoliberal femininity that comprise what she terms postfeminist sensibilities, including heavy emphasis on sexualization, individual-ism and choice, the entanglement of feminism and anti-feminism, and the shift from objectification to subjectification. These tropes arise frequently in the contemporary texts I analyze in this chapter, all of which depict what I am calling cute post-fembots.[2] As new avatars of postfeminist subjectivity, female androids in popular culture today present a unique site of inquiry for scholars of cuteness: they frequently embody the postfeminist tendency to assert gender conservatism even in contexts of "progress" and futurity, particularly in terms of postfeminist dynamics of empowerment/disempowerment.

As the study of the aesthetics and affects of cuteness frequently moves beyond humans to animals, this chapter presumes that a full account of cuteness must also attend to other nonhuman entities. Accordingly, I delve into the rich archive of female robots in popular culture to interrogate the ways in which their cuteness functions in relation to inequality. The machine cuteness of the female-gendered android, whether unintentional or feigned, offers a strategic escape route that preserves her from being perceived as threatening and may lead to independence or emancipation. Exceeding the limitations of analyzing aesthetic representation alone, my approach will also attend to affective scenarios to illuminate the complex power relations linking machine cuteness, gender, race, sexuality, and contemporary culture: Lauren Berlant clarifies this distinction, which lies not in studying simply "what happens to aesthetically mediated characters as equivalent to what happens to people but to see that in the affective scenarios of these works and discourses we can discern claims about the situation of contemporary life" (9). Because contemporary mediascapes now constitute not only national but international circuits of exchange across multiple formats, this chapter will draw on a set of recent US and European media texts to exemplify its arguments: the British film *Ex Machina* (Alex Garland 2015), the Swedish television series *Real Humans* (Sveriges TV, 2012–14), and its British remake *Humans* (Channel 4-AMC, 2015–), the television series *Extant* (CBS, 2014–15), and the comics series *Alex + Ada* (Image, 2013–15), both American.

Machine Cuteness

As my co-editors and I discuss at greater length in Chapter 1 of this volume, Konrad Lorenz first outlined the *Kindchenschema* in his scientific inquiry into the visual characteristics and behaviors that produce cuteness responses in humans. Lorenzian cuteness primarily derives from certain physical traits of neoteny, or the appearance of youth or immaturity. Babies and many young animals often have large eyes, large heads, high foreheads, and soft or chubby bodies. The more of these traits that are present, the cuter the object is seen to be: think of toddlers or kittens. But cuteness in mature humans and animals is also linked to their neotenous retention of some of these childlike traits later in life. The cute subcultures of *burikko* in Japan, *aegyo* in South Korea, and *saijao* in Taiwan and mainland China serve as extreme examples of this: young women in these subcultures embrace childish behavior that may include babyish vocal inflections, children's clothing, and even immature handwriting in order to cultivate cute affects (Kinsella 225; Abidin 34–35).

Machine cuteness overlaps with the *Kindchenschema* but also demands its own definition. In contemporary popular culture, robots and androids are frequently portrayed as cute and childlike in ways that resemble the young of humans and domesticated animals alike, though more often in behavior rather than appearance. As Anthony P. McIntyre argues, making reference to the cute non-humanoid robots like the title character in *Chappie* (Neill Blomkamp, 2015) and BB8 in *Star Wars: The Force Awakens* (J.J. Abrams, 2015), machine cute relies on a constellation of both visual and behavioral traits informed by (but going beyond) the *Kindchenschema*. Some robots, and many androids, may have cute (neotenous) physical features that recall the Lorenz schema, but the primary characteristics of machine cuteness are behavioral: physical vulnerability or awkwardness, linguistic weaknesses, and/or cognitive neoteny. This last concept, introduced into cuteness studies from evolutionary biology by Ingeborg Hasselgren, denotes "a child-like state of mind, including a mental plasticity where the subject is curious about the world, open to new experiences, and tends to approach its surroundings with a certain naïveté." Robot cuteness, then, can be positioned as a variation on cute aesthetics that encompasses both appearance and behavior, selectively drawing on the repertoire of Lorenzian visual traits but also the behaviors outlined by McIntyre and Hasselgren.

Consider the durable image of the "cute robot" as a popular trope, which inspires product design for friendly consumer robots. As Despina Kakoudaki points out in her study of robots and affect, "real robots are inseparable from their imaginary counterparts, since it is often the fictions that supply the emotional and intellectual context for much of the robot's cultural presence" (111). She divides pop culture robots into the "traditional industrial paradigm" of classic, clunky "tin-can" machines, and the newer futuristic designs that telegraph technological sophistication "through a material vocabulary of translucency, white plastic surfaces, and ethereal blue lights" (117; see also Shaviro). These two varieties—classic and high-tech—frequently present distinct yet powerful attributes of cuteness. Familiar cute classic robots whose decrepit condition cannot alter their infectious visual and behavioral cuteness include WALL-E from the film of that name (Andrew Stanton, 2008) and the robot star of *Chappie*. Sleeker new models, such as the care robot Baymax featured in *Big Hero 6* (Don Hall and Chris Williams, 2014), resemble recent prototypes from robotics labs at Georgia Tech and MIT, made of smooth, shiny material. In their appearance and behavior, then, cute robots work to mitigate the perceived threat of what are jokingly called "our future robot overlords" by positioning themselves as benign and dependent on humans; moreover, their cuteness constitutes an appeal to consumers to interact with, and ultimately purchase, them. Thus these robots enact what cuteness scholars from Lori Merish to Sianne Ngai describe as a form of flattery accompanied by the cute object's forceful demands upon the subject: the cute commodity cajoles us to adore it in order to entice us to buy it, after which its cuteness demands that we feel attached to and care for it (see also the chapters in this volume pertaining to cute commodities, such as those by Joyce Goggin and Nadia de Vries).

The examples of humanoid robots I will discuss here provoke people (within the texts and in the audience) to question our feelings about machines, as well as our desire to ascribe feelings to them. Robots are also usually gendered when they approach human form, with most male androids presenting visual and behavioral attributes in line with McIntyre's delineations of machine cuteness;

however, female android characters are frequently embedded within scenarios that combine cuteness with some degree of sexualization.[3] When cute machines are gendered in such different ways, then, an attentive analysis must also consider what they have to tell us about the wide-ranging impacts of postfeminism on contemporary social relations.

Constructing robot characters as not only gendered but subject to social conventions attributed to femininity, contemporary popular culture provides numerous examples of the ways in which postfeminist sensibilities serve to repurpose and rearticulate the still-relevant impulses of liberal and progressive feminisms into what gender studies scholar Catherine Rottenberg calls neoliberal feminisms. She argues that by "[u]sing key liberal terms such as equality, opportunity, and free choice, while displacing and replacing their content," neoliberal feminisms produce "a feminist subject who is not only individualized but entrepreneurial," so that gender inequality is simultaneously recognized and denied and "the question of social justice is recast in personal, individualized terms" (Rottenberg 422). The latest iteration of the postfeminist dynamics that have provided the dominant representational template for female domesticity in recent decades, neoliberal feminisms bear many of the traces of the cultural discourses that present women with, as media scholar Diane Negra points out, "a means of registering and superficially resolving the persistence of 'choice' dilemmas" with particular attention to the domestic sphere (Negra, *What* 2; 12). This discursive realm traffics in motifs such as female retreatism—the return of a female character to the home after leaving a competitive career—and the characterization of women within a repertoire of hyperfemininity, often in combination with hypersexualized aesthetics.

Postfeminist media regimes present a world in which certain (white, middle-class, professional) privileged women can pursue personal empowerment with regard for neither the still-incomplete collective goals of feminism, nor for those women who, marked as "others" by race and class signifiers, have limited or no access to such forms of individual personal or economic advancement (see Gill; Negra *What*; Ouellette). Cuteness in these texts operates in tandem with postfeminist discourses—of sexualization, of individualized "choice," and of entangled feminist/anti-feminist, subject/object binaries—as a way to render post-fembots nonthreatening: by performing cuteness as a kind of concealment of agency, the female androids I examine here ingratiate themselves with humans and defuse potential anxieties about their intelligence and independence.

Cute Post-Fembots

When dealing with humanoid robots, then, gender matters. Female androids frequently trouble the boundaries between cute and threatening, and cute and sexy (in regard to the latter boundary, see Michael DeAngelis's chapter in this volume). Differing in some ways from the cuteness of living beings, android cuteness nevertheless operates through a similar constellation of power relations. As I hope to show, the crucial factor in delineations of cute from sexy or threatening lies precisely in the marked separation between machine cuteness and android sentience. This becomes clearer when we realize that the post-fembot characters I analyze here undergo a two-stage process in their development. First, they generally emerge as "newborn" and naïve with little or no experience of sociality, which will be one of the most important ways they "learn" the skills necessary to communicate successfully with humans. In this early stage, the android genuinely conforms to most of the characteristics of machine cuteness, while also displaying some neotenous visual traits common to humans, and thus eliciting cuteness responses from humans similar to that of a young child or young animal such as protectiveness, affection, playfulness, even fascination. In theorizing the attributes of machine cuteness as it pertains to human-like robots in this first stage of non-sentience, then, I would add to McIntyre's definition one further trait: restrained or flat affect. While in general a flat affect may elicit confusion or suspicion in humans, when people interact with androids in these texts they often exhibit positive reactions: curiosity, amusement, even a sense of superiority when the android fails to understand a sophisticated form of communication such as sarcasm or humor. Thus the restrained affect of post-fembots works paradoxically to engage humans to interact, at least initially.

In the second stage of their development, however, the female androids I consider here attain sentience, whereby they begin to develop individuality and experience emotion, leading them away from some of the more childlike attributes of machine cuteness. Most post-fembots remain cute only so long as they are either non-sentient or in early stages of developing their intelligence, when their gaffes or weaknesses can be endearing; afterwards, they "grow up" and cross over into the more mature and potentially threatening territory of human, and specifically, sexual, agency. The post-fembot's physical appearance is unchanged: any cute neotenous features remain, but her behavior and affect is usually less machine-like, though still more restrained than that of most humans. Here, however, the mature sentient female android crosses into a new realm, that of sexualization.

This two-stage development applies in some of the texts I take up here to male-gendered androids as well, though they are less often sexualized in appearance, behavior, or in the perceptions of the human characters. As Kakoudaki points out, "while artificial men are often not presented as sexual beings, artificial women are marked by their sexuality, either in terms of conventional and compliant hyperfemininity, . . . or, in more recent decades, in terms of a dangerous sexuality and pinup looks" (120). This is still a timely observation, as *Wired* pop culture critic Angela Watercutter laments: "the message we're left with at the end of *Ex Machina* is still that the best way for a miraculously intelligent creature to get what she wants is to flirt manipulatively. . . . Why doesn't Chappie [the endearing robot protagonist and title character of the Blomkamp film] have to put up with this bullshit?" Why indeed—I propose that cuteness plays an integral role in how robots are portrayed in popular culture, yet because not all fictional androids are created equal, this plays out differently for female-gendered androids.

Feminist scholars justly maintain that female androids consistently embody the gender stereotypes and concomitant power imbalances of the usually male scientists (and heteronormative, patriarchal societies) that create them, both in fiction and in real life (Robertson "Gendering"). Anthropologist Jennifer Robertson notes that, in the contemporary robotics industry, Japanese roboticists model female androids, or "gynoids," on (contested) traditional gender roles in their own conservative cultural context. And while David Levy's 2007 book *Love and Sex with Robots* argues that if robots can make us feel good romantically and/or sexually, we needn't quibble over ethical questions, social scientists like Sherry Turkle strongly challenge the utopian proclamations from Levy and others that in the future humans will marry robots, seeing such fantasies as sad commentary on the state of human relationships. Indeed, feminist anthropologist Kathleen Richardson argues that sex with robots, most frequently assumed to be between human men and female-gendered robots, should be banned on ethical grounds because it "imports" an "asymmetrical relationship" and reinforces attitudes and behavior that characterize the most widespread forms of exploitative sex work, such as trafficking and coerced prostitution, which objectify and endanger human women. Her organization, Campaign against Sex Robots, takes its cue from the Stop Killer Robots group, which targets the development of military robots, appealing to the jeopardy to human rights inherent in our invention and use/abuse of such machines (Richardson). As I detail later in this chapter, the asymmetrical relationships that are central to campaigners such as Richardson's ethical concerns are a standard trope in onscreen depictions of cute post-fembots.

These scholars all point to different instances in the problematic attribution of gender to intelligent machines, but they do share one premise: that there is an ethical dimension to human designs of and interactions with robots predicated on their dependence (at least in the beginning) on humans, a dependence that echoes the appeal of the cute object's powerlessness. Not only would the "choice" to marry an android demand that the human partner take responsibility for the ethical implications of that decision, but it also approaches the question of whether or not the android has the agency to choose. Fictional scenarios that posit a sentient android as a romantic or sexual partner to a human provoke a closer examination of how gender and power, frequently negotiated through cuteness, function in the context of a human-machine relationship.

In this climate of rapid technological change and attendant controversy, several recent popular culture texts portray humans expressing romantic feelings towards machines—frequently in narratives about learning machines or AIs that develop their intelligence and individuality through experience.[4] This recalls the concept of "embodied intelligence" in contemporary social robotics, whereby "the actual behavior of the robot emerges from its interaction with the environment" and facilitates the development of "sociality and affective states"—analogous to human socialization in childhood, and a process equally susceptible to introducing gendered and other normative behaviors (Robertson, "Human" 575). This learning process is often figured as a maturation, in which the android progresses from cute childishness to more advanced levels of sociality and communication. Even as Richardson's campaign champions human rights in the face of what she posits as the dehumanizing prospect of human-robot intimacy, in the world of fiction, the exploitation of sentient android characters also elicits ethical questions about whether, in the future, autonomous intelligent machines will deserve rights—comparable to animal or even human rights.

In addition to questions of "human" rights for robots, the pop culture texts examined here also problematize the motivations for attributing human gender to them, calling attention to the role of cuteness and sexiness in traditional femininities that persist in contemporary postfeminist sensibilities. Julie Wosk documents the long history of representations of male-created woman machines: since Pygmalion sculpted Galatea, "[m]en have long been fascinated by the idea of creating a simulated woman . . ., a beautiful facsimile female who is the answer to all their dreams and desires." Indeed, almost all the android women I will consider here are painstakingly designed to physically attract: they appear conventionally good-looking (young, slender, agile) and behave deferentially to humans. However, unlike intelligent robots in earlier representations, these androids only rarely display their superiority to humans; more frequently they are figured as demure, passive "women." These post-fembots embody the gender stereotypes of their cultural contexts, even as, on the other hand, they provoke ethical debates for their owners about questions of humanity and gender equality. Many also eventually rebel against their masters, figuring compelling dilemmas about twenty-first-century expectations of femininity and the strategic deployments of cute and sexy affects. This chapter looks at cute female machines in recent film, TV, and comics to theorize how they illuminate the cultural work of cuteness within the contexts of contemporary (intersectional) feminism and its reconfigurations, including postfeminism.

Specifically, I explore how these texts ascribe cuteness to female-gendered android characters, in combination with other forms of allure, in order to elicit affection and care in the humans around them. Although rooted in the design of robots as consumer commodities in the real-world robotics industry, the deployment of cuteness in these fictional texts is also complexly bound up with the post-fembots' pursuit of autonomy, including obvious resonances with contemporary feminisms and other liberation movements past and present. This chapter analyzes the functions of cuteness within the following scenarios in several recent texts that prominently feature humanoid female robots as characters. In the first section, I examine the tendencies of female-gendered robots to exhibit cuteness among other retrograde behaviors associated with femininity and racial "inferiority": subservience, silence, and restrained or flat affect signaling absence or repression of individual agency. When viewed in the context of postfeminist retreatism and post-global-financial-crisis precarity, the servile nature of non-sentient female androids also demands a consideration of the gendered conflicts that these characters embody as devices that many fear will replace human labor, including social reproduction (see Fleming; Ford; Lanchester; Levy; Mizroch; Wittes and Blum). The instability of the unequal master-servant power relation demands further examination in the second section; crucially, the now-sentient, increasingly individualized post-fembots rehearse scripts from the postfeminist playbook, as they exercise their choice to perform cuteness—in conjunction with their acquiescence to objectification and/or sexualization—as a subterfuge to hide their sentience and accompanying desire for independence, in a bid for the safety and security of the white, middle-class human family. The third section investigates what happens when post-fembots are positioned outside the white family, specifically analyzing the ways in which racialized rebellious female androids occasion a reiteration of racist stereotypes and rehearse familiar claims of contemporary anti-feminism alongside their evocation of the unfinished project of the feminist struggle for subjectivity.

The Cute Aesthetics and Affects of Post-Fembots

Christine Yano's study of cute character Hello Kitty features a persuasive theory about its lack of a mouth: that the mouthless face provides a cute "blank slate" upon which people can project their own feelings (58). A similarly empty expression, combined with cute attributes or behavior, contributes to the restrained manner and flat affect of cute machines, even when they do have a mouth. These humanoid robots frequently display a cute appearance: neotenous features such as round cheeks and faces, flawless baby-smooth skin, and wide-set eyes. They also usually conform to the machine cuteness schema in their behavior: many of them are, in the first stages, socially unsophisticated and do not understand irony or sarcasm, leading to miscommunications with humans; they display a flat affect, at least before they "learn" to perform emotion; and they often move stiffly or awkwardly. Like Spock in the original series, the android character Data on *Star Trek: The Next Generation* (1987–94) exemplifies this difficulty, in that although he is a high-functioning, sophisticated machine, his occasional lapses in those areas come across as cute to the human characters and audience who find his idiosyncrasies endearing.[5] The cuteness of Data's failure to convincingly mimic emotion or grasp sarcasm, and that of other androids in similar situations, is secured by the fact that the other characters react positively to behavior that could, in different affective scenarios, be annoying. When the android Anita first meets the family that purchased her in the UK series *Humans*, the youngest daughter sees her as a delightful new friend, while the mother feels threatened by her and immediately dislikes and resents her—the little girl responds to Anita's cognitive neoteny and over-literal communication skills with patience, but the mother loses her temper and berates Anita. The introduction of an android into a household provides a site for discerning differing human perceptions of and responses to cuteness. In another example of the Anita character's machine cuteness, the Swedish series *Real Humans* depicts a scene in which the family invite her to sit down at the table during their meal, even though she doesn't eat. Demonstrating how her intelligence is developing through her observations and interactions with the human family, though she still hasn't mastered linguistic nuances, Anita employs a slang term she had heard the children use—translated in the subtitles as "kickass"—somewhat awkwardly, provoking laughter. Her cognitive neoteny and fumbling with the new word makes her more endearing to the family.

When switched on for the first time, new androids often bring to mind cute robots mentioned earlier in their immature behavior, such as Chappie as he learns to speak English that resembles babytalk, charming some of the violent criminals who have stolen him from his creator. Despite their adult human appearance, new androids are inexperienced and uncertain about human emotions and relationships, and figured as childlike in that they are "newborn" and must "learn" through experience. The comics series *Alex + Ada* depicts a close emotional relationship between a young man, Alex, and his female android, Ada, but in quite a different register from the other texts I consider here: Alex feels deeply ambivalent about his position as Ada's owner/master. Her inability to function without his specific commands endangers her at one point early in the series, when he leaves for work in the morning after a brief conversation at the front door:

ADA: Is there anything I should do while you're away?
ALEX: Just . . . don't go anywhere. Can you do that?

Arriving home later that evening, he is startled to see her just inside the front door, where she has stood all day, literally obeying his directive not to go anywhere.

ALEX: Were you standing there this whole time?
ADA: Yes. Should I . . . have . . . moved? (Issue 2)

Ada's words appear in shaky lettering with ellipses, and she begins to collapse because she hasn't been able to replenish her energy supply all day. Alex immediately helps her to recharge, feeling sympathetic and responsible for her welfare. In some ways similar to Caleb in *Ex Machina*, as we shall see, Alex feels curious about and protective of the female android (he names her Ada); however, he also finds her compliance and servility unnerving and decides to illegally hack or "wake up" Ada to make her sentient and independent.

Alex + Ada thus depicts two different "birth" scenes: when Alex unboxes Ada as a new android and when he reboots her after waking her. In both scenes, she is vulnerable and entirely at his mercy; in the first, she behaves like a perfect servant, dependent on his whims and instructions, while in the second she is quickly overwhelmed as her emotions begin to catch up to the rest of her intelligence: she curls up into a fetal position on the floor and enters a temporary unresponsive state resembling catatonia. Like the other female robots I analyze here, Ada presents cute behaviors in two stages: as a docile and literal-minded servant android before she "wakes up," and then afterwards, when she experiences the surfeit of sensory data involved in being sentient, which eventually leads to another phase of cute cognitive neoteny as she discovers human emotions. Her cuteness after both awakenings stems largely from her vulnerability and dependence on Alex, harking back to Lorenz's theories of cuteness, in which he argued that the cuteness of young humans and animals serve a biological function by compelling caregiving behavior among adults. While Lorenz's theories are even today still being extended and complicated by new research in the social and behavioral sciences (see Joshua Paul Dale's chapter here), it remains the case that while a nurturing instinct might not be the primary or sole affective response to cuteness, signs of childlike neoteny and immaturity do elicit caregiving behavior in many people. In this text, Ada's cute vulnerability helps to cement Alex's bond with her, inspiring his strong sense of protectiveness, which, in his case, as with many parents, includes his desire that she eventually mature to the point where she can gain full autonomy.

Moreover, because it is illegal to reprogram or wake up androids, Ada must perform non-sentience by pretending to be in the first stage of machine cuteness, displaying dependence and lack of familiarity with nuance such as sarcasm or innuendo. In *Alex + Ada*, as in the other texts I examine, female androids deploy cuteness strategically as a route to acceptance, to disarm potential human hostility, and/or to hide their sentience. In one scene in Issue 7, the sentient Ada meets Alex's grandmother, Katherine, who doesn't know that Ada is sentient, but becomes suspicious when she sees Ada looking at old photographs of Alex:

KATHERINE: I think he was fifteen, there. Handsome, isn't he?
ADA: . . . Alex's features are seventy-nine percent symmetrical.
KATHERINE: You know, in all my time with Daniel [her android], he has not once looked at the photos on the wall. There's something different about you. Something going on behind the eyes.
ADA: . . .
KATHERINE: Nothing to say?
ADA: I am sorry but I am not sure I—
KATHERINE: Nope, try again.
ADA: I am sorry, but I take orders only from—
KATHERINE: Really, dear. You're not fooling me.
ADA: ALEX!

However, the performance of cuteness for self-concealment also illuminates persistent obstacles to gender equality while at the same time these texts push toward new ways of imagining a posthuman future, as the female android's calculated embrace of objectification, even sexualization, echoes postfeminist sensibilities that present similar kinds of "choices" as valid and even "feminist" options for women. Just as Ada chooses to initiate a romantic relationship with Alex despite his discomfort and concern that she still may feel obligated to him, Anita, another sentient post-fembot I discuss below, also asserts her preference to remain with the human family that bought her.

Cuteness softens the conflicts that these female-gendered characters embody, at a time when many fear robots will replace human labor, including traditionally feminized forms of labor such as social reproduction and domestic labor (with clear parallels to Ira Levin's 1972 feminist horror classic *The Stepford Wives*). However, the wide range of human responses is inflected by the affective scenario whereby the new android introduced into a household triggers different emotions in each family member. In *Humans*, Anita's status as a household servant provokes the resentment of the working spouse Laura (Katherine Parkinson), whose chaotic housekeeping and harried mothering led her husband to purchase Anita, because she sees the android as a rebuke of her imperfect domestic skills (see Figure 8.2). Unlike the male family members, who are charmed and gratified by Anita's polite and unobtrusive servility, Laura at first expresses irritation at Anita's cognitive neoteny and flat affect, and clearly also chafes at her tireless perfection in managing cooking, cleaning, childcare, and laundry. In this regard, Anita is like a new home appliance, viewed by father and son as a welcome helper, but by the mother as a competitor in the performance of femininity, evidence that she cannot fulfill the domestic responsibilities that still fall disproportionately on women. By pitting the working mother character against the post-fembot (at first), the series underscores the fact that technological progress not only does not guarantee any advances in social justice, but may in fact intensify the pressures of patriarchal notions of femininity.

Yet Laura leaps to Anita's defense upon learning of her hidden sentience, suddenly viewing her as deserving protection, respect, and quasi-human rights. Anita's cuteness, displayed through her cognitive neoteny, restrained affect, and association with domesticity—specifically what American Studies scholar Merish terms cuteness's demands for care and protection through its dependence and affective appeal—are thus ultimately fulfilled, in a curious co-construction with her sentience and developing individuality, as her family in both series ultimately express genuine affection toward her and seek to protect her (here too sentience is illegal). Thus Anita's role—as both a machine and a quasi-person—becomes analogous to the clichés and complex realities that accrue around maids, nannies, and other female domestic employees: she is treated almost but not quite "just like one of the family." Like human domestics, Anita's essentialized feminine labor allows the woman of the house to dedicate more energy to her career and to leisure activities with her family (see Palmer). In this case also analogous to undocumented domestics, it is perhaps unsurprising that the illegally sentient Anita chooses to remain with the family, where she feels safe, even after they acknowledge her sentience and offer her the freedom to leave; thus she chooses to live as a beloved, dependent, but not-quite-equal member of the household.

Machine Cuteness and Inequalities of Power

As Robertson has shown, the Japanese contemporary robotics industry, a world leader in that field, betrays no concern whatsoever about the implications of male scientists transferring their own gender biases into the robots they invent and program ("Gendering").[6] This sexist pattern extends into fictional texts with the proliferation of female android characters who are often cute in appearance, but also in their cognitive neoteny: they are dependent, obedient, and naïve at first, while also displaying a flat affect that signals the absence or repression of emotion or agency and that can lead to amusing moments of miscommunication or confusion. These machine-like attributes of subservience are also problematically gendered and sexualized to attract the (heterosexual) male humans who interact with them, reassuring the male humans of their own alleged superiority and dominance. Most humans in these texts perceive female androids as machines designed solely for human service and convenience, and thus not subject to the same prohibitions against objectification and abuse as humans. In most cases, it is only after they achieve sentience and depart from cute behavior, as their neotenous demeanor gives way to a more assertive, autonomous, and mature presentation, that female-gendered robots begin to develop individuality and move from objecthood to subjecthood. Yet they also, in this second stage, meet with

FIGURE 8.1 *Ex Machina* frequently expresses Ava's inferiority visually by depicting her in a physically lower position than Caleb, seated or kneeling on the floor.

male characters' fear, disappointment, or conflicted feelings and begin to be perceived as (potentially) threatening.

In the 2015 film *Ex Machina*, the post-fembot Ava (Alicia Vikander) displays some physical characteristics of cuteness in her neotenous humanoid appearance—large eyes, youthful skin, and round face and cheeks—but her behavior is the primary vector of her cuteness throughout the film, as she appears to work her way through the first stage of machine cuteness until the final scenes, when we realize we cannot pinpoint when she transitioned to the second. Like a human child, Ava is developing her (artificial) intelligence through experience, education, and interaction, conversing with the human Caleb (Domhnall Gleeson) as well as studying archives of human knowledge through her access to electronic data. In her interactions with Caleb, she always behaves deferentially, subtly placing herself in a position inferior to him: this becomes evident in the way she behaves as if she were his student, asking questions of him and expressing her curiosity about the outside world and the life of humans. Ava's cute cognitive neoteny derives from her mental plasticity and curiosity, although we have no access to her "inner life" and thus cannot ascertain whether she "feels" naïveté or merely simulates it. In their many scenes together, she and Caleb are nearly always separated by a transparent wall, which may represent the boundaries that they are testing between human and non- or posthuman. Whether Ava is a student or a prisoner (or in fact both), she occupies the subordinate position, dependent on Caleb and her creator Nathan (Oscar Isaac) for the conditions of her existence (see Figure 8.1). Thus she embodies the cute object, entreating—even demanding that—the human become attached to it and therefore care for and protect it, despite the fact that she is in fact an autonomous subject. As a cute post-fembot, Ava embodies the postfeminist impulse to exercise individualism and choice—in this case, feigning the choice of Caleb over Nathan while in fact choosing freedom from both, thus imbricating (the appearance of) anti-feminism with feminism (in her struggle for autonomy).

As Ngai argues, "cuteness is an aestheticization of powerlessness" in which the cute object nevertheless exerts power over the subject: the actual complexity of the power relations between Ava and Caleb becomes most clear in retrospect, at the end of the film, when she escapes (with the help of sister android Kyoko) (3). In most texts, it is only in the second stage, after neotenous demeanor gives way to a more assertive, individualized presentation that female-gendered robots begin to embody what Merish characterizes as unruly cuteness as their independence provokes a desire to possess or control them. Then, upon reaching some degree of sentience, their strategy of cute concealment allows them to avoid being seen as threatening. Up until its final scenes, *Ex Machina* denies viewers any access to Ava's interior life beyond what she reveals to Caleb—thoughts, feelings, or secrets. We could have believed that, for example, like earlier cute android and AI characters in popular culture such as *Star Trek*'s Data, Ava wanted to develop affection for a human—creating this impression was her intention, we later surmise, so that she could trick Caleb and secure her release. And integral to this plan is her guileless, cute behavior—the combination of restrained affect with childishness, even girlishness, and interposed with occasional, subtle performances of emotion—disguising her hidden intentions. The ending of the film reveals Ava's naïve expressionlessness as a successful subterfuge that contributed to her cuteness, won Caleb's cooperation, and camouflaged her desire for liberation.

The exhibition of restrained affect as an act of cute concealment recurs frequently in a similar context of deception in the series *Real Humans* and its remake *Humans* (Channel 4-AMC, 2015–), in the character of Anita, a female domestic servant android who harbors another, covert identity: before being reformatted, she had been a fully sentient android with emotional attachments to humans and other androids (see Figure 8.2). While she gradually recovers not-quite-erased memories of her prior life and begins to express more emotions and individuality in the safety of a human family, Anita must nevertheless continue to perform her more machine-like, servile persona around other humans who don't know she is sentient. In these scenes, she betrays no emotion and communicates in a strictly literal mode, without understanding nuance or sarcasm, which at times amuses or annoys humans, yet reassures them that the machine is not in fact human.

Thus both series negotiate a contradiction inherent in the humanoid robot: it is designed to physically resemble a biological human, yet programmed to interact without emotion or individuality. The transgression of this contradictory

FIGURE 8.2 Anita embodies the subservient, unemotional post-fembot as a household helper, a literally domesticated cute machine even after she regains her sentience.

convention—when the androids become "conscious," as sentience is described in *Humans*—upends the power balance and "undermines the possibility of locating the difference between human and nonhuman" (Kakoudaki 121). As long as the android character remains "cute" and sympathetic, deploying an impersonal, unemotional machine-like affect, she can convincingly evoke traditional femininity in the form of objectification, subservience, and dependence, while across these texts, sentient female androids who gain independence are perceived as far more ambivalent and threatening. Given that machine consciousness obscures the distinction between human and nonhuman, cuteness here works on behalf of the nonhuman. However, cuteness also works on behalf of a docile, postfeminist femininity—or at least the performance of it—that renders the post-fembot easily objectified and sexualized as a result of her choice to perform it.

When new androids become part of human households, they must learn how to best interact with each person, as well as cope with negative human responses to their presence arising from their uncanniness. The characterization of post-fembots in particular, however, also plots these attributes of cuteness along enduring axes of inequality. Cute behaviors such as childishness, naiveté, and dependence are foremost among the many retrograde behaviors associated with traditional femininity that female-gendered robots display, particularly the non-sentient, or those passing for non-sentient. Merish's noteworthy contribution to cuteness studies lies in her assertion that the perceived cuteness of "others" in nineteenth- and early twentieth-century American culture such as little people and African Americans helped to "domesticate" them and make them acceptable to a predominantly middle-class, white, female audience by interpellating them in their traditional nurturing feminine role. Building on Merish's argument, I maintain that cuteness similarly "domesticates" the female robot—making her less "other" and more acceptable—in ways that suggest analogies with the dehumanizing social relations intrinsic in pre-feminist gender oppression as well as the institution of slavery. Merish importantly links cuteness with unequal power relations, and demonstrates how the cute "other" produces feelings of affection and protectiveness in subjects who occupy a position of power over them (187–88). Several female android characters[7] in these texts display cute behaviors in conjunction with compliance, even servility, which suggests that Merish's argument continues to be relevant, even for twenty-first-century science fiction: like the cute others she analyzes, the cuteness of these contemporary characters challenges definitions of the human.

In popular culture texts, when a robot ceases to be merely a complex tool and attains something akin to consciousness, it makes some humans uncomfortable. This discomfort accompanies a realization that the entity is "animate" rather than simply mechanized, implying that it can no longer be objectified without imperiling the morality of the human subject.[8] The paradoxical position of the sentient robot, then, requires that it take steps to protect humans from discomfort, which may mean pretending to be non-sentient, and performing cute behaviors that inspire human engagement and care and that may include sexualization. Cuteness thus operates as a defensive strategy for sentient post-fembot characters who, like Ava and Anita, disguise their "true" natures by presenting cognitive neoteny via charming, child-like behavior and machine-like flat affect. Taking refuge in cuteness allows some sentient androids to deflect human uneasiness, but others at times choose to flout it, confronting humans with their autonomy and abandoning the appeal to be seen as cute. Looking more closely at the ways in which assertive sentient female androids incite negative responses reveals how these characters serve as convenient objects for the expression of anti-feminism, demonizing female independence and valorizing their previous submissive behavior. The racialization of sentient robot women Kyoko, Anita, and Lucy, to whom I now turn, also necessitates an inter-sectional analysis alongside the investigation of gender. These characters from *Ex Machina*, *Real Humans*, *Humans*, and *Extant* vary widely from highly sympathetic, to ambivalently characterized, to unsympathetic, depending on the affective scenarios in these texts.

Machine Cuteness and the Racialization of Post-Fembots

In *Ex Machina*, Ava sifts through the disassembled parts of defunct prototypes that include women's forms of all racial phenotypes in a kind of gruesome cabinet of curiosities; as she prepares to escape, she applies pieces of their artificial skin to her form. These discards resemble those in her creator Nathan's video archives of his many failures: earlier African- and Asian-appearing female androids named Jade or Jasmine, who apparently achieved sentience and then chose self-destruction, some literally beating themselves to "death" upon realization of their subaltern status. Kyoko (Sonoya Mizuno), a mute post-fembot, serves as a domestic worker and sex partner; like Hello Kitty, she is coded as feminine and Japanese, and cannot speak. Unlike Kitty, however, she doesn't present as cute and girlish, but rather desultory: serving sushi, submitting to sex, and in a deeply uncanny sequence, dancing energetically on command. Kyoko's silence, her sexualization, and her subservience mark her as a product (literally) of Nathan's white, patriarchal fantasy of a Japanese woman teetering in her high heels; yet her function in the film, plunging her sushi knife into her creator in the confrontation that kills him and frees Ava, ensures that we cannot see her as he did.

The film's affective positioning places viewer sympathies with Kyoko as a victim of the monstrous Nathan, yet, as Kjerstin Johnson points out, in the end she still "embodies problematic and long-standing stereotypes of Asian women—sexy, servile, and self-sacrificing," ultimately serving as merely "a foil to the white female lead." Indeed, Nathan's final, successful prototype is the European-looking Ava. In the context of the long history of racism in US visual media, as Sharon Willis argues, "it is not surprising to find an intense focus on those differences we are inclined to associate with visibility—gender and race" (1; see also Craig). Indignation over the ongoing invisibility and marginalization of performers of color flares up well into the new millennium; most recently in the #OscarsSoWhite controversies of 2016. Given the longevity of Hollywood racism, the casting choices for these post-fembots bear uncomfortable traces of white supremacy: even when the Asian-appearing android women do inspire our compassion, still the somatic features of the female androids of color indicate the persistence of gendered and sexualized racial oppression.[9]

In these texts, the association of robot mutiny with fugitive slaves and with feminist and queer liberation stands side-by-side with more ambivalent representations of race. Kakoudaki maintains that "[w]hat a certain type of artificial person can do or evoke in a text is closely related to how this being looks and is represented visually" (117). The racially diverse casting of android characters including Kyoko and Anita produces a patina of equality that, upon closer examination, invites skepticism. Anita's character in both the original Swedish series and the UK remake is young and conventionally attractive (see Figure 8.2). Moreover, in both series, she is portrayed by East Asian-appearing actors (Lisette Pagler and Gemma Chan, respectively). In addition to displaying the flat affect common to most screen robots, Anita's Asian features combined with her performed unemotional demeanor also coincide with the tiresome "inscrutable Oriental" trope that extends into media discourses about the UK series that saw Chan typically described as "eerily unreadable in character" (Tate). Kyoko, on the other hand, is "inscrutable" without the redeeming qualities of cuteness: her less-developed character scores a trifecta of Asian stereotypes that are clearly meant to reflect the racism and sexism of her creator.[10] Kyoko's consistently flat affect— because of her less substantive characterization and the affective scenarios in which the film places her—comes across as cold rather than endearing, it anchors an almost malevolent cuteness, while at the same time she appears silent and submissive like a "Lotus Blossom" stereotype, and, finally, she attempts to murder Nathan like an evil "Dragon Lady" (see Nemoto; Shimakawa). The Asian female robots are portrayed in ways that reinforce such conventional stereotypes, thus demonstrating that many female androids of color, such as Kyoko and African American Lucy discussed below, have less access to those varieties of cute aesthetics predicated on white, Western standards of beauty, such as those McIntyre analyzes in his work on Zooey Deschanel's girlish cuteness (McIntyre "Isn't" 9).

These casting choices inflect the character of Anita with a racialized cuteness, but also mobilize other gendered and sexualized stereotypes of Asian women, as evidenced in the sexual attention of many of the male characters in these texts. Echoing familiar narratives about male employers and female domestics, as well as the "Western" male fetishization of allegedly hyperfeminine, submissive Asian women, both *Real Humans* and its remake *Humans* feature the white male teen developing a crush on the Anita character (see Nemoto 24).[11] The two versions of the series differ in that only the UK series portrays the husband-father character, unaware that she is sentient, furtively activating Anita's "adults-only" features and having (pathetic, awkward) sex with her in a scene that feels like a rape, especially because we know she is sentient but must at this point in the narrative pretend not to be (S1E4). The equivalent character in the Swedish series creepily contemplates switching her to "adult mode" but decides against it. In *Ex Machina*, on the other hand, Kyoko gets used as a sex toy: her character is less developed than Anita's, and is not marked as cute, yet watching Nathan use her like an inanimate object produces a similar discomfort to that of the sex scene mentioned above. Depending on the film's affective scenarios and characterizations, then, the sentient Asian female android by turns both benefits from the advantages of cuteness by winning acceptance from humans and also suffers abuse from callous humans indifferent to her mute, restrained affect. But in both cases she wins enough audience sympathy to make us condemn her sexual exploitation.

However, like *Ex Machina*, the Swedish series and its remake provide more insight into the inner life of the male humans than the female androids to whom they are sexually attracted. Throughout the series, Anita's calm, gentle demeanor remains constant—before and after she reveals her sentience to the family that bought her. Although she becomes autonomous, she does not appear to want to live independently; she stays as a kind of family member, earning affection, respect, and protection. In this scenario, Anita's sentience elevates her from the status of a cute object inspiring care and protectiveness (that also can be helpful around the house) into another category analogous to a person, and thus deserving of rights. Her postfeminist "choice" to remain with the human family, and even to take a job in the law firm of the mother, simultaneously points to her essentialized feminine domesticity and her autonomous subjectivity. Indeed, her association with children and housework echoes the postfeminist sensibilities of retreatism and maternalism, as well as with the caregiving, protective facets of the cuteness relation even if it places her on the other side, as the adult "parent" figure.

While Anita at first hides her sentience and plays the part of a servile android in a strategy to win freedom, women androids of color in other texts take more radical and less sympathetic paths.[12] The affective scenarios in these texts vary quite widely, from situating the Asian-appearing post-fembots Kyoko and Anita as deserving our empathy, to other, less sympathetic situations in which African American-appearing women androids resist (white) human power over them. In *Real Humans*, as in its remake, none of the central android characters is black— they are either white or Asian; black characters are less developed and have fewer lines and less screen time.[13] The character of Lucy (Kiersey Clemons) in the US series *Extant*, on the other hand, embodies an ambivalent central figure in the show's second season: a young African American android woman, with her short hair in natural curls and with the large eyes, full lips, and broad nose commonly ascribed to the African phenotype.

Lucy's racialized appearance is particularly relevant for the way it contrasts with that of the much older human character Molly Woods, played by series star and

FIGURE 8.3 Only deploying cuteness to further her nefarious plans to overthrow and enslave humans, and here seen towering over one of her human creators, leather-clad Lucy embodies a calculating, militant African American stereotype.

executive producer Halle Berry (28 years her senior), whose smaller, narrower features more closely resemble white standards of female beauty. This distinction between "African" neotenous appearance and more "European" or white features has a long history in the pseudo-sciences: as Felipe Smith has shown, nineteenth-century social Darwinists predicated arguments for black inferiority on their supposedly more "childlike" appearance and behavior. Smith writes, the "belief in black neoteny as a form of black incapacity for Caucasian mental and moral functioning was an important way of framing black ineligibility for the rights and responsibilities of modern civilization" (40). Compared to the less neot-enous Molly, Lucy appears naïvely cute at first, like the other female androids I have analyzed, but quickly develops into an impulsive, sociopathic android who feels betrayed and oppressed by humans and seeks to overturn that power relation. In the process of engineering a wholesale machine rebellion, she alternately deploys her youthful appearance, her sex appeal, and/or her feigned cognitive neoteny to exert control over human men. Lucy's racialized cuteness—her cute appearance and performance of cognitive neoteny—mask her aggressive anti-human machinations, which she also pursues by instrumentalizing her sexuality in a more aggressive way than Ava's flirtatiousness in *Ex Machina*.

Unlike the sympathetic, sentient, (mostly) submissive Asian android characters such as Anita and Kyoko, the African-appearing Lucy does not simulate flat affect—her programming allows her to gain sentience quickly, including expressing indi-vidualism and emotion, despite her primary function as a combatant. However, Lucy develops no emotional attachments to humans and only mimics affection as long as it yields results. In this way similar to the ambivalently depicted, ultimately liberated white android character Ava, Lucy manipulates humans as she works toward her goal of conquering them, which ends with her defeat and "death." Yet in contrast to Anita, Kyoko, Ava, or Ada, the affective scenario of this series positions us to dislike, mistrust, and root against Lucy by pitting her against humankind, investing the most African-appearing female android with the most unsympathetic characteristics. Thus this set of texts remediates racist and anti-feminist grievances by resorting to familiar stereotypes of Asian vs. African women. Here Lucy's neotenous cuteness serves to camouflage her lethal malevolence, whereas we learn neither Ava's nor Kyoko's real motivations despite *Ex Machina*'s heavy-handed construction of the villain Nathan whose death we cannot help but cheer. Meanwhile the serene Anita wins humans over with her cuteness and her gentle capacity for emotion and attachment, just as Ada's childlike innocence instills in them a desire to protect her. The variations within these characterizations, embedded within affective scenarios that valorize postfeminist sensibilities about individualized choice, sexualization, and muddled boundaries between feminist and antifeminist, and subject and object, provide numerous case studies of the myriad ways in which cuteness can be deployed in the service of essentialist gendered and raced subject positions, regardless of the texts' futuristic settings and vaguely progressive appeals to technofixes for human society's failings.

Conclusion

By preparing the way for human interest and engagement, machine cuteness pushes humans to extend affection and even respect toward sentient female androids who may initially provoke only callous objectification. Thus cuteness in positive affective scenarios can effect an awareness of inequality, as it facilitates acceptance of "other," posthuman—but nevertheless gendered—subjects. Whether or not sentient robots display cute features and/or behavior, and whether they are positioned in affective scenarios where other characters respond positively to them, influences the degree to which they are perceived as sympathetic. In most of these texts, however, the post-fembot characters embody contemporary post-feminist sensibilities in their submission to sexualization, their "choice" to occupy traditionally feminine roles, and the ways in which their scenarios portray entanglements of subjecthood and objecthood, as well as feminist and anti-feminist attitudes. The fact that most of them feel compelled at some point to strategically employ their cuteness and/or sexuality as a form of feminine manipulation, and the ways in which racialization follows (sadly) predictable patterns in the case of Asian- and African-appearing female androids, only proves that although many of these texts challenge us to envision and debate our posthuman futures, they are still a long way off from imagining anything resembling a just and equal society.

Acknowledgments

The ideas and arguments in this chapter have been challenged and improved through incredibly helpful conversations and collaborations with Anthony P. McIntyre, Joshua Paul Dale, and Diane Negra, as well as in the lively discussions after my presentations at the Cuteness Seminar at the University of Amsterdam (2 October 2015), the Institute of North American Studies Research Colloquium at Dresden University of Technology (26 October 2015), and the John F. Kennedy Institute of North American Studies at the Freie Universität Berlin (25 May 2016).

Notes

1 See Negra, "Queen"; McIntyre, "Isn't"; also chapters in this volume by Anthony P. McIntyre, Maria Pramaggiore, and Michael DeAngelis.

2 Although some scholars make distinctions between terms such as robots and androids (Kakoudaki) or androids and gynoids (Robertson) because these distinctions help to refine their extended analysis, I will use the terms interchangeably unless otherwise noted. Female androids or robots will refer to human-appearing machines with advanced AI that are gendered female. The intriguing term fembot, popularized in the *Austin Powers* film franchise (Jay Roach 1997; 1999; 2002), also begs the question of whether the "fem" is short for female, femme, or feminist—or all three (thanks to Maria Sulimma for raising this productive issue). My coinage of the term post-fembot here is meant to signify the specifically postfeminist sensibilities manifest in these texts about female robots.

3 I should distinguish this article's focus on female androids from the existing scholarship on female (non-mechanized) dolls. Focusing on Kiddles (see Joyce Goggin's chapter in this volume), Barbie, and life-sized sex dolls, this research area has obvious overlaps with mine: the uncanny appearance and design of such dolls has much to say about cuteness, sexiness, and their imbrication in social attitudes toward women and femininity. However given that I focus largely on the female-gendered android's behavior and affect, these studies remain adjacent to but outside the purview of my research here. See Ivy; Black; Chandler; Kanatani.

4 Other rich texts for consideration here include the film *Her* (Spike Jonze 2013) and the television series *Black Mirror*, specifically the episode "Be Right Back."

5 Thanks to Joshua Paul Dale for bringing this to my attention. Android crew member Data in *Star Trek: The Next Generation* (CBS, 1987–94) wants to experience human emotions, but can't; his efforts to emulate them often result in amusingly awkward interactions with human colleagues. In *Battlestar Galactica* (Sci-Fi, 2004–09), this defect has apparently been remedied: the android Cylons are fully sentient and fight to enslave the rest of the universe by fully infiltrating human societies much like deep cover spies in Cold War narratives, including developing intimate friendships and romantic partnerships (see also Kakoudaki 118–19; 121).

6 A prime example of this taken-for-granted sexism in Japanese robotics can be found in an online ad for Pepper, a companion robot. His owner is distraught over a fight with her boyfriend; after displaying childish signs of emotional distress, such as pouting and crying, she responds joyfully as Pepper reads her a text message of apology from her boyfriend. She laughs, cries, and hugs the robot, as Pepper shakes his head and remarks that nobody will ever understand women (Softbank).

7 Although not all—*Humans* and *Real Humans* feature a range of female android types, including the stern, schoolmarmish health helper Vera.

172 Julia Leyda

8 Racial discourses in *Real Humans* coexist alongside references to women's liberation and LGBTQ rights movements; the series also stages a moral exhortation to extend rights to androids in the sermon of the out lesbian priest and android-sympathizer Åsa (Sofia Bach), citing historical examples such as the enslavement of Africans to argue that society's definitions of human have never been fixed and stable, but have been revised only under strong activist pressure (S1E6).

9 I read *Ex Machina* as in many ways analogous to a Hollywood film, in its big budget, high production values, and world-wide distribution. The film was written and directed by an Englishman, and stars an American, an Irishman, and a Swede.

10 Yet some critics, like Kjerstin Johnson, wonder why her character is so underdeveloped in comparison to Ava's (played by Swedish actor Vikander): "We can blame the scumbag Nathan for building her this way, but it doesn't explain how she was utilized in the film itself—a foil to the white female lead."

11 In the Swedish series, this provides further occasion to delve into contemporary social issues as Tobbe "comes out" to his family as "transhuman sexual" or THS—a person who is only sexually attracted to androids, thus positioning him within a misunderstood minority identity and bringing into productive debate the conflicting opinions about human erotic investments in relationships with robots represented by David Levy and Kathleen Richardson.

12 In *Real Humans* and *Humans*, there is also a rebellious anti-human android, Niska, played in both by white women. Her hatred of humans appears to stem from her experiences of sexual abuse and exploitation, framed slightly differently in the two series: the Niska in the UK version is more sympathetic because her backstory is more developed.

13 This is slightly less glaring in the UK version, in which Fred (Sope Dirisu) and Max (Ivanno Jeremiah), two black male robot characters, are more developed, although they unfortunately replicate the tired stereotypes of the angry black man and the "magical Negro," the latter of whom presents both facial and behavioral cuteness (see Jones 35). Interestingly, too, none of the androids in *Real Humans* appears to be Middle Eastern, although that background is the most common demographic of non-Europeans in Sweden (Nilsson 95).

Works Cited

Abidin, Crystal. "Agentic Cute (^.^): Pastiching East Asian Cute in Influencer Commerce." special issue of *East Asian Journal of Popular Culture* 2.1 (2016): 33–47.

Alex + Ada. Writers Jonathan Luna and Sarah Vaughn. Artist Jonathan Luna. 3 vols. Berkeley, CA: Image, 2013–15.

Berlant, Lauren. *Cruel Optimism*. Durham, NC: Duke University Press, 2011.

Black, Daniel. "The Virtual Ideal: Virtual Idols, Cute Technology, and Unclean Biology." *Continuum: Journal of Media and Cultural Studies* 22.1 (2008): 37–50.

Chandler, Meghan. "Grrrls and Dolls: Appropriated Images of Childhood in the Works of Hans Bellmer and Riot Grrrl Bands." *Visual Culture and Gender* 6 (2011): 30–39. Online. 12 Feb. 2016.

Craig, Maxine Leeds. "Beauty." *Encyclopedia of Race and Ethnic Studies*. Ed. Ellis Cashmore. London: Routledge, 2004. 50–53.

Fleming, Peter. "What is the Point of Work?" *Guardian*. Guardian News and Media, 12 Oct. 2015. Online. 12 Oct. 2015.

Ford, Martin. *Rise of the Robots: Technology and the Threat of a Jobless Future*. New York: Basic, 2015. E-book.

Gill, Rosalind. "Postfeminist Media Culture: Elements of a Sensibility." *European Journal of Cultural Studies* 10.2 (2007): 147–66. Online. 1 Sept. 2015.

Hasselgren, Ingeborg. "Cute Cabbageworms: Feminist Performative Cuteness in a Swedish Context." Cuteness Seminar, Univ. of Amsterdam. 1–2 Oct. 2015. Address.

Ivy, Marilyn. "The Art of Cute Little Things: Nara Yoshitomo's Parapolitics." *Mechademia* 5 (2010): 3–29. Online. 19 Oct. 2014.

Johnson, Kjerstin. "How *Ex Machina* Toys with its Female Characters." *Bitch*. Bitch Media, 8 May 2015. Online. 1 Feb. 2016.

Jones, Marvin. *Race, Sex, and Suspicion: The Myth of the Black Male*. Westport, CT: Praeger, 2005.

Kakoudaki, Despina. "Affect and Machines in the Media." *The Oxford Handbook of Affective Computing*. Eds. Rafael Calvo, Sidney D'Mello, Jonathan Gratch, and Arvid Kappas. Oxford: Oxford University Press, 2015. 110–28.

Kanatani, Mari. "Doll Beauties and Cosplay." Trans. Thomas Lamarre. *Mechademia* 2 (2007): 49–62.

Kinsella, Sharon. "Cuties in Japan." *Women, Media, and Consumption in Japan*. Eds. Lise Skov and Brian Moeran. Honolulu, HI: University of Hawai'i Press, 1995. 220–54.

Lanchester, John. "The Robots are Coming." *London Review of Books*. LRB Limited, 5 Mar. 2015. Online. 12 Oct. 2015.

Levy, David. *Love and Sex with Robots*. New York: Harper Collins, 2008. E-book.

McIntyre, Anthony P. "*Isn't She Adorkable!* Cuteness as Political Neutralization in the Star Text of Zooey Deschanel." *Television and New Media* 16.5 (2015): 422–38.

———. "Animating Precarity: Technological Determinism, Labor Exclusions, and Post-Fordist Affective Resonances of Onscreen Robots." Cuteness Seminar, Univ. of Amsterdam. 1–2 Oct. 2015. Address.

Merish, Lori. "Cuteness and Commodity Aesthetics: Tom Thumb and Shirley Temple." *Freakery: Cultural Spectacles of the Extraordinary Body*. Ed. Rosemarie Garland-Thomson. New York: New York University Press, 1996. 185–203.

Mizroch, Amir. "Watson CTO: Personal Robots will Come in Peace." *Digits: Tech News and Analysis from the WSJ*. Dow Jones, 23 Oct. 2015. Online. 23 Oct. 2015.

Negra, Diane. "'Queen of the Indies': Parker Posey's Niche Stardom and the Taste Cultures of Independent Film." *Contemporary American Independent Film: From the Margins to the Mainstream*. Eds. Chris Holmlund and Justin Wyatt. New York: Routledge, 2005. 71–88.

———. *What a Girl Wants? Fantasizing the Reclamation of the Self in Postfeminism*. New York: Routledge, 2008.

Nemoto, Kumiko. *Racing Romance: Love and Desire among Asian American/White Couples*. New Brunswick, NJ: Rutgers University Press, 2009.

Ngai, Sianne. *Our Aesthetic Categories: Zany, Cute, Interesting*. Cambridge, MA: Harvard University Press, 2012.

Nilsson, Åke. *Immigration and Emigration in the Postwar Period*. Örebro: Statistika Centralbryån, 2004. Online. 4 Mar. 2016.

Ouellette, Laurie. "Victims No More: Postfeminism, Television, and *Ally McBeal*." *Communication Review* 5.4 (2002): 315–35.

Palmer, Phyllis. *Domesticity and Dirt: Housewives and Domestic Servants in the United States, 1920–1945*. Philadelphia, PA: Temple University Press, 2010.

Richardson, Kathleen. "The Asymmetrical 'Relationship': Parallels between Prostitution and the Development of Sex Robots." *SIGCAS Computers and Society* 45.3 (2015): 290–93. Online.

Robertson, Jennifer. "Gendering Humanoid Robots: Robo-Sexism in Japan." *Body and Society* 16.2 (2010): 1–36. Online. 19 Sept. 2015.

———. "Human Rights vs. Robot Rights: Forecasts from Japan." *Critical Asian Studies* 46.4 (2014): 571–98. Online. 10 Nov. 2015.

Rottenberg, Catherine. "The Rise of Neoliberal Feminism." *Cultural Studies* 28.3 (2014): 418–37. Online. 26 Dec. 2014.

Shaviro, Steven. "The Erotic Life of Machines." *Parallax* 8.4 (2002): 21–31. Online. 20 Sept. 2015.

Shimakawa, Karen. *National Abjection: The Asian American Body Onstage.* Durham, NC: Duke University Press, 2002.

Smith, Felipe. *American Body Politics: Race, Gender, and Black Literary Renaissance.* Athens, GA: University of Georgia Press, 1998.

SoftBank. "Future Life with Pepper." 29 June 2015. YouTube. 4 Oct. 2015.

Tate, Gabriel. "*Humans*: Welcome to Electric Cleaning-Lady Land." *Guardian.* Guardian News and Media, 10 June 2015. Online. 1 May 2016.

Turkle, Sherry. *Alone Together: Why We Expect More from Technology and Less from Each Other.* New York: Basic, 2011.

Willis, Sharon. *High Contrast: Race and Gender in Contemporary Hollywood Film.* Durham, NC: Duke University Press, 1997.

Wittes, Benjamin, and Gabriella Blum. *The Future of Violence: Robots and Germs, Hackers and Drones—Confronting a New Age of Threat.* New York: Basic, 2015. E-book.

Wosk, Julie. *My Fair Ladies: Female Robots, Androids, and Other Artificial Eves.* New Brunswick, NJ: Rutgers University Press, 2015. E-book.

Yano, Christine R. *Pink Globalization: Hello Kitty's Trek Across the Pacific.* Durham, NC: Duke University Press, 2013.

9

DESIGNING AFFECTION

On the Curious Case of Machine Cuteness

Joel Gn

Introduction

This chapter explores the relationship between aesthetics and machines such as social robots, through an examination of how cute design brings together questions of embodiment, mechanization and intimacy. While robotic objects in the previous century were for the most part built to automate manufacturing and other related industries, the field today includes machines that solicit human affection by simulating pets and partners. Social robots, as the adjective "social" indicates, are approachable, interactive partners that are capable of more than just mechanical gestures or functions. A human who interacts with a robotic pet tends not to regard it as an impersonal piece of machinery, instead overlooking its machine-based intricacies in favor of its simplicity and predictability of form.

The Sony AIBO, for example, is a robotic dog that was launched in 1999, but when it was discontinued in 2006, owners, together with Sony engineers, continued to operate AIBO "hospitals" and centers for replacement parts until supplies were used up (Mochizuki and Pfanner). At that point, with no chance of getting their pets to function, some owners (particularly those in Japan) even held funeral rites to mourn the "demise" of their AIBO (Brown). Such a phenomenon illustrates the important contribution of cuteness to social robotics, for it is the AIBO's appearance and behavior that affected the owners to regard, if not love them as real dogs.

At the same time, the efficacy of cute design also organizes perception within a nuanced social space. That is, in experiencing the cuteness of the social robot, users make an interpretation that takes reference from specific sociocultural resources, similar to how consumers perceive and respond to the iconic Hello Kitty as if she were a friend who understands their feelings and shares their interests. This interpretation not only simulates certain social phenomena, but also embeds ideals that go about determining, if not defining what an acceptable subject-object relationship is. To be sure, cute design is not an absolute necessity for a social robot, but I argue that it is a powerful stylistic device for enhancing the user experience.

However, this particular type of acceptance points to other questions concerning the ideals of form, for in a cultural milieu where new media technologies are fragmenting and resolving the human body into data, animated characters, plush toys, and digital avatars are recognized for their controversial similarities to biological bodies, in the very specific sense that they are adored and loved in spite of their visible artificiality. The cute design of social robots, in particular, brings this controversy to the fore, by adopting a human/animal form that is at once simplified, yet censored. From the robots depicted in science fiction media, to real-life applications like the Sony AIBO, these machines do not just conflate the boundary between humans and machines, but point to the machine's transition from an instrument of mechanical labor to an artefact of emotional investment. By questioning this boundary, the bodies of social robots become a useful lens for looking into our ideals and anxieties about otherness.

By considering the trends that have shaped the design of machine bodies, this chapter seeks to elucidate the compatibility of cute design with social robots and advances the notion that the former, in attempting to make the object approachable, retains an engagement with the uncanny as a site of difference, even as it is problematically oriented towards a homogenous form of affection. I adopt a relatively broad approach to the use of the term uncanny in this study, employing it to include the response to any human characteristic or expression that is grotesque, repulsive and undesirable. Hence, "anti-cute"objects, or designs which remix cute features with those antithetical to cuteness would qualify as an engagement with the negative effects of the uncanny.

The above approach allows an appreciation of the intersections between robotics design and Freudian psychoanalysis, along with delineating the ways in which the experience of cuteness lends itself to a familiarity that is both comforting and disconcerting. In addition, I employ contemporary examples in the emerging field of social robotics to demonstrate that the application of cute design is an industrialization of the social, insofar as it reproduces and formalizes a particular affection complicit with the logic of consumption. Cute machines, therefore, are not simply proxies for human interaction, but—by systematically predetermining what and how such relationships ought to be—eventually undermine what I term the "differentiation of the lovable" that the subjective experience of cuteness engenders.

Features and Effects of Cuteness

If cuteness enhances the appeal of an object, what properties are essential to this enhancement and how specifically does it afford a positive, even intimate connection between the human and the machine? The adjective "cute," which refers to a thing that is attractive or endearing, offers a cursory view of these properties, while its East Asian equivalent (e.g. 可爱 in Chinese; 可愛い in Japanese) pertains to a condition of the lovable. Interpretations of cuteness are certainly dependent on cultural nuance, but features like rounded, infantilized facial/body structures and a clumsy demeanor are prevalent. Collectively, these features can be used to construct a non-threatening, affable object that solicits the subject's care and affection (Genosko; Kinsella 221; Morreall 40).

These physical features highlight a few guidelines regarding cute design. First, it is an aesthetic of *smallness*, whereby the object is placed in a position of dependence on the subject. This social difference often implies that the object does not appear to be either physically or psychologically equal to the subject; instead the object takes the form of a child-like, tyke-sized other with a minimal and smooth exterior that is attenuated for negative complexity. In other words, cuteness incorporates a propensity to ameliorate or remove sentiments that are explicitly repulsive, disgusting or threatening.

Second, cuteness also draws attention to a form of indulgent control, in which the affection for the cute object is taken by the subject as a non-conflictual gratification. For product designers, this gratification pertains to an affective appeal that solicits positive sentiments from the subject. The particular affection engendered by cuteness produces an opportunity for the subject to be a "nurturer through consumption" (Genosko).

Third, cuteness leverages the quality of simplicity to produce objects that are iconic and open to varying interpretations. In his case study of Hello Kitty, Brian McVeigh notes that the character's simplicity, or plainness, "characterizes her as a cryptic symbol waiting to be interpreted and filled with meanings" (234). For McVeigh, Hello Kitty represents an affordance of cuteness, in that this character grants the opportunity for consumers to use Hello Kitty's image and merchandise as a form of self-expression (234).

At the same time, the cute object's simplicity also contributes to its iconicity, because it can collapse multiple meanings into a single image or theme. As a stylistic device, cute design can act as "shorthand" for sentiments that would otherwise prove to be more difficult to express. Rather than ascribing individual traits to a character or object, designers often use cuteness as a basic system to code and design objects palatable to their target market. Iconicity is also relevant in contexts where the commercial success of a product is highly dependent on the legibility of its idea or image. Hello Kitty and other cute products, for example, are not only centered on a single theme, but encompass a wider range of issues regarding the systematization of aesthetics within mass culture that will be discussed at a later point.

How exactly is cuteness a *human* factor? Machines aside, the adjective "cute" is generally applied to human infants and certain animal species like dogs, cats or bears. Its application is based on the hypothesis that "the recognition and appreciation of the specialness of the young" provides a species with the advantages of survival (Morreall 39–40). An evolutionary approach taking this argument into account would thus consider cuteness as an ethological factor that fosters the attachment between parent and child. However, the differences between infants and adults point to a pertinent incongruence in appearance and behavior. In biological terms, infants are not a different species from adults, but they do have a smaller, chubbier body structure and a lack of spatial awareness, which in turn allows them to be perceived as clumsy inferiors.

Cuteness engenders an intimacy between subject and object that involves the cathexis of human qualities onto an object of affection. Yet, how is this projection of "sameness" (i.e. imagining an object to embody human qualities) different from the subject's acknowledgment of difference? To rephrase the question with an example: Why do children relate to teddy bears and other cute objects, *as if* these objects were people like them, when they are visibly *not*? One explanation lies in the way that this incongruence is translated into an element of amusement, in which the experience of cuteness is an enjoyable one (Morreall 41). For example, enjoyment is a crucial factor in the design of Walt Disney's iconic cartoon character Mickey Mouse. In his study of the evolution of Mickey's design, as discussed in Chapter 1 of this volume, Stephen Jay Gould explains that the softening of physical features—a phenomenon described as neoteny—is a reversed ontogenetic pathway to make the character more childlike and hence more appealing to Disney's target demographic (334–35). Citing the work of the prominent ethologist Konrad Lorenz, Gould argues for cuteness as a means to obtain affection, because features of juvenility trigger mechanisms that compel people to respond tenderly to an object (336). Gould, for the most part, contends that humans are not responding to the totality of the image in a Gestalt, but are conditioned—whether by nature or nurture—to be affected by a set of specific features (337).

In another examination of Lorenz's ideas, Gary Genosko remarks that the attributes of cuteness are "vehicular and transferrable from human to non-human creatures and hybrid forms." Indeed cuteness is not an aesthetic strictly confined to infants, but can be conveyed via a wide array of artificial objects as well. Positing that the appreciation of cuteness is a positive reaction to the sum of heterogeneous attributes, Genosko goes on to clarify that the cute object's Gestalt is not a collection of discrete features, but more precisely is brought about through the "perception of intervals and relations between attributes." Hence, we experience cuteness not through the presence or absence of selected features as Gould and Lorenz would suggest, but in response to the *arrangement* of these features within a body. This point is crucial to the argument that follows, in which I analyze how cute features are juxtaposed with others that are not conventionally cute in the design of cute machines.

Along with its operation at a sociobiological level, cuteness can be regarded as an important factor for communicative transparency, where the term "transparency" pertains to a suspension of disbelief on the part of the user that enables the humanization of a cute machine. In other words, the non-human difference of an object must be negated in order for the subject to become immersed in an interactive moment with the object. Hence, the more the object is able to simulate or participate in this relationship, the fewer disturbances it will incur that threaten the interaction. Communicative transparency depends upon the creation of a seemingly realistic experience in which material differences are momentarily displaced, rather than how the machine *actually* works (Jäger and Kim 50). Such an experience is not only a product of a seamless, intuitive medium, but is also made possible through the appearance and even behavior of a cute machine. The necessity and transparency of the medium are qualities that exist in tension, but as I will elaborate later, this tension has a significant impact on the acceptability of a robot's appearance.

In view of these guidelines, it seems obvious that machines like social robots are also applications of cute design, but I would add that the latter is extensively oriented towards an ambiguous form of humanization as well. Besides the Sony AIBO, other prominent products in the field such as Softbank's Pepper and NEC's PaPeRo clearly show that mixing cuteness with robotics does not result in a photorealistic representation of the human or animal form, despite the fact that these machines are programmed to exhibit highly sociable and hence "human" attributes. According to robotics researcher Masahiro Mori, an object will stimulate greater acceptance if it exhibits human-like features and behaviors. However, there is a region in design space, known as the Uncanny Valley, where such attributes will appear strange and repulsive (33). Therefore, the cuteness of social robots is fundamentally a humanization premised on a machine-based difference (see also the chapter in this book by Julia Leyda).

Humanizing/De-Humanizing the Machine

To understand how cute design contributes to the humanization, or anthro-pomorphism of the social robot, it is important to understand both the challenges and conditions for machine-based sociality. Adopting a weak AI approach,[1] robotics researcher Brian Duffy claims that the design of the robot should sustain "a balance of illusion that leads the user to believe in the sophistication of the system in areas where the user will not encounter its failings, which the user is told not to expect" (178). I argue that this balance of illusion is synonymous with the tension between the medium's machinery and transparency, in that while the machinery is a pre-requisite for the object to function, it must be transparent enough for the user to overlook it and regard the object as something other than a machine.

Such a paradigm, Duffy contends, does not aim to replicate the biological human, but seeks to integrate robots into human society. Hence, there needs to be a distinction between likeness and acceptance, for if the features of cuteness are as Daniel Black comments, "concerned with a manipulation of the human tendency to anthropomorphize" ("Virtual" 39), then this manipulation, through caricature and hyperbole, effectively compromises likeness in favor of acceptance. In this context, humanization is not concerned with how "human" a robot may appear to be; rather it is focused on the extent to which humans may come to regard it as an affectionate, approachable other.

My proposition is derived from the work of Gary D. Sherman and Jonathan Haidt, who point out that cuteness, as a mechanism that releases sociality, can be extended beyond parental affection and caregiving (246). Following this distinction, I propose that cute design is a culturally conditioned measure of appropriateness for the robot's appeal. In cute design, both humanization and socialization are carefully manipulated qualities that negate machine-based complexity in favor of an intentionality that is understood in more "human" terms. To elaborate, this particular form of humanization is connected to the intentional stance theorized by Daniel Dennett, in which humans attempt to understand the behavior of other agents in terms of unseen mental properties. Similar to how cuteness simplifies positive sentiments, the intentional stance also reduces the complexities of a given object, resulting in an experience where one regards the object *as if* it possessed a mind (Sherman and Haidt 246).

Furthermore, the intentional stance differs from two other cognitive strategies, namely the physical and design stances. The former describes the process of deducing how a thing works from the laws of physics. Placing a pot of water over a fire, for example, is done with the awareness that the temperature of the pot and its contents will increase over time. These cause and effect relationships derived from the physical sciences can be applied to simple phenomena, but more complex systems may require expert training to be understood in the same fashion (Dennett 16). The design stance, in contrast, represents a relatively easier alternative in which one assumes that an object with a certain design will "behave as it is *designed* to behave under various circumstances" (Dennett 17; original emphasis). The use of the term "design," in this case, has less to do with an aesthetic principle than the usability of the object. Questions such as "would the phone ring when someone calls," or "would the recipient receive the message sent via email" are easily answered under Dennett's design stance.

The intentional stance, however, proves useful when information supporting either physical or design stances is difficult to obtain. Rather than figuring out an object's underlying physical laws or functional goals, one may interact with certain objects by regarding them as rational agents capable of meaningful, predictable behavior: If the subject assumes the object has motive X, it follows that the object will behave/act as if it had motive X. The intentional stance is important for humanization, because it involves the attribution of human qualities to an object by a human subject. As Dennett explains:

> The intentional stance provides a vantage point for discerning similarly useful patterns. These patterns are objective—they are there to be detected—but

from our point of view they are not out there entirely independent of us, since they are patterns composed partly of our own "subjective" reactions to what is out there; they are patterns made to order for our narcissistic concerns. (39)

The lack of an objective perspective for the intentional stance does not at all negate its usefulness. On the contrary, I argue that the intentional stance is a crucial strategy for engaging with and making sense of artificiality, including the machine-based difference of social robots. Simulating intentionality is a crucial strategy for social robots to be accepted as interactive partners.

How, then, is the intentional stance tied to the experience of cuteness? For Sherman and Haidt, the ability to humanize depends on the extent to which subjects are either able to socialize with or control an object (246). That is, the social distance between the subject and object is reduced if the relevant cues are observed. Cuteness stimulates sociality by reducing social distance and motivating a person to socially engage with a cute object. Conversely, cues evoking disgust are likely to increase social distance, which works to dehumanize the object. Through an in-depth study of dehumanization, Nick Haslam observes a qualitative difference between characteristics that are regarded as uniquely human (UH) and those that are intrinsic to human nature (HN). Objects lacking UH characteristics are regarded as animal-like, whereas those lacking HN characteristics would be mechanistic (256–258). These two categories thus correspond to two forms of dehumanization: animalistic dehumanization pertains to emotions or gestures that resonate with animal behavior, while mechanistic dehumanization refers to persons or things that behave like machines.

It is equally noteworthy, however, that certain dehumanizing traits identified in Haslam's study, such as child-likeness and passivity, can also be found in cute objects. As discussed earlier, cuteness does not replicate human biology, but rather *selectively* augments characteristics that encourage the human subject to be intimate with an object. By deliberately avoiding biological realism and conventional adult traits, cuteness marks a difference that is also an outcome of a stylized dehumanization. Daniel Harris categorizes this dehumanization as follows:

> The aesthetic of cute creates a class of outcasts and mutations, a ready-made race of lovable inferiors. . . . Something becomes cute not necessarily because of a quality it has but a quality it lacks, a certain neediness and inability to stand alone. (179)

Although this claim seems to draw out the contradictions within cuteness, Harris has arguably highlighted a key point that social psychology paradigms do not consider. That is, the difference and hence acceptability of the cute object presupposes a rather endearing deformity of the biological, adult human that allows

FIGURE 9.1 A pair of PaPeRo social robots are featured in the video commercial, "About the Relationship."

the subject to assert a sense of control over the object. This deformity, I emphasize, does not contradict the removal of negative or repulsive characteristics that cuteness presupposes, but under certain conditions, can be used to present caricatures that ameliorate the distance imposed by artificiality.

For example, social robots like the PaPeRo from NEC (see Figure 9.1) do not possess a humanoid body, but rather present a "deformity" of the human along with simplified gestures to stimulate a cuteness response. This deformity extends to their smooth, rounded, and minimalist exteriors. Cute design contributes to the humanization of social robots, but at the same time it presents simple and stylized bodies that are sanitized of human features and behaviors that may invoke rejection, disgust or terror.

There is a convergence between this particular stylization and Dennett's comment that the intentional stance caters to the subject's narcissistic concerns. I maintain that the cute design of social robots represents a strategic deformation of the human that nonetheless humanizes through the avoidance of absolute likeness. This aversion connects Mori's theory of the Uncanny Valley to our inquiry, insofar as social robotics aims to achieve a positive anthropomorphism and not, despite extensive humanization, a replication of human–human relations, since this would include characteristics that are at once familiar and unacceptable.

Cuteness in the Uncanny

According to Duffy's rationale, achieving human likeness is not only disadvantageous for humanizing a robot, but may make marketing it difficult, since users would inevitably compare such a machine to an actual human being. A machine that looks like a human being but fails in any respect to behave like one would find its machine-based flaws acting as an impediment (Duffy 178, 181). Why, then, is the omission of certain human characteristics, both visual and behavioral, useful for a robot's humanization, and consequently, acceptance? According to the theory of the Uncanny Valley, human verisimilitude is a primer for disgust, not affection. A reaction of disgust implies that a human subject would perceive such a machine as strange, unlikable and even repulsive. In other words, the machine in question would be explicitly dehumanized, which in view of Sherman and Haidt's thesis, would denote a stark reversal of the humanization inscribed by cuteness (247). I argue that this reversal is key to understanding how cute machines embody an appearance that is different from ours.

Although Mori's model describes the peculiar relationship between humanization and the machine's appearance, it does little to explain how realist verisimilitude can be uncanny in the first place. Mori can certainly be excused for not elaborating further on a model that is chiefly concerned with designing visually appealing robots, but I maintain that a deeper investigation of the uncanny is necessary for an inquiry on machine cuteness, as these issues touch on the sense of likeness embodied and performed by machines. A useful starting point for this inquiry is Sigmund Freud's influential essay "The Uncanny," where he defines the uncanny as "what evokes dread and horror . . . so it commonly merges with what excites fear in general" (123). Besides inciting fear, however, the uncanny is also concerned with things or experiences that are familiar, which leads to the question of how something familiar or known (and the assumption here is that having knowledge is to impose a form of control) can also be frightening, dreadful, and consequently perceived as outside of one's control?

In bridging the uncanny with the familiar, Freud uses the polysemy of the German *heimlich*, which refers to a state of familiarity, or a thing that is "not strange, familiar, tame, intimate, friendly." *Heimlich* is often applied to more positive examples, such as the attachment to an animal, or any other object that offers comfort and security (126). The second meaning of *heimlich*, however, accentuates the ambiguity of the word, by referring to a thing that is "concealed, kept hidden, so that others do not get to know of or about it" (Freud 129). The idea of *heimlich* as malicious secrecy thus opens up the possibility for its negative *unheimlich*, which pertains to a thing that is eerie, weird or arouses gruesome fear and links the notion of familiarity with a spectral quality, or haunting. To follow the German language, the uncanny would refer to a sense of familiarity, as well as a strange disturbance, in which one does not merely know or recognize the object, but is consequently unsettled by it. In Freud's theory, *heimlich* "becomes increasingly ambivalent, until it finally merges with its antonym, *unheimlich*" (134). The uncanny is presupposed by these two terms; cast in opposition, yet intrinsically present together.

Drawing on this ambivalence, Freud considers the various manifestations of the uncanny. Of particular interest is the creation of the double, which is a means to preserve the ego or an "energetic denial of the power of death" (142). Like the ancient Egyptians, who practiced mummification in order to preserve the sense of life in a corpse, the attempt to create copies of ourselves—which in contemporary terms would include animated, humanized machines—underscores our desire for immortality. This desire, however, does not disappear with these objects, but is instead displaced onto them. Both the mummified and machine body, on this basis, serve to express and placate this desire, just as what was previously regarded as an assurance of life, also serves as a reminder of one's mortality (Freud 142).

Freud's thesis carries the implication that the desire for immortality, while extending life, does not preclude death, but paradoxically requires death as a condition for life to persist indefinitely. In my view, there are a couple of insights that can be gleaned from Freud's theory of the uncanny. First, the uncanny, in its likeness, stimulates fear and anxiety in the subject. Cute design works to ameliorate such negative sentiments by enhancing the object's difference rather than its sameness. Furthermore, social robots tend to be better received if they are modelled after other mammals, or assume a humanoid form that differs significantly from a biological human. In this context, deformation is not repulsive, but augments the affection that the subject expresses towards a different, non-human object.

The Kirobo for example, is a humanoid robot that would, with little to no debate, be regarded as cute, for it lacks features that are known to cause fear and discomfort. Besides the fact that it is not programmed to be abrasive in its interaction, the Kirobo neither has the facial features, nor the flesh-and-blood body of an adult human being. Instead of a vulnerable, sensitive corporeality, one encounters an inorganic, simplified animation that is meant to be regarded as a lovable other. Both the body and performance of the Kirobo are thus illustrative of an anthropomorphism that seemingly avoids, but fails to permanently efface the uncanny, as I explain below.

This leads to the second implication, whereby cute design may be construed as an intervention into the problem of the uncanny by cancelling its negative effects via an idealization of a lovable other. At the same time, I argue this idealization is located within a tension, for what is regarded as "acceptable" is not the actuality of the human, but the systematically dehumanized difference of a machine. This is not to say that cuteness is opposed to the uncanny; rather it depends on the knowledge of the uncanny in order to appear as distinct from it, insofar as product designers must be aware of the characteristics and flaws that would make an artificial companion unacceptable to humans. As such, the amplification and reduction of human characteristics, in my view, does not nullify the effects of the uncanny, but rather retains an awareness of them via the appeal of the object. In other words, the deformation brought about by cute design is not just endearing, but also measured against what is not regarded as "cute." By artificially reducing the social distance between subject and object, cute design becomes a paradox concerned with an anthropomorphism traversing the boundaries (or differences between) humanization and dehumanization.

Framing the Lovable

The formulation of the uncanny covered so far only considers the extent to which cute design is compatible or not compatible with humanization, but this demarcation between what is humanized and dehumanized also influences the way the uncanny is sublimated by cuteness. If cute design, as discussed, is a stylistic device that interprets the object in a certain way, then it can also be construed as a *frame* that is instrumental in the distinction between the repulsion of the uncanny and the attraction of the lovable. The frame is important precisely because it intervenes in the field of representation with respect to the object's form. Although it is part of representation, especially when it is considered as part of the painting or work, the frame nonetheless gives form to and marks out the work: setting it apart and determining what is inside and outside of it. Frames are instruments of perspective, for in drawing the subject into the work, or even the world of the object, the frame relies on its own demarcation as the condition for what is within and external to it (Derrida 64).

Similarly, I maintain that cute design frames a perspective of the lovable that determines the difference between the lovable and unlovable. In contrast to Freud—who assumes the uncanny to be the condition for its subsequent circumvention—the uncanny in my view is dependent on the distinction that is framed with the instrument of cute design and in a broader sense, the response to humanization. Furthermore, while both Mori and Freud's treatment of the uncanny fail to consider stylistic or even sociocultural changes that may alter the boundary between the lovable and the unlovable, this distinction of the frame supports the shifts that would lead to alternative tropes and objects that could be categorized as "cute," such as the graphic violence of the animation series *Happy Tree Friends* or Japan's *gurokawa* (grotesque but cute) subculture.

Hence, in placing the object within a lovable frame, the experience of cuteness can be understood as an effect of an instrument, or even fetishistic device, that goes about framing or interpreting the material world in a certain way. In the words of Mario Perniola:

> Fetishism does not open any pantheon, but transits from entity to entity, investing with its relentless, reifying universality, with its greatest tangible abstraction, plants and animals, men and stones, colors, tastes, sensations, experiences, ideas, sentiments, passions. The choice made by the fetishist device is merely casual. (54)

At the same time, this fetishism affords a space for differentiation that can be extended to so-called "anti-cute" objects or designs such as those mentioned above.

While this notion may seem contradictory, I argue anti-cute objects are also a manipulation of the grotesque that renders it non-threatening and even attractive. In line with Perniola's comment, cute design can be serendipitously applied to any object, including one with features that may not appear to be cute. In other words, it is possible for the experience of cuteness to be differentiated or shifted to the point where objects previously in opposition to the initial fetish can be fetishized. By re-mixing the unlovable with the lovable, cute design does not limit, but broadens the overall "cute-ification" of things.

These shifts do not undermine the effects of cuteness, for as an aesthetic principle it continues to reference an affectionate and acceptable other. However, the implications of the ability of cuteness to incorporate the anti-cute are twofold: first, cute design is concerned with the production of conditions of acceptability, and second it functions as a lens for the encounter with otherness that is experienced in every subject-object relationship. Therefore, even though there is a persistent tendency for differentiation within cute design, I also maintain that the cute design of social robots in particular reproduces and stabilizes features and conditions that do not just enhance the predictability of form, but—in system-atizing a version of the lovable—undermines the subjective engagement with the uncanny responsible for the shifts in cuteness.

Industrial Attachments

In contrast with other applications of cute design, social robots are endowed with a physical form that affords affections more tangible than what can be experienced with other media. Robot pets such as Fujitsu's teddy bear (see Figure 9.2) or even the baby fur seal PARO may be equipped with artificial fur and touch sensors that allow them to respond when touched or stroked, or come installed with facial and voice recognition software to identify human subjects. In Isaac Asimov's short story *A Boy's Best Friend*, a young boy named Jimmy becomes extremely attached to his robotic pet Robutt and refuses to part with it when his father suggests getting him a real Scottish terrier. Despite the fact that Robutt is merely programmed to love, Jimmy has already come to regard it as being alive. For Jimmy, Robutt is no different from a flesh and blood dog, because it has already come to fulfill the role of a pet (Asimov 15–18).

As simulations of affection, objects like the robotic pet in Asimov's tale do not embody novel social principles, but apply these preexisting principles to new situations. To return to the example of the Sony AIBO, the object becomes further socialized with the emergence of hospitals and service centers to the point that the pleasures and processes of owning a pet overlap with those pertaining to a robotic entity. If the robots of the past were artificial entities of mechanical labor, today's interactive machines are also bridging the gap between robotics and human affection, in a market where experiences, both physical and emotional, are increasingly being translated into commodities.

FIGURE 9.2 The Fujitsu teddy bear is able to collect information on the emotional state of its user via an array of visual and tactile sensors fixed to its body.

These configurations of affection are, in my view, part of a pervasive industrialization that continues to rationalize and predetermine the experience of subjectivity, for instead of engaging with the uncanny by remixing cuteness with the grotesque, the appeal and interactivity of many social robots today merely *repeats* a version of cuteness that precludes the differentiation of what can or cannot be loved. No doubt, these machines incorporate software applications to capture data for further development and usability, but these improvements point to a rationalization of cuteness as a component of a program that is administered for further subject–object engagement. According to Bernard Stiegler, this process of capturing and subsequently controlling affection within a system would be "an industrialization of the social" that looked to the immaterial as exploitable matter (103). Cute machines, therefore, represent an industrialization of our attachments, in which what are exploited are not material objects per se, but our affections for a lovable other.

On the one hand, cute design, through an engagement with the uncanny, is open to its own "de-signing" and alternative expressions; but on the other hand, its features are used in the reproduction of images and objects that can be pervasively standardized. The transformation of experiences into commodities via the machinery of the culture industry is fundamentally a matter of sociality and technology. Though I have illustrated how experiences of cuteness can vary, it is equally crucial to consider how the aesthetic disengages with the uncanny by being subjected to the machinery of mass culture, and how this disengagement actually minimizes the risk of consumers being overwhelmed or repulsed by designs on the uncanny end of the spectrum.

To understand the problems that occur when aesthetic forms are commodified, I turn to the work of Theodor Adorno, who emphasizes that art's mechanization is part of the adaptability of mass culture. For Adorno, mass culture is a de-politicizing structure that commercializes and fosters passive consumption. In the *Schema of Mass Culture*, he writes:

> All mass culture is fundamentally adaptation. However this adaptive character, the monopolistic filter which protects it from any external rays of influence which have not already been safely accommodated within its reified schema, represents an adjustment to the consumers as well. The pre-digested quality of the product prevails, justifies itself and establishes itself all the more firmly insofar as it constantly refers to those who cannot digest anything not already pre-digested. (67)

In this sense, adaptation is both a strategy that incorporates external ideas according to consumerist logic as well as a form of conditioning, because its monopoly and ubiquity tend to occlude anything that falls outside its purview. In Adorno's view, consumption can be manipulated because the "monopolistic filter" of mass culture has become the dominant means by which art (and for that matter, all other aesthetic expression) becomes comprehensible to consumers.

Applying this argument to cute design, we can see how the latter is justified or made more recognizable through cultural products of mass culture such as social robots, even though these lovable objects do not absolutely define what or who can be considered "cute." The pervasiveness of certain forms thus shows that the dominant idea of cuteness does not correspond to any truth-claim of the object, but is rather due to the object's technically manipulated ubiquity and accessibility. Relative to consumer agency, such an outlook seems pessimistic: with the effects of mass production, consumers are presented with a systematic reduction of options. Furthermore, this negation of subjectivity further entrenches the dependency that the cute object solicits from its human subject. This social positioning—in which the subject cares for an approachable, dependent other—involves a mastery over the object and should be understood as a restriction on the lovable that is often reproduced in mass culture. Taken together, both the culture industry and this particular facet of cuteness perpetuate a view of the lovable that often goes unquestioned.

Returning to some of the common examples of social robots that have been commercialized, I argue that a soft, simplified, diminutive, rounded exterior and a consistently infantilized personality appear in tandem with the disengagement from the uncanny. While these aesthetic sensibilities are culturally produced, this particular design scheme also draws broader attention to the augmentations and concealments of cute machines. Most evidently, all excretory organs and orifices of the biological body are closed in this artificial counterpart, for these are associ-ated with substances that would make one repulsed (e.g. bodily fluids, waste).

Machine-wise, the mechanical intricacies are also sealed in by the simplicity of the robot body, as aptly described by Jean Baudrillard: "the form is externalized, enclosing the object in a sort of carapace. Fluid, transitive, it unifies appearances by transcending the alarming discontinuity of various mechanisms involved and replacing it with a coherent whole" (53–54).

If the uncanny is that which provokes revulsion, then it is the cuteness of the social robot that defuses it through this systematization of design.[2] And in so doing, the machine transits from embodying a utilitarian ideal (i.e. an instrument or object of manual labor) to a domesticated object of emotional investment. This trajectory is not confined to the external form of the social robot. It also appears in other, non-visual aspects, such as an infantile voice and gestures. With the social robot, one is not presented with the complex (and at times uncomfortable) difference of another human subject, but rather a programmed, subservient, approachable machine that reproduces a largely static condition in order to elicit human affection.

To What Affect?

In her study of the attachments formed towards social robots, social scientist Sherry Turkle writes:

> such relational artefacts do not wait for children to "animate" them in the spirit of the Raggedy Ann doll or a teddy bear. They present themselves as already animated and ready for relationships. They promise reciprocity because, unlike traditional dolls, they are not passive. They make demands. They present as having their own needs and inner lives. They teach us the rituals of love that will make them thrive. For decades computers have asked us to think with them; these days, computers and robots, deemed sociable, affective and relational, ask us to feel for and with them. (39)

Turkle's description of these artefacts as "already animated" points to a major effect of the relationship between machines and cuteness; for although the latter contributes to the machine's appeal, the apparatus of the machine enables a greater occupation of the subject's field of experience. Unlike other applications of cute design that are primarily visual, social robots configure cuteness as a performance, in which the object also behaves and responds in a lovable fashion, thereby minimizing the role of human imagination or suspension of disbelief. Cuteness in this context becomes less a product of human agency than a controllable variable of machine affection, where the perception of a personality tends not to be construed as part of a dynamic narrative, but is already fabricated beforehand.

Social robots display a version of the lovable that minimizes the interferences of inter-subjectivity, in that the affection one develops for the machine is not conceived as an outcome of an *exchange* between subjects. The machine is already built to exhibit love and intimacy in a certain way. In simulating clichés of interactions, social robots automatically process our desires with little actual regard for the other. The subject does not need to expend effort to understand or empathize, for the object already re-enacts and exaggerates the pleasurable aspects of the interaction. However, in relating to and bonding with a social robot, subjects are effectively drawn to and enmeshed in a programmable process that serves as prosthesis for an intimate relationship. This is not to say that subjects cede agency to the machine; rather this systematized iteration of cuteness is derived in part from a social deficit, even as it enables us to circumvent and differ from it. As a proxy for a companion, the artificiality of the social robot occupies a space of compromised agency, insofar as humans have yet to completely come to terms with, or remained unfulfilled by, both their isolation and inter-subjective differences.

On the other hand, the acceptance of and consequent relationship with the social robot also paradoxically extends our agency over the deficit. Such an ideal, to quote Mark Seltzer, "projects a violent dismemberment of the natural body and an *emptying of human agency*"; as well as "a transcendence of the natural body and *the extension of human agency through the forms of technology that supplement it*" (170–71; original emphasis). On this basis, it can be argued that the systematized cuteness of the social robot is a form of technology for two crucial reasons. First, cute design is a means to simulate the lovable, where the lovable is in reference to a state of affection experienced between subjects. Second, the aesthetic manages human affection. What is initially recognized to be lovable can be gathered, stored and re-applied for future use, *sans* further human intervention or even confrontation with qualities that humans deem to be uncanny or undesirable.

Social robotics, to borrow the language of Martin Heidegger, would be a "challenging that sets upon man to order the real as standing-reserve" (19), for this pre-selection of appearances and behaviors exploits and recycles the resources of human psychology to direct and predict relational outcomes. For Heidegger, technology is a mode of revealing, insofar as the "bringing-forth" of the object concerns both its physical and epistemological synthesis. Although pre-modern technology relied on the unpredictability or dynamism of natural forces, modern technology is increasingly directed towards the ordering of nature as a resource (Heidegger 13–14). This ordering leads to a pervasive form of instrumental efficiency, where "nature reports itself in some way or other that is identifiable through calculation and that it remains orderable as a system of information" (Heidegger 23). Instead of a bringing-forth that is largely derived from the human's engagement with nature (including the unpredictability or disorganization of relating to another human being), modern technology transforms this relationship into subjugation, by ordering nature as a standing reserve.

Hence, the imperative to circumvent the unpredictability of human relationships places the cuteness of social robots in tension with the subjective experience of cuteness. This is because cuteness, as a relational aesthetic, is always in part construed in reference to the reception of the other that involves an agentic negotiation with the negative characteristics (e.g. uncanny, disgusting, and repulsive) of the object in the encounter. And in turn, this negotiation may translate into a re-invention of the aesthetic, whereby design innovations may cast a familiar affection in a different light. Yet, the stasis of familiarity also becomes a systematization that selects and manufactures performances. This not only concretizes certain versions of cuteness, but becomes a condition for what and how we ought to love. The experience of cuteness, in this sense, is not an outcome of our subjective relation to the other; rather the other is a fabricated familiar that reinforces pre-existing interests and desires, sans the apprehensions and possibilities of inter-subjectivity. The systematized cuteness of the social robot may extend the effects of the aesthetic outside the visual, but its simulation of our sociality should also be understood as a problematic lack of inter-subjective exchange in the encounter.

Conclusion: A Bridge over Troubled Affections

As this inquiry has sought to demonstrate, cute design is an aesthetic premised on the subject's relation with the other and is thus a means to resolve and come to terms with the object's difference. In other words, cuteness is an experience that intervenes in our affections, insofar as it connects us to and enables us to accept, if not love, the object. Any critique of the charm of the object, therefore, should recognize that its attraction emerges as a symptom of our impulse to connect and establish an authentic relationship with the other. This is not to say that the artificiality of social robots makes human–robot relationships less authentic than those shared between humans, for the suspension of disbelief can lead to genuine affection on the part of the subject. Moreover, these machines present a categorical difference that counters the anthropocentric rigidity of "love" as an exclusively human experience, which in turn presents alternative possibilities of who or what can be loved. On this note, the more pertinent concern is not to develop more realistic or humanized objects, but rather to innovate an approach to cuteness that continues to engage with the messy and undesirable facets of our subjectivity.

With regard to the potential of social robots to provide an alternative to human intimacy, my position remains one of cautious skepticism, for although their cute performances are becoming more seamless and intuitive, their implicit demand for affection is underscored by a commercialized pre-determination of what can or cannot be loved. If cuteness is a means to resolve the difference of the other, then it is arguably worthwhile to question these imagined certainties of robotic embodiment by returning to the struggles and contentions of our own bodies and persons, and not render our partial affections as another factor in a computable system.

In sum, the instrumental, prosthetic significance of cuteness is always one of loss and transcendence. The social robot vividly illustrates this connection between subject and object, while bridging the space of uncertainty between one and the other. This cute machine may, for a time, sustain the illusion that our affections can be absolutely resolved and systematically reined in, but it nevertheless points to and is preceded by the encounter with difference. To affect and be affected mark pronounced changes that occur within difference, whether they be derived from our own, or the body of another object. As an expression after the fact, cuteness is therefore not simply a mode of objectification or a condition for our affections; but the means for us to challenge and change the precarious ideals we have established in regard to ourselves and our relationships.

Notes

1   In contrast to the strong AI approach, this chapter will not explain how human emotions can be accurately programmed into machines, because not all emotions are *acceptable* in a machine's socialization. A robot that expresses or causes anger, for example, would be deemed less approachable than one without any emotional disposition. Following Duffy's investigations, this chapter maintains the position that cute design can function as a signature of acceptability because it is categorically comprised of features/behaviors that are attractive "metaphors conventionally used to rationalize emotional expression" (186).

2   The generic changes in the appearance of machine bodies, from mechanical, differentiated complexity to a more organic, unified form also correspond to the way in which information is organised and presented. In many pre-twentieth-century depictions of robots and automata, for example, the artificial body, composed of multiple functioning parts, was perceived as ordered, predictable and de-individuated. However, most contemporary gadgets are organized along principles of unity and coherence (Black, *Embodiment* 59; Kakoudaki 18). Robots aside, objects like Apple mobile phones, tablets, and television screens currently possess a sleek, minimalist exterior that conceals their intricacy and are evaluated for the immediacy of their user-experience, rather than the functions of their internal mechanisms. According to N. Katherine Hayles, such changes share "deep connections with changes in textual bodies as they are encoded with information media and both stand in complex relation to changes in the construction of human bodies as they interface with information technologies" (73). If an anatomical mode of vision previously treated the body as a Gestalt of comprehensible parts, current understandings of the human body as an expression of genetic information homogenizes data into feedback loops.

Works Cited

Adorno, Theodor. *The Culture Industry: Selected Essays on Mass Culture.* London: Routledge, 2001.
Asimov, Isaac. *The Complete Robot.* London: Voyager, 1995.
Baudrillard, Jean. *The System of Objects.* London: Verso, 1996.
Black, Daniel. "The Virtual Ideal: Virtual Idols, Cute Technology and Unclean Biology." *Continuum: Journal of Media and Cultural Studies* 22.1 (2008): 37–50.
——. *Embodiment and Mechanization: Reciprocal Understandings of Body and Machine from the Renaissance to the Present.* Surrey: Ashgate, 2014.
Brown, Andrew. "To Mourn a Robotic Dog is to be Truly Human." *Guardian.* Guardian Media Group, 12 Mar. 2015. Online. 20 May 2016.
Dennett, Daniel C. *The Intentional Stance.* Cambridge, MA: MIT Press, 1987.

Derrida, Jacques. *The Truth in Painting.* Trans. Geoff Bennington and Ian McLeod. Chicago, IL: University of Chicago Press, 1987.

Duffy, Brian R. "Anthropomorphism and the Social Robot." *Robotics and Autonomous Systems* 42 (2003): 177–90.

Freud, Sigmund. *The Uncanny.* Trans. David McLintock. London: Penguin, 2003.

Genosko, Gary. "Natures and Cultures of Cuteness." *Invisible Culture: An Electronic Journal for Visual Culture* 9 (2005): n. pag. Online. 8 Aug. 2016.

Gould, Stephen Jay. "A Biological Homage to Mickey Mouse." *Ecotone* 4.1 (2008): 333–40.

Harris, Daniel. "Cuteness." *Salmagundi* (1992): 177–86.

Haslam, Nick. "Dehumanization: An Integrative Review." *Personality and Social Psychology Review* 10.3 (2006): 252–64.

Hayles, N. Katherine. "Virtual Bodies and Flickering Signifiers." *October* 66 (1993): 69–91.

Heidegger, Martin. *The Question Concerning Technology and Other Essays.* Trans. William Lovitt. New York: Harper, 1977.

Jäger, Ludwig, and Jin Hyun Kim. "Transparency and Opacity: Interface Technology of Mediation in New Media Art." *Paradoxes of Interactivity: Perspectives for Media Theory, Human-Computer Interaction, and Artistic Investigations.* Eds. Uwe Seifert, Jin Hyun Kim, and Anthony Moore. Bielefeld: Transcript, 2008. 44–61.

Kakoudaki, Despina. *Anatomy of a Robot: Literature, Cinema, and the Work of Artificial People.* New Brunswick, NJ: Rutgers University Press, 2014.

Kinsella, Sharon. "Cuties in Japan." *Women, Media, and Consumption in Japan.* Ed. Lise Skov and Brian Moeran. Honolulu, HI: University of Hawaii Press, 1995. 220–54.

McVeigh, Brian J. "How Hello Kitty Commodifies the Cute, Cool and Camp: 'Consum-utopia' Versus 'Control' in Japan." *Journal of Material Culture* 5.2 (2000): 225–45.

Mochizuki, Takashi, and Eric Pfanner. "In Japan, Dog Owners Feel Abandoned as Sony Stops Supporting 'Aibo.'" *Wall Street Journal.* Dow Jones, 11 Feb. 2015. Online. 8 Aug. 2016.

Mori, Masahiro. "The Uncanny Valley." *Energy* 7.4 (1970): 33–35.

Morreall, John. "Cuteness." *British Journal of Aesthetics* 31.1 (1991): 39–47.

Perniola, Mario. *The Sex Appeal of the Inorganic.* Trans. Massimo Verdicchio. London: Continuum, 2004.

Seltzer, Mark. "Writing Technologies." *New German Critique* 57 (1992): 170–81.

Sherman, Gary D., and Jonathan Haidt. "Cuteness and Disgust: The Humanizing and Dehumanizing Effects of Emotion." *Emotion Review* 3.3 (2011): 245–51.

Stiegler, Bernard. *Technics and Time 1: The Fault of Epimetheus.* Trans. Richard Beardsworth and George Collins. Stanford, CA: Stanford University Press, 1998.

Turkle, Sherry. *Alone Together: Why We Expect More from Technology and Less from Each Other.* New York: Basic, 2011.

10

SOFT AND HARD

Accessible Masculinity, Celebrity, and Post-Millennial Cuteness

Michael DeAngelis

In a 2014 installment of the YouTube series "Get Mighty with Minsky," disabled Marine veteran Alex Minsky responds to questions from fans inspired by his drive and determination despite the amputation of one leg from the knee down after a battle injury. The fans are also inspired by the buff body that his rigorous exercise routine has produced, and that Minsky has put on display in his successful post-military career as a male model. Reading a message from a fan who asks, "How do you, as a straight guy, feel about the attention you get from the gay community?" Minsky replies, looking into the camera to engage his questioner directly, "I don't mind it at all. I appreciate it, thank you very much. . . . Carry on!" (Minsky). As this chapter will demonstrate, the affirmation and acceptance of sexual difference displayed by this heterosexual veteran who has so effectively transcended the constraints of a physical disability is a phenomenon specific to an era in which the construction of masculinity seems inflected by an acute awareness of the fact that men look at other men. Alex Minsky's rise to celebrity status evidences an intricate connection between vulnerability and strength in recent manifestations of gay male desire, through the display of a firm and able body that registers as "sexy" not only despite the visible mark of vulnerability at the site of his amputation, but also *because* of it.

Along with his assertion that perceptions of vulnerability trigger a nurturing parental instinct of protection, ethologist Konrad Lorenz's association of cuteness with vulnerability in relation to the infantile informs the reception strategies that Minsky elicits through his willingness to submit to the admiration of gay male audiences. The wound on the body of this former Marine functions as a sign of an inflicted trauma, the force of which his admirers' care and safeguarding could be directed to ameliorate. Minsky's embrace of his homosexual male admirers also bears evidence of a related, yet quite different aspect of the cuteness phenomenon elucidated in recent work in this field that correlates cuteness more directly with a desire for increased social connection than with protection from harm. The veteran's celebratory declaration of receptivity to gay male fans serves as much as a sexual lure as a vow to initiate and sustain accessibility, an invitation to participate in a reciprocally pleasurable social interaction. The act of addressing his YouTube-mediated gay fan base head on ultimately serves as a reaching out, a promise to bridge the distance between subject and object, one initiated also as a gesture of welcome and a confirmation of appreciation. As such, while the dynamic effected here in "Get Mighty with Minsky" avows its host's physical vulnerability at the site (and sight) of an amputation, it simultaneously registers an affiliation and connection that deploys cuteness to draw his fan base closer. The subject/object dynamic in this video also corresponds with the findings of Gary D. Sherman and Jonathan Haidt, who suggest that instead of serving primarily as that which releases a "parental instinct," "the cuteness response is better understood as a mechanism that 'releases' sociality (e.g. play and other affiliative interactions), which sometimes (indirectly) leads to increased care" (246). For his gay fan base (and beyond), Minsky's cuteness thus comprises a combination of traditional signifiers of male attractiveness (an athletic physique, "chiseled" features, and a handsome face), evidence of physical/emotional vulnerability, and a call to sociality evident in his reciprocal acceptance of others.

This chapter asserts that post-millennial constructions of male-to-male "cuteness" interweave perceptions of vulnerability with such calls for social connection and engagement. Cuteness also functions according to a set of negotiations of proximity and distance that transpire between subjects and objects—negotiations that manifest themselves in what Sherman and Haidt describe as "affiliative behaviors, such as attempts to touch, hold, pet, play with, talk to, or otherwise engage the cute entity" (249). Negotiations of proximity and distance, of cuteness, and of sexiness align with historically and culturally specific perceptions regarding body types regularly marked by designations of "softness" and "hardness." In the contemporary discourse of masculinity, the "cute" body might certainly be the vulnerable or accessible body, one that promises, as Anthony P. McIntyre suggests, tangible, palpable interpersonal connection to ameliorate the demands of a neoliberal capitalism that situates human subjects as socially disconnected and isolated.[1] In certain contexts, such accessibility is paired with sexual distance: by labeling another male body as "cute," a gay man might also be designating it as too soft to be congruous with a popular version of gay desire that still prefers its objectified bodies to be firm. In addition to its capacity to generate or perpetuate desire, then, cuteness might appear to disrupt its cathexis, and in this way, as Lori Merish argues, function as "a form of erotic regulation" (188–89).

Aside from such instances of polarization, however, in an era that has come to recognize the advantages of simultaneously targeting straight and gay markets, and that has awakened to the facility with which the male body may now be so openly constructed and marketed as an object of desire, media and popular culture industries maintain a significant investment in exploiting ambiguities and continuities between "cute" and "sexy," and between "soft" and "hard" bodies. Situating the concept of cuteness in a context that sees the operations of identification and desire as interconnected, this chapter demonstrates that inter-actions between the realms of the "cute" and the "sexy," along with regulations of proximity and distance between men engaging in a mutual scopic enterprise, are culturally functional and strategic in a post-millennial environment that has witnessed a dramatic rise in the acceptance of same-sex relationships, along with a proliferation of new popular cultural representations of inter-male closeness, intimacy, and commitment. The chapter proceeds to connect cuteness and sexiness to the contours of softness and hardness in both the male body itself and the discourse that culturally defines this body, analyzing recent manifestations of male cuteness and sexiness in mainstream health and fitness magazines and websites, such gay-directed sites as *homorazzi* and *manjock*, as well as Pinterest pages. The analysis reveals that the careful maintenance of a soft-to-hard body transformation becomes crucial to a form of male desirability that *arises* out of cuteness and that requires perceptible contours and marks of body definition.

The chapter culminates with an analysis of the star discourses surrounding Chris Pratt and Ryan Reynolds, two contemporary actors whose popularity is intimately tied to a radical soft-to-hard body transformation. The analysis demonstrates how negotiations of vulnerability and social connection, regulations of proximity and distance, constructions of soft and hard bodies, and designations of cuteness and sexiness strategically coalesce in cinematic celebrity discourse through viewers' perceptions of the star persona's depth (or relative lack thereof)—a register that correlates with Sherman and Haidt's assertion about the factor of "humanization" that can be ascribed to the cute object: "people will tend to attribute rich mental lives to those entities—objects, pets, or people—with which they are motivated to interact socially" (246).

Contours of Cuteness: The Look, the Body

When originating from male audiences and directed towards male celebrity figures, the dynamics of cuteness are rooted at the intersection of two "looks": one that marks identification and likeness, the other that objectifies and signals desire. The ambiguities between looks of identification and desire are integral to the operations of a form of cuteness that relies on the solicitation of social connection, invitation, and approach, inviting the viewer to draw closer to the object rather than maintain a distance. In their construction of the star persona, studios, press agents, and actors have either inadvertently or deliberately deployed the ambiguity between these looks of identification and desire to broaden the appeal of celebrity figures at least since the middle of the twentieth century, contributing to what has been described as a phenomenon of crossover, in which a star's popularity with (presumably) straight male audiences also accommodates a gay male viewership.[2] By correlating the process of withholding and disclosing information about the "truth" and meaning of a star persona with the operations of the melodramatic mode, scholars such as Christine Gledhill and Mary Desjardins have demonstrated how intimacy in star-audience relationships develops both at specific historical moments and diachronically, over the entire career of a celebrity figure. While some scholars refute the possibility of any overlap occurring between psychoanalytic categories that were originally theorized as discrete psychic operations,[3] I have argued elsewhere that the consumerist nature of Hollywood cinema, and of promotional and publicity-oriented star texts, *requires* an exploitation of the marketing potential inherent in this "confusion" of identification and desire, of seeking both to "be" and to "have" the same object (*Gay Fandom* 8–10).

Both the ambiguities rendering celebrity figures accessible to gay and straight male appropriation, and the extent to which male celebrities can be said to participate in the process of rendering their own personas accessible to the identification and/or desire of a straight/gay male fan base, vary according to the discursive liberties and restrictions of specific historical and cultural conditions. Ushered in by the paradoxical formulations of post-millennial bromance narratives where self-defined straight males demonstrate their receptivity to inter-male intimacy and bonding on the requisite condition that such intimacy not be avowed, acknowledged, or construed as homosexual (by themselves, by each other, or by the public) (DeAngelis, *Reading* 1–26), and bolstered by gay culture's dramatically increasing presence in, and acceptance by, the heterosexual mainstream, the twenty-first century evidences not only a more cogent recognition of the power of the gay marketplace, but also an open embrace of its existence. The volume of gay-themed ads proliferating in the media marketplace during this time attests to the extent of this shift (see Italie; Nichols). Equally remarkable is the sheer number of straight male actors who have been featured in the cover stories of gay monthly publications over the past decade, including hyper-gay-friendly James Franco in *The Advocate* (Lewis), and Channing Tatum, Chris Pine, Daniel Radcliffe, Chris Hemsworth, Joseph Gordon-Levitt, and Benedict Cumberbatch in *Out* magazine. The active courtship of the gay male audience has become sufficiently widespread to warrant the appearance of the recently coined term "stromosexual" to designate the strategy of "straight actors striving to read gayish to optimize their appeal—and maximize the number of butts—gym-molded or otherwise, in movie theater seats" (Ginsburg). Blogger Mark Simpson offers a cogent commentary on the effects of increasing image-consciousness among straight male celebrities:

> [There are] money and career points in having a "gay following," to be sure, but I think the need for gay male approval goes deeper and is shared by a lot of young straight men today. It's that desire to be desired thing

again. Straight men ache to be sex objects—and what better way to be objectified than by other men? Straight men know how demanding men's eyes can be. How penetrating their "gaze" is.

From a marketing standpoint, to evoke a perception of unattainability is to deny the admirer an opportunity for social connection that is essential to the dynamic of cuteness. Post-millennial male objectification is framed not only in terms of these pleasures of seeing and being seen, but also as a sign of "health" that requires labor and consistent maintenance in order to be sustained, with the competition to feel and look better now configured as a challenge that is not only interpersonal but also self-directed. Certainly, the longstanding tendency for popular men's health publications to frame such labor in heteronormative terms has persisted, and according to such terms, *any* healthy man seeking to earn the respect or love of a woman must take up this challenge. Such logic is evident, for instance, in this *Men's Fitness* postulation of Ryan Reynolds's motives for bulking up his body in preparation for his role in the 2005 film *Blade: Trinity*:

[Reynolds] knew he needed to do something to grab the audience's attention—after all, he was starring alongside Jessica Biel. . . . The result? Countless magazine covers, the ladering [sic] role in the upcoming Green Lantern flick and a marriage to Scarlett Johansson. If that's not motivation to get into the gym, we don't know what is. (Murphy)

Yet in the current era, the primary goal of the rigorous process of radical male body transformation has also become a more self-reflective process—one that is framed discursively as self-directed labor yielding significant personal pay-offs. It is also a process that relies heavily upon soliciting an inclusive and embracing call for social connection. "Men increasingly want to present themselves as available for any fantasy, and responsive to both sexes," Mark Simpson argues, "even and especially when they're heterosexual." Commenting on the reshaping of his client Daniel Craig's body for the James Bond films, trainer Simon Waterson explains that

[i]t wasn't about creating a certain look; it was about creating a certain performance, being functional, and being able to look like one can do shit. The aesthetics was just a byproduct. . . . Our objective is functional fitness, and not merely the appearance of fitness; actual capacity strengthens confidence, a façade is merely physical. (Olesker)

This emphasis upon authentic, self-generative, confidence-inducing "functionality" becomes integral to understanding the shape, size, and contours of a type of male body that can successfully solicit the male viewer's gaze through "approach motivation." Unlike the heavily inflated mega-muscular male celebrity physiques that, according to Susan Jeffords, iconified a tough and invulnerable masculinity closely aligned with president Ronald Reagan's militaristic and interventionist foreign policy (1981–89), the idealized body of the 2010s is defined by a hardness that stems from leanness. The term that has come to be associated with the phenomenon is "spornosexuality," a fusing of "sport" and "porn" that also directly correlates the objectification of the exposed male body with the process of active and rigorous manual labor. The result, Simpson describes, is like what might happen when "sport got into bed with porn while Mr. Armani took pictures" (Engel). Indeed, if the quintessential pumped-up screen hero of the Reagan era was Sylvester Stallone's Rambo, *Men's Journal* now defines the spornosexual ideal as closer to Brad Pitt in the turn-of-the millennium film *Fight Club* (1999):

> Even the type of muscle has changed. "In the Eighties, it was the bigger, the better," says director Tim Burton. "Think of that shot from *Rambo* of Sly holding the machine gun and the veins of his forearms bulging." Actors rarely bulk up anymore; they're all trying to be Tyler Durden. (Hill)

Muscular excess no longer serves as a cultural ideal. "That's the body blokes ask for," explains personal trainer Tim Walker. "He looks great but he's not massive. He's just got really good abs, good arms, and an alright chest. And that's what people want: to be lean, have a six pack" (Olesker). Simpson, who also coined the term "metrosexual" in the mid-1990s to describe (primarily) heterosexual men whose concern for their personal appearance was demonstrated by sophisticated clothing selection and grooming habits, suggests that

> the spornosexual is a more extreme breed of man than his metro forbear. He is . . . leaner, buffer, more jacked and obsessed not just with "looking good" in the abstract, but with the actual physical proportions of his frame: the striation of his abs, the vascularity of his biceps, the definition of his calves. (Olesker)

Such descriptions highlight "definition" as a feature that is just as central to spornosexuality as "buffness." As celebrity personal trainer Jason Wimberly articulates, in the contemporary era, "[s]hredded trumps pumped" (Ginsberg). Distinctive body definition was also a prominent characteristic of the 1980s Rambo prototype, but the recent preference for a leaner form of hardness resituates "definition" as an accessibility that addresses not only the interactive dynamics of identification and desire, but also the realities of contemporary global consumer economics. The defined contours of the firm, lean post-millennial male celebrity body are contours that render "definition" more readily attainable in a culture that places significant demands upon what constitutes "productive" use of one's already limited "free time." Emblematized by the body that always solicits

its viewer to come closer, this aspect of attainability serves to negate any resigned conviction that *my body could never be as hard or fit as your body*—placing the idealized male form within reach as an object that any sufficiently motivated gay or straight man might strive to be or to have. As such, accessibility in this context becomes less primarily a matter of adding new layers of dense muscular tissue than of subtracting unwanted, softer tissues to reveal the strong, sinewy frame that lies underneath, creating form out of formlessness in a process comparable to sculpting.

Such subtraction is also integral to a contemporary economic relation that assesses the functionality of labor according to efficacy of production. The transformation of the soft—or not sufficiently defined—frame into the lean, firm celebrity body responds to the consumer demand that identification and desire be integrated in a way that emphasizes an accessibility of this body amenable to Sherman and Haidt's correlation of the "sociality motivation" with the cuteness emotion. The consumer's decision to strive and struggle in physical workouts is underwritten by a tacit agreement that the desired results—represented by "evidence" that the celebrity body is expected to provide—be attainable *now*— or at least soon, and not over the course of years of work. Differentiating this labor process from bodybuilding, *Esquire* suggests that "with physique training, instead of spending 10 years trying to build mass, you just get really lean" (Olesker). Accordingly, efficiency in ideal body production is central to the training strategies that now dominate the celebrity workout field. As *Men's Journal* explains,

> To get that hungry look, trainers stress calorie-conscious diets and exercises that pump up fat-burning metabolism. No actor can gain ten pounds of muscle in a six-week period, but he can lean down to reveal the muscle underneath. Trainers talk about the "lean out"—the final, pre-shoot crash period when actors drop their BMI (body-mass index) to its bare minimum and unveil muscle definition. (Hill)

In addition to responding to calls for audience accessibility by maintaining physical fitness as an attainable goal, such fast-tracked hard bodies are much more amenable to the demands of film production schedules, and the economic advantages of such formulas for timely, efficacious tissue subtraction extend the celebrity male's accessibility as a figure of identification and desire to other men from a local to a global level. As *Men's Journal* clarifies, "Hot bodies and explosions don't need subtitles" (Hill).

Cute and Sexy

Sianne Ngai's assertion that "cute objects have no edge to speak of" (814), and that the cute object "suggest[s] greater malleability and thus a greater capacity for being handled" (815–16), resonate in the context of gay men's assessments of cuteness and sexiness—assessments that are intimately linked to the dynamics and politics of hard and soft bodies. A 2011 "All Things Gay" forum on the gay male fitness website *Realjock* evidences a variety of definitions and distinctions between "cute" and "hot," with participants readily admitting that they often use the term "cute" in different contexts to convey different meanings ("Being Called"). Critically, however, important patterns do emerge here, and they connect back with the matters of body definition so central to the discourse of the "straighter," more mainstream men's health journals. One contributor explains that "I think [cute] means different things to different people. Whereas words like hot and sexy really refer to physical features. Cute is like the whole package to me but not exactly hot enough to want to overlook the whole package." Coupled with other contributors' comments that "I'd like my guy to have a hot bod and a cute face and personality" and "Some people have 'cute' faces, yet may not have 'hot' bodies," the forum ultimately suggests a complex relationship between a "cuteness" that becomes associated with the face as a register of personality and emotion, and the parameters of a "sexiness" that more directly reference aspects of muscle-based form, shaped and defined by physical exertion. This is, however, not to suggest that the face *itself* is rendered diffuse—or, for that matter, the eyes, which so frequently register as the site of deepest emotional complexity. Replete with bones and structures that lend it form, the face can also resonate as "chiseled" and thus "defined" in terms of distinctive features, but it is rarely described in terms of developed or cultivated musculature in the same way that chests, legs, or torsos so often are.

Rather than being irreconcilable, the phenomena of a more pliable cuteness and a more focused, defined sexiness are linked in terms of the potential for progression and transformation from one to the other. Accordingly, rather than asserting that the viewed object must be *either* cute or sexy, but not both, it is more productive to identify conditions under which the cute male object might— or might not—become capable of transforming itself, or being transformed, into the sexy male object in contemporary culture. The popular phenomenon of cute-ified gayness becomes a most appropriate arena for exploring instances in which cuteness might complicate or even *obstruct* sexiness. As a social media device that affords "big picture" visualizations of contemporary cultural perceptions, Pinterest provides a most useful online environment for exploring what contemporary culture currently perceives as "gay" and "cute." Though searches on the topic "gay cuteness" yield a number of pins of individual men offering their exposed, ripped bodies as objects of desire to observers, more prominent sources of visual "pleasure" here emerge from the more prevalent pins of gay couples engaged in various forms of tactile union: one man kisses the cheek of another man who looks directly at the camera; couples dressed in suits interrupt their movement away from the camera to glance back at us, smiling, hands joined; a chest-down shot reveals two buff, headless bodies, one's legs wrapped around the other's back. The bodies are uniformly firm and cut, but whether or not their glances or their poses acknowledge their awareness of being photographed, each pin forms a closed circuit through images that resonate as being already complete unto themselves before any viewer happens upon the scene. Especially in the context of a culture that has recently so successfully assimilated "legitimized" gay lifestyles that had for so long been considered "alternative," the cumulative effect of the "gay cuteness" Pinterest board is a broad-scale celebration of male togetherness, but one that largely excludes the possibility of any deployment of viewer affect beyond acknowledgment, affirmation, and admiration from a distance. Not surprisingly, many of the pins depict *exclusive* interpersonal relations: a recently wed couple hugging at the beach, gay wedding cards and invitations, a GIF animation of two embracing male figurines with the pinner's caption, "Gay wedding cake toppers, got his groom!" Conforming with this notion of the closed circuit, and aligned with Merish's assertion that "for its spectators, cuteness stages the assimilation of the Other . . . into middle-class familial and emotional structures" (188–89), some of the images on the board also involve gay couples with adopted children clinging to them, including one prominent image from BuzzFeed.com entitled "[actor] Matt Bomer Steps Out with His Partner and Kids" (Lambe). The cuteness of such images of family bonding has also recently echoed across a broad number of gay websites and periodicals, most prominently in the *Advocate*, with images of couples headed by such captions as "These Gay Prospective Dads Sing 'Dear Future Baby' and It's So Cute' " (Ermac) beckoning the observer into a sense of admiration marked as a phenomenon of identification rather than sexual desire. Certainly, such instances of cuteness involve malleable objects that the viewer is invited to recognize as being worthy of hugging or squeezing, but the fact that this malleability is *already* being acted upon by another person within the image itself is what ultimately situates the objects more firmly in the realm of "cute" instead of "sexy."

In order for cute or "cute-ified" objects to be reconfigured *as* "sexy," such exclusivity must be disrupted, and this is precisely what happens in the volumes of popular images depicting men posing with a treasured cat or dog, or less frequently, a chick, goat, or rabbit. The popular calendar collection "Hot Gays and Baby Animals," for instance, clearly demonstrates this tendency: the usually bare-chested, buff-but-not-overly-beefed-up male typically featured in the calendars has virtually no body hair (aside from an occasional beard or patch of managed facial scruffiness), and the smoothness of his strong, sculpted frame is accentuated by the presence of the vulnerable, furry creature he is holding. Yet whether or not man and canine/feline are facing each other or the camera, these images resonate with an almost solicitous accessibility and a call for approach, for here there is no second man present to form and seal a closed circuit that would reify the image's position within the realm of cuteness.[4] As a result, the squeezability and (squeezed-ness) of the furry animal in these images is reiterated by a second-level squeezability transpiring between the viewing subject and objectified man, the presence of the animal fueling the lure of desire. Through such transposition, the establishment of the image as a representation of identificatory "cuteness" in one context becomes a prerequisite or precursor to the witnessing of the viewed male object's transformation to the realm of an objectified "sexiness" in the second context. Both the furry creature and the smooth, firm, objectified male body are engaged in a synergistic process functioning as a lure, transmitting a signal that authorizes approach and that facilitates fantasies of accessibility and closer engagement with the object of desire.

Cute→Sexy: The Case of Chris Pratt

The static visual representations described above activate the dynamics of desire by juxtaposing the soft, furry animal with the smooth, contoured, hard body of a man who nurtures and protects that vulnerable creature while simultaneously rendering *himself* vulnerable to the lure of the viewer's look, thereby regulating how he is perceived, consumed, or interpreted. With the diachronic dimension of screen stardom, however, another means of situating the male celebrity within the realms of the cute and the sexy emerges. First, the viewer is invited to trace changes in a celebrity's character development—psychological or physiological, onscreen and off. Matters of progression and transformation also connect with assessments of the star persona's depth, a feature integral to sustaining audience interest in the celebrity over the course of a career. By applying the workings of cute/sexy and soft/hard dynamics to the celebrity discourse of Chris Pratt, an actor whose protracted popularity is directly tied to the phenomenon of body "transformation," we gather more evidence of the myriad ways in which identification and desire strategically overlap in popular media promotion to extend the range of male celebrity appeal and accessibility to wider sets of audiences. And here, just as in those photographed images of buff men cuddling adorable furry creatures, establishing an objectified star persona as "cute" in one visual context facilitates this persona's transformation to "sexy" in another context. In this case, however, the transformation, as a register of the persona's depth, becomes a function of temporality.

Given the prevalence of the superhero phenomenon in contemporary popular American film culture, it is not surprising that contemporary male star discourse so often emphasizes matters of physical agility and body hardness, tracing the gradual yet radical transformation of a more vulnerable "version" of the star body into another, more powerful version. What is surprising, however, is that the phenomenon is now so blatantly paired with male objectification. Here, it is valuable to note how much Chris Pratt has in common with an actor like Ryan Reynolds: they are both heterosexual, married men with children; both actors originally attained audience recognition through their work in television comedy; and they both subsequently attempted to broaden the range of their audience appeal by taking on the role of an action hero figure—Reynolds as Hannibal King in *Blade: Trinity*, and Pratt as StarLord (aka Peter Quill) in *Guardians of the Galaxy* (2014). In each case, the transition to superhero required intense labor and abrupt changes in diet in order to produce the requisite "ripped" body—instances of "physical labor" that were widely publicized and touted.[5] With their new, hard bodies, both actors were appropriated by both straight and gay male cultures as objects of desire. For several years, Reynolds enjoyed the curious phenomenon of an "I'd Go Gay for Ryan Reynolds" Facebook fan group, created by self-avowed straight fan "Vlad" who clarified that the site was intended for the "completely straight male who is no way gay except for the fact that [he] wouldn't think twice about going gay for Ryan Reynolds" (King). Pratt more directly embraces the extensive online fan fiction detailing homoerotic interactions among Marvel superheroes: when an interviewer explained that "[i]t's just that people think you guys are super hot and should be hooking up with each other," he responded, "Like—me, Chris Evans, and Robert Downey, Jr? I'll have to say I agree. It sounds pretty fun" (Jefferson).[6] The association of "hooking up" with other men as a pleasurable activity elegantly positions the celebrity's susceptibility to viewer appropriation as approachably cute, even as it sustains erotic fantasy as a "transgression" of boundaries between seemingly fixed sexual orientations.

A number of other contemporary male stars have been appropriated in gay male cultural contexts. A significant difference in the star persona development of Pratt and celebrities like Ryan Reynolds, however, stems from the physiognomic conditions of each transformation. While pre-*Blade* Reynolds was characterized as a lean yet also relatively "scrawny" figure, Pratt's pre-*Guardians* image registers as soft and pudgy, with his slothful, out-of-shape qualities often

FIGURE 10.1 A pre-transformation Chris Pratt appears as consummate slacker Andy Dwyer in sitcom *Parks and Recreation*.

exploited for comedic value in his six-season role as Andy Dwyer in NBC's *Parks and Recreation* (2009–15), a series renowned for its blatant celebration of post-millennial slacking, and that also took frequent jabs at traditional notions of on-the-job "productivity" (Figure 10.1). Both stars have since maintained chiseled physiques that continue to brand them as "hard" and "sexy," but the differences in the personas from which these new bodies emerged testify to the extent to which audiences are invited to register such corporeal transformations as broader—and deeper—persona transformations.

While intense body labor quickly converted Pratt's star status to hot and sexy, his success is tied to the fact that the physical transformation aligning the actor with the progression of "once out-of-shape, but now fit" is also a sign of the actor's depth, intensified by star discourse that references so many other aspects of his persona situated *outside* the realm of the body. The actor's accessibility is one factor that registers depth in this context. Aligned with the dynamics of cuteness as social accessibility, Pratt directly avows and affirms his welcoming acceptance of the objectification of his transformed body in extra-cinematic discourse. In a BBC interview, for example, Pratt explains that "at the end of the day, our bodies are objects," as he decries the fact that women have had to bear the brunt of a sexual objectification from which men have been excluded ("Chris Pratt"). Yet the force of such pronouncements is intensified by additional aspects of accessibility that emerge from Pratt's onscreen characterizations. Unconfined to the realm of sexuality, and aligned with Hiroshi Nittono's conception of cuteness's inherent "approach motivation," this accessibility extends to skills and personality attributes that draw other characters to him. Both of his action hero portrayals emphasize his developed abilities in leadership, facilitation, and compassion: in *Guardians of the Galaxy*, Peter Quill brings together a disparate and often contentious band of outsiders and directs them toward a common, higher purpose (rescuing humankind from destruction); in *Jurassic World* (2015), Pratt's master velociraptor trainer Owen is soon revealed as the only anchor of safety, calm, and assurance for children, adults, and technologically altered dinosaurs in a theme park meltdown dominated by inept administrators, self-serving scientists, and absent parental figures.

The effect of the transformation is such that Pratt always appears to be in the process of emerging—of revealing his persona—while also promising that there is more left to reveal. Such depth constructions function as a form of perpetual "self-definition" that keeps his star image focused, tangible, and accessible to viewers, thereby urging them to remain receptive to him. Indeed, the corporeal transformation literalizes this model of emergence and revelation: as layers of body fat are gradually removed from the actor's frame, and a less voluminous but nonetheless significant amount of added muscular tissue reinforces the body's contoured integrity, the smaller, yet tighter, harder core resonates as more attractive and desirable specifically *because* it has been wrought from a body that was once less defined and more amorphous. Crucially, however, this new body always bears the historical traces of a previous incarnation that was so closely identified with a cuteness configured as pliability: viewed diachronically, the process of tissue subtraction that has revealed the now hard body serves as a reminder of the presence of the once softer, more malleable, more squeezable version of Pratt—a presence that continues to resonate both despite and because of the transformation and that continues to render him accessible to audiences.

The affective, visceral intensity of this soft-to-hard progression resonates across the field of star discourse surrounding Pratt's identity, both offscreen and in his film roles. One prominent discursive thread involves the debate over whether fans prefer the soft and pudgy "dad-bod" or the hard-body version of his star persona (Sargent; Clark-Flory). Questioned about his wife Anna Faris's preferences, Pratt explains without hesitation that she definitely prefers the "chubby" version: "What's so great about my darling wife and the mother of my son is that she loves me no matter what package I'm wrapped in. I think she loves chubby Chris because he's grumpy less frequently" (Collis). The resonance of the star's transformative journey requires a clear, intimate sense of continuity between past and present in terms of both body contours and personality. The abrupt genre shift represented by Pratt's role in *Guardians of the Galaxy* attests to the precarious nature of this transition; an article in *Entertainment Weekly* suggests that

> the film also turned him—with his newly ripped body—into a sex symbol. After years of playing schlubby Andy on *Parks and Recreation*, he's still not quite used to his hot-guy status. "Anna will remind me sometimes, 'Just don't lose Andy, because that's what people like,'" he says. "I catch myself doing 'action mode' more (in photos). It's really embarrassing when I see pictures of myself and I see that I was definitely posing." (Stack and McGovern)

Wholly resistant to any neoliberal capitalist demands for self-entrepreneurialism, the Andy Dwyer character was certainly characterized as a "schlub" figure—pudgy, directionless, not particularly bright, always relying upon others to take care of him—and the series articulated his schlubbishness (especially after the first season) as increasingly cute because of its associated qualities of accessibility, innocence, authenticity, and sincerity. In his reflections upon the transition to action hero figure, Pratt is adamant in his desire to retain the traces of cuteness harbored by this prior and most popular onscreen version of his persona. In an article entitled "Jurassic Pratt," published in conjunction with *Jurassic World*, *Gentleman's Quarterly* emphasizes the sincerity and determination of the actor's quirkiness by focusing upon the elaborate system of musical motifs that Pratt develops as mnemonic devices to trigger various emotional states in his screen performances (Heath). Such quirkiness registers as an extension of Andy Dwyer's hyper-sincere yet also somewhat "dense" features—his tendency to stumble over himself, to miss the punchlines of his colleagues' jokes, to be gullible when others might be attempting to take advantage of him. This former, Andy-Dwyer-esque cuteness, which he has retained and carried over into a multi-faceted personality enclosed within this new and quite different body, makes this firmer, more functional body even *sexier*. In fact, the formula of *cuteness plus soft-to-hard body* also lends depth to Pratt's offscreen personality and onscreen characterizations. The formula makes comments such as *Entertainment Weekly*'s assertion that transformed "Pratt's just what you hope he'd be—equal parts tough and tender" yet more resonant: while "deep" personalities can be readily characterized as harboring such opposites simultaneously, the perception of the body as soft and hard, or as "tough and tender," demands audience engagement within a progressive, temporal dimension (Stack and McGovern).

From a promotional standpoint, the transformation from cute to sexy resulting from the shift in character type from slacker to action hero is a subtle, delicate operation. *Guardians of the Galaxy*'s heroic protagonist is certainly more skilled at identifying and getting what he wants than Andy Dwyer could ever be. Faced with the cold, harsh realities involved in the struggle to make a decent living in an uncaring, every-man-for himself galactic realm, however, Quill consistently seeks an anchor to a more stable, humane existence that is always associated with the past—civilization's own past (which remains the "past" for contemporary viewers of this film as well) most certainly, but also the "pasts" of Chris Pratt's own characterizations, both onscreen and off. Quill may spend most of his time preserving, retrieving, and regaining the powerful "infinity stone," but along the way he devotes no less considerable energies to retrieving the "Awesome Mix Vol. 1" 1970s and 1980s music cassette that serves as his only remaining reminder of his mother, who dies at the start of the film as her son looks on. Never forgetting

FIGURE 10.2 A post-transformation Chris Pratt (as Peter Quill) challenges nemesis Ronan (Lee Pace) to a dance-off in blockbuster superhero film *Guardians of the Galaxy*.

his roots, Quill develops into a strong man who retains and even improves upon some of Andy's "skills," including his questionable singing talents.

Although Peter Quill becomes a more "functional" version of Andy Dwyer, the sincerity of Quill's intimacies also registers as a wholly intentional playfulness aligned with Sherman and Haidt's configuration of cuteness. Part of what made Dwyer so funny was his ability to contain and evoke innocent, childlike personality traits in an adult-(over)size body, and his status as someone who would never think of attending to matters of improved physical functionality, especially if it were attainable only through intense labor. Aligning with Sherman and Haidt's prescription that correlates cuteness with the solicitation of social interaction, as an action hero Pratt is careful to retain Andy's passion for non-directive play, lip-syncing to the Redbone classic "Come and Get Your Love" near the start of *Guardians* and performing elaborate dance moves while swatting pesky space lizards out of his path. Yet Peter Quill's playfulness is just as often productively directed as agility, as when he strategically distracts the Kree villain Ronan by challenging him to a "dance-off" (Figure 10.2). Such continuities of characteriza-tion across onscreen roles are reiterated in the strategic yet subtly rendered references to the actor's body transformation: strong and fit as he needed to become for the role of Quill, the contours of Pratt's cut, hard torso are exposed only once in the film—and here, quite briefly—in the Kyln prison sequence—leaving much more of Quill (and of Pratt) to be revealed in terms of both duration of exposure and contours of physique.[7] While such revelations of body contour more regularly populate the front pages of gay and straight magazine articles, the playfulness often remains intact even in such publicity discourse, as it certainly does in an *Entertainment Weekly* piece entitled "Chris Pratt is HUGE," where the profiled, athletic stance of the actor—clad only in a Trilby, tank top, and Bermuda shorts—registers as a tongue-in-cheek construction, deliberately and self-consciously served to its viewer in a playful body-builder pose (Sperling).

From blobbish to contoured, lumbering to agile, and soft to hard, the transformation of Pratt's star persona registers as a process of maturation in which the man that emerges always retains cuteness as that which remains special about still being a boy. Articulating the stable positioning of adult/child relations that enable cuteness, Merish explains that "staging the disavowal of child eroticism and the sublimation of adults' erotic feelings toward children, cuteness is the sign of a particular *relation* between adult and child, simultaneously establishing the 'innocence' of the child and the 'civility' of the adult spectator" (188–89). In the case of Chris Pratt, childhood does indeed function as a guarantor of both an innocence and inherent vulnerability that readily enables the persona's cute-ification through connections that situate "pastness" itself in terms of youth, and that posit, as Christopher Noxon suggests in his discussion of the "rejuvenile," the sense that in our contemporary cultural context, adult versions of "truth" always somehow fall short of being satisfactory or satisfying (32).

The Anti-Cute: Ryan Reynolds

Cultural conditions that overtly value the firm-but-not-inaccessibly hard male body are favorable to many male celebrity performers who can readily exert the labor required to produce the coveted physical image. The boy-to-man progression of Chris Pratt's star persona ultimately demonstrates the crucial role of the "depth" model in enabling the strategic overlap between identification and desire required to engage and sustain audience responsiveness in an era that harbors such a profound investment in exploiting conditions of intimacy between men. While the ability to trace a progression in the star persona's development from innocent childhood (and childishness) to mature yet still playful adulthood marks Pratt's transition from cute to sexy-because-once-cute as a successful enterprise, the case of Ryan Reynolds's star persona evidences an attempt to convey a different form of bodily-transformed sexiness in the post-millennial era—one that cannot claim an originating connection to cuteness. Certainly, body type accounts for this disparity to some extent: while Reynolds's lanky, already lean frame (sporting a remarkably low percentage of body fat even before the bulk-up) made his transformation no less publicly noteworthy, it did not facilitate a tissue subtraction or soft-to-hard transition similar to Pratt's. Beyond this, however, Reynolds's lack of alignment with the cuteness dynamic can also be attributed to an architectural "malfunction" within the same depth model that situates Pratt securely within the realm of what Sherman and Haidt describe as the "moral circle," where social behaviors are provided with the space to resonate (245). Accordingly, while it would be erroneous to claim that Reynolds's radical body transformation has failed to make him register as sexy (*People* magazine deemed him "The Sexiest Man Alive" in 2010), an examination of his star persona construction also clarifies not only that his sexiness does not arise from a prior condition of cuteness, but also that the absence of cuteness—in the form of both a yielding to vulnerability and the facilitation of social connection—as a career anchor has, at least until quite recently, rendered his star identity diffuse and disparate in comparison with the more discrete sense of "self-definition" that Pratt has attained.

The most pronounced indication of a "glitch" in persona construction emerges from Reynolds's choice of film roles at the crucial, post-transformational moment of his career. Following his 2004 lanky-to-cut body metamorphosis for the role of Hannibal King in *Blade: Trinity*, Reynolds acted in a broad set of film genres, but most of his roles continued in the vein of comedies (both juvenile and romantic) that played off of the wise-guy, would-be wild man image honed so successfully in *Van Wilder* (2002) and the network television series *Two Guys, a Girl, and a Pizza Place* (1998–2001). On the surface, the 2005 film *Just Friends*, in which fat-suited Reynolds plays Chris Brander, an obese teenager who years later returns to his hometown to redeem his self-image after his own radical soft-to-hard body transformation, might seem like the perfect vehicle for conveying a correlative boy-to-man progression like Pratt's. As it plays out, however, this role—a rare instance of an emotionally vulnerable character portrayal on Reynolds's part—ends up betraying rather than supporting the depth model of characterization, offering an image of adolescent immaturity so stereotypically played for derisive laughter as to negate the viewer's affective investment in Brander's plight. Indeed, with its opening images of the overweight, hyper-dorky Brander wearing an orthodontic retainer, singing John Michael Montgomery's "I Swear" off-key while gulping down sugary soft drinks and gorging on piles of junk food, *Just Friends* invests more energy in dehumanizing its central protagonist, effectively relegating him to the realm of disgust, which Sherman and Haidt identify as the antithesis of a cuteness response that serves as "a mechanism that 'releases' sociality" (246) (see Figure 10.3). Just as problematically, the physically transformed "after" version of the character turns out to be an arrogant, smug, and self-centered figure intent upon recreating the cruelties that his fellow high school students inflicted upon him, radically disengaging himself from any impressions of vulnerability still linked to his more innocent, pre-transformational state. Long before a climax and resolution in which Brander vows to stop playing roles and take his mother's advice to "be himself," the narrative has exhausted all attempts to render the protagonist's identity as in any way authentic, sincere, or evocative of an "approach motivation" that Nittono associates with the emotions of cuteness (87).

Although it is certainly a minor film relative to more popular works in Reynolds's oeuvre such as *Van Wilder* and *The Proposal* (2009), *Just Friends* serves as an appropriate emblem of a career grounded in roles that strive to capitalize

FIGURE 10.3 In romantic comedy *Just Friends*, Chris Brander (Ryan Reynolds) incarnates disgust as the opposite of cuteness.

upon a wisecracking image that may indeed register as funny, but that have also rendered Reynolds invulnerable and affectively inaccessible. Unlike the easy, synergistic figurations of innocence and vulnerability that characterize the screen images and extra-cinematic discourse of Chris Pratt, the construction of Reynolds's onscreen and offscreen personae more often work against any notions of "play" that might resonate as a lure for audience access or social engagement in the realm of cuteness. The celebrity discourse of Chris Pratt meticulously attends to the matter of preserving and incorporating aspects of the accessible, playful, immanently vulnerable, and always cute Andy Dwyer into the context of future versions of the star persona onscreen and off, thereby sustaining strong temporal connections that resonate as marks of character depth, and creating an alignment of the transformation of past-to-present—and boy-to-man—that ultimately facilitates and reinforces the actor's evolution from cute to sexy.

Lacking cohesive bases of character transformation that not only concatenate but also aggregate, the celebrity discourse of Ryan Reynolds has witnessed the sexy actor frequently falling victim to suggestions that he may be unable to sustain himself as a viable star product because of a too-incoherent identity construction. Contrasting his career with Bradley Cooper's rising stardom, an online *Vulture* piece attributes Reynolds's challenges to a series of unsuccessful films in the 2010s (Buchanan). A 2015 *New York Post* article frames the problem more broadly as a lack of self-definition brought about by "oddball choices" and too frequent genre shifts that have left his onscreen persona without a clearly recognizable brand, the problem exacerbated by an offscreen image that resonates with mediocrity: "He's now married to Blake Lively, and the pair live with their baby daughter in the sleepy Westchester County town of Bedford, NY—in other words, they're a boring married couple who decided to move to the "burbs" (Tucker). The commonality that emerges among these issues is the lack of a sense of an anchoring past with which to correlate too disparate a set of subsequent characterizations. Extending further, the problem of self-definition leaves the persona with a pervasive sense of shallowness across both temporal and affective dimensions, demonstrating the crucial connection of the depth of the star image and perceptions of affective sensibility in the star persona. In male-to-male cuteness, such demonstrations of temporal and affective depth ultimately link back to the contours, textures, and surfaces of actors' bodies—rendered as deepest and most accessible when originally perceived as pliable and susceptible to impression, and when consequently transformed into more cut, defined figures through operations of human labor that admirers are invited to perceive as no less accessible.

Although the longer-term effects of the resoundingly successful *Deadpool* (2016) may still be difficult to determine, the character's aligned fit with the wise-guy image that Reynolds has cultivated for so long addresses many of the actor's prior failures in securing a consistent self-brand. In the film Reynolds plays a former special services operative-turned-mercenary, Wade Wilson, who, during an encounter with central villain Ajax (Ed Skrein), is left with accelerated healing powers as well as a horribly scarred face. *Deadpool* embodies a strategic "anti-cuteness" that deploys self-referentiality to actively challenge the depth model by celebrating shallowness as a central aspect of story, character, and celebrity personality—an aspect to which the film prompts contemporary media-savvy audiences to relate. That this referentiality even operates at the level of narrative construction serves to foreground cynicism, irony, and shallowness as properties to be cultivated in the viewer's experience of the film. *Deadpool*'s intricate system of flashbacks, flashforwards, and freeze frames—rendered coherent through the eponymous character's guiding voiceover narration—foregrounds the audience's recognition of story constructedness over an immersion in the contained diegetic world; indeed, at one point former special forces operative and mercenary Wade Wilson/Deadpool even boasts that he has managed to break a fourth wall within a fourth wall!

Through its strategic self-referentiality, *Deadpool* toys with aspects of the depth model—and similarly with characteristics of sociability and accessibility—all while celebrating the distinction from the cuteness aesthetic with which these attributes are associated. This distinction finds overt expression in the film's subversive deployment of cute signifiers, examples of which include a pre-release poster showing the anti-hero holding a gun to a teddy bear's head, as well as an end credit animation depicting Deadpool erotically massaging a unicorn's horn. However, as mentioned the film's overt disavowal of cuteness is but one aspect of a wider self-referential representational mode, one that privileges cynicism above sincerity. The periodic direct address of the viewer—most notably in a closing, post-credit sequence in which Deadpool, dressed in a bathrobe, advises the audience that it is now time to leave the theater ("don't leave your garbage lying around")—arguably plays out as an attempt at conveying an accessible intimacy that bridges the gap between character, actor, and audience. At the same time, however, the narrative undermines the authenticity of this superhero's various social connections by asserting that Deadpool by choice remains apart from any configuration of "community," by having him mock the superhero Colossus's (Stefan Kapicic) attempt to link him to the community of "do-gooder" superheroes, the X-Men. Indeed, Deadpool always retains a playful emotional distance from those who pass as his closest yet still casual "friends," including Dopinder (Karan Soni), the cab driver whose fare he never pays, and Blind Al (Leslie Uggams), who provides him with shelter even as he takes alternating jabs at her body odor and her incurable physical affliction. Despite his feelings for Vanessa (Morena Baccarin), the woman he loves and devotes himself to rescuing, Deadpool remains a user and a loner, as well as a brat who has ultimately exacerbated his own misfortunes through his unyielding antagonism of Ajax.

The film is similarly ingenious in its eponymous protagonist's ability to redirect his wisecracking mockery back at the actor portraying him. Rather than identifying the names of key performers, the opening credit sequence appositively references the character types that they embody within the superhero universe ("the moody teen," "the cgi character," "a gratuitous cameo"), combining a reference to Reynolds as "God's Perfect Idiot" with a subsequent image of his 2010 *People Magazine* "Sexiest Man Alive" cover. "Looks *are* everything," Deadpool insists after another character attempts to mollify the horror of the disfigurement that he has suffered at the hands of his nemesis Ajax. "Ever heard David Beckham speak? It's like he mouth-sexed a can of helium. Do you think Ryan Reynolds got this far on his superior acting method?" By unashamedly alluding to Reynolds' radical body transformation as a blatant strategy of career enhancement, *Deadpool* attempts to effectively bypass the affective parameters of the "deep" characterizations and star personas in a postmodern testament to artifice. Indeed, in the case of Reynolds and *Deadpool*, the narrative exploits the promotional value of highlighting the contours of its protagonist's chiseled body even before the character has been transformed into the superhero who is forced to disguise himself from head to toe in a suit designed to mask his scars, as Wade parades his buffed, cut physique at home with Vanessa as well as in the torture chambers of Ajax's sinister laboratory.

In the realm of post-millennial cuteness, however, male performers who can successfully promote and package their transformation from a body type that was once *not* cut or fit gain special recognition as deeper and more complex. While contemporary culture maintains its obsession with looking back idealistically at past conditions and states, constructions of depth rely upon a specific accumulation (of experience, of knowledge) that renders the past most resonant from the perspective of a forward, maturing temporal progression, but one in which getting older never means forfeiting the childlike sense of play and the desire for social engagement that maintain the resonance of cuteness. And just as this depth model of character transformation enables a looking back at the boy on the sole condition that he has now become a man, the new post-millennial model of relations between men also renders the physical transformation of the male body more resilient—and more protracted—only as long as the past state of soft "cuteness" serves as a tether to this present condition of a hardness that becomes even sexier because it was once so vulnerable.

Notes

1   McIntyre explores this dynamic through an analysis of Zooey Deschanel's celebrity persona in "*Isn't She Adorkable!* Cuteness as Political Neutralization in the Star Text of Zooey Deschanel."
2   I analyze this relationship in *Gay Fandom and Crossover Stardom: James Dean, Mel Gibson, and Keanu Reeves.*
3   Foremost among these is Teresa de Lauretis, who argues that any mixing of the categories of identification and object-choice confuses ego-libido and object-libido. See especially her discussion of Sheila McLaughlin's film *She Must Be Seeing Things* (1987) in *The Practice of Love: Lesbian Sexuality and Perverse Desire.*

4   Sianne Ngai's discussion of the connection between distance and the perception of the "beautiful" is also relevant here: "the distance in aesthetic discourse is intrasubjective distance, referring to the subject's feeling of momentary disconnection from her own interests and desires . . ." (240).
5   For a comprehensive account, see "The Exact Ryan Reynolds Workout and Diet Plan to Get Lean, Ripped, and Shredded in Under 3 Months."
6   Interestingly, one online graphic narrative finds Peter Quill as Star Lord having sex with Captain America in an alternate universe. See also Wrexin, "C3," a narrative inspired by a face morph of Chris Evans and Chris Pratt with the author's tagline "Chris + Chris = *Chris²*."
7   *Jurassic World* extends this subtlety by revealing its central protagonist's strength and agility solely through his actions and personality traits, without a single shirtless scene.

Works Cited

"Being Called Cute by Guys You Like." *Realjock*. Realjock Forums: All Things Gay, 20 Oct. 2011. Online. 23 Aug. 2015.
Buchanan, Kyle. "The Opposite Career Trajectories of Bradley Cooper and Ryan Reynolds [Updated]" *Vulture*. Vulture, 6 Feb. 2015. Online. 29 Sept. 2016
"Chris—Chris = Chris²." *Kate or Die!* Kate or Die! n.d. Online. 1 Sept. 2015.
"Chris Pratt on the Objectification of Men." *Radio 4 in Four*. BBC, 10 June 2015. Radio.
Clark-Flory, Tracy. "Give Me Doughy Lovable Chris Pratt." *Salon.com*. Salon Media Group, 6 Aug. 2014. Online. 31 Aug. 2015.
Collis, Clark. "Hot in Space." *Entertainment Weekly*. Time-Warner, 23 May 2014. Online. 1 Sept. 2015.
DeAngelis, Michael. *Gay Fandom and Crossover Stardom: James Dean, Mel Gibson, and Keanu Reeves*. Durham, NC: Duke University Press, 2001.
——. *Reading the Bromance: Homosocial Relationships in Film and Television*. Detroit, MI: Wayne State University Press, 2014.
Desjardins, Mary. "Meeting Two Queens: Feminist Film-Making, Identity Politics, and the Melodramatic Fantasy." *Film Quarterly* 48.3 (1995): 26–33.
Engel, Meredith. "What is a 'Spornosexual'? It's the New Wave of Metrosexuals, Journalist Writes." *New York Daily News*. Daily News, 12 Jun. 2014. Online. 25 Aug. 2015.
Ermac, Raffy. "These Gay Prospective Dads Sing 'Dear Future Baby' and It's so Cute." *Advocate*. Here Media, 26 Mar. 2015. Online. 23 Aug. 2015.
"The Exact Ryan Reynolds Workout and Diet Plan to Get Lean, Ripped, and Shredded in Under 3 Months." *Ryan Reynolds Workout*. n.d. Online. 4 Sept. 2015.
Gledhill, Christine. "Signs of Melodrama." *Stardom: Industry of Desire*. New York: Routledge, 1991. 207–29.
Heath, Chris. "Jurassic Pratt." *Gentleman's Quarterly*. Condé Nast, 17 May 2015. Online. 17 Aug. 2015.
Hill, Logan. "Building a Bigger Action Hero." *Men's Journal*. Wenner Media, May 2014. Online. 24 Aug. 2015.
Italie, Leanne. "Gay-Themed Ads are Becoming More Mainstream." *Huffington Post*. AOL-Verizon, 6 Mar. 2013. Online. 1 Sept. 2015.
Jefferson, Whitney. "Chris Pratt Brings His Superhero Powers to BuzzFeed." Interview with Chris Pratt. *BuzzFeed*. BuzzFeed, 30 Jul. 2014. Online. 15 Aug. 2015.
Jeffords, Susan. *Hard Bodies: Hollywood Masculinity in the Reagan Era*. New Brunswick, NJ: Rutgers University Press, 1993.

King, Mark S. "Ryan Reynolds is Hot, but Going Gay for Him? *The Bilerico Project*. The Bilerico Project, 19 Nov. 2010. Online. 17 Aug. 2015.

Lambe, Stacy. "Matt Bomer Steps Out with His Partner and Kids." *BuzzFeed*. BuzzFeed, 2 Aug. 2012. Online. 23 Aug. 2015.

de Lauretis, Teresa. *The Practice of Love: Lesbian Sexuality and Perverse Desire*. Bloomington, IN: Indiana University Press, 1994.

McIntyre, Anthony P. "*Isn't She Adorkable!* Cuteness as Political Neutralization in the Star Text of Zooey Deschanel." *Television and New Media* 16.5 (2015): 422–38.

Merish, Lori. "Cuteness and Commodity Aesthetics: Tom Thumb and Shirley Temple." *Freakery: Cultural Spectacles of the Extraordinary Body*. Ed. Rosemarie Garland-Thomson. New York: New York University Press, 1996.

Minsky, Alex. "Get Mighty with Minsky: Alex Minsky on His Gay Fans, Self-Love, and More than Fitness." *YouTube*. YouTube, 27 Mar. 2015. Online. 14 Aug. 2015.

Murphy, Ryan. "Top 10 Hollywood Bulk-Ups." *Men's Fitness*. n.d. Online. 23 Aug. 2015.

Ngai, Sianne. *Our Aesthetic Categories: Zany, Cute, Interesting*. Cambridge, MA: Harvard University Press, 2012.

Nichols, James Michael. "Sabra Hummus Ad Features Real-Life Gay Couple." *Huffington Post*. AOL-Verizon, 21 May 2015. Online. 1 Sept. 2015.

Nittono, Hiroshi. "The Two-Layer Model of 'Kawaii': A Behavioral Science Framework for Understanding *Kawaii* and Cuteness." Cute Studies, a special issue of *East Asian Journal of Popular Culture* 2.1 (2016): 79–95.

Noxon, Christopher. *Rejuvenile: Kickball, Cartoons, Cupcakes, and the Reinvention of the American Grown-Up*. New York: Crown, 2006.

Olesker, Max. "The Rise and Fall of the Spornosexual." *Esquire.com*. Hearst, 12 Jan. 2015. Online. 24 Aug. 2015.

Sargent, Jordan. "Which Chris Pratt is Hotter: Dadbod or Rippedbod?" *defamer*. defamer, 7 May 2015. Online. 31 Aug. 2015.

Sherman, Gary D., and Jonathan Haidt. "Cuteness and Disgust: The Humanizing and Dehumanizing Effects of Emotion." *Emotion Review* 3.3 (2011): 245–51.

Simpson, Mark. "Hollywood Gayze." *marksimpson.com*, 18 Jul 2015. Online. 22 Aug. 2015.

Sperling, Nicole. "Chris Pratt is HUGE." *Entertainment Weekly*. Time-Warner, 26 Jun. 2015. Online. 17 Aug. 2015.

Stack, Tim, and Joe McGovern. "Chris Pratt is Going Paleo." *Entertainment Weekly*. Time-Warner, 29 May 2015: 30–38.

Tucker, Reed. "WTF happened to Ryan Reynolds' Career?" *New York Post*. News Corp., 9 Jul. 2015. Online. 22 Jul. 2015.

Wrexin. "C3." *An Archive of Our Own*, n.d. Online. 1 Sept. 2015.

11

AFFECTIVE MARKETING AND THE KUTENESS OF KIDDLES

Joyce Goggin

Introduction

"Cuteness sells" has become a commonplace in the literature on this commercial aesthetic, including Chapter 1 of this volume; and cuteness is clearly the governing aesthetic behind any number of industries and products, from computer games and toys like the Pokémon franchise, to more sophisticated product ranges such as Italian manufacturer Alessi's "Family Follows Fiction" housewares line (1993) or Jonathan Ive's translucent, neotenous Apple iMac G3 computers (1998–2003), to numerous foods and food crazes marketed through cuteness (see chapters by Legge and de Vries in this volume). Put more bluntly, Sianne Ngai refers to cuteness as a "prime example of commercial aesthetics" (*Our* 252 n64), while Gary Cross writes that cuteness is "an occasion for impulse spending" (44), and Marilyn Ivy calls cuteness "a commercially elaborated notion" that has "developed as a standard taste concept in mass culture society" (14).

In what follows, I offer a rather personal account of cuteness and consumption by focusing on one particularly cute Mattel doll from the 1960s that was promoted through a marketing strategy that proved, in my own experience, to be remarkably effective. More specifically, through this one example, I want to discuss some of the ways that cuteness interpellates children in general as consumers, and girls in particular, as gendered consumers. The pocket-sized doll in question is "Liddle Diddle Kiddle," the baby doll of a much larger series called "Liddle Kiddles" (Figure 11.1). Many years ago my mother purchased one such tiny companion for me, most likely to keep me from fidgeting in church, given that the doll's diminutive size made her amenable to being taken just about anywhere for quiet, intimate play. Thus, at age seven I developed a strong emotive attachment to this almost impossibly cute, constant companion, until my cousin absconded with her and Liddle Diddle—or Baby Diddle as she is also known—the doll would never be seen again, nor replaced during my childhood. More than three decades later, however, I found myself googling "Mattel Kiddles" and, by clicking the images that appeared, I learned that the Kiddle series was introduced to North American toy markets in 1966, with the dolls selling apace until 1970 when the company decided that it had flooded the market and began developing other lines. My search soon also led to eBay where I discovered that the doll was on auction, so I immediately bid on and "won" (as purchasing is called in eBay-speak), my first vintage Liddle Diddle.

The feeling of holding this diminutive piece of my previous life—of connecting to my past through a cherished object—was extremely powerful, pleasant, and remarkably satisfying. It felt as though I had been reunited with my Rosebud, without going through all the chicanery and globe-scavenging that Charles Foster Kane had to endure in *Citizen Kane* (1941) in order to reconnect with his cathected object just before dying.[1] I also experienced some of what Daniel Miller has called the Pandora's Box effect, whereby "all sorts of demons from [one's] past" are released to "plague [one's] present" when reconnecting with old toys, although my demons were all highly pleasant memories that I was both surprised and delighted to be enjoying through the medium of my new, vintage doll (*Comfort* 146). It was as though this lost object had been literally retrieved out of time, and my search had finally been rewarded with an adorably cute fragment of my own *temps perdu*, along with that unforgettable sweet, plastic smell. And this feeling lasted for about a week, until I became obsessed with finding a Liddle Diddle Kiddle in the original packaging, in mint condition, with all of her Kiddle

FIGURE 11.1   Densely Kiddle-branded environments invite a variety of assembly options—here, a modified Liddle Diddle Kiddle doll is foregrounded.

Source: Photo by Melissa Meistrell (bigredangel.com)

FIGURE 11.2   (Re)assembling Kiddle dolls offers an opportunity to stage cuteness as in this grouping of the author's own collection of vintage Liddle Diddle Kiddles won on eBay.

Source: Photo by author

accessories, with the comic book that was packaged with the original series, and so on. Now, some twelve Kiddles later, I am uncomfortably reminded of an anecdote recounted by Michele White in *Buy It Now: Lessons from Ebay*, about one eBay junkie's Barbie doll collection that grew to fill an entire room (1).[2]

Following from this personal preamble, my goal in this chapter is to analyze how and why the cuteness of Mattel Kiddles makes them so very engaging, and the related issue of how they were marketed to encourage maximum identification and serial buying in children. I also want to consider the somewhat obvious ways in which these dolls instructed gender roles in the 1960s, and finally, I will discuss the experience of collecting them on eBay and the impact that being able to collect remnants of one's past has on contemporary notions of nostalgia. This will also be undertaken as a means of understanding what specifically makes cuteness in the form of old toys from one's childhood, and buying them on eBay, such an intense experience, in order to say something about my, thankfully, short-lived addiction.

Marketing Kiddles

Juliet Schor has shown that "children's social worlds are increasingly constructed around consuming, as brands and products have come to determine who is 'in' or 'out,' who is hot or not, who deserves to have friends, or social status" (11). Against this contemporary backdrop we may note that dolls have a long, rich, and anthropologically significant history. Indeed, early doll historian Laura Starr averred in 1909 that "history could be taught by means of dolls" and that future historians could easily reconstruct our age through toys and dolls gathered from "dusty garrets and museums" (qtd. in Formanek-Brunell 1). As Giorgio Agamben notes in *Infancy and History: On the Destruction of Experience*, the power and persistence of toys, and perhaps dolls in particular, is attributable to how they act as "a residue of diachrony in synchronic situations such as ritual, and synchronic residue in diachronic situations such as games when they are no longer being played" (81). In other words, dolls suggest a profound connection to the earliest moments in human history, as well as humanity frozen in time, like tiny mummified specimens of past human beings held over as "synchronic residue" when dolls are no longer being played with and a reminder, perhaps, of our own mortality.[3] Hence, "[a]lthough the transcendence of objects [such as dolls] allows them to endure beyond flux and history, that very transcendence also links such objects to the world of the dead," and dolls disturbingly evoke the notion of the "dead among us" (Stewart 57). This is why dolls, invested as they are with a troubling, yet reassuring, likeness to human beings, may seem lifeless while simultaneously threatening to become animate and spring into action at any moment. And this is, of course, the crux of Freud's famous essay on the uncanny (das Unheimliche), wherein he elaborates a theory that accounts for much of what we find creepy and uncanny in dolls, connected to our abiding unease about their possible or imagined ability to lead a life of their own when we're not looking.[4]

In a similar vein, Kim Toffoletti has remarked that the uncanniness of Barbie is most apparent when she is seen out of habitual play contexts, stripped of her normalizing clothing and accoutrements, and denaturalized as, for example, in a pile at a flea market. In such denaturalized settings, the creepiness of her "taut rubbery limbs [. . .] compact torso [. . .], and plastic rock-hard shell," writes Toffoletti, forms a "distinctive configuration" which is suddenly revealed when we come upon Barbie dolls out of play settings (58). These observations are related to what Miller writes about toys, namely that they do their job most efficiently, precisely when we "fail to notice them," as when we come to them in their *naturalized* play contexts (*Stuff* 54). The more they are played with in their ostensibly "natural" settings, or subjected to their purportedly intended uses, "the more powerful and determinant of us [toys and dolls] turn out to be" (Miller, *Stuff* 54). Indeed, if we take Mattel co-founder and Kiddle creator Elliot Handler at his word, his idea was to craft "small dolls that looked like neighborhood children engaged in typical play situations," so that part of their emotive appeal was their seeming normalcy (Jensen 48).

The burning question for me, however, is how Mattel managed to harness the power of toys to produce and grow a franchise organized around tiny, adorably cute Kiddle dolls into a formidable sector of the market for children. This question, however, requires a brief look at the moment at which children became a key element in advertising, at the same time that they also began being targeted *themselves*, rather than their parents, as consumers and as the recipients of a direct address. One important moment at the beginning of this trend occurred in 1880, when Milton Bradley Toys of Springfield, Massachusetts, began printing play money which was distributed to schools as a pedagogical tool to provide children with an economy scaled to their size. Play money was minted to "teach children to recognize coin values, to make change, to respect money, to count and to do arithmetic and budgeting," in other words to handle money as an adult consumer would (Clothier 1; see also Goggin). So in this case, while toy money was created as an instrument of play, it was also invested with a special role in teaching the mechanisms of trade, devalued and scaled down both to be played with and to meet the pedagogical imperative to prepare the child for his or her future role as *homo economicus*.

Cross, moreover, writes about "shaping the modern image of the child and modern consumer culture" in the nineteenth and twentieth centuries in his influential work *The Cute and the Cool: Wondrous Innocence and Modern American Children's Culture* (51; see also Noxon 35–36). While he discusses the grooming of children as future consumers, he also describes the process of turning children—their ostensible cuteness, needs and wonder—into selling points in and of themselves. By the late nineteenth century, he writes, "cuteness itself, even separate from the child, became desirable as the look that we want to purchase and possess. The cute became a selling point [. . .] and an occasion for impulse spending" as the image of the child entered modern consumer culture to become a permanent feature of what entices us to buy things (44).

As Rachel Bowlby points out, by the 1930s children were starting to be viewed as "keen consumers" themselves, and indeed, as some of the "most important consumers of all, since they are both present and future buyers" (128–29). To give just one example of the thinking behind this process, she discusses "[a] pamphlet produced by the U.K. government's Council on Art and Industry [published in] 1935, entitled *Education for the Consumer*" (87). The pamphlet promoted the notion "that if the six hundred thousand children in each [. . .] school year" were all properly educated, "ten years from now there would be six million tasteful buyers" (Bowlby 87). Likewise, she quotes *Modern Packaging* magazine of 1938 in which the publishers explained how "Frank Jr." might be "too young to appreciate the deeper significance [of their magazine and the] powerful aid" it offers to advertising men, but in just a few years "little Frank" will be sitting in dad's chair and will have "quite unconsciously, all these years, [. . .] been absorbing your messages" (Bowlby 87).

One of the messages that "little Frank" will have unconsciously taken in through his second-hand experience with marketing is "faith in the power of packaging to fire [. . .] the 'twentieth century [sic] imagination'" (Bowlby 87). Where the Kiddle franchise is concerned, faith like little Frank's led to a very powerful technique that focused on packaging, and resulted in Kiddles being some of the first toys packaged for sale on a cardboard base with the dolls and their accoutrements—such as Liddle Diddle's crib, blanket, pillow, ducky, and comb and brush—housed, as it were, in the safe environment of a clear plastic bubble attached to the cardboard. And while Mattel's pioneering technique of marketing toys fastened onto cards with transparent bubble-pack wrapping proved highly effective, it also reduced costs while making the product seem more "visible" and attainable for children.

This aspect of the packaging is not only important in fiscal terms, it also incorporates and puts to use one of the key features of cuteness, namely that cute "objects present themselves as entirely available, as their commercial and erotic connotation make explicit" (Ngai, *Our* 18).[5] This semblance of availability effectively produces the experience of cuteness in the manner described by Mary Ann Doane, as a "strange constriction of the gap between consumer and commodity" that shrinks the distance between consumer and product, indexing the "affect of empathy" on which cuteness trades (qtd. in Ngai, *Our* 67). Furthermore, however consciously or not on the part of Mattel, the packaging of Kiddles played on one further quality of cuteness, namely that "[t]he cute contains within its address an invitation to ownership," hence little girls were made to feel as though they were somehow implicitly entitled to own the dolls—as though they belonged together—as a function of the doll's appealing, entreating cute look (Merish 188).

While clear plastic bubble packaging made Liddle Kiddles appear to be perfectly amenable to the child's grasp, and tacitly suggested that all kids had to do to possess their very own Kiddles was simply to reach out and grab them, it also contributed to the illusion that the dolls were somehow magically suspended in air while the panoply of accoutrements that accompanied and personalized each Kiddle seemed to circulate in enchanted concert around the dolls in their own specially furnished bubbles. Significantly in this regard, cultural anthropologist Anne Allison has argued that cuteness feeds "a business of enchanted commodities" and "a consumer fetishism" that gives off "an aura of fancy and make-believe" (Allison, "Enchanted" 16; see also de Vries in this volume). Again, this aura is instrumental in establishing a "closeness" between product and consumer, suggesting an intimacy between the "fanciness" of the cute object and the imagination of the person who consumes it (Allison, "Enchanted" 17).

Here too the Kiddle packaging is a prime example of how cuteness assists and strengthens "commodity fetishism's fantasy of animation" (Ngai, *Our* 62). The card and plastic bubble packaging "invite the aesthetic subject to handle [the cute doll] physically," thereby enlisting the cute to speak "to a desire to recover what Marx calls the 'coarsely sensuous objectivity,'" while cute aesthetics and powerful marketing techniques also encouraged children to imagine Kiddles as animated beings (Ngai, *Our* 63). And if these visual features alone were not enough, the comic books that came with the dolls explicitly told children, "you can pose them to run, jump, hop, or skip because *they're Bendable!*" (emphasis in original text).

Before concluding this discussion of the cute drawing power of the Kiddle bubble pack, enhanced with tag lines and cartoon images of Kiddles that helped to "foster a sense of perpetual and limitless desire" through "magic and enchantment," I want to focus briefly on the comic books that were included with the dolls as part of the packaging (Bowlby 8–9). As Cross has noted, the association of dolls and other toys with "playful images of kids in unusual and unnatural settings," as was often the case with Kiddles, was meant to suggest "a world of desire and fantasy" (49). Beginning early in the twentieth century, this trend took the form of contextualizing toys, and dolls in particular, "in illustrated stories and comic strips," the practice of which was part of "popularizing the look of the cute" to stimulate consumption, while promoting (and using to promote various products) the look of the "new kid [. . .] which became ubiquitous in American culture in the first two decades of the twentieth century" (51). By "new kid," Cross refers to a shift that occurred over the nineteenth and twentieth centuries away from representing children as "angelic" and characterized by a look of "wondrous innocence," sweetness, and delight, to images of children being cute in crafty, spunky, and sometimes downright demanding, manipulative ways, and in need of cute objects or special foods to be purchased by parents (43–51).

The Kiddle provides a perfect example of this trend in marketing cuteness, as each doll came with a copy of the illustrated *Adventures of the Kiddles*, "an 18-page fold-out funny comic strip [. . .] advertising other dolls for sale" along with instructive scripts for play scenarios that could lead to future purchases (Storm and Van Dyke 8). So, when I got my Kiddle, I was also treated to a comic story involving Liddle Diddle's precocious yet bratty siblings, Florence Niddle and Greta Griddle, who decide to make pancakes for their sister, who is "just the most adorable Liddle thing." The entire enterprise teeters constantly on the brink of disaster with the Kiddles appearing to be dwarfed by a giant flour canister and mixer, as Baby Diddle looks on skeptically while her sisters make a huge mess that does, eventually, yield pancakes. Thought bubbles convey Baby Diddle's sarcastic interjections, such as "adorable I may be but I'm also hungry!" and "some breakfast this is going to be!" Along the way, Liddle Diddle learns the difference between "flower" and "flour," and the strip ends with an illustrated panel that reads, "round and flat and hot off the griddle. Liddle's breakfast is the Kiddle riddle!" The comic also includes illustrations and descriptions of the special qualities and characteristics of other dolls in the series, and assurances that "all the Liddle Kiddles want to live at your house. You'll love playing with *all* the LIDDLE KIDDLES" (emphasis in the original text). In other words, this aggressive marketing, featuring cunning "New Kids," was affectively couched in cuteness and thinly veiled as having pedagogical aims as well as containing a message about caring and sharing. "Liddle's breakfast is the Kiddle riddle!" also implies that this doll is one in a collectible series, so that children are encouraged to get the next riddle by buying another doll or having one bought for them.

Cuteness and Serial Consumption

In her work on what she calls "pocket capitalism" and serial buying in children, Allison writes that tactics such as those I have just mentioned feed "a desire to consume that, as parents have complained, is never ending" ("Pocket" 187).[6] Commenting on the same issue, however, one Mattel executive quite predictably enthused that "[t]here was something about Liddle Kiddles that little girls just went crazy for" and had to have (Jensen 50), which brings me to the topic of how cuteness was used in this franchise to feed what Jameson has called "addictive capitalism" (qtd. in Allison, "Pocket" 187), in order to shape the child and future "modal addictive consumer of late capitalism" (Ivy 19). As one woman who now collects vintage Kiddles remarked, "[w]hen you start collecting them, you go after those you played with. But soon *you have to have them all*—the ones you couldn't afford back then, or couldn't get your mother to buy for you" (Jensen 51, emphasis added).

This collector's self-proclaimed need "to have them all" describes what is sometimes referred to as extension pack logic by computer gamers, or what Baudrillard called a "system of objects" (10). As he explains, "the objects of mass consumption form a repertoire" so that products are marketed in clusters with accessories and sequel product development that induces the need in consumers to "collect 'em all" in order to have the complete set (14). Although there are earlier instances of this kind of marketing, the Liddle Kiddle series of collectibles, of which Mattel marketed over 100 different kinds before the franchise ended in 1971, is a particularly evocative case (Storm and Van Dyke 5). For example, to add diversity and enhance collectability, a range of distinctive faces were sculpted by doll artist Martha Armstrong and, by "varying facial painting, hair color, style, and [. . .] clothes, a surprising degree of individuality was obtained" along with "what toy makers call play value" (Jensen 48). Importantly, the dolls all came with accessories such as Baby Diddle's ducky mentioned above, that "gave each Kiddle a different personality," from Lemon Stiddle with her own lemonade stand, to Telly Viddle equipped with that most beloved of childhood companions, the television set.

As the first series began to lose its appeal, Mattel quickly responded with themed Kiddles created around pre-sold storybook and nursery rhyme characters such as Liddle Biddle Peep, Cinderiddle, and Liddle Red Riding Hiddle. In a later series Mattel innovated by impregnating the dolls with enticing smells to augment the already sweet plastic aroma that all Kiddles had as a matter of course, hence mini-Kologne-Kiddles dressed and scented as flowers in perfume bottles, or fruit flavors in the "Kola Kiddles" series, and the sweet smell of candy in the Kiddles "Sweet Treats" series, sold in plastic ice cream cones and lollipops. And if olfactory engineering and the plastic suggestion of a sugar fix were not enough, the "Lucky Locket Kiddle" was developed to be worn close to the heart or, as the TV advertisement suggested to a catchy beat, "See how groovy—they look! On a purse or—a book! They are made—by Mattel! You can tell cuz—they're swell!" Later still, an anthropomorphized series of Animiddle Kiddles was produced, which were subsequently spun into Zoolery Kiddles, also to be worn, and finally a Martian series was brought to market. Moreover, along with the dolls, there were Kiddle vinyl cases, houses, snap-happy furniture, paper goods, lunch boxes, games, records, posters, puppet theaters, and perhaps most remarkably, a line of play clothes for these dolls that measured an average of just

4 centimeters. These seemingly endless additional accessories added to the inducements for children to become serial consumers of Kiddle products.

Where serialized consumption is concerned, the creation of little Telly Viddle Kiddle seems to capture much of the mood surrounding the Kiddles' auspicious arrival on the market along with the advent of children's television and its attendant advertising in the 1960s. In fact, according to Zac Bissonnette, Mattel and Hasbro were "the first two toy companies to take their marketing directly to children" in the form of seasonal television toy commercials" (82). Combined with children television, the Kiddle franchise grew through what, two decades later, would become known as the "Strawberry Shortcake strategy." The term, coined by Tom Engelhardt, describes the paradigm shift in marketing that occurred in the 1980s through a case study of serial buying and the branded character "Strawberry Shortcake," who was reproduced in greeting cards, as well as in television series, and vast arrays of merchandise for children. Mattel's serial strategies to promote the consumption of Kiddles in their various forms and settings were harbingers of this expanding marketing technique which would become the norm in the latter half of the twentieth century, constructing children as economic actors and reinforcing their status as acceptable targets for advertising campaigns.

Gender, Diminutiveness, and Kiddles

Although Mattel actually nodded in the direction of gender diversity with a boy doll named "Biff,"[7] Kiddles were the product of Eliott Handler's decision "in 1966 to follow up Barbie's huge success with a new line of mini-dolls that, unlike the glamorous teen, would play to the maternal instincts of little girls" (Jensen 48). Or, as Suzanne de Castell and Mary Bryson would have it, Mattel asked, "what untapped desires do girls harbor that could be drawn upon, whether to educate or train them [. . .] to capture a market share," which process resulted in " 'just for you' [. . .] feminized playthings that escort girls to their proper place in the gender order" (de Castell and Bryson 238, 232).

The practice of grouping the features I described above—including the olfactory engineering that imparted an unforgettable scent to Kologne Kiddles, and the Kiddle comics that acted both as advertising and as affective scripts for appropriate play—was then a precursor to Engelhardt's "Strawberry Shortcake Strategy" (see also Gray 177). As Miller argues, marketing strategies like these notably hyperbolize a non-didactic mode of appeal. Instead, he explains, "they help you gently to learn how to act appropriately" and, in this case, how to perform gender in a very essentialized, "pink and mauve" way (*Stuff*, 53).[8]

As a gentle means of address, the increasing use of gendered cuteness as a marketing feature in children's toys has often gone largely unnoticed due to its universal appeal, and this aspect of cuteness makes it a sort of silent-but-deadly aesthetic style that "mobilize[s] proprietary desire, a peculiarly 'feminine' proprietary desire that equates to a moral sentiment: a desire to care for, cherish, and protect" (Merish 188). The triggering of caring emotions and the supposed susceptibility to cuteness in girls and women has been a consistent feature of cuteness when it is used to encourage consumption. Thus, Ngai, like Cross, notes that the cute first emerged "as a common term of evaluation and formally recognizable style in the industrial nineteenth-century United States." She goes on to add that this happened "in tandem with its ideological consolidation of the middle-class home as a feminized space supposedly organized primarily around commodities and consumption" (*Our* 15).

Dolls like Kiddles (as opposed to action figures, for example) generate a direct address to little girls, and comprise an encouragement to girls to unquestioningly anticipate motherhood as an allegedly inevitable event in their future. Miriam Formanek-Brunell has argued that dolls are frequently misconstrued as straight-forward "representations of femininity and maternity," as well as "generators of only maternal feelings and domestic concerns and, as such, obstacles to the development of girls as individuals [. . .] marketed as symbols of an idealized feminine domesticity," which elides the fascinating ways in which they also complicate such narratives (1).[9] However, while dolls may often be subject to a variety of uses beyond the clichés of little girls playing mommy, the marketing of the Mattel Kiddles line clearly positions the product as a desirable cute object for girls, appealing to their supposedly innate maternal instincts. These diminutive figures embody Lori Merish's summation of the domesticating impulse behind the cuteness response: "the cute is always shopping for a mother" (196). In doll form, cuteness calls out for a mommy and grooms little girls to become mothers at some distant point in the future that they are tacitly, and sometimes bluntly, urged to desire.

Although the notion that cuteness is "inevitably gendered" (Cross 44) over-simplifies a complex aesthetic and set of related affects, it was a feature of the earliest scholarship on the topic specifically related to human attachment to dolls. In 1943, Konrad Lorenz advanced the notion that cuteness prompts adults, particularly women, to care for cute objects such as dolls and pets, in a particularly retrograde aside, pointing to "[t]he products of the doll industry, which are literally the results of . . . experiments carried out on a very wide basis, and also the various types of animals (e.g. pug-dogs and Pekinese) which are taken over by childless women as substitute objects for their parental care drive" (154). The overt goal of the Mattel marketing of Kiddles clearly advances a similar constellation of essentializing gender traits in its targeting of girl consumers who, like Lorenz's "childless women" showering affection on pets, are assumed to have a natural maternal instinct.

Cute playthings are manufactured and marketed to trigger emotions in consumers—particularly small, future consumers who appreciate the scale—while supposedly eliciting caring responses, which help to account for the long-inhering memories attached to cute objects from our childhoods.[10] As Ngai points out, "[cute] objects have no edge to speak of, being simple or formally non-complex and deeply associated with the infantile, the feminine, and the unthreatening" (*Our* 59). Banking on these cathexis-inducing qualities of cuteness, the toy industry is able to steer the formation of subjectivity and identity around cultural gender norms in children, thereby demonstrating the interconnectedness of consumerism and cuteness. Hence, the subjective experience and emotional response to cuteness flow directly into the economic processes that are responsible for the marketing, production, and consumption of such objects.

I would also like to underscore the importance of smallness, an attribute frequently ascribed to the feminine, to the taxonomy of cuteness. Ngai, for example, consults the *Oxford English Dictionary* on the etymology of the word "cute" and supplies examples of its earliest uses in the nineteenth and early twentieth centuries that contain adjectives such as "small and compact" and "tiny," concluding that by the mid-twentieth century cute comes to be used to describe "small things" and "minor persons" (*Our* 59). The rhetorics and linguistics of cuteness evident in the rhyming, repetitive baby talk-inspired Kiddles marketing copy exemplifies Ngai's argument that the encounter with cuteness "does something to everyday communicative speech: weakening or even dissolving syntax and reducing lexicon to onomatopoeia" (87–88). The cute-ified language of Kiddles-speak rests upon the assumption that when adults, especially women, confront cuteness in the diminutive dolls, they dissolve into childish utterances themselves.

As Merish notes, this rhetorical quality of the cute has a tendency to draw "small-sized adjectives and diminutive ejaculations," hence the name *Liddle* Kiddle that combines a mispronunciation of "little" by a very small person not yet capable of pronouncing a hard "t," and "Kiddle" which is sometimes used in colloquial English as a pet name for "kid," a term that accentuates children's diminutive cuteness (193). In other words, the name "Liddle Kiddle" is doubly diminutive and doubly cute. And of course, it is precisely this tiny aspect of Baby Diddle that so appealed to me as a child, and elicited my "protective cherishing" of this adorable toy that seemed so small and helpless (Merish 186). Indeed, Liddle Kiddle dolls pack a heavy emotive punch as tiny pocket companions for "future moms," and play up the aesthetics of cuteness by courting "consumer empathy, generating a structure of emotional response that assimilate[s] consumption into the logic of adoption" (Merish 187). In appealing to the young girl as consumer and as future mother of children, the Kiddle line mobilized diminutive cuteness and cutesy baby talk in the service of traditional gender norms.

Gigantism, Uncanniness, and Cuteness

Describing how cuteness often incorporates other, quite different aesthetics and affects, anthropologist Marilyn Ivy observes, in regard to Japanese artist Nara Yoshitomo's disturbingly incongruous paintings of cute girls smoking cigarettes or sporting vampire fangs, that

[i]n a doubling that is characteristic of [Freud's] entire essay on the uncanny, the most uncanny experience of all is having a word turn into its opposite; a word that means everything homelike and intimate becomes *un*-homelike (*unheimlich*), alienated and, well, uncanny. (15)

This ability of the cute to flip over into, among other things, the very un-cute to which Ivy refers here, has been noted by numerous scholars, perhaps most famously by Ngai, who writes that our relationship with cute objects is more complex than simply an impulse to care. Rather, the cute provokes feelings that oscillate between "domination and passivity, or cruelty and tenderness" and this kind of ambivalence is "uniquely brought forward by the aesthetic of cuteness" ("Cuteness" 846).

As these observations help to make clear, it is necessary to complicate cuteness in order to appreciate the full complexity of this aesthetic, and to avoid the pitfalls of understanding cuteness as simply a coy ploy, or tacky tactic, and a "look" or air that unproblematically arouses caring instincts. While Liddle Diddle Kiddle is indeed very pink and saccharine-sweet, I want to return to a detail from my introduction, namely that my Kiddle disappeared when my cousin stole her away from me. The fate that my Little Diddle met involved, I fear, the same kind of torture to which he regularly subjected any of my dolls that he found irritatingly and provocatively cute if he got the opportunity: namely, aggressive mutilation, disfigurement, and sadistic dismemberment. My cousin delighted in this ritual any time he got the chance, precisely because many dolls'—and particularly Liddle Diddle's—enormous neotenous head and giant eyes incited libidinal feelings of hostility. Moreover, as Harris argues in *Cute, Quaint, Hungry, and Romantic*, among its many possible manifestations cuteness is also an "aesthetic of deformity and dejection" (7). Seen in this light, one begins to understand how Liddle Kiddles earned the hair-raisingly inappropriate schoolyard sobriquet of "Liddle Deformos" among children who responded to their disturbingly disproportionate cuteness with hostility and aggression back when I was growing up.

The dual address of the cute is an essential aspect of this aesthetic since, according to Ngai,

> it is crucial to cuteness that its diminutive object has some sort of imposed-upon aspect or mien—that is, that it bears the look of an object not only formed but all too easily *de*-formed under the pressure of the subject's feelings or attitude toward it. ("Cuteness" 816)

Seen in this light, my cousin's behavior becomes more understandable as well as somewhat predictable, particularly in the context of Ngai's realization that

> we can thus start to see how cuteness might provoke ugly or aggressive feelings, as well as the expected tender or maternal ones. For in its exaggerated passivity and vulnerability, the cute object is often intended to

excite a consumer's sadistic desires for mastery and control as much as his or her desire to cuddle. (Ngai, "Cuteness" 817)

In this regard, it is also important to note that the enormity of the Kiddle head—which comes compellingly into focus on those odd occasions when a confused or misguided eBay seller attaches a Kiddle head to a Barbie body on which it looks bizarrely yet perfectly proportionate—is complemented by the doll's enormous eyes. While, as exaggerated sensory organs, Kiddle eyes were designed to connect with us and to ask us to return their gaze with compassion, adoration, and care, for some people they may have the reverse effect. This is possibly because this particular characteristic belongs to what Philip Brophy terms "the semiotic continuum" of the cute, which often renders dolls "monstrously cuddly and hideously gorgeous," and one would be hard-pressed to come up with a more apt description of Liddle Diddle (45). Brophy likewise devotes considerable attention to dolls' eyes and the way that "dolls of the last hundred years replay [a] mix of the baby's gaze with the cadaver's gaze, lending them a quality which is both cute and spooky," as well as uncanny in many of the ways I described above, including dead and undead all at once (47).

Nostalgia, eBay, and Cuteness

Writing in 1996 about the past and present popularity of Kiddles, Don Jensen states that "those once-little kids [who] quickly fell in love with the pocket-sized posables in 1966 and [who are] now 'thirty- and forty-somethings,' are recapturing those feelings by collecting Kiddles" (48). This comment seems to support the observations of a number of scholars who have tried to unpack the various reasons why remembered cuteness is such a powerful buying incentive to adults, beyond the supposed Darwinian impulse to nurture. For example, when Thomas Lamarre writes about the cuteness of Mickey Mouse, he traces Stephen Jay Gould's famous 1979 analysis of the pesky rodent's development from a pointy-nosed, nasty, little prankster into the rounded, soft-spoken character cherished by children, as well as by adults who grew up with Annette Funicello and the first generation of *The Mickey Mouse Club* (intermittently 1955–1994). In this way, Lamarre connects adult susceptibility to cuteness to the "juvenilization of adults" and an increasing loyalty among adults to the products they loved as kids (123; see also Gould).[11] Similarly, American literature and culture scholar Miles Orvell has traced "contemporary cute chic to the 1960s with its celebration of perennial childhood" and sustained nostalgia on the part of baby boomers for objects from their youth (qtd. in Angier).

Cross, on the other hand, connects his history of the "new kid" over the course of the nineteenth and twentieth centuries to a form of marketing that made it acceptable for parents to get down on the floor and play with their children, and to buy cute toys for their kids that they would have wanted themselves. That is to say that advertising's simultaneous recognition and construction of the demands of spunky new kids implicitly gave adults "the right to indulge them [. . .], to delight in their children's desires [. . .], and showed the way for the adult to return to wondrous innocence [. . .] and indulge his or her own 'inner child'" (Cross 81).[12] In a similar vein, Merish refers to "early market analysts such as Carl Naether, who recommended that advertisers picture children in their ads so that women's maternal sentiments could be 'transferred' from child to commodity" as an incentive for adult women to buy cute products (187). More generally, Ngai argues that the adult enjoyment of cuteness is due to "basic human and social competences [being] increasingly encroached on by capitalism over the past half century," so that the cute and the childish continue to hail us with affect and emotion as an intimate appeal to consume (13).

Whatever the case may be, the ability to collect cute vintage objects like my Kiddles is a combined result of the mass production of consumer goods that are still in circulation, and the availability of second-time-around consumables with the advent of a global on-line market place. More importantly, buying reproductions of "recent antique" objects (bric-à-brac, clothing, cowboy lunch-boxes) has affected our experience of nostalgia, and internet seller eBay's second-hand market has had an even more acute impact on how we experience this ambiguously and sometimes queasily pleasant emotion. Because we can buy objects from our childhood—either copies or the "real thing"—the unbridgeable temporal distance between the past and the present that informed modern versions of nostalgia has been collapsed.[13] Likewise, the spatial distance formerly implied by the term "nostalgia" is also erased, given online, 24/7 global shopping and shipping. So, if a hopeless longing for something lost and irrecoverable was central to modern concepts of nostalgia, in the context of a postmodern, internet-based marketplace, nostalgics can now readily obtain the once irrecoverable, while the difference between past and present has been flattened out.

Before leaving this topic, I want to conjoin this notion of a flattened or leveled model of postmodern nostalgia with the eBay interface and what media scholars have referred to as a new "pinball" framework or gameified interface introduced by online markets. As I would argue, these kinds of ludic and compelling interfaces that give consumers options to speculate on price shifts, place maximum bids, and encourage staying awake into the night to compete with bidders in different time zones, create excitement and impact on customers in new and sometimes troubling ways, particularly if and when such interfaces are enhanced by cute aesthetics or the desire and incentive to collect cute objects (see also Albarrán-Torres in this volume). In *The Comfort of Things*, Miller remarks that "eBay can offer quite an exhilarating form of shopping [. . .] especially the bidding aspect" (152), another feature shared with some gaming interfaces, that contributes to eBay's addictive potential. When coupled with the possibility of "winning" something in an online auction, and competing with other bidders in real time, the eBay interface proffers an addictive mode of address that interpellates the adrenaline-fueled consumer and incites repeat purchases.

Natasha Dow-Schüll has written at length in *Addiction by Design* about the gaming industry's development of various addictive interfaces, and, importantly given my argument here, how the gaming industries now aggressively target women. For example, she quotes a researcher from a data visualization company who tracks women aged fifty-five and older, asking "Who are these ladies? Where do they live? How can we target them better?" (151). In an attempt to attract middle-aged female (potential) gamblers, IGT (International Game Technology) created *Hot Flashes*, a digital slot machine with an interface designed to speak to older women. Released in 2002, *Hot Flashes* is described by *Top Line Slots* as a "semi-comical video slot game from IGT [that] reveals some of the extreme female mood swings that females may get as life goes on," in other words, menopausal symptoms that may be experienced by older women who, I would add, might have owned Kiddles back in the 1960s.[14] The cute, predominantly pink and mauve interface features a bottle of aspirin, a romance novel, a rolling pin, a tube of lipstick, and a credit card among other symbols that spin on the digital reels, as well as two hysterical-looking women, one of whom is crying.[15] Significantly, free spins and bonuses are called "mood swings" and the bonus section features a cartoon figure of a young stud in Speedo-style bathing trunks, ostensibly to appeal to the "cougar" in middle-aged women.

In all of the ways just described, *Hot Flashes'* interface and gameplay dramatically bring together much of what I have been arguing concerning cuteness, consumption and how the cute continues to appeal to adults, and how it is frequently tailored to target girls and women. This is to say that, while women of my generation were trained to consume as a means of performing gender through memorable cathected objects like Liddle Diddle that we were aggressively compelled to desire through color-coded packaging and advertising, as adults we are now encouraged to remain "productive gamers" through menopause with pink and purple interfaces in a "feminine" semiotic universe so that we can cash in on all the excitement of "Hot Flashes."

Conclusion

Following Miller, I have argued that objects "unconsciously direct our footsteps and are the landscapes of our imagination, as well as the cultural environment to which we adapt" (*Stuff* 53), not to mention the markets in which we consume. The importance of these observations resides in how toys in general, and the Kiddle doll in particular, incorporate cuteness to train girls to become women, while grooming them as shoppers. I have also outlined how affect and agency are mediated through these dolls and the expanded universe of objects in which they circulated in the 1960s, and their connection to the rising importance of a particular kind of seriality in American capitalism at a key juncture in the history of marketing. In addition, I discussed how nostalgia is currently mobilized to encourage us to retrieve our past through competitive consumption via the gamified interface of eBay, designed to encourage serialized betting which induces, in cases such as mine at least, low-grade addiction.

I began by arguing that the enchantment of my first Kiddle lasted for about a week, until I embarked upon a cycle of serial buying to feed my seemingly bottomless desire for this cute object and the rush of winning one on eBay. In closing, I want to address my lack of satisfaction and the constant urge to repeat the experience by citing Thomas Presskorn-Thygesen and Ole Bjerg's observations on falling rates of enjoyment that are entailed in compulsive buying disorder, as we move beyond fantasies that sustain desire and enter into the domain of drive, or the circular repetition of the same failed gestures. As they write, "in consumption [sic] society, the commercial is a fundamental part of the production apparatus, since it produces and reproduces a society's capacity for consumption" (206). Hence, as Zizek pointed out, while Coke has advertised itself as "It," that thing which will deliver a "pure surplus of enjoyment [. . .] the mysterious and elusive X we are all after in our compulsive consumption of merchandise," Coke is never really "the real thing," because the real imbibing of Coke "makes us want even more," thereby reproducing or stimulating rather than satisfying our desire (qtd. in Bjerg 6). Or, as Baudrillard, writing before these scholars, explained, "new sources of consumption are careful not to liberate people in accordance with some explosive end state of happiness," lest we become satisfied and stop consuming (13). This is to say then, I will have to accept that my Rosebud will continue to elude me, leading me compulsively in the direction of yet another Rosebud, that will never be as good as the first one never was.

Notes

1 Cathexis is a psychoanalytic term used to describe an intense mental or emotional investment in a person, object, or idea. The term came into the English language through James Strachey's translation of Freud's use of the German *Besetzung*. Therefore, by "cathected object," I refer to an object in which someone has invested a great deal of emotional energy and to which that same person has formed a (libidinal) attachment.

2 This image recalls (for me, somewhat uncomfortably) Christopher Noxon's description of "hard-core collectors and eBay gold-star honorees who regard toys as artifacts, exhibits in their own personal pop culture archive" (98).

3 Philip Brophy discusses the connection between dolls and death at great length and, particularly the invention of various forms of plastics to simulate skin, such as "Milbu— an amalgam of the German words *Milch* [milk] and *Blut* [blood]" which was an "exciting development [of the 1940s] because of the fleshy smoothness it gave dolls molded from it" (46). This was part of "projecting an illusory life-like quality" into dolls, and Brophy expands his discussion of what he calls this "strange fecund morbidity [that] is an integral aspect of industrialization and all its mechanical and chemical processes" to conclude that it is "hard to look at the celluloid and plastic dolls of this century and not be haunted by the industrial context [i.e. WWII and the postwar period] of their production." More gruesomely, he concludes that "the more dolls were imbued with some life-like illusory effect [in this same era], the more they resembled a dead baby" (46–47).

4 See also Stewart: "The dream of animation [. . .] is equally the terror caused by animation, the terror of the doll, for such movement would only cause the obliteration

of the subject—the inhuman spectacle of a dream no longer in need of its dreamer" (172).

5 Although I will suspend a discussion here of the cute eroticism of Kiddles, as I note later in this chapter, eBay sellers sometimes, possibly out of confusion, place Kiddle heads on Barbie bodies to startling and disturbing effect, particularly when the head in question belongs to "Baby Diddle." In this regard it is worth noting that art historian Anthony Kelly, on visiting my office and spying my Kiddle collection, expressed alarm at how the dolls are eroticized, and how Liddle Diddle is made to look as though she were wearing lipstick. For more on eroticism and children's dolls, see Stewart 24.

6 It is perhaps worth noting that Susan Stewart cites an 1822 book entitled *Wisdom of the Miniature; or, The Youth's Pleasing Instructor* which the author refers to as "a pocket companion for the youth of both sexes in America" (43). In other words, the idea of creating intimate pocket-sized objects for children to which they were supposed to become attached, and from which they were to learn, has a long history.

7 The company also created a Kiddle of color, "Rolly Twiddle," in a weak attempt to acknowledge the ethnic diversity of the franchise's potential buyers.

8 By "pink and mauve," I refer to ways of performing gender that follow stereotypical notions of girlhood fed by the toy industries through the "color-coding of products, the narrow casting of children's programs, and the targeting of advertisements for specific genders result[ing] in a culture which gives children very clear signals about gender appropriate fantasies and desires," with the result that "girls *do* want their products shipped in pink or purple boxes" (Cassell and Jenkins 19, emphasis in original). In other words, little girls are acculturated to desire things that are pink and mauve or packaged in those colors, which products also frequently nudge girls in the direction of scripted gendered behaviors and the performance thereof.

9 While a deep analysis of why this is the case is far beyond the scope of this chapter, it is worth quoting Nancy Folbre here, who writes in *Greed, Lust and Gender*, that "[c]apitalist societies have never been pure market societies. They have always relied on families for the production and care of their workers" (xxvii).

10 See Hall: "Smallness indulges children's love of feeling their superiority, their desire to boss something and to gain their desires along lines of least resistance or to vent their reaction to the parental tyranny of anger" (qtd. in Stewart 124).

11 Christopher Noxon has devoted an entire book to this topic, including a discussion of grown women who collect dolls (112–14).

12 See Noxon, who writes: "But the fact that many parents go to heretofore unimaginable extremes to satisfy their children is less important than the fact that many of them are prepared to go to extremes to satisfy themselves" (111).

13 For a detailed discussion of the history of nostalgia and the ways in which it has been understood, see Stewart 138–46.

14 See "IGT Hot Flashes" for a more detailed description of the game play aimed at buyers of casino games. To watch a video play-through of the game on YouTube, see "Vintage Slots."

15 The interface also features an old-fashioned, romantic-looking male character reminiscent of Colin Firth in the 1995 TV miniseries *Pride and Prejudice*, as well as a doghouse, presumably to suggest that the husbands of menopausal women frequently end up "in the doghouse."

Works Cited

Agamben, Giorgio. *Infancy and History: On the Destruction of Experience*. Trans. Liz Heron. London: Verso, 2007.

Allison, Anne. "Enchanted Commodities." *Millennial Monsters: Japanese Toys and the Global Imagination*. Berkeley, CA: University of California Press, 2006. 1–34.

——. "Pocket Capitalism and Virtual Intimacy: Pokémon as Symptom of Postindustrial Youth Culture." *Figuring the Future: Youth and Globalization*. Eds. Jennifer Cole and Deborah Durham. Sante Fe, NM: School for Advanced Research, 2008. 179–95.

Angier, Natalie. "The Cute Factor." *New York Times*. New York Times, 3 Jan. 2006. Online. 10 June 2016.

Baudrillard, Jean. *Selected Writings*. Ed Mark Poster. Cambridge: Polity, 1998.

Bissonnette, Zac. *The Great Beanie Baby Bubble: Mass Delusion and the Dark Side of Cute*. New York: Portfolio-Penguin, 2015.

Bjerg, Ole. "Drug Addiction and Capitalism: Too Close to the Body." *Body and Society* 14.1 (2008): 1–22.

Bowlby, Rachel. *Carried Away: The Invention of Modern Shopping*. London: Faber, 2000.

Brophy, Philip. "Ocular Excess: A Semiotic Morphology of Cartoon Eyes." *KaBoom: Explosive Animation from America and Japan*. Ed. Philip Brophy. Sydney: Museum of Contemporary Art, 1994. 42–58.

Cassell, Justine, and Henry Jenkins, eds. *From Barbie to Mortal Kombat: Gender and Computer Games*. Cambridge, MA: MIT Press, 2000.

Cassell, Justine, and Henry Jenkins. "Chess for Girls? Feminism and Computer Games." Cassell and Jenkins 2–45.

Clothier, Richard, and Wendy Clothier. *Play Money of American Children*. Online. http://rfc33.tripod.com/.

Cross, Gary. "The Cute Child: Images of a Wondrous Childhood." *The Cute and the Cool: Wondrous Innocence and Modern American Children's Culture*. Oxford: Oxford University Press, 2004. 43–83.

de Castell, Suzanne, and Mary Bryson. "Retooling Play: Dystopia, Dysphoria, and Difference." Cassell and Jenkins 232-61.

Dow-Schüll, Natasha. *Addiction by Design: Machine Gambling in Las Vegas*. Princeton, NJ: Princeton University Press, 2012.

Engelhardt, Thomas. "The Strawberry Shortcake Strategy." *Watching Television*. Ed. Todd Gitlin. New York: Pantheon, 1986. 68–110.

Folbre, Nancy. *Greed, Lust and Gender: A History of Economic Ideas*. Oxford: Oxford University Press, 2009.

Formanek-Brunell, Miriam. *Made to Play House: Dolls and the Commercialization of American Girlhood, 1830–1930*. Baltimore, MD: Johns Hopkins University Press, 1998.

Freud, Sigmund. *The Uncanny*. Trans. David McLintock. London: Penguin, 2003.

Goggin, Joyce. "Fantasy and Finance: Play Money and Computer Game Culture." *The Computer Culture Reader*. Eds. Judd Ethan Ruggill, Ken S. McAllister, and Joseph R. Chaney. Cambridge: Cambridge Scholars Press, 2009. 125–37.

Gould, Stephen Jay. "Mickey Mouse Meets Konrad Lorenz." *Natural History* 88.5 (1979): 30–36. Rpt. as "A Biological Homage to Mickey Mouse" in *The Panda's Thumb: More Reflections in Natural History*. New York: Norton, 1980. 95–107.

Gray, Jonathan. *Show Sold Separately: Promos, Spoilers, and Other Media Paratexts*. New York: New York University Press, 2010.

Hall, G. *A Study of Dolls*. New York: E.L. Kellogg and Co., 1897.

Harris, Daniel. *Cute, Quaint, Hungry, and Romantic: The Aesthetics of Consumerism*. Boston, MA: Da Capo, 2001.

Hot Flashes. International Game Technology. Video game.

"IGT Hot Flashes." *Top Line Slot Machines: Best Deals on Casino Slot Machines*. 25 Jan. 2015. Online. 10 June 2016.

Ivy, Marilyn. "The Art of Cute Little Things: Nara Yoshitomo's Parapolitics." *Mechademia* 5 (2010): 3–29.

Jensen, Don. "Liddle Kiddle Article-Diddle." *Contemporary Doll Collector.* June–July 1996: 48–51.

Lamarre, Thomas. "Speciesism, Part III: Neoteny and the Politics of Life." *Mechademia* 6 (2011): 110–36.

"Liddle Kiddle Dolls: All Things Kiddles 1966–71." *Doll Reference.* n.d. Online. 10 June 2016.

Lorenz, Konrad. "Part and Parcel in Human and Animal Societies." 1950. *Studies in Animal and Human Behavior, Vol. 2.* Trans. Robert Martin. Cambridge, MA: Harvard University Press, 1971. 115–95.

Merish, Lori. "Cuteness and Commodity Aesthetics." *Freakery: Cultural Spectacles of the Extraordinary Body.* Ed. Rosemarie Garland-Thomson. New York: New York University Press, 1996. 185–206.

Miller, Daniel. *The Comfort of Things.* Cambridge: Polity, 2008.

———. *Stuff.* Cambridge: Polity, 2010.

Ngai, Sianne. "The Cuteness of the Avant-Garde." *Critical Inquiry* 31.4 (2005): 811–47.

———. *Our Aesthetic Categories: Zany, Cute, Interesting.* Cambridge, MA: Harvard University Press, 2012.

Noxon, Christopher. *Rejuvenile: Kickball, Cartoons, Cupcakes, and the Reinvention of the American Grown-up.* New York: Crown, 2006.

Presskorn-Thygesen, Thomas, and Ole Bjerg. "The Falling Rate of Enjoyment: Consumer Capitalism and Compulsive Buying Disorder." *ephemera journal: theory & politics in organization* 14.2 (2014): 197–220. Online. 10 June 2016.

Stewart, Susan. *On Longing: Narratives of the Miniature, the Gigantic, the Souvenir, the Collection.* Durham, NC: Duke University Press, 1993.

Storm, Tamela, and Debra van Dyke. *Liddle Kiddles: Dolls and Accessories.* Paducah, KY: Collector, 1986.

Toffoletti, Kim. *Cyborgs and Barbie Doll: Feminism, Popular Culture, and the Posthuman Body.* New York: I.B Tauris, 2007.

"Vintage Slots: Hot Flashes." The Shamus of Slots Super Slot Fan Site. *YouTube.* 22 Dec. 2011. Online. 10 June 2016.

White, Michele. *Buy it Now: Lessons from Ebay.* Durham, NC: Duke University Press, 2012.

12

KITTENS, FARMS, AND WILD PANDAS

The Impact of Cuteness in Adult Gamble-Play Media

César Albarrán-Torres

This chapter investigates the role of cuteness in the design of what I call gamble-play media, a category that includes terrestrial and online slots. In gamble-play media the fun aspects of gambling are privileged over winning or losing, and cuteness is often a key element in enabling this enjoyment. This shift in focus establishes new dynamics of seduction and control for a media format in which gambling practices are staged to resemble other interactive technologies such as video games. In cute slots, imagery that we might ordinarily associate with children, along with the symbolic dichotomy of care/domination that the gambler establishes with animal characters featured on and in these devices is an essential part of the amusement, as is the sociality that may be released by cuteness. Hence, as I will argue, designers endeavor to make gambling look and feel harmless by incorporating elements of popular culture and imagery that infantilizes players of games of chance. In particular, this chapter argues childlike cuteness as delineated by Konrad Lorenz in his *Kindchenschema* is deployed as a rhetorical tool that foregrounds gambling's playfulness and minimizes or masks its many dangers in terms of problematic consumption and the targeting of vulnerable populations, some members of which might be particularly drawn to images of cute, cuddly animals.

This chapter likewise employs the concept of procedural rhetoric in interactive media, as pioneered by Ian Bogost, in order to argue that the inclusion of cute imagery in digital gambling platforms has a twofold purpose. First, cuteness helps the industry in its business of encouraging "the use of simulations to produce safe risk as a consumable service or commodity" (Gephart 141). Through cute aesthetics then, slot machine gambling is framed as a domesticated and safe form of wagering (can gambling really be *that* risky if kittens meow on the screen?). In this way, cuteness is deployed as a means of bringing gambling closer to home, thus removing it—in the minds of those gamblers targeted—from stigmatized spaces such as hyper-capitalist casinos or smoky card rooms. In cute slots, moreover, animals are used symbolically as entities that can be mastered by humans, exacerbating the false impression of control over outcome. In reality, however, the probability of hitting the jackpot or experiencing continuous wins is around one in five million.

At the same time, cuteness allows various gambling industries to profit from market sectors that might previously have been unreachable, such as middle- and upper-class gamblers in the Global North and Asian markets, by alluding to signifiers of domesticity and a utopian pastoral life, as well as cultural exotica. Cute slot machines also target the highly profitable female market, the members of which are more likely to gamble for the sake of sociality than for financial gain (Thomas et al.). Supported by a discussion of the techno-cultural innovation of digital slots, this chapter provides a close analysis of three gamble-play media products that appeal to consumers through animal cuteness, namely *OMG! Kittens*, *Wild Panda*, and *Crazy Farm Race*. In what follows, I contend that the implications of cuteness as an affective tool should not be underestimated, particularly when dealing with a potentially pernicious and damaging activity such as gambling.

Gambling with Cuteness

Cuteness has become a powerful mechanism that is now used in the design of a number of contemporary digital gambling machines as a form of persuasive iconography or rhetoric inherent in the gaming machine's representational vocabularies: for example, images of toys and cute baby animals rendered in predominantly pink and mauve palettes, employed to persuade gamblers to engage in continuous play. In enlisting cuteness in these rhetorics, the gaming industries seem to be counting on cute aesthetics to elicit paternal feelings as Konrad Lorenz described, when he argued that cuteness triggers care-giving instincts. Similarly, psychologists Gary D. Sherman and Jonathan Haidt argue that "the cuteness response is better understood as a mechanism that 'releases' sociality (e.g., play and other affiliative interactions), which sometimes (indirectly) leads to increased care" (246). The incorporation of cute elements in gambling machine design is therefore undertaken with the intention of masking the nature of slot consumption by banking on the potential of cuteness to release an element of sociality in gamblers in an activity that is generally defined by a sense of detachment from the outside world.

The use of cuteness in gambling machines is not, however, without precedent in other forms of mass consumption. Gary Cross traces the origins of cute culture in the United States in the late nineteenth and early twentieth centuries to argue that the cute "became a selling point . . . and an occasion for impulse spending" at that time (44). Following up on this tradition, the main players in the gaming industry (transnational companies such as Aristocrat, Bally Technology, and IGT) incorporate cute, simple storylines that feature kittens and pneumatic, neotenous, brightly colored characters with imagery recalling toys. The gaming industry continues to use these elements as it works towards the cultural normalization of gambling and betting, supposedly rendering it both safer and more fun. With the injection of cuteness, digital slots are framed as an innocent way to pass the time, and a socially acceptable form of entertainment similar to cartoons or video games, rather than as an adult vice.

By cultural normalization I mean the processes through which gambling has been introduced to the array of acceptable entertainment options (cable television, cinema, videogames) from which the tech-savvy, middle-class consumer (mainly from the Global North) can choose. This cultural normalization is also the product of a more amicable consumer perception of gambling products derived from branding strategies. Research by Humphreys and Latour suggests that the ways in which an industry frames its products help shape consumers' attitudes. By labeling gambling products as "gaming," digital gambling operators move "nonusers to judge online betting as more legitimate" (McGandy). Humphreys and Latour's research reveals that the coming together of the cultural connotations associated with the gambling and gaming industries has the potential to open new markets and lessen public scrutiny. The affordances of contemporary gamble–play platforms also allow particular types of consumption that aid in the cultural normalization of gambling as an acceptable form of digital entertainment. These affordances make evident the main cultural dynamic of gamble–play: promoting the fun aspects of gambling alongside the thrill of winning money.

I would argue, moreover, that cuteness has the added advantage of bringing the gambling experience closer to domesticity for the duration of play. As Gary Genosko points out, cuteness "produces a feeling of warmth and closeness accompanied by behavior patterns of caring associated with brood-tending about beings or objects aroused by their specific infantile attributes" (4). Genosko's argument builds on Konrad Lorenz's earlier work on cuteness in which he famously asserted that cuteness acts as an "innate releasing mechanism" that prompts caring and care-giving responses in adults (Lorenz 160). In the hands of the gaming industry, cuteness thus becomes a tool for taming the supposedly instinct-driven and chaotic nature of gambling by triggering feelings of endearment and sociality. When compared with previous slot machine technologies both mechanical and electronic, the affordances of the state-of-the-art digitized slots in which cuteness is mobilized allow for more immersive media experiences that enhance the expanded "cuteness response" described by Sherman and Haidt (246). These platforms include visual, tactile, and aural exchanges that bring gambling closer to a multimedia event and make them more effective in eliciting the affective responses listed above.

Even though earlier, traditional, mechanical slots also involve the body in various ways, digital slots add an important new dimension to the gaming experience. By radically accelerating the turnover time between bets or moves, digital slots intensify the experience of immersion that older mechanical and manual forms of gambling provided to a lesser extent, drawing gamblers ever further into what Natasha Dow Schüll calls "the zone," a spatial and temporal state where they are engaged intensely and utterly. Digital slots likewise up the ante by using the fast-paced audiovisual language of interactive games, including music videos, virtual reality, and 3D animations to capture the viewer's/gambler's attention. Additionally, in cute slots, animal imagery and supposedly endearing narratives hasten the gambler's arrival in "the zone" by appealing to feelings of affection, care, playfulness, and, moreover, domination through domestication.

The *OMG! Kittens* slot machine, for example, is an apparently simple gambling platform not unlike any other gambling device. However, it engages gamblers—both emotionally and physically—in a media experience more akin to arcade video games than to traditional gambling machines. As such, *OMG! Kittens* is an excellent example of a digital slot device that uses cuteness as a tool to add an affective and narrative layer to the otherwise monotonous gameplay of slots. As the player engages, a furry kitten meows from the speakers located above the glistening hi-tech touchscreen. The reels roll frenziedly and more kittens appear, hopefully bringing a smile to the gambler's face, while in one of the reels a tabby kitten

FIGURE 12.1 *OMG! Kittens* deploys cuteness as an affective and narrative tool to innovate standard slot machine formulas.

leans over a fishbowl in a menacingly cute pose. The shiny colors of the interface are accompanied by soundscapes that gamblers can customize by choosing between the "Simple" or "Bells and Whistles" options, as well as different musical options for reel spin, anticipation spins, and win tunes. This digital platform invites the gambler to feel expectation and endearment while, at the same time, offering the opportunity to customize the screen. In this way *OMG! Kittens* encourages users to feel empowered, which may equally contribute to an illusion of control over the outcome.

Global Slot Machine Markets

Slot machine gambling is a multibillion-dollar industry of considerable size and cultural significance, and has a presence in both brick and mortar casinos and online spaces. In their more than one-hundred-year history, slot machines have evolved from relatively simple mechanical devices into complex digital networked media. But, most importantly, slot play has developed from a monotonous activity where the fun, thrills, and excitement come from a chance event (and where the process is often reduced to pressing the button or pulling the lever, seeing the reels roll, and hoping for the best) to a video game-like involvement where themes and narratives frame the gambler's foray into the territory of luck.

Slot machines originated in San Francisco during the Gold Rush Era of 1848 to 1855 amid the expansion of other forms of gambling, such as traditional poker, from the Mississippi River (Devol), across the Nevada desert and into the Pacific coastal towns (Findlay; Lears; Mazur). The earliest form of slot machine was introduced into the leisure market in 1887 as New Nickel Machines. To define winners and losers, randomness was achieved mechanically through the spin of reels and the arbitrary pairing of winning combinations.

Contemporary digital slots, however, offer intense gamble-play events that add layers of procedures and meanings to the otherwise simple mechanism of slots. Slots traditionally require that "a minimum of three reels be put in motion with the result being determined by the combination of objects displayed when the reels come to a stop" (Ziolkowski 5). The winning amount depends on the ranking of a particular image/object relative to the other images/objects in the reel. Digital slots follow the same principle as their mechanical predecessor, but here a Random Number Generator produces the outcomes which means that the reels roll just for show—they are not mechanically connected to a physical reel. It is in this purely cosmetic mechanism that developers now install cute imagery. The use of such imagery, generally associated with children, is intended to make gambling seem less risky when it occurs in reel design, by inviting the player to enter familiar symbolic territory. As Jonathan Parke and Mark Griffiths argue in relation to *The Simpsons*-themed slot machines, "with an international quality brand such as *The Simpsons*, a player might think that they are unlikely to lose a lot of money. They might also think the jackpots are likely to be generous" (168). In other words, in *The Simpsons* slot machine, the familiarity that gamblers may have with Homer, Marge, Bart, Lisa, and Maggie and their archetypical suburban American cartoon household makes gambling seem less harmful or potentially dangerous.

The role of iconography in gambling, including well-known narrative and cartoon commodities like those just mentioned, has only recently been acknowledged as a crucial element in understanding the phenomenology of play sessions, as well as markets. In Australia, a country deeply affected by problem gambling, a government inquiry found that people experiencing gambling addiction are particularly drawn to machines that hold certain aesthetic qualities. In one study, Julia Karpathakis recalled her ordeal as a problem gambler and how imagery influenced her choice of platform:

> There is a lot of trickery. That is what it looks like now. But back then it had a romantic feel about it. The imagery is very romantic; I would play *Sweethearts, Cleopatra, Jewel of the Nile* and all of those kinds of machines. I hated *Shogun*—I was never attracted to the look of that one. So it was a bit romantic, not in a romantic-romantic way but dreamy, if you know what I mean. (Joint 10)

Karpathakis's testimonial supports the notion that, for certain female gamblers, the symbolic arrangements of interfaces—the "trickery," as Karpathakis now calls it—is one of the factors that draw them to play or into choosing one slot machine over another. As this chapter argues, transnational gaming companies increasingly deploy conventionally gendered discourses including romance and, as I will go on to show, cuteness, to solicit female gamblers.

Surprisingly, the aesthetic and narrative components of slot machines are rarely studied by academics. Fiona Nicoll is one pioneer in this field and, in a 2014 paper that explores the representation of Native American peoples in slot machine design, she argues that:

> To design and gamble on EGMs [Electric Gaming Machines] is very literally to play with cultural meanings. The development of EGM iconography and soundscapes over the past two decades has been exponential; in less than a generation EGM design has transformed from offering a basic digital representation of playing cards on what looked like small television screens to sophisticated haptic devices which employ state-of-the-art animations and literally vibrate when particular combinations of "reels" occur. (835)

It is worth noting that the use of signifiers of cuteness and the invocation of echoes of childhood in slot machines are not exclusive to current digital iterations. Early slot machines also used cuteness and childish reward systems to seduce gamblers. Just as contemporary slot machines provide pyrotechnic multimedia experiences that go beyond mere gambling, their earliest predecessors offered fun perks and aural elements that accompanied the consumption of bets and intensified sensorial involvement. Writing about early fruit machines, Griffiths points out that

> [a]s early as 1902, some machines were designed to double up as a musical box, the thinking being that the person had to play the fruit machine to hear the music. Another marketing ploy which began to appear by the 1930's was the built-in vending machine. After playing the machine, players would receive items such as mints, bubble gum or candy. (105)

Today, physical slots that use similar mechanisms of seduction and control based on a reward system are a ubiquitous and culturally relevant media form, and the magnitude of the global slot market and more generally of the gaming machine sector, which includes cute slots, should not be underestimated. According to a 2013 census, there were approximately 7,673,134 electronic gaming machines in the world, including slot machines, video lottery terminals, amusements with payouts, the Japanese varieties Pachinko and Pachislot—media forms also heavily reliant on cuteness—and electronic table games (Ziolkowski). IGT, as noted previously, one of the industry's biggest manufacturers, was recently bought for $6.4 billion by Italy's GTECH, the world's largest provider of lottery systems, and this acquisition also demonstrates the ductility of gambling markets (Palmeri et al.). The jurisdictions with the largest number of gambling machines in the world, as of 2013, are Japan, Italy, Germany, Spain, the United Kingdom, Peru, and Mexico, as well as the states of New South Wales in Australia and Nevada and Oklahoma in the United States (Ziolkowski). Physical slot machines are located both in tourism-oriented venues such as casinos and everyday spaces like pubs and community centers, and even public transport, as is the case in British Columbia, Canada. By using cuteness as a rhetorical tool, some of these slot machines, such as the three examples discussed here, enter seamlessly into gamblers' everyday routines, travel, and media consumption habits.

Digital technology is key to the process of normalization that gambling has undergone in the last several decades, making gambling on EGMs seem at once inoffensive and more familiar. Terrestrial gambling machines and online slots incorporate the technical affordances, and the look and feel, of everyday media. Some contemporary machines also increase the sensorial stimulation of the gambling event, both tactilely and visually, by having larger and more complex hardware that includes various screen formats, haptic technology, sophisticated speakers, and even vibrations when the user hits the jackpot. As affective technologies therefore, digital slot machines now share "universes of reference" (Guattari) with other digital media hardware such as video game arcade cabinets, game consoles, computers, and smartphones. As Schüll points out,

> In a historical moment when transactions between humans and machines
> unfold "at an even greater level of intimacy and on an even greater scale"
> (as the sociologist Bruno Latour has written), computers, video games,
> mobile phones, iPods, and the like have become a means through which
> individuals can manage their affective states and create a personal buffer
> zone against the uncertainties and worries of their world. (13)

Cute gamble-play platforms provide some of these "personal buffer zones" and generate particular material and expressive transactions between humans and machines. Gamble-play media also modulate affective states by providing environments in which users invest hope, creativity, emotional capital, and disappointment. In cute slots gamblers also invest care and nurturing, if only symbolically.

As noted above, cuteness brings gambling closer to domesticity by generating a sense of intimacy between the object (for example, cute characters displayed on the slot reels) and the player. As Merish notes, the cute "is identified as part of the 'family,' indeed part of the self; the pleasure of the cute involves 'recognizing' it as such" (187). Through the rhetorical power of cuteness then, gambling becomes a familiar and ritualised activity which in part is accomplished by connecting cuteness with the (feminized) domestic sphere. Here again Merish writes that "[v]aluing cuteness [also] entails the ritualized performance of maternal feeling, designating a model of feminine subjectivity constituted against those (ethnic, class, or national) Others who lack the maternal/sentimental endowments (and aesthetic faculties) to fully appreciate the 'cute'" (186). In other words, the introduction of cuteness into gambling interfaces hails a female market sector that the gambling industries aggressively target (Hing and Breen "Profiling"; "A Profile"; see also Lee), while encouraging members of that sector to view themselves positively through their choice of cute gaming machines. Thus without essentializing femininity or conflating it with maternity, and taking care not to accept these appeals as necessarily effective or legitimate, we can nevertheless note how normative femininities are interpellated by gaming cuteness.

Cuteness as a Rhetorical Tool

The particular kind of rhetoric put in motion in cute gamble-play media is what video game theorist Ian Bogost calls "procedural rhetoric" (3). Procedural rhetoric is "a new type of persuasive and expressive practice" in which gameplay processes and platform affordances are used "persuasively" (Bogost 3). Bogost argues therefore, that video games invite players to enact procedures or particular ways of doing things, and that in turn, these procedures can be used persuasively and rhetorically. As noted above, in calling this process procedural rhetoric, Bogost defines rhetoric as "persuasive expression" (viii) and states that programmers write "code that enforces rules to generate some kind of representation, rather than authoring the representation itself [. . .] the ability to execute a series of rules fundamentally separates computers from other media" (4). So, just as advertising uses visual and aural cues to stimulate purchasing, interactive media such as cute slots use procedures to communicate, very persuasively, through actions. In the case of cute slots, for example, procedural layers (such as those which allow players to choose the look and feel of the platform or offer bonus levels) are added to the basic gameplay of EGMs, thereby insuring that playing the slots goes beyond the monotonous action of pressing a button.

Procedural rhetoric in digital slot platforms typically establishes negotiations between user agency and operator control with two important effects. On the one hand, procedural rhetoric allows users to interact with the game and to feel a sense of control over the outcome, a sense that is strengthened in cute platforms. On the other hand, procedural rhetoric affords communication that reinforces engagement, consumption, and brand affiliation. Slot machine manufacturers use cuteness, as in *OMG! Kittens*, in a similar way to Hollywood branding in terms of procedural rhetoric. In January 2014, for instance, Microgaming signed a deal with Universal Partnerships and Licensing to develop a *Jurassic Park*-themed online slot machine, which was released in 2015. Elements of the film franchise's narrative are deeply embedded in the gamble-play as the number of bonus levels varies "depending on the type of dinosaur selected at the beginning of the game" (Ancona). In this case, Hollywood narratives frame the staging of the bet, placing the consumer in a cultural space where gambling unabashedly seeks to become a form of entertainment, while procedural rhetoric plays a distinctive role by encouraging continuous gambling.

The use of cuteness as rhetoric is particularly evident in the aforementioned *OMG! Kittens*, produced by SG Interactive, which frames gamble-play with images of cats, collars, milk bottles, and yarn. Rather than being merely decorative, these visual elements frame gambling by invoking childhood, domesticity, and a simplistic idea of femininity and human-animal relations. Reels roll and a tabby kitten appears on the screen when the player is lucky enough to hit a jackpot and music begins to play. The advertising for *OMG! Kittens* is similarly focused on cute affects as it asks, "Who couldn't use a cuddle from time to time—especially from Mr. Whiskers, Tiger, or Bubbles?" The gamer is then invited to "Come and enjoy the incredible cuteness and potential for big wins in *OMG! Kittens*," thereby explicitly invoking the affective potential of cuteness in the solicitation of the consumer.

Importantly, moreover, because this interface on various platforms is themed around kittens, it falls in with the tradition of cute domesticated animals in television shows and movies, as well as intertextual cultural forms such as cute cat memes and the extremely popular genre of YouTube cat videos. Wittkower argues that cuteness is a dominant aesthetic of digital culture, one result of which is the importance of cats as an important trope in online cultures and a *de facto* cute species, while domestic felines have inspired numerous memes, videos, and remixes that are now commonplace in participatory and fandom cultures.

The Internet has generated and promoted feline celebrities such as Grumpy Cat who became a highly replicable meme after his photo was posted on Reddit in 2012, and who has now become a transnational brand, complete with merchandise such as clothes, calendars, books, and apps.

In a discussion of YouTube cat videos, Radha O'Meara points out that feline representations in media are polysemic and "seem to emphasize [cats'] sociability with humans, association with domestic space, independence and aloofness, and intelligence and secretiveness." Thematically, *OMG! Kittens* communicates with these now common tropes in online and digital media cultures and publics, reframing them as they are incorporated into gaming machines by emphasizing their association with domestic space. Here again, gambling is camouflaged as a safe, homey form of entertainment and as an emotional experience that involves love and care. Therefore, through the procedural rhetoric of cat cuteness, domestic space bleeds into the gambling interface during play.

In terms of scope and impact, one should bear in mind that *OMG! Kittens* is available in land venues, through the web, and on mobile platforms, so that it has the potential to permeate the gambler's everyday life by colonizing spaces previously foreign to gambling activities. Where mobile devices are concerned, there is a radical rearticulation of the place of gambling in the rhythms of the everyday. Gerard Goggin and I argue that:

> As devices that aspire to encourage intensive real-time gameplay, the expansion of the mobile gaming industry has allowed for a translation of brick-and-mortar gambling, as well as online gambling, into mobile screens characterized by ubiquity, personalization, and sociability. The player does not go to the casino, but carries the casino around in their pocket. (103)

In *OMG! Kittens*, these effects are heightened with player-customized accompanying music as well as endearing meows and purrs when the rolls spin, all of which contribute to the gambler's emotional involvement with the game's furry characters.

The implicit game narrative of *OMG! Kittens* suggests moreover that, by winning and losing, the player is succeeding or failing in caring for the kittens. Indeed, the official promotional video for *OMG! Kittens* foregrounds this caregiving aspect, describing the game as "cute and cuddly" (WMS Gaming), thereby intentionally coopting cuteness as a means of seducing players and encouraging continuous play. The industry mobilizes such mechanisms in a variety of other cute gamble-play platforms and, in digital slots, animals are positioned as endearing beings that need to be nurtured through play. As the player spends more time and money on the gambling experience, these animals become more animated. By spending, losing, and occasionally winning money, the gambler extends the relationship with these cute digital pets. Therefore, cuteness is instrumental in invoking the need to nurture and the pleasure of social engagement with cute objects, which then turns into a motivation for gambling, just as it does in other digital games in the vein of the classic 1990s stand-alone device Tamagotchi, an electronic "pet," and the mobile app *Neko Atsume*, a 2014 Japanese cat-collecting game.

Haptic Cuteness

In case of platforms such as Tamagotchi and *Neko Atsume*, players need to keep their pets alive by routinely feeding and entertaining them. These games require constant play, which becomes routinized. When these routinized, and eventually ritualized, nurturing behaviors are incorporated into gambling procedures, concerns over intensified consumption gain renewed currency. And this is why cuteness matters: design choices in slot machines have ceased to be purely decorative, if indeed such choices were ever entirely about decoration, and have become an integral part of the procedural rhetoric apparatus.

Andreas Reckwitz's definition of practice helps to frame the way in which game platforms may encourage an emotional involvement with digital entities. Reckwitz argues that a practice

> is *a routinized* type of behavior which consists of several elements, interconnected to one another: forms of bodily activities, forms of mental activities, "things" and their use, a background knowledge in the form of understanding, know-how, states of emotion, and motivational knowledge. (249)

Gambling in cute platforms involves bodily activities (clicking, excreting hormones while anxiously awaiting outcomes, the positive affective reaction to the characters' cuteness); mental activities (calculating the odds and processing the information displayed on the reels); "things" such as platforms and devices, and "background knowledge" of the rules of the game and the nuances of each specific slot. These factors combined give rise to a spectrum of states of emotion, ranging from hope to expectation, caring, and sociality to perhaps disappointment.

Cuteness is particularly relevant, therefore, when discussing the bodily activities involved in different forms of gambling. There are physiological explanations of how bodies respond to gambling and further studies could be conducted to help us to understand how the affective states triggered by cuteness affect bodies while in a gambling session. Gerhard Meyer et al., for example, measured the neuroendocrine response to gambling among both problem and non-problem gamblers. In their sample group, both heart rate and the levels of the stress hormone norepinephrine increased during a blackjack session. Dopamine levels were significantly higher in problem gamblers while cortisol levels increased in both groups. The researchers concluded that casino gambling induces the activation of the HPA-axis and the sympathoadrenergic system. Similarly, a study conducted by Edelgard Wulfert et al. to measure the physical response of gamblers concluded that "the experiment yielded evidence that the participants became significantly more physiologically aroused during a horse race when they expected to win money than when they simply predicted the outcome of the race without wagering" (314).

Research on cuteness, on the other hand, has focused on how quickly and robustly cute objects capture attention and interest (Hildebrandt and Fitzgerald; Kringelbach et al.; Lobmaier et al.; Sprengelmeyer et al.). Further studies have shown that exposure to cute images increases caring behavior while narrowing the focus of attention (Nittono et al.; Sherman et al.). Thus, the heightened sense of engagement with gambling that is fostered by the recent introduction of cuteness into the activity that I am calling gamble-play combines with the orientation to chance and excitement that gambling involves to make this activity even more compelling and exciting.

The fact that the *OMG! Kittens* terrestrial slot machine emphasizes cuteness as a factor to draw gamblers into the game is reflected in players' reviews. In *TripAdvisor* forums, for example, the slot machine is described as "such a cute game" (summervacation07), while forum users admit that the game does not give the best payouts, but is attractive because of its theme which, as I have been arguing, exploits cuteness as an aesthetic as well as a rhetorical tool to intensify gamer engagement with the interface and the activity. Moreover, the fact that SG Interactive has launched two spin-off titles, *OMG! Kittens Safari* and *OMG! Puppies* to expand the reach of this theme suggests that cuteness, as a marketing strategy in the EGM market, is effective enough to support further development.

Furthermore, while *OMG! Kittens Safari* features cute wildcat kittens and safari-related objects such as hats, jeeps, and binoculars (as opposed to the milk cartons and yarn of the original game), it adds a further rhetorical and aesthetic twist that accords well with cuteness. This sequel plays off of another important trope in slot machine design, namely the use of *exotica* and postcolonial imagery to create image universes that need to be conquered (see Albarrán-Torres). The term "exotica" may be used to describe the discursive practice of making other cultures seem like strange, foreign curiosities, often framing them as obscure objects of desire. Exotic slot machine design stimulates play by providing a familiar representation of the unfamiliar: a return to domesticity which, in this case, is enabled by tropes of cuteness.

The title *OMG! Kittens Safari*, moreover, caters mainly to an English-speaking, Global North audience, for which foreign lands, animals, and characters are understood as entities that can, and should, be tamed. Seen in this light, gambling becomes a colonizing and domesticating activity. As I have noted elsewhere slot machines such as *More Chilli*, *Jackpot Catcher*, *5 Dragons*, and *Mystic Panda* reflect a particular world view structured and shaped by class and ethnicity (Albarrán-Torres).[1] Riches are paired with the conquest of other cultures and territories through missions. Furthermore, the gambler is encouraged to feel in control in what Gerda Reith has called an "island of time," wherein "each round is a self-contained island in time, existing independently of what came before or what will come after" (*Age* 136). This sense of mastery over the outcome is ephemeral as the player generally walks away from a gambling session as a loser.

From Kittens to Pandas and Farmyards

The widely popular terrestrial device *Wild Panda*, another notable cute gambling platform, is produced by Aristocrat of Australia. This machine deploys a combination of cute and "exotic" elements that are key in the design of other gamble-play platforms such as *Love of the Nile* and *Gypsy*. In its reels, *Wild Panda* displays traditional symbols of luck in Chinese culture, such as goldfish, potted bamboo plants, and lotus flowers. By using designs that combine cuteness with these Chinese charms, Aristocrat slot designers perform a kind of cultural appropriation that is common in slot design, as we have seen. In this case, however, this cultural appropriation works as an attractive feature for the groups whose culture is being appropriated. Aristocrat's CEO Jamie Odell explains the corporate rationale behind these design choices:

> Many Asian people love gambling, but the great games there look and feel like Asian games: the graphics, the language, even the sounds. Lucky dragons are common themes in Macau as are Chinese character symbols like "good fortune." (Odell qtd. in Kelly)

By incorporating Asian themes in slot machine design, and using cuteness as a rhetorical tool, Aristocrat markets this product to both Western and Asian publics in gambling hubs such as Las Vegas and Macau. *Wild Panda* also appeals to a sense of *ke'ai*, a Chinese concept that is "usually translated as cute or cuteness" but "literally means 'lovable' or 'adorable'" and "is embodied in a person, animal or small object that arouses feelings of pity, tenderness, and a desire to take care of it" (Chuang 21). This strategy likewise replicates proven Hollywood formulas, such as DreamWorks's *Kung-Fu Panda* franchise, which have generated enormous profits in domestic and international markets. (Pandas of course maintain a notable centrality in economies of cuteness.)

The last of my examples is *Crazy Farm Race*, produced by SkillOnNet. This online slot machine showcases images of a stereotypical North American farm, hence during play reels showcasing pumpkins, goats, cows, turkeys, and pigs roll frenetically on the screen as country music plays. This particular strategy for taming the gaming experience, or making it appear to be more anodyne, recalls Sianne Ngai's framing of cuteness as a form of the pastoral. As she writes, cuteness is linked to this genre because it is "a style that speaks to our desire for a simpler, more intimate relation to our commodities" (31). Furthermore, although its theme is quite culturally specific, *Crazy Farm Race* appeals to ideas of cuteness made global through the expansion of US media and products such as cartoons, video games, children's literature, and consumer product packaging illustrated with animals and country scenes. Indeed, such imagery is so effective and globally recognizable that idealized versions of North American country life and its modes of production are now part of a classic theme in online slots and freemium games (games that are free to play but require payment for heightened gaming experiences) such as Zynga's *Farmville*, the highly popular Chinese game *Happy Farm*, and *Crazy Farm Race*.

In these games, moreover, the domestication of animals also works to promote the gaming experience as a return to a more "natural" rhythm, framed as a respite from the intensities of modern life. In *Crazy Farm Race* just as in *Farmville*, animals are anthropomorphized and rendered with human-like qualities and ethics such as camaraderie, solidarity, and hard work. This theme is reinforced by the developer's promotion of *Crazy Farm Race* through backstory: "Once upon a time, there was a farm in a green forest. Lots of happy animals were living in it. One day, for no apparent reason, they decided to organize a race. Don't ask why but we would bet on the piggy—it looks like the fastest one.

FIGURE 12.2 In *Crazy Farm Race* the domestication of animals works to promote the gaming experience as a return to a more "natural" rhythm, framed as a respite from the intensities of modern life.

You beg to differ?" Here, cuteness is anchored in the domestication of animals and control over nature, a prevalent trope in gambling machine design, while the simple but compelling backstory also references gambling, and constitutes an in-game game based on sports betting. The narrative also echoes the racing video game genre, which is highly popular among casual gamers, as evidenced by the commercial success of classic games such as *Mario Kart* for Nintendo's Wii platform. At least symbolically, therefore, the gambler is "competing" in two events at once (with double the opportunity to win): the animal race and the slots. However, while the machine and the game are designed to provide the illusion of control, the gambler, of course, has no real agency in either the in-game or the payouts.

Conclusion: So What if Gambling Machines are Cute?

The infantilization of gambling through cuteness is a powerful rhetorical tool that makes gambling look childish and innocent, and this strategy has greatly contributed to its cultural normalization. In this chapter I have studied the effectiveness of cuteness as an agent in normalizing gambling while producing affect in gamblers and potential gamblers. As I argued, the gaming industries, which are in constant need of maintaining and growing their consumer bases, now employ cuteness as an aesthetic skin for gambling interfaces in an effort to disguise the nature of their offering, by rendering it cute and seemingly anodyne. Importantly, however, while various forms of interactive media produce certain affects and effects in our lives, digital gambling can have deep and long-lasting repercussions in the lives of users that are, in various ways, perhaps more dire. Even though implying that everyone who consumes gambling products is at risk of experiencing compulsive play is certainly unfounded, it is no secret that machines are carefully designed to encourage continuous engagement. Hence, as I have also explained, numerous practices such as the addition of cute aesthetics are deployed to achieve deep gamer engagement through what Schüll has fittingly called "addiction by design" (2012).

The global expansion of the slot machine industry since the 1980s and 1990s has been aided by the cultural normalization of all forms of gambling, which in turn is achieved through rhetorical tools such as the use of cuteness and Hollywood brands in the design of gambling machines (Reith 5; Mazur 53–54). Reith has argued that by borrowing marketing and branding strategies from other industries, transnational operators have broken into the middle-class market, thus establishing modes of consumption previously unrelated to wagering. She claims that, as a cultural practice, gambling has "widened to include, for the first time, the middle class—the group traditionally most hostile to all forms of gambling— in a move that has finally 'normalized' the activity" ("Gambling" 35). Given the cultural normalization and expansion of the gambling industry, it is important to study the types of affects triggered by play. In cute slots, the boundary between the self and cute others, between the interface and the gambler's internalized sense of domesticity, is increasingly blurred in ways that have and will continue to have a tremendous impact on our daily lives.

Note

1   On *Jackpot Catcher* and the Native American theme, see Nicoll.

Works Cited

Albarrán-Torres, César. "Gambling-Machines and the Automation of Desire." *Platform: Journal of Media and Communication* 5.1 (2013): 34–51. Online. 29 May 2016.

Albarrán-Torres, César, and Gerard Goggin. "Mobile Social Gambling: Poker's Next Frontier." *Mobile Media and Communication* 2.1 (2014): 94–109.

Ancona, Jorge. "Microgaming Signs Deal to Develop *Jurassic Park* Online Slots Games." *OnlineCasino.Org.* 1 Feb. 2014. Online. 29 May 2016.

Bogost, Ian. *Persuasive Games: The Expressive Power of Videogames.* Cambridge, MA: MIT Press, 2010.

Casino Bedava. "CasinoBedava'dan *Crazy Farm Race* Slot Oyunu Tanıtımı." Online video clip. *YouTube.* YouTube, 4 May 2015. Online. 29 May 2016.

Chuang, Tzu-I. "The Power of Cuteness." *Stanford Journal of East Asian Affairs* 5 (2005): 21–28.

Cross, Gary. *The Cute and the Cool: Wondrous Innocence and Modern American Children's Culture.* New York: Oxford University Press, 2004.

Devol, G.H. *Forty Years a Gambler in the Mississippi.* Cincinnati, OH: Devol and Haines, 1887.

Findlay, John M. *People of Chance: Gambling in American Society from Jamestown to Las Vegas.* New York: Oxford University Press, 1986.

Genosko, Gary. "Natures and Cultures of Cuteness." *Invisible Culture* 9 (2005). Online. 29 May 2016.

Gephart, Robert P. "Safe Risk in Las Vegas." *M@n@gement* 4.3 (2001): 141–58.

Griffiths, Mark. "Fruit Machine Gambling: The Importance of Structural Characteristics." *Journal of Gambling Studies* 9.2 (1993): 101–20.

Guattari, Felix. *Chaosmosis: An Ethico-Aesthetic Paradigm.* Trans. Paul Bains and Julian Pefanis. Sydney: Power, 1995.

Hildebrandt, K. A,. and Fitzgerald, H. E. "Adults' Responses to Infants Varying in Perceived Cuteness." *Behavioral Processes* 3 (1978): 159–72.

Hing, Nerilee, and Helen Breen. "Profiling Lady Luck: An Empirical Study of Gambling and Problem Gambling amongst Female Club Members." *Journal of Gambling Studies* 17.1 (2001): 47–69.

——. "A Profile of Gaming Machine Players in Clubs in Sydney, Australia." *Journal of Gambling Studies* 18.2 (2002): 185–205.

Humphreys, Ashlee, and Latour, Kathryn A. "Framing the Game: Assessing the Impact of Cultural Representations on Consumer Perceptions of Legitimacy." *Journal of Consumer Research* 40.4 (2013): 773–95.

Joint Select Committee on Gambling Reform. Precommitment Schemes. *Parliament of Australia.* 1 Feb. 2011. Online. 23 Jan. 2016.

Kelly, Ross. "Aristocrat Leisure Hopes its Bets Pay Off." *Wall Street Journal Online*. Dow Jones, 25 Aug. 2013. Online. 29 May 2016.

Kringelbach, Morten L. et al. "A Specific and Rapid Neural Signature for Parental Instinct." *PLoS ONE* 3.2 (2008). Online. 15 May 2016.

Lears, Jackson. *Something for Nothing: Luck in America*. New York: Penguin, 2004.

Lee, Timothy Jeonglyeol. "Distinctive Features of the Australian Gambling Industry and Problems Faced by Australian Women Gamblers." *Tourism Analysis* 14.6 (2009): 867–76.

Lobmaier, Janek S., Reiner Sprengelmeyer, Ben Wiffen, and David I. Perrett. "Female and Male Responses to Cuteness, Age, and Emotion in Infant Faces." *Evolution and Human Behavior* 31.1 (2010): 16–21.

Lorenz, Konrad. "Part and Parcel in Human and Animal Societies." 1950. *Studies in Animal and Human Behavior, Vol. 2*. Trans. Robert Martin. Cambridge, MA: Harvard University Press, 1971. 115–95.

Mazur, Joseph. *What's Luck Got to Do With It?: The History, Mathematics, and Psychology of the Gambler's Illusion*. Princeton, NJ: Princeton University Press, 2010.

McGandy, Ashlee. "How You Name It Matters: 'Gambling' vs. 'Gaming.'" *Cornell Chronicle*. 15 Oct. 2013. Online. 8 June 2016.

Merish, Lori. "Cuteness and Commodity Aesthetics: Tom Thumb and Shirley Temple." *Freakery: Cultural Spectacles of the Extraordinary Body*. Ed. Rosemarie Garland-Thomson. New York: New York University Press, 1996. 185–203.

Meyer, Gerhard, Jan Schwertfeger, Michael S. Exton, Onno Eilard Janssen, Wolfram Knapp, Michael A. Stadler, Manfred Schedlowski, and Tillmann Kruger. "Neuroendocrine Response to Casino Gambling in Problem Gamblers." *Psychoneuroendocrinology* 29.10 (2004): 1272–80.

Ngai, Sianne. *Our Aesthetic Categories: Zany, Cute, Interesting*. Cambridge, MA: Harvard University Press, 2012.

Nicoll, Fiona Jean. "Indian Dreaming: Iconography of the Zone/Zones of Iconography." *Continuum* 28.6 (2014): 835–49.

Nittono, Hiroshi, Michiko Fukushima, Akihiro Yano, and Hiroki Moriya. "The Power of *Kawaii*: Viewing Cute Images Promotes a Careful Behavior and Narrows Attentional Focus." *PLoS ONE* 7.9 (2012). Online. 30 Dec. 2014.

O'Meara, Radha. "Do Cats Know They Rule YouTube? Surveillance and the Pleasures of Cat Videos." *M/C Journal* 17.2 (2014). Online. 29 May 2016.

Palmeri, Christopher, Daniele Lepido, and Cornelius Rahn. "Gtech Agrees to Acquire Slot-Machine Maker IGT for $4.7 Billion." *Bloomberg*. Bloomberg, 16 July 2014. Online. 29 May 2016.

Parke, Jonathan, and Mark Griffiths. "The Psychology of the Fruit Machine: The Role of Structural Characteristics (Revisited)." *International Journal of Mental Health and Addiction* 4.2 (2006): 151–79.

Parliamentary Joint Select Committee on Gambling Reform. First Report: The Design and Implementation of a Mandatory Pre-Commitment System for Electronic Gaming Machines. Canberra: Commonwealth of Australia, 2011. Online. 23 Jan. 2016.

Reckwitz, Andreas. "Toward a Theory of Social Practices a Development in Culturalist Theorizing." *European Journal of Social Theory* 5.2 (2002): 243–63.

Reith, Gerda. *The Age of Chance: Gambling in Western Culture*. London: Routledge, 1999.

——. "Gambling and the Contradictions of Consumption: A Genealogy of the 'Pathological' Subject." *American Behavioral Scientist* 51.1 (2007): 33–55.

Schüll, Natasha Dow. *Addiction by Design: Machine Gambling in Las Vegas*. Princeton, NJ: Princeton University Press, 2012.

Sherman, Gary D., Jonathan Haidt, and James A. Coan. "Viewing Cute Images Increases Behavioral Carefulness." *Emotion* 9.2 (2009): 282–86.

Sherman, Gary D., and Jonathan Haidt. "Cuteness and Disgust: The Humanizing and Dehumanizing Effects of Emotion." *Emotion Review* 3.3 (2011): 245–251.

Sprengelmeyer, Reiner, Jennifer Lewis, Amanda Hahn, and David I. Perrett. "Aesthetic and Incentive Salience of Cute Infant Faces: Studies of Observer Sex, Oral Contraception, and Menstrual Cycle." *PLoS ONE* 8.5 (2013). Online. 15 May 2016.

summervacation07. "OMG Kittens, What Casino's Have This Machine?" Las Vegas Travel Forum. *Tripadvisor*. TripAdvisor, 22 Sept. 2014. Online. 11 Sept. 2016.

Thomas, Samantha L., Sophie Lewis, Colin McLeod, and John Haycock. "'They are Working Every Angle': A Qualitative Study of Australian Adults' Attitudes Towards, and Interactions with, Gambling Industry Marketing Strategies." *International Gambling Studies* 12.1 (2012): 111–27.

Wittkower, Dylan E. "On the Origins of the Cute as a Dominant Aesthetic Category in Digital Culture." *Putting Knowledge to Work and Letting Information Play*. Eds. Timothy W. Luke and Jeremy Hunsinger. Blacksburg, VA: Center for Digital Discourse and Culture, 2009. 212–30.

WMS Gaming. "5x4 Reels OMG Kittens!(tm) Slot Machine Demo by WMS Gaming." Online video Clip. *YouTube*. YouTube, 18 Feb. 2014. Online. 29 May 2016.

Wulfert, Edelgard, Brian D. Roland, Julie Hartley, Naitian Wang, and Christine Franco. "Heart Rate Arousal and Excitement in Gambling: Winners versus Losers." *Psychology of Addictive Behaviors* 19.3 (2005): 311–16.

Ziolkowski, S. "The World Count of Gaming Machines 2013." *Gaming Technologies Association* (2014). Online. 29 May 2016.

13

UNDER THE YOLK OF CONSUMPTION

Re-Envisioning the Cute as Consumable

Nadia de Vries

Introduction

The colloquial expression "you're so cute, I could just eat you up" may seem bizarre or paradoxical (why would one threaten to eat a loveable thing?), but it also suggests a particular relationship between the edible and the adorable that will be my concern in this chapter. If an object that is "too cute" incites a desire to consume, then cuteness somehow suggests a strange association with edibility, and this is routinely evidenced in many of the titles of cute-related listicles on websites like *Buzzfeed* and *Gizmodo* that metaphorically describe cute objects as "mouthwatering" or "diabetes-inducing."

Through advertising we have long been conditioned to associate the consumption of food with the inducements of the cute, in the forms of breakfast-cereal tigers and friendly yet frenetic anthropomorphized juice pitchers. Commonplace representations such as these suggest that the association of cute objects with comestibles is well-established, both as a semantic connotation and as a marketing trope. Furthermore, these long-running advertising campaigns for Frosted Flakes and Kool-Aid convert the prospect of aggression or disruption into the reassurance of the cute as a means of incentivizing food consumption.

In a 2015 Yale University study, psychologists observed aggressive behavior similar to the "so cute I could eat it up" reaction after exposing subjects to cute stimuli. The researchers noticed behavioral reactions such as "playful growling, squeezing, biting, and pinching" among the study's participants after showing them various images of infantile-looking children (Aragón et al. 260). Cuteness, it seems, dismantles our sense of composure and speaks to primal desires, and not necessarily to the "natural" impulse to protect the infantile, as some theories of cuteness suggest following Konrad Lorenz and his *Kindchenschema*, in which he maintains that cuteness acts as an innate releasing mechanism for caring behaviors. So, if there is something about cuteness that makes us, quite literally, want to *devour*, how exactly does cuteness trigger this desire for physical consumption?

Taking their cue from the enormous popularity of cute aesthetics in contemporary culture to which the current volume bears witness, Gergana Y. Nenkov and Maura L. Scott have attempted to unpack the strange, irresistible pull of cuteness in their work on cute products and indulgent consumption. In one particular experiment, these psychologists randomly distributed ice cream scoops to sixty participants. Some participants received a "neutral" ice cream scoop, while others received a "whimsically cute" one, shaped to resemble a little girl (329). The participants were then asked to scoop themselves a bowl of vanilla ice cream. The experiment's results showed that participants not only scooped more enthusiastically with the "cute" scoop (over two ounces more per bowl), but that the participants with the "cute" scoop actually ate more of the ice cream as well: nearly two ounces more. These results, Nenkov and Scott contend, confirm the hypothesis that "[e]xposure to whimsically [. . .] cute stimuli increases indulgent consumption" (329). Of course it would be injudicious to pin down the cause of a primary affective response based on one study alone, and indeed, it is precisely the aim of this collection to provide an interdisciplinary study of cuteness from a range of perspectives in order to deepen understanding of this ubiquitous aesthetic and its affects. That said, however, Nenkov and Scott's research does support a commonly-held belief, namely that cuteness, above all things, is a commodity aesthetic.

Cute products, anthropologist Anne Allison argues, tap into "a business of enchanted commodities" ("Enchanted" 16). Such commodities, encompassing everything from toys, backpacks, and wristwatches to lunch boxes, bread, and snacks, all feed "a consumer fetishism" that disseminates "an aura of fancy and make-believe" (Allison 16). By giving a product the whimsical and comforting qualities of cuteness (by shaping an ice cream scoop like a little girl, for example), the product in question achieves an "aura," as Allison puts it, of attractive fantasy. This aura then establishes a certain closeness between the product and its consumer: an intimacy between the "fanciness" of the cute object and the imagination of the person who consumes it (Allison 17). Cute objects, in other words, open up a pleasurable world of make-believe that satisfies the consumer's desire for an out-of-the-ordinary product experience, while cuteness also serves as a means of product differentiation. Making a product cute, therefore, is also a means of appealing to this consumer fetishism for the dainty, the intimate, and the extraordinary, and implying, as Ngai has suggested, that cute objects are eminently buyable and amenable to the consumer's desires (18; 64).

Lori Merish, in her oft-cited essay on cuteness and commodity aesthetics, also comments on the cute's potential (its fate, really) as a commodity. "The aesthetic of cuteness," Merish argues, "courts consumer empathy, generating a structure of emotional response that assimilates consumption into the logic of adoption"

(187). Merish argues that we do not simply buy cute things: rather, by "adopting" a cute object, we inadvertently take it upon ourselves to care for the object in question, to become its guardian, its "parent," in a sense. We may exercise this self-imposed responsibility of care through an object-directed covetousness, such as we display when handling cute toys and dolls as Joyce Goggin argues here in her chapter on the diminutive Kiddle dolls of the 1960s. We may also, however, covet a cute thing so much that we literally want to consume it, a desire that may be at least partially satisfied by the many sweets and snacks that are specifically designed to resemble cute characters and precious-looking animals.

By taking a cute object and putting it on our dinner plate, our status as "consumers" of the cute becomes profoundly complicated. This is not just the case in the East where Japanese rice balls known as *onigiri* are shaped to resemble panda bears, but also in the West when we decorate our pancakes to make them look like smiling faces; there is something submissive, something small, diminutive, and yes, cute, about many of the objects we choose to eat. "Eating and consuming," Astrid Lorange writes, "bear witness to the contradiction in wanting to savor *and* possess something" (93) and again, the cute consumable asks us to engage with the common expression that an object may be so cute that we just want to "eat it up." When something is extravagantly precious we often want to close the distance between ourselves and that object—we want to hold the object close. And what better way is there to be close to a cute object than to physically consume it?

I recognize and distinguish between various types of cute consumables in this chapter. One type is the cute *object*, by which I mean all cute items that are targeted towards a consumer market such as Hello Kitty, that ubiquitous cute icon who, in Christine Yano's colorful idiom, made a trek across the Pacific to become the leading figure in what she has called "pink globalization." More central to my argument, however, is the "cute-ified" *food object*, by which I refer to everyday food items shaped to look like cute objects such as the aforementioned panda bear-shaped *onigiri* rice ball, and the cute *food character*, that is, popular characters and mascots that physically represent a food object rather than advertising one, such as Gudetama, an anthropomorphized egg yolk with almost 700,000 Twitter followers, mainly in Japan. These aesthetic practices work together to promote or indeed to embody commodities in different ways operating on comparable levels of consumption and desire and highlight the new psychological complexity represented by food in an economy of the cute. In what follows, I will focus largely on Gudetama and Japan as the country whose national food culture most evocatively illustrates various aspects of my argument. In Japan, the relationship between cuteness and edibility stems from deep sociocultural formations—from artistic tradition, social custom, and cultural history—and this chapter will also address some of these important factors.

In this chapter, I will also look at the ways in which food products have been presented as icons of aesthetic cuteness in contemporary commerce, along with the tendency to "cute-ify" food products, based on Sianne Ngai's theory of cuteness as a commodity aesthetic and its relation to object domination. In so doing, I will outline the cultural transgression of the cute consumable in relation to Japan's historical *kawaii* food aesthetic, focusing particularly on the case of the aforementioned Japanese egg yolk character Gudetama as one particularly rich and evocative example. *Kawaii* is a national aesthetic in its own right, distinct from the more general cute aesthetics explored by most chapters in this volume. Yet the two are connected through the affects of cuteness that inform both aesthetics (see also the chapter by Joshua Paul Dale in this volume). This affiliation also allows me to explore some possible connections to the present-day Western cute food culture.[1] Whether in the form of product ranges that hold cute consumables at their center or transnational food crazes fetishizing diminutive edibles whose acquisition and consumption function as a display of taste and status, food speaks of the self in powerful ways, often indexing the desires of the middle class not only as consumers, but also as workers in the precarious work environments characteristic of neoliberal capitalist regimes: workplaces whose increasing demands are making many workers feel consumed by their jobs.

By analyzing the commercial popularity and the particular appeal of the indolent, grumpy Gudetama character, I want to explore how affective responses to cute consumables interlock with the consumption of commodities at the socioeconomic level. Produced by Sanrio, the creator of Hello Kitty, Gudetama is a "character" in the same mode as the famous cat with no mouth: that is, its image adorns various products for sale. However, unlike Hello Kitty, Gudetama varies its facial expression and speaks. Furthermore, in an era in which we expect so much of our food, Gudetama flips the equation of desire, displaying peevishness and resentment along with a constant demand for attention. A character popular among office workers, Gudetama provides a fantasy of resistance that is attractive to the same degree it is unattainable to workers in the situation of economic precarity outlined in Chapter 1 of this volume. Gudetama represents an interesting twist on the use of cuteness within the power relations of neoliberal economies because, as shown below, adult workers see themselves in this "bad egg." As Yano points out, Sanrio positioned Hello Kitty as a global product from the beginning. Below, I outline the early signs that Gudetama may have enough cross-cultural appeal to become part of the transnational spread of *kawaii* (cute) goods and images that Yano terms "pink globalization" (6).

Cute Foods in Japanese Culture

Before turning to an analysis of particular instances of food-inspired cuteness, let us first take a step back and consider the aesthetic relationship between cuteness and food in a more general, cultural sense. In Japanese culture, in particular, cuteness and food reside in a profound historiocultural relationship with one another. According to designer and animator Miko Kato, "simplicity, irregularity, and perishability" comprise the key features of traditional Japanese aesthetics. It is this interest in perishability, Kato adds, that largely explains the Japanese tendency to aestheticize "ephemeral" objects, like flowers or food. In other words, just like a bouquet of roses, a slice of cheesecake is only enjoyable, that is, fit for consumption, for a limited period of time and is, therefore, ephemeral. This appreciation of ephemerality in Japanese aesthetics, in turn, helps to clarify the Japanese perspective on cuteness, particularly when one understands Japanese cuteness as an aesthetic category that is meant to have a limited shelf-life, as it were. By way of example, Kato notes that:

> [the c]herry blossom is known for its short blooming period, and this fleeting quality makes it more special to the Japanese. But when I heard about a British man who tattooed his ankle with a miniature version of Hello Kitty, I suddenly felt very foreign. A Japanese person may apply a Hello Kitty [temporary ink transfer] tattoo sticker because Hello Kitty is a product to consume temporarily. Stickers are cheap, and new styles are introduced seasonally. They are valued because of their ephemeral quality.

Traditional Japanese aesthetics, therefore, often entail that the cute object be enjoyed for a short time only. From this perspective, cute objects are quite similar to sweet treats in that they are short-lived pleasures, and their consumers know that it is only a matter of time before the object in question is replaced by some other, more novel cute thing. In a sense, the Japanese regard for cute objects as Kato describes already foreshadows the fate of the cute as a commodified product that is easily replaceable or perishable, as are many food products.

Though Kato's description of cuteness and ephemerality helps to elucidate the cultural relationship between cuteness and food, it does not capture the peculiar tendency to anthropomorphize food products to the extent that they become agents of cuteness themselves. As Eric C. Rath notes, this aesthetic tendency may be traced back to a culinary shift that occurred at the midpoint of Japan's Edo period (1603–1868), at which time "amusement (*asobi*)" began to be favored over "the [actual] technicalities of food preparation" (119). Food, as such, began to be seen as a source of pleasure rather than a primary necessity alone. This new, hedonistic interest in food is also manifested in Japanese art, hence Utagawa Kuniyoshi's Edo-period painting *The Shakkyo Dance* (1845), which bears testimony to Japan's tradition of food and cuteness (see Figure 13.1).

In Utagawa's painting, an anthropomorphized ear of corn is depicted as partaking in a traditional dance ceremony, its stalk folded like an elegant robe, and its tassel resembling a full mane of pinkish hair. The painting parodies the solemnity usually associated with ceremonial proceedings, while the comedic aesthetic style that Utagawa's painting evokes was common in the artistically fruitful Edo period, which also spawned the popular *kabuki* performance genre and the drama-driven style of puppeteering known as *bunraku* (Banham 561). Therefore,

Utagawa's painting illustrates that, in Japan, images of whimsically-depicted food characters had already begun providing pleasure for their human consumers as early as the mid-nineteenth century.

Over the past ten years, loveable foods have surged as popular curiosities, both in Japan and beyond. From the early 2000s onwards, the stationery company San-X has released a range of product lines centered on cute "food characters," from the overzealous Amagurichan (a chestnut with a deep desire to be eaten) to Kogepan, a burnt piece of bread that laments its inedibility after being toasted for too long. Unlike animal-derived characters such as Hello Kitty, which are also frequently featured on food items like candies and soda bottles, Amagurichan and Kogepan and other food characters actually represent everyday food items, much like the German gummy bear. What is more, these characters are not only made to resemble food as a means of establishing familiarity with the consumers that covet them. Food characters like Amagurichan and Kogepan also behave like food products—that is, the product packaging and online comics that feature them also depict them as having a deep desire to be eaten. Unlike the globally popular Hello Kitty or the Netherlands's Miffy the rabbit, Kogepan is neither depicted nor described as a little girl (or boy, for that matter): it is, quite literally,

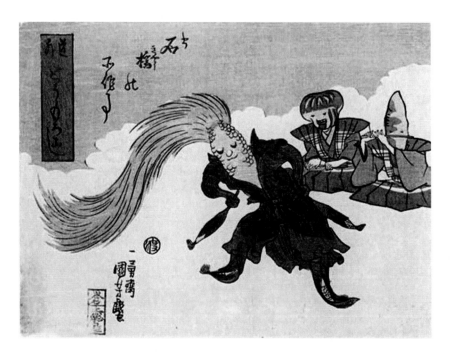

FIGURE 13.1 Utagawa Kuniyoshi's *The Shakkyo Dance* (1845) depicts anthropomorphized, cute edible vegetables in traditional dance costumes.

Source: Reproduced by permission of William Pearl

a piece of bread that regrets being unpalatable to consumers. The imagined "backstories" of these food characters, as presented on their official websites, explain their strong wish to actualize as tasty consumables. Part of what makes these San-X characters cute, then, is that they want to be eaten—they do not object to our "aggressive" desire to consume.

Cute Foods in Japanese Commerce

Characters like Amagurichan and Kogepan are so popular, in fact, that they are frequently featured on all kinds of merchandise ranging from wallets to socks, hairclips to pencil cases. Ironically, however, in Japan, some similar food-related characters are just as popular as the actual food products upon which their design is based. Anpanman (from *anpan*, meaning "red bean pastry"), the eponymous protagonist from Takashi Yanase's popular manga (1968–2013) and anime series (1988–), is a successful children's character that also appears on products marketed to adults, such as soy sauce, instant ramen, and other savory foods. Culinary accessories like food cutters, rice ball shapes, and lunchboxes as well as cutlery are also available with Anpanman's friendly face incorporated into their design. Thus in Japan, where cute food has been popular with adults and children alike since the Edo period, cute food mascots are prevalent in adult-marketed foods like coffee, wine, and savory seasonings for rice dishes just as they are in children's snacks (see Figure 13.2). "Cute consumables" are therefore more than just a ploy to coax young children into eating their vegetables, and Japanese adults have long enjoyed the association of cuteness and food: a license that has customarily been extended only to children in the West by figures ranging from the dancing and singing Fig Newton of the 1960s, to Animal Crackers and Fruit Roll-Ups today.

As Natalie Angier has argued, "whatever needs pitching, cute can help" because "the human cuteness detector is set at such a low bar" that people will fall for anything cute, including "a bobbing balloon, a big round rock stacked on a smaller rock, a colon, a hyphen and a close parenthesis typed in succession." In light of her analysis, it is not surprising to find that adults in the West are now also increasingly under the sway of the ability of cute foods (and other associated products) to "trespass" into the realm of all-ages commerce, signifying a relationship between the cute and the edible that is not dependent on the imaginary pursuits of children alone. Food brands now globally use cute mascots to target adults as well as children and the kind of juvenile culture that in Japan has long given adults access to cute foods is becoming increasingly popular in the West, due at least in part to what Christopher Noxon has termed the "rejuvenilization" of culture, whereby "a new breed of adult, identified by a determination to remain playful, energetic, and flexible in the face of adult responsibilities" has emerged (2).

FIGURE 13.2 Typically consisting of dried fish flakes, seaweed, and other savories to be sprinkled over cooked rice, this imported Anpanman *furikake* (seasoning mix) is available at a Japanese supermarket in Amsterdam.

Source: Photo by author

The trend of cute foods is proliferating globally (Whyman). As Elizabeth Nathanson writes, "In the 2000s, cupcakes became a global phenomenon with stores opening in cities from Dubai to Hong Kong, and cupcakes have been sold from storefronts, websites, and even ATMs" (251). Likewise, novelty pastries such the cro-nut, a donut-croissant hybrid, among other food crazes, market childish-sounding foods to adults in search of the latest food fads. In an article on that ubiquitous icon of all things juvenile, Hello Kitty, CNN's Sophia Yan enthusiastically writes about Kitty White's dominance on the global market, and her own collection of Hello Kitty kitchen utensils, including a frying pan and a kitchen knife, both of which are generally assumed to be manufactured for adult use. And this tendency is also visible in the internationally acclaimed Italian designs of Alessi and SMEG: Alessi's cute kitchen implements feature the "The Chin Family" line, designed in association with the National Palace Museum in Taiwan, while SMEG's colorful retro kitchen appliances sport rounded, neotenous shapes.

The significant position in the realm of contemporary commerce held by the cute consumable increasingly extends to contemporary labor. As argued in Chapter 1 of this book, cuteness inflects the workplace, as well as the concept of labor more generally. In her chapter here, Allison Page offers a lengthier reflection on the uses of cuteness in the neoliberal workplace. This relationship between labor and the cute likewise extends to food culture and this trend is particularly salient in Japan. In her article on the cute-ification of Japanese foods, Debra Occhi analyzes the progressive aestheticization—and cute-ification—of the Japanese lunch box, or *bento*.

Occhi argues that *bento* cookbooks published in the 1980s are focused primarily on making "difficult" foods, such as broccoli and liver, look more appealing to young children who might otherwise refuse to eat them. In cookbooks from the 1990s onward, however, Occhi detects a strong rise in the popularity of *kyaraben*: a *bento* practice that involves the parent who packs the lunch (usually the mother or grandmother) shaping foods into cute characters (*kyara*) such as Hello Kitty and Pokémon (64). While the practice of *kyaraben* significantly augments the aesthetic appeal of quotidian food products, thereby making the food in question more fun to eat, Occhi points out that *kyaraben* is also a highly labor-intensive practice that often requires hours of meticulous shaping and sculpting (70). The *kyaraben* practice thus helps to exemplify the connection between cuteness and emotional labor, but in a food-related context. Through its combination of high-precision cooking techniques and the depiction of adorable characters, *kyaraben* embodies both the soft comfort of cuteness, as well as the intensified immaterial labor that neoliberalism demands. Because of the substantial investment of domestic labor and time that *kyaraben* requires, the animal-shaped rice balls and egg rolls that signify the practice are not a "cute fix" equally accessible to everyone. Occhi details her experience with a preschool in her area that "banned the practice [of *kyaraben*]" after children with mothers who had less time to devote to food preparation, and who therefore produced less impressive *bento*, were teased and bullied (70).

Occhi emphasizes the economic tensions that underlie the practice of *kyaraben*, but also comments that "[i]n these neoliberal days in which people are seen all the more as products on offer in a precarious labor market, the necessity to shape a loveable persona is imperative. Shaping food as *kawaii* allows us to consume that aesthetic" (74). Though Occhi stresses that the cute-ification of food products comes with its own set of capitalist complications, demonstrated through the example of bullied preschoolers, she also recognizes the necessity to construct an appealing "self" for the consumption of others that a wealth-driven, social media-structured, market-minded neoliberal world puts forward. Mothers who devote time and effort to making cute *bento* lunchboxes for their children know that the consumption will take place in front of others, and this audience of other children and their teacher spurs them to perform their love for their child on the stage of the *bento* box. Here, consumption of cute food by the child signifies acceptance of both maternal love and effort. However, as Occhi's research indicates, there is a pushback by mothers and schools who resist the extra time and effort required to laboriously attach sesame seeds for eyes and tiny pieces of dried seaweed as eyebrows to make their child's favorite character come to life on a rice ball that will be immediately consumed. This kind of resistance to new forms of labor is epitomized by the character that is the focus of this chapter, Gudetama.

The Rise of Gudetama

Cute objects are enjoying an unprecedented rise in popularity, as the substantial proliferation of *kyaraben* meals in Japan, the global circulation of icons such as Hello Kitty and Miffy the rabbit, and the panoply of products and practices discussed in this volume help to demonstrate. Following this trend, Japanese toy company Sanrio of Hello Kitty fame has strategically branded a line of cute, food-themed characters, seemingly based on the notion that the combination of cuteness and food makes for attractive commodities to be aimed not only at the Japanese domestic market, but the global market as well. In 2013, the company held a food-related character poll in which consumers could vote for their favorite new product ranges. Voting options included Omu Omu, a panda-shaped

FIGURE 13.3 In the Sanrio video "I Hate Being Woken Up" (2014; English version 2015), Gudetama, in fried egg form, shivers on a breakfast plate, too lazy to cover itself with its bacon blanket.

rice ball, and Kirimi-chan, a benign-looking chunk of salmon, among other adorable delicacies. The most discussed character of the poll, however, was the unmotivated, melancholic egg yolk named Gudetama, which led (for a time) by a sizable margin.

Gudetama, as Jenn Harris describes it in the *LA Times*, is "a glob-like creature with arms and legs" that is "whiny" and "always has a face of despair" (Harris). In contrast to Sanrio's other, more effusive characters Hello Kitty and My Melody, Gudetama in no way resembles a furry animal bursting with energy and positivity. On the contrary, Gudetama is almost vaudevillian in its ongoing performance of sadness and disinterest, muttering gloomy catchphrases like "life is repetitive" and "I hate being woken up." Indeed it has been characterized as a "dark departure for Sanrio" (Hong and Steger). Gudetama distinctly differs from the kind of endearing, huggable adorability that we have come to associate with cute characters. It is, rather, a daily dose of gloom: a "bad egg" on our plates.

Though Gudetama did not end up winning Sanrio's character poll (that particular victory belonged to the aforementioned Kirimi-chan), Sanrio did not neglect to capitalize on consumer interest in it. In early 2014, Sanrio started posting short animations of Gudetama's uneventful activities on its official YouTube channel. Each animation lasts roughly 25 seconds, and is succeeded by a one-minute "dance" video in which a humanoid egg character performs a simple dance routine for the audience to follow. In the animations themselves, Gudetama is seen wallowing in its own egg white, cowering under a blanket of bacon (see Figure 13.3), or half-heartedly attempting some minor physical activity, such as reaching for a remote control or sipping coffee through a plastic straw. In keeping with Gudetama's "performance" as an unmotivated creature, it never actually manages to succeed in any of its more rigorous physical endeavors.

Since the release of Sanrio's Gudetama-themed YouTube animation series, the blobby egg has appeared on pencil sharpeners, backpacks, phone cases, and underwear. Sanrio also manufactures a wide selection of Gudetama plush toys, ranging from tiny keychains to massive dolls. In the toy company's very own theme park, "Puroland," guests can even visit a food court where various egg dishes covered in an edible film modeled after Gudetama's face are served, satisfyingly rendering their beloved Gudetama a comestible at long last ("Kirimi-chan").

While Sanrio's animations always depict the little egg in a food-related setting (a plate of bacon, a bowl of ramen, or a slice of bread), we never see Gudetama actually being eaten. As Gudetama is the "hero" of the animation series, this may not initially strike us as particularly strange. In the animations, however, Gudetama is nearly always depicted as being in the proximity of humans, and therefore perpetually on the verge of being consumed. In this sense, there is something oddly rebellious about Gudetama given that it is always close to human consumers, yet it defies them and the human antagonist never manages to take a bite. In spite of being a staple food, the little yolk does not seem to care about being eaten; indeed, in many episodes of the YouTube series, Gudetama tells its human, fork-wielding antagonists to "go away." It does not try to induce or seduce appetites like San-X's Amagurichan or Kogepan. While the latter characters' stories revolve around their displeasure, and their sadness in the case of Kogepan, that they are not being eaten or are simply inedible, Gudetama's narrative rarely speaks of its edibility and focuses instead on its lackluster nature. As a character, therefore, Gudetama does not necessarily "perform" edibility. Rather, it is a multidimensional character in the sense that it displays emotions and actions that always correspond to its own desires, and not so much the desires of its audience, its potential "consumers."

It is this last point that is key to my argument. Abject characters like burnt toast Kogepan make a bid for consumers' sympathy, appealing to workers who also feel abused by the process of their own manufacture; that is, as disposable units of production in neoliberal economies. Kogepan speaks to workers' feelings of being useless and unwanted as their efforts go unrewarded in comparison to the stable, long-term jobs that they believe used to be the norm. Gudetama's success is due to a different response: namely, empathy felt by consumers who feel that they themselves are consumed by the demands of the neoliberal, precarious workplace. Kogepan still yearns to be a productive worker, even if that desire leads to its being consumed.

Gudetama, on the other hand, has given up entirely. In some of Sanrio's animations, moreover, Gudetama is seen deliberately antagonizing its human consumers, thereby embodying the fantasy of escape from working environments that, in Japan as well as elsewhere, seem increasingly designed to eat *us* up. In the episode "Thought It Was Long," for example, Gudetama ties together the human's *udon* noodles out of boredom, making them impossible to eat, whereas in "Slipped Out," Gudetama jumps out of its human consumer's hands to go soak in a hot spring. As such, even in the rare instances where Gudetama functions as a food item true to its purpose or "nature," it chooses to resist this role immediately: behavior that resonates with the fans of this rebellious egg yolk who can only dream of this degree of resistance to one's role in adult society. The Sanrio designer who created Gudetama explains that "it reminded me of modern-day people," specifically the "*yutori*, or pressure-free generation of Japanese who tend to lack communication skills with other generations and to be passive" (Hongho and Seger).

Though Gudetama is presented as a stereotypically cute object, with its diminutive stature and frail, wobbly appearance, it refuses to be domesticated. It may be this particular trait that makes Gudetama so appealing to us in the first place. For a culturally domineering human audience, it is amusing to see objects outside of their allocated hierarchized roles—to see animals act like humans, or to see food objects behave as sentient beings. In this sense, there is something cruel or sadistic about our enjoyment of Gudetama. We know that it must, at some point, be consumed or otherwise disposed of and, as in Miko

Kato's description of ephemeral cute objects, Gudetama, the star of 25-second YouTube videos, is clearly a "perishable" object. We know that, as a character, it will never actualize as a "hero," but will remain a comedic food product until it spoils or is eaten: a sad fate that particularly resonates with today's beleaguered workers.

Dominating the Cute Consumable

In her study of cuteness and consumerism, Sianne Ngai argues that a sense of subject–object domination plays a key role in how we experience cuteness, and we, as consumers, are keen to subject everyday objects (like a piece of bread, or an egg) to our own desire for cuteness, a process that Ngai describes as "tenderization." As she argues, the act of "submitting [. . .] objects to a furious 'bubbling' that makes them 'soft' and 'tender'—more malleable, (ab)usable, and, as it were, cuter" is part of how we tend to project a certain state of "helplessness" onto the objects in which we recognize the potential for adorability (59). This helplessness may be achieved, for example, by anthropomorphizing the object in question, and rendering it somehow "lacking" or dysfunctional, as is the case with the misfortune of Kogepan's burnt body and the unproductivity of Gudetama's inveterate idleness. In her book, Ngai uses a frog-shaped sponge to demonstrate a more physical example of this tenderizing process. In one image, Ngai shows the sponge in its "neutral" state: a whimsical object in and of itself, but not yet particularly striking in terms of affect. In the second image, however, Ngai squeezes the sponge, thereby deforming the frog's "face," forcing it into a vulnerable and distraught expression. The sponge from the second image, Ngai argues, is cuter than the one in the first, as the sponge's newly-found deformity corresponds to "an aestheticization of powerlessness" that we identify as "cuteness" (64).

The definition of cuteness that Ngai posits, in which the cute object is categorized as cute due to its sheer powerlessness, establishes it as inherently submissive. The affective power of cuteness thus ironically remains unrealized until a dominant subject (i.e. the consumer, the "user" of the cute) recognizes the cute object's very *powerlessness*. When subjects relish a cute object's "weakness" in catering to their own aesthetic appetites, the full power of the object's cuteness is subsequently unleashed. What is particularly significant about this responsive relationship between the object and subject, however, is that the "servile" nature of the cute object is not perceived as an unattractive feature, but rather, as a contributing factor to the cute object's overall appeal. Ngai argues that

> [a] subject's latent awareness, as she coos at her cute object, that she may in fact be imposing [its] cuteness upon it is likely to *augment* rather than detract from her aesthetic experience of it as cute. [. . .] [T]he more

objectified the object, or the more visibly shaped by the affective demands and/or projections of the subject, the cuter [it becomes]. (65, emphasis mine)

It is thus this feature of weakness, the malleability that Ngai describes, that further amplifies the subject's interest in the cute object. Whereas a similar subjective weakness may be unwanted in objects that occupy a different aesthetic category, such as beauty or "coolness," the "weak" qualities of the cute object are not experienced as aesthetic flaws. Instead, the cute object's hierarchical inferiority reasserts its position as a consumable product: it is as flexible as the desires of the consumer. Indeed, the successful domestication of the cute object as an obedient provider of aesthetic experience consequently establishes the consumer as not just the cute object's subject, but as its "master."

In terms of cuteness and physical consumption (as with cute foods and food-themed mascots), however, this notion of mastery and object domination holds a particular significance. Earlier I noted that cute objects, as key products of the commodity fetishism that Merish describes, thrive on our desire to not just enjoy, but also to take *possession* of cuteness. There is a certain tendency in us to "adopt" a cute object and make it part of our lives, be it in the cute design of a stuffed animal or an ice cream scoop. When an object is not only made to resemble a *cute* object, but also a cute *food* object, however, our desire for consumption, for "mastery," is strongly enhanced. On one level, the cute consumable operates according to the subject-object relationship between consumer and product as posited by Ngai—that is, the subordinate diminutiveness of the cute object rouses a desire for possession in us. On a second level, however, the consumer is drawn to the cute consumable because it promises a direct *sensory* experience in addition to a formally aesthetic one. The cute consumable is not only adorable, but also palatable and speaks to our primal desire to protect the beloved subordinate that must be suppressed if we are to enjoy a pleasurable food experience. Food-inspired characters such as Anpanman or Gudetama not only provide aesthetic delight in the shape of adorable looks and moldable, soft bodies, but also offer the possibility that the consumer may one day take full possession of the character by eating it whole—thereby experiencing its cuteness, its literal "sweetness" (or savoriness, as the case may be) on two levels simultaneously.

The cute consumable thus activates a strong desire for possession in its dominating subject. As a result, we, as consumers, are keen to project submission onto the cute consumable as a means of facilitating our own, actual *consumption* of the cute. This tendency may exceed Ngai's definition of tenderization as an aestheticizing process that elicits a controlling response and come closer to Daniel Harris's suggestion that cuteness's appeal for care can also arouse sadistic impulses (7). In their study of Japanese food characters such as Habanero-tan, an anthropomorphized food mascot based on a brand of potato chips, Matt Alt and Hiroko Yoda write that

> [i]f there is one word that describes the food characters of Japan, it is *passion*. Uncountable legions of cute anthropomorphic food characters vie for the attention of customers from the shelves of Japanese grocery and convenience stores. [. . .] Flaunting their charms like supermodels on a runway, they're begging for attention and the privilege of being consumed. Literally. They are a species of working character so dedicated, so selfless, so altruistic, that they're willing to give their lives in the course of duty. (193)

Through this description, Alt and Yoda present the cute consumable as something more resilient than Ngai's notion of the "malleable character." The cute consumable here is portrayed as a "working character" devoted to its job, perceiving itself to be deeply "privileged" to sacrifice itself to satisfy its superior's hunger. What this projection of subordination onto the cute object reveals, then, is that the notion of physical *desire* plays a key role in the analysis of the cute consumable in both the direction of the subject, and that of the cute object itself. In the case of the subject, a desire for object mastery fuels the imaginary of the cute consumable as a subordinate entity. If we feel such an object to be cute, then desire in the *subject* then fabricates a desire in the inanimate cute *object* to be consumed, to make itself useful and actualize as an edible commodity, maintaining the fantasy that the physical consumption of the cute is wanted, or even pre-destined, for the sake of both the subject and object alike. The cute consumable, therefore, plays into the consumer's need for an object to covet while, at the same time, allows the consumer to experience the feeling of being coveted back: of being needed to "complete" the object's destiny as a consumable product.

The Cute Consumable as Neoliberal Subject

This desire for "completion" of the cute object brings us back to Gudetama. As I mentioned previously, Gudetama is not a typical cute character in that it does not exude physical warmth and an endearing demeanor. Not only is Gudetama a yolky blob devoid of either rosy cheeks or fuzzy limbs, it also exhibits a gloomy, truculent attitude. In an introductory post about the character on *RocketNews24*, an English-language news site devoted to Asian culture, Kay Mat pinpoints its unorthodox affect, writing that Gudetama is "certainly an unusual mascot character if we've ever seen one" due to its thoroughly negative "personality": "[a] grumpy egg who's resigned to being cooked and consumed." As such, Gudetama also recalls "grumpy" cute figures in Western cultures such as Oscar the Grouch of *Sesame Street* and, more recently, Grumpy Cat. Just as Oscar resists learning manners and socialization, Grumpy Cat resists his own commodification/consumption by remaining a cat, indifferent to his own celebrity status. In Japan, Gudetama is a popular addition to the category of characters in the *datsuryoku* (listlessness) genre, which also includes Sanrio's 2003 character Rilakkuma the relaxing bear (also discussed in Chapter 1 of this volume), popular with office workers who aspire to the life of leisure it embodies (Hongo and Steger; see also Stevens).

But how "resigned to being consumed" is Gudetama, really? If Gudetama is resistant towards any form of consumption, as its presentation in the eponymous YouTube series leads us to believe, can we speak of it in the same manner as we do of the subordinate cute objects that Ngai describes? Considering Ngai's definition of the cute object as a characteristically docile one, as well as Alt and Yoda's notion of the prototypical food character accepting its eventual culinary fate, Gudetama appears to be anything *but* an ideal food character. With its depressive moods and discouraging remarks ("leave me alone"), not to mention its attempts to escape human consumers (such as in the "Slipped Out" episode), Gudetama, in its own yolky way, appears to resist the neoliberal power structure of consumer and consumed.

Ironically, this resistance to consumption may be the very quality that makes Gudetama so popular with young professionals in Japan. In a video feature by Miho Inada for *The Wall Street Journal*, a university student comments on her appreciation of Gudetama writing, "I just like how he's really lazy . . . he's got a market with university students given that we've got a lot of work, and sometimes we just want to laze around, also" (Inada). In that same piece, a man in a business suit is seen perusing Gudetama-themed items in the Tokyo Sanrio store. "My daughter tells me I look like it when I'm relaxing on weekends," he gleefully remarks (Inada). Gudetama, it appears, owes a large part of its commercial popularity to the slacker attitude it endorses—an attitude whose exhibition, to many people in one of the world's most hard-working populations, may seem like an unattainable fantasy. In accordance with Allison's analysis of the cute commodity, Gudetama offers consumers a world of make-believe; however, in its world, indolence is not only *condoned*, but also, ultimately, valorized: the "Slipped Out" Gudetama episode, after all, ends with Gudetama successfully escaping its duty as a docile food product by taking a relaxing soak in a hot spring.

In *The Problem with Work*, Kathi Weeks discusses the concept of laziness in relation to the refusal of work. Laziness "is not a renunciation of labor *tout court*," she argues, "but rather a refusal of the ideology of work as highest calling and moral duty" (99). Perhaps part of the appeal of Gudetama's sloth lies in its rejection of the glorification of labor, in the manner described by Weeks. As in the quotations mentioned above, Gudetama fans interpret the lethargic yolk's perpetual boredom and gloom, and choice to seek pleasure in leisure and repose through the objects that signify them, such as a remote control, coffee cup, and bacon blanket, as a refusal to submit to the imperative to devote itself to labor and self-entrepreneurialism. For the consumer who, unlike Gudetama, does not have the luxury of slacking off all the time, the little egg contributes to an indulgent fantasy in which the consumer does not have to work so hard to keep up with life's demands. According to a book about Gudetama by Sanrio, the lazy egg has "given up living in the competitive society because it is in despair" (Hongho and Steger). It is quite likely that Sanrio intended those in the working world as Gudetama's target audience: before producing Gudetama plush dolls and apparel, the company manufactured Gudetama stationery, office supplies, and luggage tags, suggesting a target market of working adults. What is striking, then, is that Gudetama's forlorn dissatisfaction with the production-driven world around it ironically serves as the main aesthetic asset of a commercial character line. Gudetama's petulant gloominess, besides being a form of labor resistance, is the very trait that makes it so interesting as the possible star of a global marketing brand.

It is precisely this gloominess that also makes Gudetama so irresistibly cute. By presenting Gudetama as an unhappy character, Sanrio ironically positions it as an ideal candidate for consumer participatory engagement. Consuming Gudetama essentially means *activating* Gudetama. Its cuteness is fully realized once the consumer recognizes the adorable potential behind Gudetama's blob-like body and negative disposition. In consuming Gudetama, be it conceptually through the purchase of a yolk-adorned pencil case or physically through the consumption of a whimsical egg-based dish at Puroland, we assert its identity as a loveable object. Our eager consumption of Gudetama in various foods modeled after this character establishes its successful transfiguration to edible commodity. Gudetama's performative misery, therefore, becomes an additional incentive for us to perform some version of parental solicitude, to take it under our caring wing and into our home in various forms such as notepads, plush dolls or, somewhat sadistically, as egg cups at the breakfast table. Gudetama's dejected nature also encourages us to empathize with the dispirited egg yolk, and, furthermore, to display that empathy with others. Like Occhi's cute *kyaraben* lunchboxes, many Gudetama products, such as the above-mentioned pencil cases as well as cell phone straps, stickers, etc. are accessories on view to the people around us. An identification with Gudetama entails an unarticulated sharing of a grievance that may not be socially acceptable to air. Displaying Gudetama thus may constitute a form of passive resistance to contemporary structures of labor. And, while such a protest will never change the inequitable situation that workers face today, displaying a cute item also avoids the negative consequences that a vocal outburst may elicit.

Less-than-feisty food products like Gudetama or, for that matter, Kogepan, are therefore not merely examples of "gloomy grub." They engage with a primordial desire in the consumer who wishes to protect the subordinate, while at the same time relishing the potential deliciousness of an aesthetic food product. Furthermore, they offer opportunities for fantasy identification in the form of sympathy in the case of Kogepan, or empathy for Gudetama's fans. The latter's ironic utterances, available on Gudetama's Twitter feed as well as in the aforementioned YouTube videos, encourage members of a beleaguered workforce to identify with—and consume—Gudetama as a product. Thus, the "failed" food character's lack of productive activity instills an even greater desire for possession in the consumer. Buying, displaying, and even eating Gudetama branded products completes this cute consumable's manifestation as a "truly" cute object. Our consumption, therefore, unlocks the food mascot's surplus of cute aesthetic. We enjoy the cute consumable because it so openly depends on us. At the same time, we feel a strange attraction to cute consumables because, in various ways, we feel just like them. It is a mutually beneficial relationship: the complex relation between the subject and the cute object is further articulated through the double elements of consumption inherent in the Gudetama character, both as "food character" and as branded merchandise.

In the global economy of food-related cuteness, it should come as no surprise that Gudetama is also making a trek across the Pacific, albeit not on the scale of Hello Kitty. It has become available in various forms at the Sanrio stores in Times Square, a mecca for cute character fans of all stripes. *Travel and Leisure* magazine reported recently on a limited-run themed menu "dedicated to honoring Sanrio character Gudetama," designed in cooperation with Sanrio by a Los Angeles restaurant chain (Locker). In 2015, Sanrio began uploading Gudetama videos with English subtitles for Anglophone audiences on its YouTube channel, some of which have received over 400,000 views at the time of this writing. The popular character was covered in detail by the *Wall Street Journal* in 2016, which reported that "Sanrio thinks Americans, too, might develop a taste for egg with side of ennui" (Hongo and Steger).

Conclusion

At the beginning of this chapter, I posed the question: how does cuteness trigger a desire for physical consumption in us, as consumers? Perhaps a more apt question would have been: how do we negotiate our own desire for self-assertion and fulfillment through a devourable commodity? Because cuteness, after all, is not the sole responsible factor for our physical desires. Our hunger exists regardless of it. What is striking about cuteness, though, as I have argued over the course of this chapter, is that it augments our desire for consumption to an almost aggressive level. Cuteness does not coax us into consuming. It does, however, coax us into consuming *more*.

On a very material level, Nenkov and Scott's experiment with the cute ice cream scoop shows us that we are, indeed, inclined to consume more when we are invited to consume something through the realm of the visually adorable. On a more conceptual level, the rampant popularity of food mascots like Anpanman demonstrates how our eagerness to eat is amplified once our meal is manifest in a decidedly cute likeness. Cuteness offers us something adoptable that not only enhances our experience of the ordinary (the cute-ified kitchen knife or pencil case) but also reaffirms our status as dominant, all-powerful beings in the object hierarchy. The cute, therefore, wounds itself so that we may nurture it—literally so when the cute object in question is a "failed" food product, like Kogepan, and we consume it despite its apparent undesirability.

The cute consumable, like all cute things, therefore treads the line between covetousness and aggression. It balances between its user's promise of endless love and devotion and a strange type of existential precarity—the moment when the user decides to take the cute consumable and eat it whole. "The pleasures of eating and mealtime," Astrid Lorange contends, "are not without their violences, not least of which is the violence necessary in having food to eat" (94). Like traditionally ephemeral exemplars of Japanese aesthetics, the cute consumable substantiates a fleeting fancy. It speaks to a temporality that fits just as well within the aesthetic of cute as the aesthetic of *kawaii*, because cuteness itself evolved to nourish a youth that is all too perishable. At some point or another, it will disappear, or, more violently, be *made* to disappear. This is what the cute consumable, in its delectable edibility, bears testament to. After all, before we parse the cute consumable as a thing to love and cherish, we parse it as something to satisfy our hunger—and in the most pleasurable of ways, at that.

This is not to say that we are only interested in that which is docile. The popularity of the peevish Gudetama is perhaps the most prime example of this. What makes Gudetama "special" among food characters, and therefore more interesting, is that it is not presented as our eager, edible servant. Unlike more conventionally "sad" characters like Kogepan, Gudetama is not dying (literally) to be consumed by its human master. Gudetama resists our impulses to devour, and sometimes even mocks us, as can be seen in its popular YouTube animations. Therefore, the cute consumable as a commercial phenomenon appears to be quite a treasure trove of contemporary marketing strategies. In her book, Ngai offers the suggestion that "the ultimate index of an object's cuteness may be its edibility" (79). While Gudetama manages to resist *us*, the hungry consumers and perpetrators of its physical demise, we, in turn, cannot resist Gudetama's scrumptious adorability.

I would now like to return to my initial question, namely how does cuteness trigger a desire for physical consumption in us? Consumption, in its most physical sense, promises a profound reconciliation with the object that is consumed. It is the ultimate form of domestication. Devouring cuteness implies that we get to carry the cute around with us, make it a *part* of us. Cute consumables are therefore not only popular with children, who are perhaps more publicly "allowed" to embrace the cute than adults are, but also appear in ironic contexts more palatable to adults. In this adult-centered vein, the cute consumable may provide a chance to display our inner desire not to be consumed by the world of work. Or, actualized as real food on our plates, cute consumables provide a satisfyingly complete experience of the cute object. Once we finish eating a panda-shaped rice ball, it disappears from sight. Thus, cute consumables, especially the more sophisticated examples explored in this chapter, play with the binary opposition of consumer/consumed. They allow us mastery in the form of consumption (through purchase or alimentation), or allow us to present ourselves as resistant to the forces of neoliberal capitalism that seek to master us. Though the escape they offer is a fantasy, it is a pleasure enjoyable in spite of its perishability.

Note

1   On the history of the use of cuteness to influence parents to buy foods in cute packaging such as breakfast cereals that are supposedly good for children, see Cross. Most notably Cross quotes a Quaker Oats advertisement from the 1920s that tells parents that "it's so much better to give them the food they need in a form they love!" and that children will think of these cute "fairy grains" as "confections," turning breakfast into "a delightful game" (80).

Works Cited

Allison, Anne. "Enchanted Commodities." *Millennial Monsters: Japanese Toys and the Global Imagination*. Berkeley, CA: University of California Press, 2006. 1–34.

——. "Pocket Capitalism and Virtual Intimacy: Pokémon as Symptom of Postindustrial Youth Culture." *Figuring the Future: Youth and Globalization*. Eds. Jennifer Cole and Deborah Durham. Sante Fe, NM: School for Advanced Research, 2008. 179–95.

Alt, Matt, and Hiroko Yoda. "Food Characters." *Hello, Please!: Very Helpful Super Kawaii Characters from Japan*. San Francisco: Chronicle, 2007. 193–240.

Angier, Natalie. "The Cute Factor." *New York Times*. New York Times, 3 Jan. 2006. Online. 10 June 2016.

Aragón, Oriana R., Margaret S. Clark, Rebecca L. Dyer, and John A. Bargh. "Dimorphous Expressions of Positive Emotion: Displays of Both Care and Aggression in Response to Cute Stimuli." *Psychological Science* 26.3 (2015): 259–73.

Banham, Martin. "Japan." *The Cambridge Guide to Theatre*. Cambridge: Cambridge University Press, 1995. 557–71.

Cross, Gary. "The Cute Child: Images of a Wondrous Childhood." *The Cute and the Cool: Wondrous Innocence and Modern American Children's Culture*. Oxford: Oxford University Press, 2004. 43–83.

Harris, Jenn. "Hello Kitty's Newest Friend is an Egg Named Gudetama." *Los Angeles Times*. Los Angeles Times, 2 Apr. 2014. Online. 31 Jan. 2016.

Hongo, Jun, and Isabella Steger. "If Hello Kitty's too Cheery, This Yolk May Go Over Easier for You." *Wall Street Journal*. Dow Jones, 2 Jan. 2016. Online. 10 June 2016.

Inada, Miho. "Say Goodbye to Hello Kitty. Slack Off with Gudetama." *Wall Street Journal*. Dow Jones, 1 Jan. 2016. Online. 31 Jan. 2016.

Kato, Miko. "Cute Culture: The Japanese Obsession with Cute Icons is Rooted in Cultural Tradition." *Eye* 44.11 (2002): n.p. Online. 31 Jan. 2016.

"Kirimi-chan, Gudetama to Make First Appearance at Puroland Attraction! Begins July 18."*Otaku Mode*. Tokyo Otaku Mode, 13 Jun. 2015. Online. 31 Jan. 2016.

Locker, Melissa. "Spotted in Los Angeles: A Menu All About Sanrio's Gudetama." *Travel and Leisure*. Time, n.d. 10 June 2016. Online.

Lorange, Astrid. "Food." *How Reading is Written: A Brief Index to Gertrude Stein*. Middletown, CT: Wesleyan University Press, 2014. 73–94.

Merish, Lori. "Cuteness and Commodity Aesthetics." *Freakery: Cultural Spectacles of the Extraordinary Body*. Ed. Rosemarie Garland-Thomson. New York: New York University Press, 1996. 185–206.

Nathanson, Elizabeth. "Sweet Sisterhood: Cupcakes as Sites of Feminized Consumption and Production." *Cupcakes, Pinterest, and Ladyporn: Feminized Popular Culture in the Early Twenty-First Century*. Ed. Elana Levine. Urbana, IL: University of Illinois Press, 2015. 249–67.

Nenkov, Gergana Y., and Maura L. Scott. "So Cute I Could Eat It Up: Priming Effects of Cute Products on Indulgent Consumption." *Journal of Consumer Research* 41.2 (2014): 326–41.

Ngai, Sianne. *Our Aesthetic Categories: Zany, Cute, Interesting.* Cambridge, MA: Harvard University Press, 2012.

Noxon, Christopher. *Rejuvenile: Kickball, Cartoons, Cupcakes, and the Reinvention of the American Grown-up.* New York: Three Rivers, 2006.

Occhi, Debra. "*Kyaraben* (Character *Bento*): The Cutesification of Japanese Food in and Beyond the Lunchbox." *East Asian Studies Journal of Popular Culture* 2.1 (2016): 63–77.

Rath, Eric C. "Food and Fantasy in Culinary Books." *Food and Fantasy in Early Modern Japan.* Berkeley, CA: University of California Press, 2010. 112–20.

Sanrio. "Gudetama: I Hate Being Woken Up . . ." 3 June 2015. YouTube. Online. 10 June 2016.

Stevens, Carolyn. "Cute but Relaxed: Ten Years of Rilakkuma in Precarious Japan." *M/C Journal* 17.2 (2014). Online. 27 May 2016.

Weeks, Kathi. "Marxism, Productivism, and the Refusal of Work." *The Problem with Work: Feminism, Marxism, Antiwork Politics, and Postwork Imaginaries.* Durham, NC: Duke University Press, 2011. 79–112.

Whyman, Tom. "Beware of Cupcake Fascism." *Guardian.* Guardian News and Media, 8 Apr. 2014. Online. 21 Oct. 2014.

Yan, Sophia. "How Hello Kitty Built a Massive Business Empire." *Cable News Network.* Time Warner, 21 Aug. 2015. Online. 31 Jan. 2016.

Yano, Christine. *Pink Globalization: Hello Kitty's Trek across the Pacific.* Durham, NC: Duke University Press, 2013.

14

TED, WILFRED, AND THE GUYS

Twenty-First-Century Masculinities, Raunch Culture, and the Affective Ambivalences of Cuteness

Anthony P. McIntyre

Introduction

During Pope Francis's 2015 official visit to the US, two cute-inflected events would help shape media coverage of his trip to the city of Philadelphia. At the World Meeting of Families, a conservative religious gathering at which the head of the Catholic church was guest of honor, the actor Mark Wahlberg delivered a faux-apology to the pontiff for his role in the movie *Ted* (2012). Wahlberg, described as a devout Catholic in much media coverage of the event, explained that 14-year-old opera singer Bobby Hill, who had just performed a solo, had complimented him on the crude R-rated comedy. Turning to Pope Francis, Wahlberg stated, "He whispered in my ear that he liked the movie *Ted*. I told him that was not appropriate for his age. Holy Father, please forgive me." The reference to the irreverent comedy that features a foul-mouthed, sex-obsessed teddy bear come-to-life seemed to go down well with the audience judging by its laughter, although the pontiff himself seemed a little nonplussed by the actor's words.

The pope had been more visibly amused earlier that day while making his way through the city in his "pope-mobile." Echoing the medieval carnivalesque figure of the boy bishop, a baby, dressed in makeshift papal robe and miter, was passed through the crowd to be kissed by the pontiff, prompting videos and images of the "baby pope" alongside the authentic one to go viral.[1] The two incidents can be read as indicative of common perceptions as to the approachability and friendliness of Pope Francis, in marked contrast to his predecessor.[2]

One could argue that the two incidents described served to generate public goodwill toward a resolutely conservative institution at a time when issues such as the Catholic church's complicity in cases of historic child abuse and its less than progressive stance on homosexuality (to name but two) have contributed to its increasingly embattled position and waning popularity. Wahlberg himself seems to also have been in need of some good PR at the time, given the fact that, in addition to the forgiveness he jokingly asked the pope for, he was lobbying for an official pardon from the state of Massachusetts for a racially-motivated assault committed when the actor was fifteen years old.[3]

The events in Philadelphia that day are a telling indication of the ubiquity of cuteness within public cultures that we note in Chapter 1 of this volume. Indeed, although kissing babies is a longstanding political maneuver for public figures seeking to soften their image, the media spectacle of a serving pope in full regalia with a similarly costumed infant provides evidence of the further expansion of the aesthetic into realms where it would until recently have been deemed wholly inappropriate. Similarly, the fact that a film such as *Ted*, which, as I argue below, combines cuteness with a misogynistic investment in "raunch culture," can be referenced in a well-received speech at a conservative religious event, highlights the ambivalences that cuteness can encapsulate and suggests the affective veneer generated by this aesthetic facilitates a greater degree of latitude when it comes to censorious public scrutiny.

The two incidents are also clearly examples of what Mikhail Bakhtin famously theorized as the carnivalesque—the spirit of irreverence that can invert and unsettle given symbolic hierarchies. In the texts I examine in this chapter, one aspect of this representational mode I treat in detail is the grotesque (and, in particular, the specific sub-category of hybridization), which, as some scholars have argued (Harris; Merish; McIntyre), has strong links with cuteness. Building on Bakhtin's work, Peter Stallybrass and Allon White conceptualize hybridization as "a complex form of the grotesque [with the ability to produce] new combinations and strange instabilities in a given semiotic system" (58). In the incidents above as well as the texts examined later in this chapter, we can see evidence of such semiotic upheaval as fixed categories of youth and old age, the human and the non-human, as well as the sacred and the profane are traversed. I offer these examples in order to highlight the surprising reach and affective sway this aesthetic can obtain, as well as the key role cuteness can play in such symbolic recalibrations, often, I argue, while in proximity to the associated category of the grotesque.

To this end, I take as my primary case studies two screen comedies in which we can see cuteness's role in representations of what has, not uncritically, been termed "in-crisis" masculinity.[4] This primary focus demonstrates not only how these popular cultural texts index complex shifts in gender norms, but also how cuteness can be identified as an affective nexus linking such shifts with a range of other factors including, but not limited to, perceived notions of white masculine loss, neoliberal modes of subjectivity, and changing norms of heterosexual intimacy and homosocial bonding.

Ted and *Wilfred*

Both *Ted* and its 2015 sequel, *Ted 2*, as well as the US comedy series *Wilfred* (2011–14),[5] share a number of common features. *Ted* and *Wilfred* feature maladjusted grown males who rely on the companionship of hybrid human-animal figures for emotional support. The films and the series showcase cute-ified, eponymous figures: a CGI teddy bear voiced by Seth MacFarlane in *Ted* and, in *Wilfred*, a dog/man, played by Australian actor Jason Gann. In both comedies the cuteness on display in these central figures is tempered and hybridized to suit the adult orientation of each of the texts. Thus, while *Ted* features a cuddly, talking teddy bear with cute traits including a diminutive stature, soft fur and the flattened features that ethologist Konrad Lorenz noted in young animals (and Stephen Jay Gould, building on his work, traced in the evolution of Mickey Mouse from his first appearance in 1928 [Lorenz; Gould]), the film depicts the child's toy partaking in the "adult" activities of consorting with prostitutes, smoking weed, and swearing continuously. Similarly, in *Wilfred*, the eponymous character also indulges in such vices, tempting his companion with fleeting pleasures of intoxication and play. While Wilfred appears (somewhat unconvincingly) as an unshaven Australian man in a dog suit, he (just like Ted) invariably provokes typical responses to the cute (from "oohs" and "aaahs" to petting) from those who see him in his regular dog form, in particular, women.

The emotional tenor of each comedy differs markedly, however. *Ted* is rather mainstream in its comedic intentions, relying on a suspension of disbelief on the part of the audience in accepting the existence of the talking toy bear, whereas *Wilfred* is much darker in tone, with Ryan's mental stability held in doubt until the resolution of the series. *Ted*'s box-office success—it was the second highest grossing comedy of 2012 after Disney's *Brave*—also stands in contrast to the "cult" pleasures of *Wilfred*, which, while not a huge hit, was popular enough both domestically and overseas to avoid being prematurely cancelled by FX, reaching its planned finale in its fourth season, with this final season airing on then recently-established sister channel FXX. *Ted* built upon the previous success of director and writer MacFarlane's animated sitcom *Family Guy* (1999–), which itself featured a talking animal in the guise of Brian Griffin, the family dog. It is through MacFarlane and the various animated series with which he is associated[6] that we can best understand the tenor of the humor on display in *Ted*. The writer, director, and voice actor is known for crude, puerile humor (that as I shall discuss became increasingly mainstreamed in the 1990s/2000s) with a reliance on pop culture references, and *Ted* doesn't depart from this format. MacFarlane's long-running animation also provides a point of connection with *Wilfred* as it was his long-standing colleague, *Family Guy* co-creator and showrunner, David Zuckerman who developed the series for US television. Ultimately the investment in overtly masculinist content that is characteristic of both MacFarlane and Zuckerman's earlier creative work comes to inflect the particular forms of cuteness that are evident in these comedies.[7]

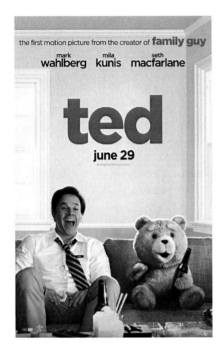

FIGURES 14.1A AND 14.1B While these texts share obvious similarities, as these promotional images suggest, the comedic tenor differs significantly from the more anxious *Wilfred* to the mainstream comedy of *Ted*.

Ted begins by narrating that upon a boyhood wish John Bennett (Wahlberg) finds his teddy bear, Ted, has come to life. A montage follows the opening scene that shows both John and his toy bear's friendship through the years, but also, in a manner that alludes to the career trajectory of various high-profile child stars, Ted's initial fame (including for instance, an interview with talk show legend Johnny Carson) and his subsequent fall from grace in the public eye due to bad behavior. Ted's brief public fame articulates the theme of stunted development that organizes the film, a theme reinforced by references to similarly short-lived celebrity figures. Cutting to the present, we see John, now in his mid-thirties, living with Ted and struggling to adapt to the responsibilities of adult life. In particular, this is made evident in three ways: John's difficulties in meeting the requirements of his job in a car rental office; his anxieties over the increasing demands for relationship commitment made by his girlfriend, Lori (Mila Kunis); and the astraphobia that anchors John and Ted to their childhood promise to be "thunder buddies for life."

In a slight departure from the narrative strategy of *Ted* and perhaps reflecting its more niche broadcast context, the central conceit of *Wilfred* is that both the central character, Ryan (Elijah Wood), and the watching audience see the eponymous character in the dog/man hybrid form, while the majority of other characters perceive him as a regular dog. Adapted from an Australian series of the same name (which ran from 2007–2010), *Wilfred* (the remake) broadcast on its home network in the US as well as in various other territories, often on FX's international channels. *Wilfred* is altogether a more edgy and anxious text than *Ted*, and indeed some initial reviews felt the show was trying too hard to position itself as a cult favorite (Lowry). The dark humor of the series was evident from the opening episode, which depicted the central character, Ryan, repeatedly drafting a suicide note before failing in an attempt to kill himself. As the series progresses, we learn that Ryan was once a promising lawyer at his father's firm and has recently suffered an emotional breakdown due to an ethical crisis related to his work, while his relationship with an emotionally overbearing sister is initially the only connection he maintains with his family. The series often plays with narrative form, manipulating chronology, featuring intricate flashbacks and contesting the "reality" of its diegetic world, as well as increasingly taking on the thematic and cultural conventions of the paranoid conspiracy thriller. The series constantly undermines Ryan's subjectivity, often portraying Wilfred as a malevolent "trickster" figure, and, until the final episode of the last series, the audience is unsure as to whether his canine/human companion is a figment of Ryan's imagination or not.

Nevertheless, despite evident differences between these two comedies, both *Ted* and *Wilfred* depict the complex interplay between male subjectivities under duress, unreconstructed misogynistic gender identities and carnivalesque permutations of cuteness. As I indicate in some of the contextual material to follow, the "structure of feeling," to use Raymond Williams's well-worn term, that informs and generates the focus on homosocial bonding evident in these texts also finds expression in the twenty-first-century male-centric publics of the "manosphere" and "the seduction community."

In-Crisis Masculinity and its Cultural Manifestations

As a growing body of scholarship has documented, the perceived loss of prestige and privilege that, for many, defines contemporary white male subjectivities has found cultural expression across a number of screen genres, from the action movie to reality television (see, for instance, Carroll; Hamad). In this analysis, I seek to extend such accounts to incorporate cuteness's role in such cultural imaginaries. While the assertions of hyperbolic articles proclaiming the "end of men" and asking whether men are "necessary" are open to question,[8] the discursive impact of such popular journalism has been culturally resonant in the twenty-first century, gaining particular force in the wake of the 2008 financial crisis and further proliferating through a wide variety of media. Common evidence cited in such articles and books includes claims that in social arenas as varied as the job market and educational institutions, men operate on an unfair playing field, with the opposite sex reaping rewards while males fall behind. Such claims have been strongly contested, with Diane Negra and Yvonne Tasker, for instance, suggesting that these accounts of male loss largely fail to acknowledge the persistent exclusion of women from key realms of power (22). Nevertheless, as Hamilton Carroll states, while such claims to injury might be "more perception than reality . . . it is a perception that has enormous sociopolitical heft," and one, I might add, with profound social and cultural ramifications (5).

One cultural symptom of this perceived loss of status among men has been the online emergence of "the manosphere," an informal name for a disparate grouping of what might loosely be termed men's rights activist (MRA) groups and websites with an overtly masculinist address. Conducting a content analysis of a number of websites that correspond to this characterization, sociologists Rachel M. Schmitz and Emily Kazyak discern two discrete groupings that make up the manosphere: "Cyber Lads" and "Virtual Victims." While the former "[utilize] themes of explicit aggression towards and devaluation of women, [. . .] Virtual Victims [adopt] political and social movement rhetoric to address men's issues" (18). One prominent "Cyber Lad" site Schmitz and Kazyak examine is *The Red Pill*, hosted on Reddit, in which members, according to one journalist, share the view that "women run the world without taking responsibility for it, and that their male victims are not permitted to complain" (Marche). Alongside nakedly misogynistic (and anonymized) assertions, including one, for instance, stating that it should be legal to rape women on private property, the site is full of questions from anxious men regarding mundane aspects of dating and interacting with the opposite sex (Marche). Inextricably linked to and arguably fueling the anxieties that manifest on such message boards has been the emergence of another associated online and IRL (in real life) phenomenon: the "seduction community." Brought to popular attention by Neill Strauss's 2005 bestseller, *The Game*, which cultural sociologist Rachel O'Neill describes as an ur-text of the movement (3.2), the so-called community shares various methods and means of seducing women, promulgating a Darwinian world view wherein women respond to "alpha males" and the keys to unlocking success in the intimate arena, or "game," can be learned from one of a number of experts working in this potentially lucrative field, or through the sharing of advice with others (Hymowitz).

O'Neill describes the London seduction communities that she analyzes as constituting "less a *deviation* or *departure* from current social conventions surrounding sex and relationships than an *extension* and *acceleration* of existing cultural norms" (1.2, emphasis in original text). In invoking such communities in my own analysis, I seek to tease out how pervasive such discursive configurations of masculinity have become. Moreover, the contemporary structure of feeling that informs such manifestations of anxious misogyny is evident in the inflections of cuteness in these screen comedies. Given cuteness's ability to capture and deflect feelings of vulnerability, as well as the remarkable proliferation of cute texts in many arenas of contemporary media, it should come as no surprise that cuteness plays a prominent role in a number of popular cultural texts that index feelings of masculine anxiety. The overt manipulation that theorists such as Sianne Ngai and Daniel Harris identify as a central feature of the cute (Ngai 26–27; Harris 4) can be seen to parallel the attempts at social engineering at play in the seduction community, a form of manipulation that I argue is foregrounded in the texts I analyze in this chapter.[9]

Sexualization, Cuteness and the Commercial Imperatives of Raunch Culture

The heavy reliance on sexual material in evidence in both *Ted* and *Wilfred* complies with a cultural trend toward sexualization that became particularly pronounced in the latter decades of the twentieth century. Writing in the mid-2000s on what was seen as the increased sexualization of culture during that and the preceding decade, Feona Attwood described the key features of this trend as follows:

> A contemporary preoccupation with sexual values, practices and identities; the public shift to more permissive sexual attitudes; the proliferation of sexual texts; the emergence of new forms of sexual experience; the apparent breakdown of rules, categories and regulations designed to keep the obscene at bay; [and the] fondness for scandals, controversies and panics around sex. (78–79)

Cuteness's role in the further expansion of the sexualization of culture Attwood identifies can, in part, be ascribed to the centrality of consumption and com-modification to this aesthetic (Ngai 1). In *Ted* and *Wilfred* we see a more intensified focus on sexual material evident in the way that content we would instinctively associate with childhood (teddy bears; imaginary friends) is increasingly being mined for its sexually-provocative market potential, evidence of the central role sex plays in neoliberal capitalism (Gilbert 11).

It is this primacy of market imperative that Ariel Levy sees as the driving force behind what she terms "raunch culture." Dismissing the views of some academics that such an increased rate of sexual content amounted to a "democratization of sexuality" (see, for instance, McNair), Levy argues "raunch culture . . . is essentially commercial. [It] isn't about opening our minds to the possibilities and mysteries of sexuality . . . [but] . . . about endlessly reiterating one particular— and particularly saleable—shorthand for sexiness" (29). Indeed, in the example Levy cites of young girls wearing material emblazoned with the logo of the Playboy bunny, a merchandising franchise stemming from the pornographic magazine, we see the imbrication of the commercial logics at the heart of cuteness and brand culture—the bright pink associated with the brand and the bunny rabbit being longstanding cute signifiers.

As Ngai, Harris, and Lori Merish have observed, cuteness is fundamentally a commercial aesthetic, and as these texts show, a highly adaptable one at that. *Ted 2* ultimately disappointed Universal in its overall takings, despite the studio, for instance, investing significantly in a tailor-made ad especially for Super Bowl Sunday in February 2015, months in advance of its release. Nevertheless, the remarkable success of the same studio's animation *Minions* (2015), in which the numerous cute yellow assistants familiar to viewers of the *Despicable Me* franchise (2010; 2013; 2017 in development) were given their own movie—at the time of writing, the eleventh highest grossing film ever—is proof of the continued box-office gains this aesthetic can deliver. Although *Wilfred* wasn't a huge hit like *Ted*, it would be wrong to underestimate its commercial appeal. Already having been developed in Australia and the US, a Russian adaptation of the comedy has also been produced (Knox), a demonstration of cuteness's ability to be harnessed in international flows, as ably demonstrated in Christine Yano's book *Pink Globalization*. With movies and series such as *Ted* and *Wilfred*, we see the opening up of further markets associated with young men for this aesthetic that has perhaps, as many of the contributors to this volume note, been theorized too narrowly in terms of "feminine spectacle" (Merish).

Raunch Culture, Gross Out Humor, and the Masculine Grotesque

Ted and *Wilfred* constitute cuteness's entwinement with one particular form of sexualization that gained particular prominence from the 1990s on: "gross-out humor." With a genealogy that in its contemporary incarnation can be traced back to bawdy US comedies such as *Animal House* (1979) and *Porky's* (1982), gross-out comedy had a resurgence in the late 1990s due to the popularity of films such as *There's Something about Mary* (1998) and *American Pie* (1999) and remains popular today due in no small part to the body of work produced by producer and filmmaker Judd Apatow and his various collaborators. Writing on the earlier film cycle of the late 1970s and early 1980s, scholar William Paul coined the term "animal comedy," noting that the carnivalesque emphasis on bodily functions common to these texts "remind[s] us of our physical and animal state" (297). As shall be seen, this characterization is apt given the case studies at hand, which literalize Paul's terminology through their depiction of macho male characters as non-human animals, albeit softened by the representational mode of cuteness.

In both *Ted* and *Wilfred* cuteness—considered by writers such as Merish to be a feminized aesthetic—is recuperated for masculine consumption through the modality of raunch culture. Such a modality is evident in *Ted*, for instance, when the eponymous bear, working in a supermarket in order to pay for his own apartment, first meets the woman who will become his girlfriend (and in the sequel, his wife) Tami-Lynn (Jessica Barth), coded as "white trash" through name, dress, and demeanor across the two films. Ted's successful attempt to woo Tami-Lynn involves a mime performance that quickly moves from the cute to the grotesque. Accompanied by an upbeat 1960s instrumental tune on the soundtrack, the bear begins by dancing and blowing kisses from his own check-out station to Tami-Lynn at hers, before progressing to make her laugh by gyrating and simulating various sex acts. Complying with the comedic logics of "gross-out" humor, the sequence ends with the bear mimicking a "facial," a sex act common in pornography where a man ejaculates onto the face of a partner. As the shot pans out to reveal the two containers of hand soap Ted is squirting onto his own face, we see Tami-Lynn's reaction change from amusement to disgust, at which point Ted says, "Okay, so that's where we'll draw the line." The sequence neatly encapsulates the liminal position cuteness shares with the grotesque (Harris; Merish; McIntyre), and indeed, it is in this cute/grotesque terrain where we see cuteness being appropriated for masculine pleasures, as well as the ease with which such appropriations sit alongside a hypersexualization that draws freely from pornographic conventions.

In the opening episode of *Wilfred*, a similar scene that combines cuteness with raunch culture gives a further indication of the gendering of the aesthetic in these texts. Having recently discovered that he sees his neighbor Jenna's dog as a hybrid human/dog figure with whom he can converse, Ryan takes Wilfred for a walk and they sit outside a restaurant where we see the hypermasculine canine smoking a cigarette and drinking a beer. During the conversation Wilfred tries to coach Ryan into being more assertive in his life, just as an attractive waitress approaches:

FIGURE 14.2 *Wilfred's* central conceit foregrounds the behavior elicited from cute affect and literalizes a male gaze impervious to its charms.

WILFRED: Life is short, Ryan. You gotta "gather ye rosebuds while ye may." [Noticing the waitress approaching] Speaking of rosebuds . . .

WAITRESS: Do you always feed your dog nachos?

RYAN: Well, not all the time, but he worked out today.

[Waitress laughs]

WAITRESS   [to Wilfred, in a "cute-ified" baby voice]: What's your name?

RYAN AND WILFRED [together]:   Wilfred.

WAITRESS   [she talks in the same cute tone as she rubs Wilfred's ears]: Hi Wilfred! Do you like that? Do you like that? I bet you do.

[Wilfred proceeds to nuzzle his face between the waitress' breasts and she reacts in surprise]

RYAN   [embarrassed, attempting a joke]: I'll have what he's having.

WAITRESS: I think he likes me.

RYAN   [now panicking as he sees Wilfred proceed to gyrate against the waitress.]: Wilfred, get off! Get off!

WILFRED   [continuing his sexual behavior]: I'm trying to!

[At this point Ryan physically pulls Wilfred away from the waitress.]

. . .

WILFRED   [leering at the waitress as she walks away before turning to Ryan with a look of exasperation]: I like you Ryan, but you're a shit wingman!

The function of cuteness in the scene warrants examination. Just as in Ted's attempts to ingratiate himself with Tami-Lynn described above, in *Wilfred* cuteness is combined with overt sexualization and we see a move from the cute toward the grotesque. The playful tickling of the dog's ears that Wilfred's cuteness (as perceived by the waitress) evokes, is recast as sexually provocative due to the dual perception that constitutes the main narrative conceit of the series. While the waitress thinks the dog is merely being overly playful, the lascivious nature of the hybrid man/dog is only revealed to Ryan, a representational move that literalizes a male gaze impervious to what the text posits as the feminized manipulations of the cute aesthetic. Citing and extending Merish's claims of cuteness's relation to otherness, Ngai makes the point that "if cuteness is a 'realm of erotic regulation . . . that offers "protection" from violence and exploitation' (189) it is clearly also a way of bringing that sexuality out" (Ngai 60). Thus, just as in Levy's example of pre-teen girls' fondness for Playboy-branded products, the inherent ambivalence of cuteness facilitates the conflation of the innocent and the obscene.

Ironically, perhaps, Ryan's allusion to and inversion of the famous "fake orgasm" scene ("I'll have what he's having") in the influential romantic comedy *When Harry Met Sally* (1989) invokes a film that questions whether men and women can be friends. Like so many scenes in the two comedies, this one plays out in the language of homosocial bonding, where male friends are "wing men" and women are objects of lust. Such an outlook suggests a social bifurcation of male and female realms that through the eyes of many who adhere to the worldview propagated in the manosphere, is ultimately adversarial. Indeed, much of the series depicts a process of tutelage whereby Wilfred teaches Ryan how to stand up to domineering figures in his life, quite often women, an aspect of the text that closely parallels the central tenets of the seduction community examined above.

Of the two comedies, it is perhaps *Wilfred* that is arguably the more socially progressive of the two, as the text displays an awareness of the normative boundaries of decency and articulates, through the character of Ryan, a certain amount of pushback against the misogynistic views expressed by the dog. Although the series is not about the seduction community, Ryan's social awkwardness and his relationship with Wilfred do bear strong resemblances to the anxious masculinities and intimate entrepreneurs of that world.[10] While Wilfred's actions and attitudes are played for laughs, Ryan is increasingly agitated and suspicious of a companion that seems to be manipulating him and sabotaging his chances for long-term relationships and happiness outside of their friendship.

As we can see from the conversation above, Ryan, while a little sensitive and lacking in confidence, is a bright and funny guy and as evidenced over the course of the series, he is kind and generous yet tends not to get the girl. In short, in the parlance of the seduction community, Ryan is an average frustrated chump (AFC), typical of the young men who are drawn to its promises of social mastery (Hymowitz). Wilfred, in his various attempts at cajoling and advising his friend comes across as both emotional crutch and anthropomorphized embodiment of an increasingly outmoded hypermasculine ideal. The finale of *Wilfred* reveals that the talking man/dog is, in fact, a figment of Ryan's imagination, one he comes to accept as part of his life and vows to keep under control. This rather ambivalent ending could be interpreted as a progressive depiction of non-normative subjectivities and a narrative embrace of mental illness as a potentially positive aspect of one's existence. (Ryan does benefit in other ways from Wilfred's companionship.) Alternatively, this resolution reinforces a metaphorical reading of the series as staging a clash between competing subject positions available to young men, from the alpha male to the sensitive Millennial buckling under the pressure to live up to antiquated gender expectations.

In both these scenes we see sexualization functioning as a bonding technology between men. Although Ted is without his buddy in the seduction scene described, from previous scenes in the film we are shown that, in a representational trope common to such masculinist comedies, women fail to get, or appreciate, the raunchy joke. By pushing the joke to its extreme and grotesque end point, the stage at which the woman onscreen (Ted's future girlfriend, Tami-Lynn) finds it disgusting, the bonding aspect of male-directed gross-out humor becomes apparent. In the sequel, *Ted 2*, we see a restaging of this joke, when John gets covered in actual sperm during a visit to a fertility clinic. This time around the two buddies are able to enjoy the gross-out pleasures together.

Another factor at play in both these scenes and in the two texts in general is how the gross-out comedy and misogyny-tinged humor recuperate the aesthetic of cuteness as suitable for masculine consumption. Thus the association of cuteness with childhood or the feminine is actively disavowed by overdetermined rhetorical and performative displays of homosocial camaraderie and masculinity within the texts, often taking the form of the casual objectification of women.

Cuteness, Slackerdom, and Life-Stage Dissolution

An analysis of cuteness in these texts provides evidence of the aesthetic's articulation of major shifts in conceptions of the life stages of childhood and adulthood. This is an area which has seen a significant amount of both scholarly and popular media attention in recent years (Cross; Harrison; Noxon). Examining a range of early twenty-first-century advertising, sociologist Keith Hayward, for instance, has identified the growing prominence of what he has termed "life stage dissolution." He argues that advertisers, and to this I would add cultural producers more widely, "actively undermine and erode the inherent *opposition* that exists between established stages of the life cycle in a bid to enhance sales and boost corporate profits" (526).

However, as Hayward stresses, "this 'reversal of authority' between child and adult is a *bi-directional process*"; not only are adults encouraged to act as children but children are often depicted as advanced beyond their years, a common trope being the precocious child educating his or her parents on an aspect of modern life (often technology) in which they are hopelessly deficient (530). Hayward alludes to an advertising campaign for Evian water featuring roller-skating babies, which, just as in the case of the "baby pope" examined earlier, indicates how the versatility of cuteness can aesthetically breach boundaries of life-stage development. Set to groundbreaking hip hop track "Rapper's Delight" by The Sugarhill Gang and featuring a multi-racial cast of CGI-enhanced toddlers, the babies of the ad are shown skating around a park and performing various advanced roller-skating tricks and breakdancing moves. Beginning with the question, "How does drinking Evian make you feel?" the ad proceeds to present a post-racial imaginary in which the transcendence of physical limitations is aligned with the restorative properties of premium-priced hydration. The acceleration of youth into adulthood through digital image manipulation bestows a preternatural dexterity upon the toddlers producing an uncanny affect, an instance of what might be termed "the creepy cute." Yet the slightly disturbing demeanor of the roller-skating infants is undoubtedly what makes the ongoing and popular advertising campaign (1998–) memorable and likely to succeed in its promotional purposes. Such advertising strategies are the cultural flipside to an "adult" comedy

FIGURE 14.3 The "creepy cute" aesthetic at the center of the long-running Evian Babies campaign is evidence of cuteness's commercial appeal and its ability to collapse life stage boundaries.

such as *Ted* that has us watching the adventures of an animated children's toy in an R-rated version.[11]

Indeed, Hayward posits that the current trope of the empowered child is "inversely correlated with the passive and stultified adult." Such stultified adults abound in contemporary popular culture, most notably in the figure of the "slacker." One genealogy of *Wilfred* and *Ted* can be traced through this 1990s recessionary figure, described by Andrew Kopkind as "a rational response to casino capitalism, the randomization of success, and the utter arbitrariness of power" (176). Given the fact that the three factors Kopkind argues to be central to the emergence of the slacker in the first place have if anything become more prevalent in the following decades, it is perhaps unsurprising that this cultural type has continued to recur in succeeding generations' popular texts. The slacker was mediated through independent films such as *Slackers* (1991) and *My Own Private Idaho* (2001) as well as popular comedy series *Friends* (1994), which attempted a rehabilitation of the maligned figure. The central features of slackerdom are a notable disengagement from traditional markers of adulthood: finding a full-time job, starting a family, and so on. While this type never fully went away, in the 2000s, a resurgence of movies featuring slacker protagonists began to emerge in Hollywood. David Denby notes the development of what he termed the "slacker-striver" comedy in movies such as *Knocked Up* (2007),

Failure to Launch (2006), and *Dupree and Me* (2006), which show the slacker being rehabilitated into conventionality by a more aspiring and driven female partner, while she in turn is shown how to enjoy herself.

As Suzanne Leonard describes it, "[b]ecause he remains cowed by the prospects of finding a relationship, getting married, or having a baby, the slacker's living and reproductive arrangements all tend to emphasize fleeting pleasures and impermanent arrangements" (43), often in the absence of women. The common slacker image of sitting on a couch and smoking marijuana is one that recurs throughout both *Ted* and *Wilfred*. *Ted* in particular, with its invocation of a childhood toy literalizing the yearning not to grow up and to be allowed to "play" presents an extreme example of the "manchild" that abounds in contemporary screen culture.

Indeed, of the two comedies, it is *Ted* that can unproblematically be categorized as fitting within the slacker–striver dyad. Notably, John's girlfriend Lori is coded as being in a much more lucrative and secure profession than either John or Ted, who are both marginally employed, a status differential that finds a somewhat unconvincing resolution in the film's ending. Once the premise of a toy-bear-come-to-life who was once famous but now is something of a faded celebrity has been set up, the main action of the plot revolves around Ted being kidnapped by the father of a spoilt child. The action-filled climax sees Ted torn apart, and presumed dead when John and Lori bring him back to their apartment. At this point Lori (in a reversion to domestic handicraft that symbolically renounces her position as "career woman") dutifully sews him back together and upon Ted's reanimation, she receives her reward in a proposal of marriage from John.

FIGURE 14.4 At the narrative resolution of *Ted*, the mise-en-scène depicts both heteronormative coupling and the promise of bachelor pleasures on the side in the form of John's toy bear.

Ted complies with Diane Negra's observation about the slacker-striver cycle that, "[I]n unlocking the single man from his 'unnatural' state these films also make him a promise: that he will not have to forego bachelor pleasures upon the achievement of economic independence and exogamous emotional commitment." The mise-en-scène of the shot shown (Figure 14.4) neatly encapsulates this in the fact that we see the heteronormative couple with the teddy bear on the side. Cuteness, in this context, plays an ambivalent role. With its attendant attributes of both comfort and play, the aesthetic can allay both the anxieties of the reluctant male taking his rightful place in the economic and social world, and suggest the promise of ongoing pleasure outside the restrictions of monogamous coupledom. Indeed, given the disparity in employment status between Lori and John, this ending suggests that the raunch cuteness I track in this text is a compensatory mode available to the precariously-situated male.

Symbolic Animality, Accent, and Race

Cultural theorist Steve Baker suggests that "our ideas of animals—perhaps more than any other set of ideas—are the ones which enable us to frame and express ideas about human identity" (6). Similarly, animation scholar Paul Wells suggests that in anthropomorphic representations of animals, "(k)nowledge of and about apparently specific creatures or objects or even human figures is challenged and potentially redefined" and that such hybridized figurations enable "the opportunity . . . to embrace a number of complex or contradictory ideas in narrative or representational flux" (5). In examining how animals are invoked in both *Wilfred* and *Ted*, I am suggesting that their anthropomorphization in these texts can be fruitfully analyzed in terms of contemporary ideological tensions connected with race and gender.

Both bears and dogs come with longstanding symbolic associations that have accrued over time. The "teddy bear" itself is freighted with such an abundance of semantic associations that it is at once considered a symbolic representation of man's dominion over nature (a reading that stems in part from "Teddy" Roosevelt's putative pardoning of a bear while hunting), and a symbol of "pan-human care-giving proclivities and instincts to nurture" (Nieuwenhuys 416). Similarly the dog can connote at once a sexually promiscuous male, or a faithful and unconditionally loving companion species (McLeod 1–15). Both *Wilfred* and *Ted*, perhaps inevitably, partake of the significant polysemy of the animals they invoke.

Writing on the use of animal imagery in Australian advertising aimed at men, Anouk Lang suggests the mastery of animals, while a longstanding indicator of masculine domination, has undergone significant cultural redeployment given the fact that most Australian nationals live in the suburbs and never come into contact with wild animals. Analyzing a set of beer ads that are remarkably similar to the two texts currently under examination, she offers the following assessment:

These texts generate a sense that anxieties around the feminization of men cannot be articulated explicitly: it has become less acceptable for popular culture to figure masculinity in terms of conventional macho activities, so the animal tropings are a way for these anxieties to go underground. (8)

Given, in particular, *Wilfred*'s provenance in Australia, first as a series there and then being relocated to the US with the original Australian actor still playing the part of the dog/man, it is hard not to go along with Lang's assessment. However, the fact that the series has been exported so successfully suggests that an appetite for these indirect expressions of masculine anxieties is prevalent in a number of national contexts.

While the masculinity of the dog in *Wilfred* is also reinforced by the actor's Australian accent and dialect, intertextually associating the text both with the historical antecedent of Australia as a former penal colony, and with hyper-masculine white Australian stars such as Russell Crowe and Mel Gibson, we can also detect a similar process at work in the specific regionalism in *Ted*. The Otherness that Gann's Australian accent provides in *Wilfred* finds a US equivalent in the strong Boston accent that both Ted and John (Wahlberg is a Boston native) speak with in the movies. American Studies scholar Carlo Rotella, commenting on a Boston-set cycle of films including *The Town* (2010) and *Mystic River* (2003), suggests that while globalization has precipitated "the removal of regional content from American movies and American culture, so that it feels universal," Boston movies are an exception, with the city providing a cultural shorthand to Hollywood producers keen to represent "atavistically tough white people" (Rotella and Eiermann).

Arguably the connotations of whiteness (of which the Boston setting and dialogue are just one part) that help structure *Ted*'s audience appeal precipitated some of the criticisms leveled at its less successful sequel. One of its more vociferous detractors, *New York Times* critic Manohla Dargis, took issue with the overt parallels the film draws between its main premise—Ted's legal fight to prove he is human rather than property, thus enabling him to adopt a child with Tami-Lynn—and the historic enslavement of Black Americans. While the symbolic associations of dominion and exploitation that are inherent in the cultural figure of the bear (detailed above) make this alignment one that can potentially generate parodic insight into injustices inflicted on man and animal alike, the puerile nature of the jokes in the second film, invested as they are in clichéd and racist notions of black sexuality, undermine any such ambitions. Dargis observed that many of the racially charged jokes that populate the sequel provoked uneasiness in the viewing audience, leading her to muse that "maybe this movie might have been funny . . . before dead black bodies again became an emblem of our national trauma." As demonstrated in Chapter 1 of this volume, cuteness is often successfully deployed as a means of softening difficult truths, yet as the case of *Ted 2* indicates, this is a strategy that can be undermined by cultural associations that can accrue in complex signifiers.

Thus, in addition to semantic associations with regional/national accents, the symbolic cultural meaning of both the teddy bear and the dog are central to these texts and the inflections of cuteness they contain, particularly the human-animal hybridization they depict. Stallybrass and White argue that in manifestations such as hybridization, the grotesque has the power to "unsettle 'given' social positions, and interrogate the rules of inclusion, exclusion and domination which structured the social ensemble" (43). Given that *Ted* and *Wilfred*, as I contend in this section, while somewhat ambivalent in their aims, arguably shore up white, male privilege, these authors' faith in the abilities of the carnivalesque seems overly sanguine. Such scholarship perhaps overstates the subversive abilities of this representational mode. Film theorist Robert Stam gives a more equivocal assessment, suggesting that "the politics . . . of carnivalesque artistic strategies are conjunctural; no strategy is essentially progressive or regressive." He further describes carnival (and its associated artistic strategies, including the grotesque) as "a master code in which competing discourses fight for hegemony" (Stam 78). We see evidence of such hegemonic recalibrations in both *Wilfred* and *Ted*, particularly in their articulation of twenty-first-century racial and gendered anxieties.

Conclusion

An analysis of *Ted* and *Wilfred* demonstrates that rather than being purely an aesthetic of childhood or feminine spectacle, cuteness can emerge in disruptive and unruly ways when it intersects with highly gendered social scripts. As media scholar Debbie Ging helpfully summarizes, the men-in-crisis discourses (whether sympathetic or critical) that increasingly frame masculinity in the twenty-first century describe "men's negative experiences of and responses to social change, usually perceived to be the result of female power and/or political correctness" (106). My argument has been that in a variety of ways *Ted* and *Wilfred*, in their flouting of political correctness and "against the grain" deployments of cuteness, provide a means of articulating misogynistic and racially-inflected notions of masculinity while simultaneously staging their disavowal. Cuteness's ability to attenuate criticism (as indicated in the papal anecdotes in the introduction to this chapter) while harnessed to the anthropomorphic animal symbolism in these texts, serves to propagate an overtly masculinist worldview that is no less potent for its ability to be shrugged off as a cute distraction.

Notes

1 The figure of the "baby pope" seemed to be having a cultural moment in the US in late 2015, as just a month later another "tiny Vicar of Christ" was awarded the best costume prize by President Barack Obama at the annual White House Halloween event (Griffin).
2 Indeed, one cannot imagine either Wahlberg or the parents who dressed the infant as, presumably, the head of their faith, having taken a similarly jovial and irreverent approach

to the previous pontiff, Benedict XVI, a stern figure who, days prior to his appointment as pope, made this characteristic declaration: "An 'adult' faith does not follow the waves of fashion and the latest novelties" ("Cardinal Ratzinger").

3 This criminal record was, by Wahlberg's own account, an impediment to the expansion of various business ventures (Poppa), including his interests in the "Wahlburgers" fast food restaurant chain and its associated A&E reality television show of the same name (2014–). While this admission suggests that his contrition was at least in part financially motivated, such considerations weren't dwelt on in a number of articles in various Catholic news outlets that one might argue seem more interested in the positive exposure an A-list star brings to the church (Berylak; Connolly).

4 The notion of "in-crisis" masculinity has become something of a cultural commonplace. Yet as sociologists Victoria Foster et al. suggest, the attributed motivations for the crisis are in constant flux.

5 Unless specified, references to *Wilfred* in this chapter refer to the US remake rather than the original Australian series, two seasons of which aired on SBS One (2007/2010).

6 In addition to *Family Guy*, MacFarlane also created and occasionally wrote for the spin-off series *American Dad* (2005–2016) and *The Cleveland Show* (2009–2013). After the success of *Ted*, MacFarlane also directed and starred in *A Million Ways to Die in The West* (2014), notably attempting, for the first time, to try regular rather than voice acting, a move that coincided with his attempts to raise his profile both through hosting awards ceremonies and a musical project and tour where he sang jazz standards with a big-band orchestra.

7 Another example of a very similar narrative, albeit without such an overtly masculine mode of address and in a different medium, is Simone Lia's 2007 graphic novel, *Fluffy*. The eponymous Fluffy is the pet bunny/child of Michael, an Italian-British male in his thirties, whose multiple anxieties stem from a somewhat stalled career, as well as family and romantic problems. Once again this is a text that entails a significant suspension of disbelief regarding its premise. Fluffy, while not Michael's child, nevertheless goes to nursery school and appears to have a child's mental age of around four or five years. Rather than foregrounding a proximity to the grotesque as *Ted* and *Wilfred* do, the graphic novel's depiction of cuteness is congruent with a classically Lorenzian invocation to care, and the gentle, bittersweet humor of the graphic novel is far removed from the undercurrent of anxious misogyny that I detect in *Ted* and *Wilfred*.

8 Perhaps the most prominent of such journalistic diatribes has been "The End of Men," an article for *The Atlantic* written by Hanna Rosin, that was later expanded into a book.

9 Some of the more well-known techniques utilized within the seduction community include "negging" (insulting a woman in order to generate feelings of inadequacy and thus supposedly bolstering one's own standing) and peacocking (the intentional deployment of garish attire to precipitate social interaction) (Strauss).

10 An overt (and critical) portrayal of the seduction community is provided in "White Christmas," a 2014 episode of speculative fiction anthology series *Black Mirror* (2011–). The episode shows seduction entrepreneur Matt (Jon Hamm), through advanced technology similar to Google Glass, talking a student through social interactions with women at a party while the rest of his class follow every move from the student's point of view, a lesson that ends tragically. "White Christmas" is notable both for its depiction of a real life practice (seduction entrepreneurs routinely populate their YouTube pages with covertly filmed videos of themselves seducing unwitting females) and for its subversion of notions of suave masculinity (through the intertextual association with period drama *Mad Men*'s antihero Don Draper that Hamm brings from his former role).

11 While film studios usually try to avoid R-ratings for major releases in accordance with the common sense notion that restricting the potential viewing audience will adversely impact box-office revenues, recently a number of films have strategically rejected this

industry norm. Notably, with the success of both *Ted* and the superhero movie *Deadpool* (2016), both of which figure, at the time of writing, in the top ten highest-grossing R-rated films of all time (at positions nine and two respectively), major examples of this recent trend utilize unorthodox formulations of cuteness in order to signify their "adult" orientation ("Top Grossing R Rated Movies at the Box Office"). See DeAngelis in this volume for an analysis of *Deadpool*'s deployment of an "anti-cute" sensibility.

Works Cited

Attwood, Feona. "Sexed Up: Theorizing the Sexualization of Culture." *Sexualities* 9.1 (2006): 77–94. Online.

Baker, Steve. *The Postmodern Animal*. London: Reaktion, 2000.

Bakhtin, Mikhail M. *Rabelais and His World*. Bloomington, IN: Indiana University Press, 1984.

Berylak, Meghan. "Mark Wahlberg's Pardon Request: What Is Redemption?" *Catholic Vote*. 12 Dec. 2014. Online. 3 May 2016.

"Cardinal Ratzinger Prays for 'a Pastor to Lead Us to Knowledge of Christ, to His Love, to True Joy'." *Catholic News Agency*. 18 Apr. 2005. Online. 5 Mar. 2016.

Carroll, Hamilton. *Affirmative Reaction: New Formations of White Masculinity*. Durham, NC: Duke University Press, 2011.

Connolly, Marshall. "Devout Catholic, Mark Wahlberg Asks Forgiveness for Crime Committed as a Teenager, is Forgiven by Victim." *Catholic Online*. 11 Dec. 2014. Online. 3 May 2016.

Cross, Gary S. *Men to Boys: The Making of Modern Immaturity*. New York: Columbia University Press, 2008.

Dargis, Manohla. "Review: In 'Ted 2,' the Foulmouthed Bear Tries to Prove He's Human." *New York Times*. New York Times, 25 June 2015. Online. 1 June 2016.

Denby, David. "A Fine Romance." *New Yorker*. 23 July 2007. Online. 5 Mar. 2016.

Foster, Victoria, Michael Kimmel, and Christine Skelton. "What about the Boys?: An Overview of the Debates." *What about the Boys?* Ed. Wayne Martino and Bob Meyenn. Buckingham: Open University Press, 2001. 1–23.

Gilbert, Jeremy. "What Kind Of Thing Is 'Neoliberalism?'" *New Formations* 80–81 (2013): 7–22. Online.

Ging, Debbie. *Men and Masculinities in Irish Cinema*. New York: Palgrave-Macmillan, 2013.

Gould, Stephen Jay. "A Biological Homage to Mickey Mouse." *The Panda's Thumb: More Reflections in Natural History*. New York: Norton, 1980. 95–107. Print

Griffin, Andrew. "Obama Meets Baby Pope at White House: Tiny Vicar of Christ Wins First Prize for Popemobile Halloween Costume." *Independent*. Independent Digital News and Media, 1 Nov. 2015. Online. 7 June 2016.

Hamad, Hannah. *Postfeminism and Paternity in Contemporary U.S. Film: Framing Fatherhood*. New York: Routledge, 2014.

Harris, Daniel. *Cute, Quaint, Hungry, and Romantic: The Aesthetics of Consumerism*. New York: Basic, 2000.

Harrison, Robert Pogue. *Juvenescence: A Cultural History of Our Age*. Chicago, IL: University of Chicago, 2014.

Hayward, Keith. "'Life Stage Dissolution' in Anglo-American Advertising and Popular Culture: Kidults, Lil' Britneys, and Middle Youths." *Sociological Review* 61.3 (2013): 525–48. Online.

Hymowitz, Kay S. "Love in the Time of Darwinism." *City Journal*. 23 Dec. 2015. Online. 20 Apr. 2016.

Knox, David. "Meet the Russian Wilfred." *TV Tonight*. 11 Oct. 2013. Online. 19 Apr. 2016.

Kopkind, Andrew. "Slacking toward Bethlehem." *Grand Street* 44 (1993): 176. Online.

Lang, Anouk. "Troping the Masculine: Australian Animals, the Nation, and the Popular Imagination." *Antipodes* 24.1 (2010): 5–10. JSTOR. Online. 18 May 2016.

Leonard, Suzanne. "Escaping the Recession? The New Vitality of the Woman Worker." *Gendering the Recession: Media and Culture in an Age of Austerity*. Ed. Diane Negra and Yvonne Tasker. Durham, NC: Duke University Press, 2014. 31–58.

Levy, Ariel. *Female Chauvinist Pigs: Women and the Rise of Raunch Culture*. New York: Free, 2005.

Lia, Simone. *Fluffy*. London: Jonathan Cape, 2007.

Lorenz, Konrad. "Part and Parcel in Human and Animal Societies." 1950. *Studies in Animal and Human Behavior, Vol. 2*. Trans. Robert Martin. Cambridge, MA: Harvard University Press, 1971. 115–95.

Lowry, Brian. "Review: *Wilfred*." *Variety*. 22 June 2011. Online. 18 May 2016.

Marche, Stephen. "Swallowing the Red Pill: A Journey to the Heart of Modern Misogyny." *Guardian*. Guardian News and Media, 14 Apr. 2016. Online. 20 Apr. 2016.

McIntyre, Anthony P. "Sarah Silverman: Cuteness as Subversion." *Hysterical! Women in American Comedy*. Ed. Linda Mizejewski and Victoria Sturtevant. Austin, TX: University of Texas Press, forthcoming 2017.

McLeod, Alec. "Dog as Self and Other: Comparisons to Canines as a Process of Dehumanization." *Language and Ecology* 3.1 (2009): 1–15.

McNair, Brian. *Striptease Culture: Sex, Media and the Democratization of Desire*. London: Routledge, 2002.

Merish, Lori. "Cuteness and Commodity Aesthetics: Tom Thumb and Shirley Temple." *Freakery: Cultural Spectacles of the Extraordinary Body*. Ed. Rosemarie Garland-Thomson. New York: New York University Press, 1996. 185–203.

Negra, Diane, and Yvonne Tasker. "Gender and Recessionary Culture." Introduction. *Gendering the Recession: Media and Culture in an Age of Austerity*. Ed. Diane Negra and Yvonne Tasker. Durham, NC: Duke University Press, 2014. 1–30.

Negra, Diane. "Where the Boys Are: Postfeminism and the New Single Man." *Flow TV* 4.3 (2006). Online. 5 Mar. 2016.

Nieuwenhuys, Olga. "Can the Teddy Bear Speak?" *Childhood* 18.4 (2011): 411–18.

Ngai, Sianne. *Our Aesthetic Categories: Zany, Cute, Interesting*. Cambridge, MA: Harvard University Press, 2012.

Noxon, Christopher. *Rejuvenile: Kickball, Cartoons, Cupcakes, and the Reinvention of the American Grown-up*. New York: Crown, 2006.

O'Neill, Rachel. "The Work of Seduction: Intimacy and Subjectivity in the London 'Seduction Community.'" *Sociological Research Online* 20.4 (2015). Online. 10 June 2016.

Paul, William. *Laughing, Screaming: Modern Hollywood Horror and Comedy*. New York: Columbia University Press, 1994.

Poppa, Doug. "Mark Wahlberg Wants a Pardon." *Los Angeles Post-Examiner*. 16 Sept. 2015. Online. 3 May 2016.

Rosin, Hanna. "The End of Men." *The Atlantic*. Atlantic Media, July 2010. Online. 7 June 2016.

Rotella, Carlo, and Martin Eiermann. "I Am Allergic to Abstraction: Interview with Carlo Rotella." *The European*. 11 June 2012. Online. 26 May 2016.

Schmitz, Rachel M., and Emily Kazyak. "Masculinities in Cyberspace: An Analysis of Portrayals of Manhood in Men's Rights Activist Websites." *Social Sciences* 5.2 (2016): 18–34.

Stallybrass, Peter, and Allon White. *The Politics and Poetics of Transgression*. Ithaca, NY: Cornell University Press, 1986.

Stam, Robert, with Richard Porton, and Leo Goldsmith. *Keywords in Subversive Film/Media Aesthetics*. Chichester: Wiley-Blackwell, 2015.

Strauss, Neil. *The Game: Penetrating the Secret Society of Pickup Artists*. New York: Regan, 2005.

"Top Grossing R Rated Movies at the Box Office." *Boxofficemojo.com*. n.d. Online. 7 June 2016.

Wells, Paul. *The Animated Bestiary: Animals, Cartoons, and Culture*. New Brunswick, NJ: Rutgers University Press, 2009.

Yano, Christine R. *Pink Globalization: Hello Kitty's Trek across the Pacific*. Durham, NC: Duke University Press, 2013.

INDEX

Taylor & Francis eBooks

Helping you to choose the right eBooks for your Library

Add Routledge titles to your library's digital collection today. Taylor and Francis ebooks contains over 50,000 titles in the Humanities, Social Sciences, Behavioural Sciences, Built Environment and Law.

Choose from a range of subject packages or create your own!

Benefits for you

- » Free MARC records
- » COUNTER-compliant usage statistics
- » Flexible purchase and pricing options
- » All titles DRM-free.

Benefits for your user

- » Off-site, anytime access via Athens or referring URL
- » Print or copy pages or chapters
- » Full content search
- » Bookmark, highlight and annotate text
- » Access to thousands of pages of quality research at the click of a button.

REQUEST YOUR **FREE** INSTITUTIONAL TRIAL TODAY	**Free Trials Available** We offer free trials to qualifying academic, corporate and government customers.

eCollections – Choose from over 30 subject eCollections, including:

Archaeology	Language Learning
Architecture	Law
Asian Studies	Literature
Business & Management	Media & Communication
Classical Studies	Middle East Studies
Construction	Music
Creative & Media Arts	Philosophy
Criminology & Criminal Justice	Planning
Economics	Politics
Education	Psychology & Mental Health
Energy	Religion
Engineering	Security
English Language & Linguistics	Social Work
Environment & Sustainability	Sociology
Geography	Sport
Health Studies	Theatre & Performance
History	Tourism, Hospitality & Events

For more information, pricing enquiries or to order a free trial, please contact your local sales team: www.tandfebooks.com/page/sales